Freedom of Overflight

Aerospace Law and Policy Series

VOLUME 20

Editors

Pablo Mendes de Leon, Professor of Air and Space Law, and Tanja Masson-Zwaan, Assistant Professor of Space Law, Leiden University, The Netherlands.

Introduction

The *Aerospace Law and Policy Series* critically examines the fundamental changes that international aviation and space activities have undergone since the last century, growing up as mature industries while freeing themselves from traditional regulatory constraints and displaying a variety of innovative applications that call for creative legal solutions.

Objective

The objective of the Series is to make a contribution to legal thinking on public international air and space law and policy, and their implementation at the regional and national levels, responsibility and liability of public bodies and service providers, competition law, insurance law, company law, and the complex relationship between EU law and public international law.

Readership

Aviation and space lawyers, academics, representatives of governments, international organizations, and companies involved in aviation and space activities.

The titles published in this series are listed at the end of this volume.

Freedom of Overflight

A Study of Coastal State Jurisdiction in International Airspace

Merinda E. Stewart

Wolters Kluwer

Published by:
Kluwer Law International B.V.
PO Box 316
2400 AH Alphen aan den Rijn
The Netherlands
E-mail: international-sales@wolterskluwer.com
Website: lrus.wolterskluwer.com

Sold and distributed by:
Wolters Kluwer Legal & Regulatory U.S.
7201 McKinney Circle
Frederick, MD 21704
United States of America
E-mail: customer.service@wolterskluwer.com

ISBN 978-94-035-3804-4

e-Book: ISBN 978-94-035-3805-1
web-PDF: ISBN 978-94-035-3810-5

You are fortunate in having before you one of the great lessons of history. Some centuries ago, an attempt was made to build great empires based on domination of great sea areas. ... We do not need to make that mistake again. I hope you will not dally with the thought of creating great blocs of closed air, thereby tracing in the sky the conditions of future wars. I know you will see to it that the air which God gave to everyone shall not become the means of domination over anyone.

Franklin D Roosevelt
The International Civil Aviation Conference,
Opening Plenary Session
Chicago, 11 November 1944

Table of Contents

List of Figures

List of Table

List of Abbreviations

ADC	Air Defence Clearance
ADIZ	Air Defence Identification Zone
AIP	Aeronautical Information Publication
ASA	Air Services Agreement
ATC	Air Traffic Control
ATFM	Air Traffic Flow Management
ATM	Air Traffic Management
ATS	Air Traffic Services
CAA	Civil Aviation Authority
CANSO	Civil Air Navigation Services Organisation
CBDRRC	Common But Differentiated Responsibilities and Respective Capabilities
CORSIA	Carbon Offsetting and Reduction Scheme for International Aviation
DIC TA	Diplomatic Clearance Technical Arrangement
EASA	European Union Aviation Safety Agency
EDA	European Union Defence Agency
EEZ	Exclusive Economic Zone
EU	European Union
FAA	Federal Aviation Administration
FIR	Flight Information Region
GAT	General Air Traffic
IAMSAR	International Aeronautical and Maritime Search and Rescue
IATA	International Air Transport Association
ICAO	International Civil Aviation Organization
ICJ	International Court of Justice
IFALPA	International Federation of Air Line Pilots' Associations
IFR	Instrument Flight Rules

IHO	International Hydrographic Organization
ILA	International Law Association
ILC	International Law Commission
IMO	International Maritime Organization
ITLOS	International Tribunal for the Law of the Sea
km	Kilometre
MBM	Market-Based Measure
MILAMOS	Manual of International Law Applicable to Military Uses of Outer Space
NATO	North Atlantic Treaty Organization
nm	Nautical Mile
NORAD	North American Aerospace Defense Command
NOTAM	Notice to Airmen
OAT	Operational Air Traffic
PANS	Procedures for Air Navigation Services
PCA	Permanent Court of Arbitration
PCIJ	Permanent Court of International Justice
RANP	Regional Air Navigation Plan
RPA	Remotely Piloted Aircraft
SARPs	Standards and Recommended Practices
SES	Single European Sky
SRR	Search and Rescue Region
TASA	Template Air Services Agreement
UAE	United Arab Emirates
UASSG	Unmanned Aircraft Systems Study Group
UK	United Kingdom
UN	United Nations
UNCLOS	United Nations Convention on the Law of the Sea
UNCOPUOS	United Nations Committee on the Peaceful Uses of Outer Space
UNMIK	United Nations Interim Administration Mission in Kosovo
UNSC	United Nations Security Council
US	United States
VFR	Visual Flight Rules

CHAPTER 1

Introduction

1.1 CONTEXT OF RESEARCH

The concept of 'creeping jurisdiction', or the assertion by coastal States of 'sovereignty and/or jurisdiction in adjacent waters beyond the rights they strictly enjoy under the law of the sea',[1] is not a new phenomenon. On the contrary, as Rothwell describes, 'a common thread throughout world affairs over the past 100 years has been a gradual encroachment by coastal states over their adjacent maritime domain'.[2] There are many instances over this period where the practice of coastal States of extending their jurisdiction has subsequently been codified in international law: the expansion of the territorial sea from 3 nautical miles (nm) to 12 nm,[3] the drawing of straight baselines,[4] the extension of exclusive economic jurisdiction over maritime resources through the continental shelf[5] and the exclusive economic zone (EEZ),[6] and the formal recognition of the concept of archipelagic States.[7] Many of these changes have resulted in large maritime areas falling under State sovereignty while others, such as the EEZ and the continental shelf, do not expand sovereignty but involve the extension of coastal State

1. Natalie Klein, *Maritime Security and the Law of the Sea* (OUP 2011) 3. The term 'creeping jurisdiction' in this context has been traced back to the US Navy in the 1960s (Erik Franckx, 'The 200-Mile Limit: Between Creeping Jurisdiction and Creeping Common Heritage – Some Law of the Sea Considerations from Professor Louis Sohn's Former LL.M. Student' (2007) 39 Geo Wash Int'l L Rev 467, 476-477).
2. Donald R Rothwell, 'Maritime Security in the Twenty-First Century: Contemporary and Anticipated Challenges for Australia and New Zealand' in Natalie Klein, Joanna Mossop and Donald R Rothwell (eds), *Maritime Security: International Law and Policy Perspectives from Australia and New Zealand* (Routledge 2010) 248.
3. *See* Section 2.2.3.1.
4. *See* Section 2.2.3.1.
5. *See* Section 2.7.4.
6. *See* Section 2.7.3.
7. *See* Section 5.4.

jurisdiction and sovereignty rights.[8] On this basis, Gavouneli describes the United Nations Convention on the Law of the Sea (UNCLOS)[9] as:

> the culmination of the tug-of-war between the sovereignty of the coastal State, which atavistically purports to expand its power further and further away from land; and the freedom of the high seas, a principle partly created as a reflexion of the impossibility to subdue the vast expanse of water for long centuries in human history.[10]

The tendency of coastal States to assert growing claims over maritime areas adjacent to their territory is well acknowledged,[11] including by the International Civil Aviation Organization (ICAO),[12] the United Nations (UN) agency responsible for managing the 'administration and governance of the Convention on International Civil Aviation'[13] (Chicago Convention).[14] Despite this broad acknowledgement, a comprehensive, contemporary examination of the impact of assertions of coastal State jurisdiction beyond that which is explicitly granted under international law, on overflight rights, specifically, was elusive. It is this set of circumstances that led to the research that forms the foundation of this book.

The initial impetus to question the application of the law in respect of coastal State rights vis-à-vis the right of overflight was the realisation of a number of current events reflected in the media[15] that involved disputes between States over the use of

8. As discussed in, Nico Schrijver, *Sovereignty over Natural Resources: Balancing Rights and Duties* (CUP 2009) 203-214; JA Knauss, 'Creeping Jurisdiction and Customary International Law' (1985) 15(2) Ocean Dev Int'l L 209, 210. *See also*, specifically in relation to the EEZ and the continental shelf, Barbara Kwiatkowska, 'Creeping Jurisdiction Beyond 200 Miles in the Light of the 1982 Law of the Sea Convention and State Practice' (1991) 22 Ocean Dev & Int'l L 153.
9. United Nations Convention on the Law of the Sea (Montego Bay, 10 December 1982) 1833 U.N.T.S. 3, 21 I.L.M. 1261 (1982), *entered into force* 16 November 1994 ('UNCLOS').
10. Maria Gavouneli, *Functional Jurisdiction in the Law of the Sea* (Brill Nijhoff 2007) 1.
11. *See* further, for example, Stuart Kaye, 'Maritime Security in the Post-9/11 World: A New Creeping Jurisdiction in the Law of the Sea?' in Clive H Schofield, Seokwoo Lee and Moon-Sang Kwon (eds), *The Limits of Maritime Jurisdiction* (Martinus Nijhoff Publishers 2013) 347; AMJ Heijmans, 'Artificial Islands and the Law of Nations' (1974) 21(2) Neth Int Law Rev 139, 148; Jon M Van Dyke, 'Military Exclusion and Warning Zones on the High Seas' (1991) Marine Policy 147, 155; Alex G Oude Elferink, 'Artificial Islands, Installations and Structures' (Max Planck Encyclopedia 2013) 8; Ivan L Head, 'ADIZ, International Law, and Contiguous Airspace' (1964) 3 Alta L Rev 182, 196.
12. ICAO WP/5-1, *Secretariat Study on Agenda Item 5: Consideration of the Report of the Rapporteur on 'United Nations Convention on the Law of the Sea – Implications, if any, for the Application of the Chicago Convention, its Annexes and other International Air Law Instruments'*, Presented at the Legal Committee 26th Session, Montreal (4 February 1987), reproduced in (1987) 3 Int'l Org & L Sea: Documentary YB 243, 245.

    Note: this book is written using UK English but the terms and quotations that are used, including articles of treaties and names of organisations, reflect the diversity of spelling and phraseology in the English language. No further signposting will be included where the language of a quotation differs from UK English.
13. ICAO, 'About ICAO', available at www.icao.int/about-icao/Pages/default.aspx accessed 12 February 2020.
14. Chicago Convention on International Civil Aviation (Chicago, 7 December 1944) 15 U.N.T.S. 295, 61 Stat. 1180, T.I.A.S. No. 1591, *entered into force* 4 April 1947, *as amended by* 1175 U.N.T.S. 297, *entered into force* October 1998 ('Chicago Convention').
15. Richard Milne, 'Scandinavians Warn Russia after Air Near-Miss' (Financial Times, 15 December 2014), available at www.ft.com/content/95751ff2-837e-11e4-8a84-00144feabdc0 accessed 12

international airspace, that is, airspace outside a State's national airspace.[16] These examples demonstrated, at one end of the spectrum, disapproval by coastal States over the way in which the aircraft of another State operated in international airspace off the first State's coast, such as in the case of northern European States with respect to Russian fighter jets in the Baltic.[17] At the other end of the scale, the items reported on the coastal State prohibiting the aircraft of another State from operating in international airspace off the first State's coast such as was reported in relation to China and the overflight of military aircraft of the United States (US) in the South China Sea.[18] These reports stimulated an interest in the international law framework that applies to overflight rights in international airspace. At the very basic level, the aircraft of all States enjoy freedom of overflight in international airspace, but what rights this entails in practice for the operation of aircraft is not clear. Furthermore, these examples all involved military aircraft, which raised the question of whether freedom of overflight applies differently depending on whether the aircraft is a State aircraft, on the one hand, or a civil aircraft, on the other.[19] These questions are necessarily tied to the consideration of legitimate restrictions on the right of overflight, whether from other States exercising their freedoms in the maritime area or the coastal State, in the exercise of its specific rights and jurisdiction as provided under international law. Such concepts are not static and, as will be evident, the development of customary international law plays a significant role in shaping the answers to these questions.

June 2015; 'Report on Occurrences over the High Seas Involving Military Aircraft in 2014' (EASA, 14 April 2015); 'China and Japan Trade Barbs after Close Encounter over South China Sea' (The Guardian, 25 May 2014), available at www.theguardian.com/world/2014/may/25/china-japan-jets-south-china-sea accessed 28 June 2015; 'South China Sea: China's Navy Told US Spy Plane Flying over Islands to Leave "Eight Times", CNN Reports' (Australian Broadcasting Corporation, 22 May 2015), available at www.abc.net.au/news/2015-05-22/us-spy-plane-in-south-china-sea-warned-to-leave-by-china/6488690?nw=0 accessed 28 June 2015; 'US Fighter Planes Intercept Russian Combat Jets off Alaska, Sweden Protests "Violation"' (Deutsche Welle, 20 September 2014), available at www.dw.com/en/us-fighter-planes-intercept-russian-combat-jets-off-alaska-sweden-protests-violation/a-17936231 accessed 2 May 2015.

16. *See* Section 2.2.2.1 for a discussion of what constitutes national airspace in accordance with the Chicago Convention, and what subsequently constitutes international airspace. *See also*, Section 2.2.1 (n 83) for discussion of territory that does not fit into one of these categories.
17. This issue will not be addressed further in the context of this research because it did not involve claims that the coastal States were permitted to prohibit or restrict the operation of the aircraft.
18. The name 'South China Sea' will be used throughout this book as the term most commonly used for this maritime area in English.
19. *See* Section 2.4 for a detailed discussion on the distinction between civil aircraft and State aircraft, and the implication of this for the application of international civil aviation law. Throughout this book, the term 'aircraft' will be used to refer to both State and civil aircraft in those situations where the distinction is not relevant. *See also*, Section 1.3.1 for a discussion of the importance of the distinction to this book.

1.2 SCOPE OF THE BOOK

1.2.1 Central Research Question

The central research question of this book is: What jurisdiction does a coastal State have over the operation of the aircraft registered in other States in international airspace adjacent to its coast?

Freedom of overflight, like the freedom of the high seas in general, is a fluid concept. While being a foundational principle of the law of the sea, it is broad and difficult to define. O'Connell, discussing the difficulty of defining the legal characterisation of the high seas as a concept itself, argues that, in the vagueness of the freedoms it is the practice of States that gives meaning to them: '[a]t any particular moment the concept of the high seas will embody a balance achieved by State practice between the freedom of the seas and national jurisdiction'.[20] As he explains, it is determining this balance at a given time that allows for an understanding of the scope of each. In this sense, this proposition is not an answer to what the scope of the freedom is, or consequently, what the rights of the coastal State are, but rather a methodology for confronting the question.[21] It is this approach that has been taken to this book. Freedom of overflight is in large part uncontroversial: an international network of civil aircraft makes use of the ocean space every day, as do State aircraft engaged in transport and military exercises and, considering the volume of traffic, disputes are relatively few. The events in the media, referred to above, though, and subsequent research on freedom of overflight and the exercise of coastal State jurisdiction in international airspace, revealed three key aspects of coastal State jurisdiction in international airspace where this balance with freedom of overflight is currently unclear.

First, China's opposition to US aircraft flying in international airspace in the South China Sea over its artificial islands, a matter that is ongoing but which gained prominence in 2015, instigated research into whether safety zones over artificial islands, installations and structures – termed 'maritime constructions' in the context of this book – could be legitimately imposed in the airspace above the construction in addition to on the surface of the sea around them.[22] UNCLOS expressly provides that a coastal State, in its EEZ and on its continental shelf, has the right to establish safety zones around its maritime constructions,[23] but is silent on whether they can extend to the airspace above the constructions. The facts of this case are used as a basis from which to examine the law in this area from a hypothetical perspective: China did not attempt to restrict overflight on the basis of safety zones. The artificial islands at the centre of the overflight dispute between China and the US are a useful starting point from which to analyse the law on safety zones because their legal status was addressed

20. DP O'Connell, *The International Law of the Sea – Vol II* (OUP 1982) 796.
21. *Ibid.*
22. This book does not consider overflight over the number of natural islands in the South China Sea beyond the general discussion on the law applying to overflight in national airspace.
23. UNCLOS, Article 60(4).

in the 2016 decision, *In the Matter of the South China Sea Arbitration (Philippines v. China)* (*'South China Sea Arbitration'*).[24] The decision provided clarity on whether human modification of a maritime feature could change the status of that feature, and thus, the nature of the rights associated with it. As will be further discussed in Section 1.3.2, this helps to inform when safety zones apply around maritime constructions. The examination of the legitimacy of extending these safety zones to the airspace follows on from this.

Second, the Gulf States' ban on Qatari-registered aircraft from international airspace within their flight information regions (FIRs),[25] introduced in 2017, led to the question of what in international civil aviation law, if anything, prohibits a State from discriminating against the aircraft of another State in this airspace. As will be addressed in Chapter 2,[26] freedom of overflight is understood to provide all States with the right to use international airspace, consistently with international law, and therefore as prohibiting any State from precluding the aircraft of another State from operating in the airspace. It is presumably on this basis that flights through the portions of international airspace were quickly reinstated in the case of the Gulf States' ban.[27] International civil aviation law, on the other hand, despite providing the legal basis governing the coastal State's responsibility in international airspace within an FIR, provides no express non-discrimination principle in relation to this responsibility in terms of its application to international airspace.

Third, the adoption by China of its air defence identification zone (ADIZ) in 2013 resulted in opposition from other States based on a number of features of the ADIZ, despite similar procedures for ADIZs imposed by other States.[28] ADIZs have no foundation in codified international law and serve as an example of the possible dynamic nature of freedom of overflight, on the basis they were to be deemed legitimate. If ADIZs are accepted as customary international law, they represent a significant shift in the international community's acceptance of coastal State jurisdiction in international airspace. The legality of ADIZ has been debated for decades, and this book does not aim to revisit and examine each ground of justification. Instead, the purpose here is to consider the legality of ADIZ in light of the most prominent justifications that represent potentially significant diversions in the understanding of States of freedom of overflight moving forward.

This book approaches its central research question from the perspective of these three matters, as the areas in the law that have been identified as involving ambiguity in respect of the balance between coastal State jurisdiction and freedom of overflight. The book also, briefly, considers coastal State jurisdiction in international straits and archipelagic sea lanes as maritime areas which, while constituting national airspace, involve aspects of regulation more akin to international airspace. As mentioned at the beginning of this chapter, coastal States have demonstrated a tendency to assert

24. P.C.A. Case No. 2013-19, 12 July 2016.
25. *See* Section 4.2.1.1 for the definition of FIR.
26. *See* specifically, Sections 2.7.1 and 2.7.3.2.
27. *See* Section 4.2.2.2.
28. *See* Section 4.3.1.

jurisdiction over increasingly greater maritime areas adjacent to their coasts. The three cases of expanding coastal State jurisdiction identified above, which form the basis of this book, each demonstrate how this 'creeping jurisdiction' encroaches upon the rights of other States and specifically, in these cases, on freedom of overflight.

On a final, terminological note, jurisdiction in this book is used in the context of both prescriptive jurisdiction, or the capacity of the State to make law, and enforcement jurisdiction, the capacity of the State to ensure compliance with the law.[29] The terms 'jurisfaction' and 'jurisaction', coined by Cheng, are commonly used in air and space law.[30] The term 'jurisaction' is broader than the concept of enforcement jurisdiction though and refers to the ability of the State 'to exercise the functions of a State' as a whole; it encompasses the 'State's power in international law to set up machinery to make, implement and enforce, and physically to make, implement and enforce its laws, judicial pronouncements and other legally binding decisions'.[31] This book will use the more widely employed terms 'prescriptive' and 'enforcement' jurisdiction. Functional jurisdiction will also be addressed, in respect of the provision of air traffic services (ATS) in international airspace.

1.2.2 Aims and Objectives of the Study

Fragmentation of the law in this area has led to consideration of matters impacting overflight in international airspace from the perspective of international civil aviation law or the law of the sea, but rarely through a combined lens. With a focus on these two areas of law, and with consideration to their place in public international law more broadly, the objective of this book is to present a comprehensive analysis of the legality of contemporary attempts by coastal States to exercise jurisdiction in international airspace adjacent to their coasts over aircraft registered in other States in cases where the legal basis for the exercise of that jurisdiction is ambiguous. In doing so, the book aims to determine the contemporary understanding of what freedom of overflight entails by establishing the legitimate limitations to it. As set out in the International Law Commission's (ILC) 2006 report on the fragmentation of international law:

> [a]ny technical rule that purports to 'develop' the freedom of the high seas is also a limitation of that freedom to the extent that it lays down specific conditions and institutional modalities that must be met in its exercise.[32]

Through its examination of specific instances of coastal State limitations to overflight, it is hoped that this book will also be able to serve as a basis from which to examine the actions of other States engaged in similar practices in future in an attempt

29. Malcolm Shaw, *International Law* (6th edn, CUP 2008) 645-646.
30. Bin Cheng, 'Crimes on Board Aircraft' (1959) 12 Curr Leg Probl 177, 177-202.
31. Bin Cheng, 'International Responsibility and Liability for Launch Activities' (1995) 20(6) A&SL 297, 301. *See also*, Bin Cheng, 'The Extra-Territorial Application of International Law' (1965) 18 Curr Leg Probl 132, 136.
32. 'Report of the Study Group on Fragmentation of International Law: Difficulties Arising from the Diversification and Expansion of International Law', finalised by Martti Koskenniemi (ILC 58th Session, 13 April 2006) 22.

to provide greater legal certainty regarding the right of overflight and of coastal State actions in respect of overflight, in international airspace.

The extension of coastal State jurisdiction is often underpinned by political motives. Where a group of States – in this case, coastal States – have an incentive to act in a concerted manner for their own benefit, and to the disadvantage of other States – States whose rights and freedoms are consequently curtailed – the actions must be closely scrutinised under international law. This book will consider whether the exercise of coastal State jurisdiction it examines is consistent with international law and, in instances where this is not found to be the case, whether the law seems likely to develop to support the specific extensions of coastal State jurisdiction.

Although this book is approached from the perspective of overflight, its relevance extends beyond aircraft. In particular, the legal issues discussed in the context of Chapter 3 are not restricted to maritime areas but have consequences for the development of the legal framework governing activities in outer space: the US recently proposed the establishment of safety zones around areas of space activity as part of its Artemis programme, which restricts the ability of other space actors to operate in the vicinity of the activity.[33] This situation raises similar questions on conflicting rights to those that arise in relation to safety zones around maritime constructions. Chapter 3 is also relevant to the development of space activities in respect of the launch of rockets from mobile maritime platforms, that is, from maritime constructions. These platforms have the advantage of being able to be positioned in equatorial areas which enables more efficient access to the geostationary orbit,[34] and they also minimise the risk to third parties on the ground associated with land launches.[35] The first orbital-class rocket was launched from an ocean platform in 1999.[36] China recently launched its first rocket from a maritime platform,[37] and SpaceX has announced plans to move away

33. Leonard David, 'NASA Proposes New Rules for Moon-Focused Space Rules' (Scientific American, 21 May 2020), available at www.scientificamerican.com/article/nasa-proposes-new-rules-for-moon-focused-space-race/ accessed 3 June 2020; Joey Roulette, 'Trump Administration Drafting "Artemis Accords" Pact for Moon Mining' (Reuters, 5 May 2020), available at www.reuters.com/article/us-space-exploration-moon-mining-exclusi/exclusive-trump-administration-drafting-artemis-accords-pact-for-moon-mining-sources-idUSKBN22H2SB accessed 3 June 2020.

34. This is the ideal orbit for communication and meteorological satellites because it enables them to maintain their position relative to the Earth's surface (NASA Science, 'Basics of Spaceflight: Planetary Orbits', available at solarsystem.nasa.gov/basics/chapter5-1/ accessed 3 June 2020).

35. *See*, respectively, Louis de Gouyon Matignon, 'Sea Launch and Launching States' (Space Legal Issues, 19 June 2019), available at www.spacelegalissues.com/sea-launch-and-launching-states/ accessed 23 June 2020; Dave Mosher, 'Elon Musk: "SpaceX Is Building Floating, Superheavy-Class Spaceports" for Its Starship Rocket to Reach the Moon, Mars, and Fly Passengers Around Earth' (Business Insider, 17 June 2020), available at www.businessinsider.nl/elon-musk-spacex-starship-ocean-spaceports-offshore-engineer-job-posting-2020-6?international=true&r=US accessed 23 June 2020.

36. Jeff Foust, 'Sea Launch "Frozen" after Ships Moved to Russia' (Space News, 24 April 2020), available at spacenews.com/sea-launch-frozen-after-ships-moved-to-russia/ accessed 3 June 2020; de Gouyon Matignon (n 35).

37. Rui C Barbosa, 'China Conducts First Sea Launch Mission with Long March 11 Launch of Seven Satellites' (NASASpaceflight.com, 5 June 2019), available at www.nasaspaceflight.com/2019/06/china-first-sea-launch-long-march-11-seven-satellites/ accessed 3 June 2020.

from land-based launches in favour of launches from maritime platforms.[38] In this sense, the analysis in this book is more far-reaching than the specific instances that it addresses.

1.3 STRUCTURE OF THE ANALYSIS

1.3.1 Part I

The first part of this book consists of one chapter - Chapter 2 - which serves as a preliminary chapter: it provides the legal framework for the analysis that forms the remainder of the book. The two key treaties that are involved in the book[39] are the Chicago Convention and UNCLOS. Chapter 2 describes the concept of the right of overflight which, in the context of international civil aviation law, refers to the privilege granted to a State for its aircraft to operate across the territory of the State making the grant, without landing, on a scheduled air service or non-scheduled flight.[40] Over international airspace, in contrast, the right of overflight has its basis in the customary international law principle of freedom of overflight, as codified under Article 87(1)(b) UNCLOS, and all States, coastal or landlocked, enjoy this freedom. The freedom also applies in the EEZ.[41]

Chapter 2 is divided into two main parts. The first part establishes the regime for overflight over sovereign territory. This is further divided into two key parts, as dictated by the legal framework that applies to them: civil aircraft, which fall within the scope of the Chicago Convention and its annexes, and State aircraft, which fall outside its scope. The distinction between these two groups of aircraft is not unambiguous, but the Chicago Convention provides that aircraft used in police, military and customs are considered to be State aircraft.[42] The chapter will address the right of overflight in respect of, in turn, civil aircraft and State aircraft.[43]

The second part of Chapter 2 sets out the various maritime areas that are recognised under UNCLOS with implications for overflight. It establishes the legal foundation and fundamental rights associated with these areas, as a basis for the chapters to follow. In doing so, this part also introduces the interaction between international civil aviation law and UNCLOS, which sits at the heart of the book. While freedom of overflight exists in international airspace, it does not mean that overflight is unregulated. In contrast, the regulation of overflight is necessary to ensure the safety of the aircraft to which the regulation applies, the safety and security of other users of

38. Mosher (n 35).
39. *See*, Appendix to Chapter 1: list with basic data on the principal treaties, for a list of the core treaties applied in this book and principal information about them as relevant to this research.
40. Scheduled services and non-scheduled flights are discussed in Section 2.3.3.
41. UNCLOS, Article 58(1). *See* Sections 2.7.1 and 2.7.3.2 for further discussion on the legal basis of freedom overflight and, in the latter section, for the implications of the EEZ for the application of international civil aviation law.
42. *See* Section 2.4.2.
43. This research does not address non-State actors, which fall outside the legal framework of the Chicago Convention and UNCLOS.

the maritime area, including other aircraft, and to ensure the coastal State is able to exercise its rights in the area.[44] Freedom of overflight applies to both State and civil aircraft and so this part does not distinguish between the two. At the same time however, State aircraft are, in general,[45] not subject to the rules in the annexes to the Chicago Convention that apply over the high seas that are discussed in this part, given that they fall outside the scope of the Convention. Leaving aside the applicable international law, the distinction between State and civil aircraft is relevant to this book because, as indicated above,[46] the instances of coastal State interference with overflight in international airspace predominantly involve State aircraft being targeted. There are a couple of main reasons for this, taking into account both the intention of the coastal State and of the State of registration of the aircraft operating in the international airspace. As to the former, attempts to extend coastal State jurisdiction to regulate overflight tend to be for the purpose of, at least explicitly, protecting national security and State aircraft, specifically military aircraft, pose the greatest threat in this respect. This is particularly relevant to the second part of Chapter 4, addressing ADIZs.

States also assert jurisdiction beyond their national airspace to support territorial claims. The legitimacy of these territorial claims will not be explored in this book, but it is mentioned here to demonstrate the complex and often political undercurrent of the coastal State actions that will be addressed. This is not to disregard other coastal State intentions, which will be addressed throughout the book. Importantly for Chapter 3, a State may attempt to impose restrictions or prohibitions on overflight, particularly at lower altitudes, in order to protect the safety of its maritime constructions. As will be seen in Chapter 4, a coastal State responsible for international airspace within its FIR will also make decisions affecting the movement of aircraft registered in other States to ensure the safety and efficiency of operations in that airspace.

1.3.2 Part II

The second part of the book comprises three chapters - Chapters 3-5 - which form the central analysis.

Chapter 3 considers the question of whether safety zones may be established in the airspace over maritime constructions in the EEZ and on the continental shelf. Safety zones are well accepted in the law of the sea as mechanisms for the protection of maritime constructions. This chapter begins by establishing the legal framework under UNCLOS applying to safety zones in a State's EEZ or on its continental shelf, including the definitions and uses of the maritime constructions to which they are relevant.

44. *See*, for instance, Thomas Gammeltoft-Hansen and Tanja Aalberts, 'Search and Rescue as a Geopolitics of International Law' in Thomas Gammeltoft-Hansen and Tanja Aalberts (eds), *The Changing Practices of International Law* (CUP 2018) 190: '... despite its name, the *Mare Liberum* is hardly a space devoid of regulation. The law of the sea imposes a complex set of norms on the maritime environment, charting out a web of intersecting rights and obligations for both states and private actors'.
45. *See* Section 2.4.3 for details of this qualification, and also Section 4.3.5, specifically in respect of interception of civil aircraft.
46. *See* Section 1.1.

Safety zones are strictly regulated under UNCLOS, including the limitation of their breadth to no more than 500 metres from the construction, unless otherwise permitted. There is no express provision allowing the State to establish them in the airspace. In establishing the maritime constructions to which safety zones apply, the chapter addresses the *South China Sea Arbitration*. In this case, the Arbitral Tribunal established in accordance with Annex VII UNCLOS and serviced by the Permanent Court of Arbitration (PCA), henceforth referred to in respect of this case as 'the Tribunal', confirmed the legal status of the relevant artificial islands constructed using natural maritime features, hence clarifying the constructions to which the question of safety zones is relevant.

The chapter then proceeds to interpret the provisions of UNCLOS applying to safety zones in light of their drafting history and in consideration of both State practice and academic opinion, to ascertain the scope of the provisions. The chapter addresses whether the extension of safety zones to the airspace above maritime constructions may be justified using existing provisions regarding air traffic management (ATM) under international civil aviation law and whether, this not being the case, coastal State jurisdiction in the airspace could amount to an unjustified interference with freedom of overflight. Regardless of its consistency with existing international law, the right to do so may develop as customary international law. In this case, the extension of safety zones to the airspace above maritime constructions may exist in parallel with the safety zone provisions under UNCLOS or may reflect the States' interpretation of the UNCLOS provisions; each of these circumstances is explored. There has been considerable discussion in the past on the jurisdiction over airspace above artificial islands facilitating aircraft operations. Without revisiting this analysis in detail, this chapter briefly examines its consistency with the analysis in the previous sections of the chapter.

Finally, this chapter addresses the extension of coastal jurisdiction over international airspace on the basis of human modification in the context of land fortification and reclamation. In doing so, it considers the distinction in the law between human modification amounting to a maritime construction – with its corresponding safety zone – and human modification amounting to an extension of a State's coastline and therefore, possibly, of the State's national airspace. While maritime constructions do not generate maritime zones, State practice indicates that land reclamation leads to a change in the delimitation of the territorial sea and thus may have implications for the delimitation of national and international airspace. These questions are particularly relevant given rising sea levels. This section is briefly discussed as it does not form part of the central analysis but rather complements it by demonstrating that human modification does have the capacity to shift airspace boundaries.

Chapter 4 examines, in two parts, FIRs and ADIZs. In particular, it considers whether a State is, under international civil aviation law, prohibited from discriminating in the provision of ATS in international airspace and, second, whether ADIZs are consistent with international law. The *first* part of the chapter, addressing FIRs, establishes the legal framework governing the provision of ATS in international airspace, which is the purpose for which airspace is divided into FIRs. In doing so, it defines the legal characteristics of an FIR and the scope of responsibility of the coastal State within its boundaries. The chapter then sets out the relevant facts of the case involving the Gulf States' prohibition of Qatari-registered aircraft in their FIRs, as a foundation for the examination of a possible implied principle of non-discrimination in the provision of ATS in international airspace, which the chapter subsequently turns to examine. In the absence of an express principle of non-discrimination in Annex 11, as the foundation for FIR responsibility, it takes a step back to consider its context within international civil aviation law more broadly, in particular considering the application and purpose of the principle of non-discrimination under the Chicago Convention to aspects of air navigation in national airspace. This first part of the chapter ultimately questions whether, on the basis of the explicit application of the principle in the regulation of air navigation aspects in national airspace, it can be argued that the principle is implied in the rules governing FIR responsibility in international airspace.

The *second* part of Chapter 4, addressing the legality of ADIZs, consists of three main elements. The first introduces ADIZs, providing a brief overview of their development and of the most common procedures associated with them. The second examines a number of legal bases that are used to justify ADIZs. These bases have been chosen for both their prominence in ADIZ discourse and their potentially significant impact on the balance between coastal State jurisdiction and freedom of overflight beyond ADIZs in the case that they were to be accepted as a legitimate legal basis for ADIZs. This part of the chapter also considers whether the right to establish ADIZ may have developed into customary international law. Up until this point, the chapter considers the legality of ADIZs in terms of whether States are able to rely on a legal basis under international law for their exercise of prescriptive jurisdiction in establishing the zones. The chapter here undergoes a shift, examining whether, in light of *The Case of S.S. Lotus (France v. Turkey)* ('*Lotus Case*'),[47] the question is rather whether States are prohibited under international law from establishing ADIZs. The enforcement of ADIZ procedures within international airspace is dealt with separately on the basis of extraterritorial *enforcement* jurisdiction unequivocally requiring a permissive rule in international law.

Chapter 5 complements the previous chapters in addressing, in turn, transit passage through international straits and archipelagic sea lanes passage. The application of both of these passage regimes under UNCLOS results in conflicting views between, on the one hand, the coastal States to whose national airspace the passage applies and, on the other, the airspace users passing through the lanes. This chapter will examine the inconsistent application of the regimes, both on the basis of reservations by States to the provisions under UNCLOS and as a result of ambiguity in the law, in the case of archipelagic sea lanes passage.

Chapter 6 reflects on the previous chapters of the book in light of the central research question and brings the different elements of the book together to provide the resulting conclusions and recommendations.

47. (1927) P.C.I.J. Series A, No. 10.

1.4 METHODOLOGY

This book involves classic doctrinal research. It is the result of normative analysis of the Chicago Convention and its annexes, and UNCLOS, together with public international law more broadly as the body of law within which these conventions function. It takes a positivist and, to a certain extent, formalist approach to international law.

The interaction between UNCLOS and the Chicago Convention is unusual in that it results naturally on the basis of the two bodies of law governing the same physical space – maritime airspace – but there was little cross-input from the perspective of air law in the process of the codification of UNCLOS. While ICAO was present at the Third UN Conference on the Law of the Sea between 1973 and 1982, at which UNCLOS was adopted, it did not contribute to the process:

> during the more than nine years of deliberations at the Third United Nations Conference on the Law of the Sea, ICAO has not formulated or addressed to the Conference any specific policy with respect to international civil aviation to be taken into account in the drafting of a new convention.[48]

At first, this seems curious considering the importance of maritime areas to international civil aviation. Beyond the principle of freedom of overflight though, UNCLOS provides very few explicit provisions related to aviation. It is perhaps on this basis that the ICAO representatives were removed from the negotiations, in that the direct subject matter was largely outside the scope of their competence.[49] As will be seen in Chapter 3, at least one State representative involved in the law of the sea conferences likewise, and for the same reason, demonstrated a reluctance to engage in negotiations for provisions governing aviation.[50] Together, the two conventions govern the same physical space but there are many aspects of governance that have developed, and continued to develop, externally to the conventions, whether through the annexes to the Chicago Convention, or State practice interpreting the conventions or otherwise contributing to the law governing international airspace. In any case, it is with this in mind that these conventions are considered.

In terms of the approach to treaty interpretation taken in this book, it follows the customary international rules[51] set out in Articles 31 and 32 of the Vienna Convention on the Law of Treaties[52] which the ILC clarifies, 'must be read together as they

48. ICAO (n 12) 244.
49. As will be addressed in Chapter 5, provisions regarding overflight in the archipelagic sea lanes regime are designed primarily for State aircraft, which are outside the scope of the Chicago Convention and so, even in this case where aviation is directly affected, it is not within the scope of ICAO's competence.
50. *See* Section 3.3.1.
51. *Arbitral Award of 31 July 1989 (Guinea-Bissau v. Senegal)*, Judgment, I.C.J. Rep. 1991 (12 November), p. 53, p. 70 para. 48; G.A. Res. 202, U.N. GAOR, 73rd Sess., Supp. No. 49, vol. 1, at 1118, U.N. Doc. A/73/202 (vol. 1) (2018) 1119; Panos Merkouris, 'Introduction: Interpretation Is a Science, Is an Art, Is a Science' in Malgosia Fitzmaurice, Olufemi Elias and Panos Merkouris (eds), *Treaty Interpretation and the Vienna Convention on the Law of Treaties: 30 Years On* (Martinus Nijhoff Publishers 2010) 5.
52. Vienna Convention on the Law of Treaties (Vienna, 23 May 1969) 1155 U.N.T.S. 331, *entered into force* 27 January 1980 ('Vienna Convention on the Law of Treaties').

constitute an integrated framework for the interpretation of treaties'.[53] Article 31, which provides the 'general rule of interpretation', requires a treaty to be '... interpreted in good faith in accordance with the ordinary meaning to be given to the terms of the treaty in their context and in the light of its object and purpose'.[54] Article 32 allows for the consideration of 'supplementary means of interpretation', to confirm the meaning resulting from the application of Article 31 or to determine the meaning in the case that the meaning resulting from the interpretation under Article 31 is 'ambiguous or obscure' or 'manifestly absurd or unreasonable'.[55] These supplementary means, as indicated under Article 32, frequently involve recourse to the drafting materials of the treaty, commonly referred to as the *travaux préparatoires*. The purpose of Article 32 is restricted to circumstances where clarification of the meaning of the terms is required beyond the application of the rules under Article 31; it is well accepted that 'there is no occasion to have regard to preparatory work if the text of a convention is sufficiently clear'.[56]

There are three broad approaches generally recognised to treaty interpretation: textual or objective, purposive or teleological, and subjective or intention-based.[57] Article 31 itself prioritises a literal interpretation, with 'the ordinary meaning to be given to the terms of the treaty' as the starting point for interpretation.[58] The International Court of Justice (ICJ), as the primary judicial body of the UN, has also made clear through its judgments that treaty interpretation is based on the primacy of the text of the treaty.[59] In practice, the methods of interpretation are not distinct though: the literal and teleological approaches are means of establishing the intention of the drafters at the time of the treaty's conclusion[60] and, as set out in Article 31(1), the ordinary meaning of the terms of a treaty is to be considered in light of the object and purpose of the treaty, necessarily requiring reliance on the teleological approach in undertaking a textual approach. The general rule of interpretation is not a checklist,[61] but is rather formed of a number of aspects to be taken into account, as determined by

53. YILC (2013) Vol. II, Part 2, 18.
54. Vienna Convention on the Law of Treaties, Article 31(1).
55. *Ibid.* Article 32(a) and (b).
56. *The Case of S.S. Lotus (France v. Turkey)* (1927) P.C.I.J. Series A, No. 10, p. 16.
57. YILC (1966) Vol. II, 218. *See also*, GG Fitzmaurice, 'The Law and Procedure of the International Court of Justice: Treaty Interpretation and Certain Other Treaty Points' (1951) 28 Brit YB Int'l L 1, 1; Irina Buga, *Modification of Treaties by Subsequent Practice* (OUP 2018) 80-81.
58. Jean-Marc Sorel and Valérie Boré Eveno, 'Article 31 Convention of 1969' in Olivier Corten and Pierre Klein (eds), *The Vienna Conventions on the Law of Treaties: A Commentary (Vol I)* (OUP 2011) 829.
59. Oliver Dörr, 'Article 31 General Rule of Interpretation' in Oliver Dörr and Kirsten Schmalenbach (eds), *Vienna Convention on the Law of Treaties: A Commentary* (2nd edn, Springer 2018) 580, with reference to, *Territorial Dispute (Libyan Jamahiriya/Chad)*, Judgment, I.C.J. Rep. 1994 (3 February), p. 6, p. 22 para. 41; and, *Legality of the Use of Force (Serbia and Montenegro v. Belgium)*, Judgment, I.C.J. Rep. 2004 (15 December), p. 279, p. 318 para. 100; *see also*, Buga (n 57) 80: '... the textual or objective method, which emphasizes the literal meaning of the text, rooted in Article 31(1) VCLT, ... is favoured by the ICJ'; Sorel and Boré Eveno (n 58) 829: 'In conformity with its line of conduct privileging textual interpretation, the ICJ has accorded minimal space for the intention of the parties.'
60. Richard Gardiner, *Treaty Interpretation* (2nd edn, OUP 2015) 9.
61. *Ibid.* 157 and 10, respectively.

the circumstances, resulting in a holistic – or integrated – approach to the interpretation of the terms, reiterating the statement of the ILC, above.[62] In this sense, Article 31 has been described as 'a true example of compromise': '[t]he objective is to find an interpretation that is simultaneously obvious (the ordinary meaning of the terms), logical (an *acte clair*), and effective (a useful effect)'.[63] The pursuit of these objectives through an integrated application of Article 31 is echoed by Gardiner, who emphasises the danger of focusing too much on a particular method of interpretation at the expense of applying the rules as set out in the Vienna Convention on the Law of Treaties.[64]

This book favours a holistic approach to treaty interpretation in that it gives primacy to the ordinary meaning of the terms of the treaty to the extent that they are taken as the starting point for interpretation but, consistent with the rules of interpretation under Article 31, and Article 32 where necessary, it determines the meaning of the text in consideration of its place within the treaty more broadly, as well as in consideration of the other sources relevant to its interpretation, as applicable, including through the use of systemic integration.[65]

62. In other words, Article 31(1) consists of 'three separate principles ... for a single combined operation taking account of all named elements simultaneously' (Dörr (n 59) 580).
63. Sorel and Boré Eveno (n 58) 808.
64. Gardiner (n 60) 9.
65. For the definition of systemic integration and for a more detailed description of how it relates to this book, *see* 2.2.2.1.

APPENDIX TO CHAPTER 1

List with basic data on the principal treaties

United Nations Convention on the Law of the Sea (Montego Bay, 10 Dec. 1982) 1833 U.N.T.S. 3, 21 I.L.M. 1261 (1982), *entered into force* 16 Nov. 1994 ('UNCLOS')

Number of parties: 167 States and the European Union

Provisions reflecting customary international law that are central to this book: the 12 nm breadth of the territorial sea under Article 3 and freedom of overflight under Articles 87(1)(b) and 58(1)

Vienna Convention on the Law of Treaties (Vienna, 23 May 1969) 1155 U.N.T.S. 331, *entered into force* 27 Jan. 1980 ('Vienna Convention on the Law of Treaties')

Number of parties: 116 States

Provisions reflecting customary international law that are central to this book: the principle of *pacta sunt servanda* under Article 26, the general rule of interpretation under Article 31 and supplementary means of interpretation under Article 32

Charter of the United Nations (San Francisco, 26 Jun. 1945) 1 U.N.T.S. 16, *entered into force* 24 Oct. 1945 ('UN Charter')

Number of parties: 193 States

Provisions reflecting customary international law that are central to this book: the prohibition on the use of force under Article 2(4) and the right of self-defence under Article 51

Chicago Convention on International Civil Aviation (Chicago, 7 Dec. 1944) 15 U.N.T.S. 295, 61 Stat. 1180, T.I.A.S. No. 1591, *entered into force* 4 April 1947, *as amended by* 1175 U.N.T.S. 297, *entered into force* Oct. 1998 ('Chicago Convention')

Number of parties: 193 States

Provisions reflecting customary international law that are central to this book: Article 1 recognising a State's sovereignty over the airspace above its territory and, linked to this, Article 2 recognising that the territory of a State includes the land areas and territorial waters under its sovereignty

International Air Services Transit Agreement (Chicago, 7 Dec. 1944) 84 U.N.T.S. 389, *entered into force* 30 Jan. 1945 ('Transit Agreement')

Number of parties: 133 States

Provisions reflecting customary international law that are central to this book: None

Convention relating to the Regulation of Aerial Navigation (Paris, 13 Oct. 1919) 11 L.N.T.S. 173, *entered into force* 31 May 1920 ('Paris Convention')

Number of parties: 33 States at the time of the signing of the Chicago Convention

NB: This convention was superseded by the Chicago Convention

CHAPTER 2

The International Legal Framework

2.1 INTRODUCTION

This chapter presents the international legal framework that forms the basis of the analysis in the following chapters of this book. It examines the development of the relevant laws and the interaction between international civil aviation law and the law of the sea, and of these two bodies of law within public international law more broadly insofar as it is relevant to overflight. In introducing and examining the application of the relevant law, this chapter also confirms the scope of the book, complementing Chapter 1 in this role.

The chapter will first outline the relationship between territory and sovereignty in international civil aviation law. In doing so, it will examine the development of the relationship between sovereignty and overflight rights, from the Convention Relating to the Regulation of Aerial Navigation (1919) (Paris Convention)[66] to the Chicago Convention (Section 2.2.2), as well as the delimitation of territory for the purpose of defining the scope of a State's sovereignty, in terms of both its vertical and horizontal limits (Sections 2.2.3 and 2.2.4).

Section 2.3 will then set out the legal framework governing the exchange of overflight rights between States in their national airspace. In international civil aviation law, the right of overflight is the right or privilege granted to a State for its aircraft to operate across the territory of the State making the grant, without landing, on a scheduled air service or non-scheduled flight.[67] The legal basis for overflight rights in national airspace differs depending on whether the flight is part of a scheduled service or is non-scheduled, whether the aircraft is manned or unmanned, and whether it is a State aircraft or a civil aircraft.

66. Convention relating to the Regulation of Aerial Navigation (Paris, 13 October 1919) 11 L.N.T.S. 173, *entered into force* 31 May 1920 ('Paris Convention').
67. Scheduled services and non-scheduled flights are discussed in Section 2.3.3.

Article 6 of the Chicago Convention is the natural starting point in establishing the legal framework for the exchange of overflight rights in sovereign territory: it is pursuant to this provision that the exchange of these rights is made separately among States for scheduled international services. Most States exchange such rights through the International Air Services Transit Agreement (1944) (Transit Agreement),[68] which was adopted at the same time as the Chicago Convention and which regulates the multilateral exchange of the right of overflight and of technical stopovers. A great majority of flights falling under the Chicago Convention today are scheduled services conducted by manned aircraft and while non-scheduled flights have decreased in significance in recent decades,[69] unmanned aircraft, or pilotless aircraft as they are referred to in the Convention, are taking on an ever-greater role in international civil aviation. This section of the chapter will address the distinction between scheduled services and non-scheduled flights, recognising the exchange of transit and traffic rights for non-scheduled flights under Article 5 of the Chicago Convention. It will then explain why, in accordance with Article 8, there is a necessity for the exchange of overflight rights to be made separately among States for pilotless aircraft, regardless of whether the flight is scheduled or non-scheduled.

As a terminological side note, Article 96(a) of the Chicago Convention defines 'air services' as 'any *scheduled* service performed by aircraft for the public transport of passengers, mail or cargo' (emphasis added). For this reason, the term 'services' will be used throughout this book to encompass both scheduled and non-scheduled services, while the term 'air services' will be restricted to scheduled services. Further to this, non-scheduled flights include both commercial and non-commercial flights. In this respect, the term 'non-scheduled flight' will be used to refer to non-scheduled flights generally, while the term 'services' will only be used in relation to non-scheduled flights when referring specifically to those that are commercial.

Section 2.4, still focusing on national airspace, will examine the grant of overflight rights in relation to the operation of State aircraft, which falls outside the scope of international civil aviation law. This part will begin by outlining the development of the distinction between civil aircraft and State aircraft, from the Paris Convention to the Chicago Convention, and then consider in more detail the definition under Article 3(b) of the Chicago Convention. Overflight rights over sovereign territory for State aircraft are generally negotiated bilaterally at a diplomatic level for individual flights.[70] In international airspace, there is no distinction made between State aircraft

---

68. International Air Services Transit Agreement (Chicago, 7 December 1944) 84 U.N.T.S. 389, *entered into force* 30 January 1945 ('Transit Agreement').
69. Section 2.3.3.
70. *See*, for example, US Department of State, 'Diplomatic Aircraft Clearance Procedures for Foreign State Aircraft to Operate in United States National Airspace', available at www.state.gov/diplomatic-aircraft-clearance-procedures-for-foreign-state-aircraft-to-operate-in-united-states-national-airspace/ accessed 1 August 2020; Australian Government, Department of Foreign Affairs and Trade, 'Diplomatic Clearances: Aircraft and Ships', available at dfat.gov.au/about-us/foreign-embassies/protocol/Pages/diplomatic-clearances-aircraft-and-ships accessed 5 January 2019; Government of Canada, 'Global Affairs Canada: State, Military or Scientific Overflight Authorization', available at www.international.gc.ca/protocol-protocole/policies-politiques/overflight_clearance-autorisation_survol.aspx?lang=eng accessed 1 August 2020;

and civil aircraft for the purpose of freedom of overflight. The distinction is relevant though because, as will be seen throughout this book, coastal State actions in attempting to restrict freedom of overflight are predominantly focused on State aircraft and, more accurately, on military aircraft.

Section 2.6 will address a State's right to revoke or suspend overflight flights in its territory and to establish prohibited or restricted areas, as well as danger areas, which may be established in national and international airspace. It will also examine whether a State may, in certain circumstances, have an obligation to close its airspace. Finally, this section will consider the closure of national airspace through legal mechanisms outside international civil aviation law, including by way of a UN Security Council resolution and in the form of a countermeasure.

Section 2.7 sets out the foundation of freedom of overflight in international airspace, which is expressly provided under UNCLOS and which flows from the freedom of the high seas. With reference to Chapter 1, freedom of the high seas means that no State can claim sovereignty over any part of those seas and that all States have the right to enjoy them, including freedom of navigation and the related freedom of overflight.[71] The seas are however, at the same time, 'an object of the law of nations', a state without which 'the consequence would be a condition of lawlessness and anarchy on the open sea'.[72] Accordingly, while freedom of overflight means that no grant of overflight is required to operate in international airspace, it does not correspond to the operation of aircraft through international airspace without regulation. This part will establish the limited application of international civil aviation law to international airspace through Article 12 of the Chicago Convention and the related annexes. Annex 11, governing ATS, will be examined in further detail in Chapter 4 in relation to the rights of a coastal State in its FIR.[73] This section furthermore introduces the EEZ, the continental shelf and the contiguous zone, all zones recognised under UNCLOS which are located in international waters and therefore over which freedom of overflight exists. Each of these zones grants certain rights to the coastal State. These rights will be outlined in this part as a basis for the chapters to follow which will critically assess the interaction between the rights of the coastal State and the right to freedom of overflight.

Two additional maritime areas codified under UNCLOS with implications for overflight are archipelagic waters and international straits, with their corresponding archipelagic sea lanes passage and transit passage. These areas are anomalies in that national airspace exists over them, but the coastal State does not have the same rights in respect of overflight as it does in other national airspace. They are considered in the

Switzerland, Federal Office for Civil Aviation (FOCA), 'Diplomatic Clearances', available at www.bazl.admin.ch/diplomaticclearances accessed 1 August 2020. *See* Section 2.4.4 for further discussion on diplomatic clearances.

71. Under UNCLOS, the term 'navigation' applies to vessels, while 'overflight' is used with respect to aircraft.
72. Robert Jennings and Arthur Watts, 'The Freedom of the High Seas' in Robert Jennings and Arthur Watts (eds), *Oppenheim's International Law: Volume 1 Peace* (9th edn, OUP 2008) 726.
73. *See* Section 4.2.1.1 for the definition of ATS and the relationship between it and other aspects of airspace management.

context of this book as maritime areas that, although constituting national airspace, involve rights regarding overflight that are in some ways akin to those in international airspace. In this context, archipelagic sea lanes passage and transit lane passage are introduced and analysed separately in Chapter 5.

At the conclusion of this chapter, the legal basis of the right of overflight in both national airspace and international airspace will be clear. In relation to the latter, the interaction between international civil aviation law and the law of the sea, as they apply to the maritime areas beyond the territorial seas, will be evident. Coastal States rely on their rights and responsibilities in these maritime areas to justify - legitimately or illegitimately, as will be examined in subsequent chapters - the exercise of jurisdiction over aircraft in international airspace within them. Thus, it is the second part of the chapter addressing international airspace that will be referred back to frequently throughout the book in examining the legitimacy of coastal State actions in restricting and prohibiting overflight.

2.2 DEFINING 'SOVEREIGNTY' AND 'TERRITORY'

2.2.1 Sovereignty and Territory under General Public International Law

The concept of territory is central to international civil aviation law as it provides the delimitation for the exercise of State sovereignty over airspace. As in public international law more broadly, the concepts of sovereignty and territory are integrally linked. A territorial unit forming a State necessarily involves the exercise of sovereignty by that State over the territory, a key principle of public international law as recognised in Article 2(1) of the Charter of the United Nations (UN Charter).[74] On the other hand, territory that does not constitute a State or part of a State is not subject to the sovereignty of any State.[75]

In the words of Crawford, '[t]he term "sovereignty" has a long and troubled history, and a variety of meanings',[76] but it is generally understood as 'the right to exercise therein, to the exclusion of any other State, the function of a State'.[77] The concept of sovereignty has its basis in the political philosophy of, influentially but among others, Bodin, Hobbes, Locke and Rousseau.[78] The Peace of Westphalia (1648) is also frequently cited in relation to the emergence of sovereignty as we understand it

74. Charter of the United Nations (San Francisco, 26 June 1945) 1 U.N.T.S. 16, *entered into force* 24 October 1945 ('UN Charter').
75. Although a State may have sovereign rights or jurisdiction in the territory (*see* Section 2.7).
76. James Crawford, *The Creation of States in International Law* (2nd edn, OUP 2006) 32.
77. *Island of Palmas (US v. Netherlands)* (1928) II R.I.A.A. 829, 838.
78. JL Brierly, *The Law of Nations* (6th edn, OUP 1963) 7-16; Luke Glanville, *Sovereignty and Responsibility to Protest: A New History* (The University of Chicago Press 2014) 61-68; for Bodin and Hobbes specifically *see*, William A Dunning, 'Jean Bodin on Sovereignty' (1896) Polit Sci Q 82.

today,[79] although the role of this event in forming the modern concept of sovereignty is increasingly downplayed.[80]

A defined territory is one of the four necessary elements of a State, as provided in the Montevideo Convention of 1933, along with a permanent population, government, and the capacity to enter into relations with other States.[81] As described above, territory that forms a State is under the sovereignty of that State, where sovereignty 'is not … a criterion of statehood … [it] is an attribute of States, not a precondition'.[82] Under international law, territory generally falls within one of three categories: territory that is under the sovereignty of a State or territory that does not belong to a State, being either *terra nullius* or *res communis*.[83] *Res communis*, as territory that is incapable of

---

79. *See*, for example, Brierly (n 78) 5-6: 'The Peace of Westphalia, which brought to an end in 1648 the great Thirty Years War of Religion, marked the acceptance of the new political order in Europe. This new order of things gave the death-blow to the lingering notion that Christendom, in spite of all its quarrels, was in some sense still a unity, and there was a danger that the relations between states would be not only uncontrolled in fact, as they had often been before, but henceforth uninspired even by any unifying ideal. The modern state, in contrast with the medieval, seemed likely to become the final goal of unity … .'
80. Andreas Osiander, 'Sovereignty, International Relations, and the Westphalian Myth' (2001) 55(2) International Organization 251, 252 and 281; Stéphane Beaulac, *The Power of Language in the Making of International Law: The Word Sovereignty in Bodin and Vattel and the Myth of Westphalia* (Martinus Nijhoff 2004) 70.
81. Convention on the Rights and Duties of States adopted by the Seventh International Conference of American States (Montevideo, 26 December 1933) 165 L.N.T.S. 19, *entered into force* 26 December 1934, Article 1(b), together with Article 1(a), (c) and (d) ('Montevideo Convention'). The Montevideo Convention is a restatement of customary international law and therefore applies to the international community as a whole rather than just to its signatory States. However, '[d]espite its wide acceptance in the practice of states (far beyond its sixteen parties), it [the Montevideo Convention] has come under scholarly criticism, especially the fourth element ("capacity to enter into relations with other states"). Many scholars do not include that condition among the elements of statehood, considering such capacity to be a consequence, not a condition, of statehood, or holding that the essence of that capacity is independence' (Aristoteles Constantinides, 'Statehood and Recognition' in André Nollkaemper, August Reinisch, Ralph Janik and Florentina Simlinger (eds), *International Law in Domestic Courts: A Casebook* (OUP 2018) 32).
82. Crawford (n 76) 32.
83. The classification of certain territory under these categories has been, and in many cases continues to be, ambiguous under the law, not just because territory is disputed, as to which see this note below, but also because the application of the legal concepts themselves are unclear. This is the case, for example, regarding the application of *res communis* to the high seas, as will be discussed later in this section. Regarding *terra nullius see*, for example, the case of *Mabo v. Queensland (No. 1)* [1988] HCA 69 (1988) 166 CLR 186, in which the High Court of Australia overturned the classification of the Murray Islands having been *terra nullius* at the time of colonisation, over a hundred years later. It ruled that the Meriam people held, and continue to hold, native title over the territory.

    Furthermore, not all territory falls within one of these categories. Consider, for example, airspace over occupied or contested territory, such as that over Northern Cyprus (Mark Franklin and Sarah Porter, 'Sovereignty over Airspace and the Chicago Convention: Northern Cyprus' (2010) 35(1) A&SL 63; Alexis Heraclides, *Greek-Turkish Conflict in the Aegean* (Palgrave MacMillan Limited 2010) 193-198; Nicholas Grief, 'The Legal Principles Governing the Control of National Airspace and Flight Information Regions and their Application to the Eastern Mediterranean' (European Rim Policy and Investment Council 2009)); and, the Autonomous Republic of Crimea (ICAO WP/245, *ATM Aspects Within Simferopol and Dnipropetrovs'k FIRs*, Presented by Ukraine at the 13th Air Navigation Conference, Montreal (28 September 2018)); consider also, the airspace over Antarctica. Antarctica is partly *terra nullius* but over its other

being placed under sovereignty,[84] is often understood to apply the high seas and outer space,[85] while the only remaining example of *terra nullius* – as 'a territory belonging to no-one'[86] – is Marie Byrd Land, unclaimed territory lying in the west of Antarctica between territory claimed by New Zealand and Chile.[87] While the high seas are referred to as *res communis*, this is not without objection. As discussed by O'Connell, Grotius identified that the terms '*res nullius*', '*res communis*' and '*res publica*' were all used to refer to the seas,[88] with each having since been subject to criticism, as well confusion over the precise implications of their application to the high seas.[89]

territory, seven States – Argentina, Australia, Chile, France, New Zealand, Norway and the UK – have made territorial claims. There is a 'thin legal basis to fly over Antarctica' provided by the Antarctic Treaty (Peter Haanappel, 'Aerial Sovereignty: From Paris 1919, Through Chicago 1944, to Today' in Pablo Mendes de Leon and Niall Buissing (eds), *Behind and Beyond the Chicago Convention* (Wolters Kluwer 2019) 28, referring to Article 7(4) of the Antarctic Treaty (Washington, 1 December 1959) 402 U.N.T.S. 71, *entered into force* 23 June 1961: 'Aerial observation may be carried out at any time over any or all areas of Antarctica by any of the Contracting Parties having the right to designate observers'); Finally, the UN Charter recognises non-self-governing territories as 'territories whose people have not yet attained a full measure of self-government' (Article 37). There are seventeen of these States recognised by the UN today (United Nations, 'Non-self-governing Territories', available at www.un.org/dppa/decolonization/en/nsgt accessed 18 June 2019) including, for instance, Western Sahara: Morocco claims sovereignty over the territory, which no other State recognises. The ICJ has ruled that Morocco's claim is not valid and that the people of the territory are entitled to form an independent State (*Western Sahara*, Advisory Opinion, I.C.J. Rep. 1975 (16 October), p. 12, p. 68 para. 162). A referendum determining the will of the people on this question is yet to be held and, in the meantime, Western Sahara is classified as a non-self-governing territory with the liberation front for the people of Western Sahara, Polisario, as the legitimate international legal representative of its population.

84. James Crawford, *Brownlie's Principles of Public International Law* (9th edn, OUP 2019) 237-238.
85. For the high seas, *see*: UNCLOS, Article 89; Crawford (n 84) 237; Malcolm Shaw, *International Law* (6th edn, CUP 2008) 492; for outer space, *see*: Treaty on Principles Governing the Activities of States in the Exploration and Use of Outer Space, including the Moon and Other Celestial Bodies (London, Moscow, Washington, 27 January 1967) 610 U.N.T.S. 8843, *entered into force* 10 October 1967, Article 2 ('Outer Space Treaty'); Stephan Hobe, Bernhard Schmidt-Tedd, Kai-Uwe Schrogel and Gérardine Meishan Goh (eds), *Cologne Commentary on Space Law: Vol I* (Carl Heymanns Verlag 2009) 27. The law of the sea and outer space law also recognise the concept of the 'common heritage of mankind' applying to the seabed (UNCLOS, Article 136) and the Moon (Agreement governing the Activities of States on the Moon and Other Celestial Bodies (New York, 5 December 1979) 1363 U.N.T.S. 3, *entered into force* 11 July 1985, Article 11 ('Moon Agreement')); the principle of the common heritage of mankind is not clearly defined under international law, although it is understood to consist of four elements: prohibition on sovereign claims, use for peaceful purposes, sharing in management, and distribution of benefits (Edward Guntrip, 'The Common Heritage of Mankind: An Adequate Regime for Managing the Deep Seabed?' (2003) 4(2) Melb J Int'l L 376, 393; Cheryl Chan, Fatima Noor Khan and Sajida Awan, 'Bigger Issues in a Smaller World' in Blake Hudson, Jonathan Rosenbloom and Dan Cole (eds), *Routledge Handbook of the Study of the Commons* (Routledge 2019) 403).
86. *Western Sahara*, Advisory Opinion, I.C.J. Rep. 1975 (16 October), p. 12, p. 39 para. 79; *see also*, *Legal Status of Eastern Greenland*, Judgment (1933) P.C.I.J. Series A/B, No. 53, p. 63.
87. Robin Churchill, 'The Piracy Provisions of the UN Convention on the Law of the Sea – Fit for Purpose?' in Panos Koutrakos and Achilles Skordas (eds), *The Law and Practice of Piracy at Sea: European and International Perspectives* (Hart Publishing 2014) 20, the author at the same time recognising that the validity of the claims to sovereignty over the other territory of Antarctica is debated (*see* above n 83).
88. Grotius wrote, '[a]s the seas is commonly described in (Roman) law as *res nullius*, as common property, or as public property according to the law of nations …' (Hugo Grotius, *Mare Liberum* (Lodewijk Elzevir 1609) 13). Regarding the concept of *res publica*, or public property, '[i]t is

2.2.2 Sovereignty as the Foundation of International Civil Aviation Law

2.2.2.1 Sovereignty over National Airspace under the Chicago Convention

The principle of sovereignty sits at the heart of international civil aviation law and 'airspace sovereignty over national territory ... is well recognised by States as part of international customary law'.[90] The airspace, and more specifically the territorial classification of airspace, determines the physical extent of the exercise of a State's sovereignty. Reflecting their paramount position as the basis of international civil aviation law, the Chicago Convention deals with sovereignty and territory in Articles 1 and 2, respectively. Article 1 is declaratory of the above-mentioned customary law, recognising that '... every State has complete and exclusive sovereignty over the airspace above its territory'. In order to define the physical space over which a State has sovereignty as referred to in Article 1, it is necessary to establish both the horizontal and vertical limits; that is, what 'territory' encompasses and then to what altitude above the territory the 'airspace' extends. The first of these will be termed 'horizontal territory', while the second will be termed 'vertical territory'. The horizontal and vertical limits of a State's airspace will be addressed in Sections 2.2.3 and 2.2.4, respectively.

Article 2 is the starting point for establishing what is meant by 'territory' in Article 1:

> For the purposes of this Convention the territory of a State shall be deemed to be *the land areas and territorial waters adjacent thereto* under the sovereignty, suzerainty, protection or mandate of such State (emphasis added).

While the phrase 'suzerainty, protection or mandate' represented the relationships between certain States and other entities at the time of the drafting of the Chicago Convention, it is now 'a vestige of colonial times' which 'has no legal relevance at present' and will therefore not be further considered as part of this book.[91]

---

unclear to what extent the concept of the high seas as public domain coincides with its characterization as *res nullius* or *res communis* or with neither' (DP O'Connell, *The International Law of the Sea – Vol II* (OUP 1982) 794).

89. O'Connell (n 88) 792-794.
90. Bin Cheng, *The Law of International Air Transport* (Stevens & Sons Ltd 1962) 120; Eugène Pépin, *The Law of the Air and the Draft Articles Concerning the Law of the Sea Adopted by the International Law Commission at Its Eighth Session* (A/CONF.13/4) – Extract from the *Official Records of the United Nations Conference on the Law of the Sea, Volume I* (Preparatory Documents), United Nations Conference on the Law of the Sea, Geneva, 24 February-27 April 1958, 65.
91. Michael Milde, *International Air Law and ICAO* (3rd edn, Eleven International Publishing 2016) 37. The term 'mandate' is used in the UN today with a number of different meanings, all of which are to be distinguished from the context in which it is used in the Chicago Convention, referring to the League of Nations' reference of 'the system of international supervision over colonial territories' (United Nations, 'UN Documentation: Researching UN Mandates', available at research.un.org/en/docs/mandates#s-lg-box-2829995 accessed 5 May 2020). One of the ways in which it is used by the UN is in reference to the establishment of a peacekeeping mission, such as the mandate of the United Nations Interim Administration Mission in Kosovo (UNMIK), which established and enumerated the responsibilities of that mission (UNSC 1244 (10 June

Although the concept of sovereignty is not static or even capable of a universally accepted definition at a single point in time, such debate is outside the scope of this book and an area 'under the sovereignty of a State' is taken to be that forming (part of) a State accepted as such, consistent with the criteria in Article 1 of the Montevideo Convention.

As identified in Section 1.1 and as will be revisited at various stages throughout this book, the law of the sea has developed so that the maritime areas under the sovereignty of maritime States have increased over time. The interpretation of 'territory' under Articles 1 and 2 of the Chicago Convention has shifted as a result. This method of interpretation involves 'systemic integration',[92] or 'the process ... whereby international obligations are interpreted by reference to their normative environment ("system")'.[93] Systemic integration is recognised under Article 31(3)(c) of the Vienna Convention on the Law of Treaties which states that, as part of the general rule of interpretation, 'any relevant rules of international law applicable in the relations between the parties' shall be taken into account. It is presented as a remedial measure against the fragmentation of international law.[94] In relation to the changes to the concept of territory that have resulted from developments in the law of the sea, many of these have been recognised as customary international law.[95] This is important because the rules that fall within the scope of Article 31(3)(c) are only those 'applicable in the relations between the parties'. The State parties to the Chicago Convention and UNCLOS do not align – notably, there are more State parties to the Chicago Convention – and so the capacity for its rules to bind these non-State parties rests on their recognition as customary international law.[96] The use of customary international law as a tool for interpretation in systemic integration is further discussed in Section 3.3.4.5.

This leaves the question of whether a rule under UNCLOS that is not customary international law can ever be used for the interpretation of a provision under the Chicago Convention. The ILC has examined this matter and determined that the best solution 'is to permit reference to another treaty provided that the *parties in dispute* are

1999) UN Doc S/RES/1244). In carrying out its responsibilities, UNMIK entered into the Multilateral Agreement on the establishment of a European Common Aviation Area, as an 'additional Associated Party' to the agreement (Multilateral Agreement on the Establishment of the European Common Aviation Area [2006] OJ L285/3). Despite the distinction between the UNMIK mandate and the term as it was used under the League of Nations, UNMIK has been described in colonial terms, as having 'assumed almost complete governing authority, essentially designating the Balkan province a UN protectorate' and exercising 'neocolonial powers as a third-party sovereign authority' (Alexander Cooley and Hendrik Spruyt, *Contracting States: Sovereign Transfers in International Relations* (Princeton University Press 2009) 200).

92. Campbell McLachlan, 'The Principle of Systemic Integration and Article 31(3)(c) of the Vienna Convention' (2005) 54(2) ICLQ 279, 280; 'Report of the Study Group on Fragmentation of International Law: Difficulties Arising from the Diversification and Expansion of International Law', finalised by Martti Koskenniemi (ILC 58th Session, 13 April 2006) 208.
93. ILC (n 92) 208.
94. Adamanita Rachovista, 'The Principle of Systemic Integration in Human Rights Law' (2017) 66 ICLQ 557, 559.
95. For the extension of the territorial sea from 3 nm to 12 nm and the drawing of straight baselines, *see* Section 2.2.3.1.
96. *See also*, Section 2.7.1.

also parties to that other treaty'.[97] Recognising that this allows for divergence in the interpretation of a treaty, the report acknowledges that this is a fundamental element in the functioning of treaties in any case, as is evident in the various reservations that attach to them.[98] In the alternative, the absurd situation would result where a treaty that is widely ratified, such as the Chicago Convention, would increasingly be isolated from the wider body of international law, as any treaty with fewer State parties would be unable to be taken into account in interpreting the Chicago Convention, at least insofar as the rules were not codification of customary international law.[99] As mentioned in Section 1.1, and as will be further discussed in Section 5.4, the concept of archipelagic States was codified in UNCLOS and has led to an extension of the area that comes under the sovereignty of such State.

The provisions under UNCLOS relating to archipelagic States built on maritime claims by States, such as Indonesia and the Philippines, that predated the Convention[100] and State practice has broadly been consistent with the regime under UNCLOS since its adoption.[101] This has led to a debate that the archipelagic State regime and the related archipelagic sea lanes passage are customary international law[102] and indeed, the US, as a non-State party to UNCLOS, has declared archipelagic sea lanes passage to be customary international law.[103] As will be discussed further in Sections 5.4.3 and 5.4.4, despite broad consistency with the UNCLOS regime, there are significant variations to State practice that are restrictive in finding a status of customary international law and rather the regime for archipelagic States is more likely 'based on interaction between custom and treaty'.[104] Despite this, ICAO stipulated upon the adoption of UNCLOS that 'territory' under the Chicago Convention now includes archipelagic waters.[105] Considering the foregoing discussion on the scope of Article 31(3)(c), it is difficult to see how non-State parties to UNCLOS would be bound by this interpretation of 'territory' under the Chicago Convention unless, like the US, they have specifically declared their intention to be bound by the provisions, or until the provisions are formally accepted as customary international law. At the same time, in the absence of express and ongoing opposition to it, ICAO's position on the role of UNCLOS in interpreting the Chicago Convention in this instance may ultimately contribute to evidence of the customary international law status of the archipelagic State regime under UNCLOS, at least in part.

97. ILC (n 92) 238.
98. *Ibid.*
99. *Ibid.* 237.
100. Alina Miron, 'The Archipelagic Status Reconsidered in Light of the *South China Sea* and *Düzgit Integrity* Awards' (2018) 15(3) Indones J Int Law 306, 308.
101. Carlos Jiménez Piernas, 'Archipelagic Waters' (Max Planck Encyclopedia of Public International Law 2009) 29. State practice is arguably too varied to establish customary international law, as to which *see* Sections 5.4.3 and 5.4.4.
102. Miron (n 100) 309-311.
103. Hugo Caminos and Vincent P Cogliati-Bantz, *The Legal Regime of Straits* (CUP 2014) 472.
104. Jiménez Piernas (n 101) 29.
105. *See* Section 5.4.2.

2.2.2.2 *Article 1 of the Paris Convention (1919) to the Chicago Convention (1944)*

The principle of complete and exclusive sovereignty over airspace for all States has been the foundation of international civil aviation law since the beginning: it was codified in the first multilateral agreement governing civil aviation, the Paris Convention, signed in 1919. Article 1 of the Paris Convention reads:

> [t]he High Contracting Parties recognise that every Power has complete and exclusive sovereignty over the airspace above its territory.

No objections were offered to the recognition of the principle in the Paris Convention during its drafting process, and no further discussion was recorded at the Chicago Conference regarding the principle as it appears in Article 1 of the Chicago Convention.[106] Despite this, the principle of sovereignty over airspace had been a point of contention between States in the lead-up to the Paris Convention, from the early 1900s. At this time, there were four main schools of thought on the matter.[107] One of these, not surprisingly, advocated exclusive sovereignty while, in direct opposition, another was a proponent of absolute freedom of air navigation. In between the two extremes was the belief that sovereignty should be accepted but with a vertical limitation, and finally, that sovereignty should be accepted but with functional limitations. The last of these - sovereignty with functional limitations - appeared to be the most dominant although opinion 'widely differed on the question of the degree of limitation', from innocent passage through national airspace to limitations by way of international agreement.[108] World War I or, more so the paramount importance of national security during this time, led to States[109] prohibiting the flight of foreign aircraft over their territories, which resulted in the creation of State practice that 'evidenced a recognition of the principle of State sovereignty in the air'.[110] It was this practice that came to be reflected in Article 1 of the Paris Convention and later under the Chicago Convention. In reaching the decision, States were required to consider whether the airspace above their land is part of their territory or whether, like the high seas, it is *res communis*.[111] The final decision to regulate international civil aviation

106. Milde (n 91) 36.
107. Peter H Sands, Jorge de Sousa Freitas and Geoffrey N Pratt, 'An Historical Survey of International Air Law Before the Second World War' (1960-1961) 7(1) McGill L J 24, 28. The authors address these views as those of 'publicists of international air law'. Refer to the source for the names of the most prominent publicists in each group.
108. *Ibid.*
109. *Ibid.* Including the Netherlands, Switzerland, Denmark, Sweden, Norway, Greece, Spain, Italy, Romania, Bulgaria and China.
110. *Ibid.* 33.
111. Ronald I C Bartsch, *Aviation Law in Australia* (4th edn, Thomson Reuters 2013) 6. Although freedom of the high seas was not codified until the Convention on the High Seas in 1958, it existed as customary law well before: 'The oceans had long been subject to the freedom of the seas doctrine - a principle put forth in the seventeenth century essentially limiting national rights and jurisdiction over the oceans to a narrow belt of sea surrounding a nation's coastline. The remainder of the seas was proclaimed to be free to all and belonging to none' (United Nations Division for Ocean Affairs and the Law of the Sea, 'The United Nations Convention on

with the sovereignty of States as the baseline principle ultimately quashed the voices of those who willed a law of the sea-inspired freedom of the air; in the words of Havel and Sanchez, 'there would be no global commercial airspace'.[112]

The Paris Convention provided, alongside the principle of sovereignty, freedoms in relation to overflight that did not withstand the Chicago negotiations. Specifically, under Article 2 of the Paris Convention, each State to the treaty was 'in time of peace to accord freedom of innocent passage above its territory to the aircraft of the other contracting States'. This appears to be a functional limitation to sovereignty but it was in fact 'granted as a privilege ... not conceded as a natural right', and was therefore consistent with absolute sovereignty.[113] With this in mind, the corresponding Article 15 was somewhat obscurely phrased, providing that '[e]very aircraft of a contracting State has the *right* to cross the air space of another State without landing' (emphasis added).

2.2.2.3 The Implications of Sovereignty over National Airspace

National security was a central consideration again during the drafting of the Chicago Convention,[114] but over the intervening decades from the Paris Convention to the Chicago Conference, the development of the commercial aviation industry meant that the 'economic protection of the national air transport industry ... became the dominant factor' in the negotiations.[115] This shift is reflected in the Chicago Convention under which *inter alia* the right of overflight has been restricted to non-scheduled flights under Article 5, and the more controversial matter of the right of overflight for scheduled air services - the first freedom of the air - is omitted, to be agreed upon separately by States.[116]

At the Chicago Conference, the United Kingdom (UK) was of the opinion that certain economic aspects[117] of air transport should be tightly regulated at the international level in order to allow States to protect their national carriers.[118] That is, States should impose economic restrictions on the operation of international services by foreign carriers to and from points in the first State's territory. This view was met with

the Law of the Sea: A Historical Perspective' (paper prepared for the International Year of the Ocean, 1998), available at www.un.org/depts/los/convention_agreements/convention_historical_perspective.htm accessed 21 August 2018). *See* Section 2.7.1 for further discussion on the Convention on the High Seas 1958 and of the customary status of freedom of the high seas.

112. Brian Havel and Gabriel Sanchez, *The Principles and Practice of International Aviation Law* (CUP 2014) 38.
113. Sands, de Sousa Freitas and Pratt (n 107) 33.
114. The Chicago Convention was, like the Paris Convention, negotiated in the wake of a world war and, particularly in World War II, the use of aircraft had a devastating impact.
115. Peter H Sands, James T Lyon and Geoffrey N Pratt, 'An Historical Survey of International Air Law Since 1944' (1960-1961) 7(2) McGill L J 125, 126.
116. The distinction between scheduled air services and non-scheduled flights and the exchange of overflight rights in respect of each will be discussed in Section 2.3.3.
117. Namely, routes, rates and frequencies (Proceedings to the Chicago Convention: Vol. I, Pt I 'Verbatim Minutes of Second Plenary Session, November 2' (Document 42) 65); Bin Cheng, 'The Right to Fly' (1959) 42 Trans Grotius Soc 99, 109.
118. Peter Haanappel, 'Bilateral Air Transport Agreements – 1913-1980' (1980) 5(2) Md J Int'l L 241, 243.

direct opposition by, most prominently, the US which at the time of the Chicago Conference had a strong international air transport network and civil aircraft fleet relative to the European States present, including the UK.[119] Other States fell on either side of the debate, but not necessarily for the same reasons. New Zealand[120] and Australia,[121] supported by France and Afghanistan,[122] advocated for the internationalisation of the ownership and operation of air services. This position was incompatible with the UK's restrictive approach and placed these States together with the US in their opposition to the UK approach, although the US was also unequivocally opposed to the international ownership of carriers.[123] On the other side of the debate, Canada supported the UK's position of international control of certain economic aspects of air transport.[124] The US ultimately received insufficient support from other States for its pro-market position to succeed,[125] and international air transport has, as a result, traditionally been highly regulated in the economic sphere through a system of restrictive bilateral air services agreements (ASAs). In essence, complete and exclusive sovereignty of airspace led to national airspace being '*de jure* closed for foreign aircraft and their operators'.[126]

In addition to national security and economic interests, State sovereignty is also at the heart of ensuring the safety of international civil aviation. Each State has a responsibility for safety oversight based on aircraft nationality and territorial jurisdiction, both of which stem from sovereignty.[127] This entails both rights and obligations of a State. States are required to ensure that international civil aviation is operated consistently with the international minimum Standards set out in the annexes to the Chicago Convention and that the aircraft bearing their nationality mark meet these Standards and comply with the laws and regulations of the States over whose territory they operate.[128] States have the right to exclude aircraft from their territory in the case

119. Peter Haanappel, 'Bilateral Air Transport Agreements – 1913-1980' (1980) 5(2) Md J Int'l L 241, 243; Pablo Mendes de Leon, *Introduction to Air Law* (10th edn, Wolters Kluwer 2017) 9-10.
120. Proceedings to the Chicago Convention: Vol. I, Pt I 'Verbatim Minutes of Second Plenary Session, November 2' (Document 42) 79.
121. *Ibid.* 83.
122. Proceedings to the Chicago Convention: Vol. I, Pt II 'Verbatim Minutes of Joint Plenary Meeting of Committees I, III, and IV, November 22' (Document 372) 457.
123. Proceedings to the Chicago Convention: Vol. I, Pt II 'Verbatim Minutes of Plenary Session, November 8' (Document 117) 545-546; Cheng (n 117) 109.
124. Proceedings to the Chicago Convention (Document 42) (n 120) 70-71.
125. Havel and Sanchez (n 112) 38. A compromise of sorts was reached by the States at the Chicago Conference, in that it was decided that 'the first Freedom and the second Freedom be unconditionally embodied in a separate agreement', which went on to be the Transit Agreement (Proceedings to the Chicago Convention: Vol. I, Pt II 'Minutes of Meeting of the Joint Sub-Committee of Committees I, III, and IV, December 2' (Document 463) 514).
126. Mendes de Leon (n 119) 10.
127. Jiefang Huang, *Aviation Safety and ICAO* (Kluwer Law International 2009) 31.
128. This is provided in ASAs between States, including in the Transit Agreement (*see* Section 2.6.1). These rights and obligations stem from various provisions in the Chicago Convention. Article 11 reads that 'the laws and regulations of a contracting State relating … to the operation and navigation of such aircraft while within its territory … shall be complied with by such aircraft … while within the territory of that State'. Regarding specifically the Rules of the Air, '[e]ach contracting State undertakes to adopt measures to insure that every aircraft flying over or maneuvering within its territory and that every aircraft carrying its nationality mark,

that they act inconsistently with those laws and regulations, by revoking a carrier's operating permit.[129] At the same time, the fact that States are required to implement internationally agreed Standards with the aim of achieving international uniformity in the regulation of the safety of international civil aviation is also a restriction on sovereignty.[130] As Huang explains: '[i]t follows from the principle of sovereignty that a State is free to enact aviation law in whatever form it prefers, *provided that the enactment is compatible with its international obligations under the Chicago Convention* and other applicable rules of international law' (emphasis added).[131] The extent to which this applies depends on the degree to which a State views itself to be bound by Standards adopted in the annexes to the Chicago Convention which are, as discussed in Section 2.3.2, generally understood to be binding.

The concept of sovereignty over airspace is firmly entrenched in international civil aviation law but it is by no means static. In more recent years, the third school of thought mentioned above – sovereignty with a vertical limitation – has been recognised by the space law community as a solution to the uncertainty of the physical scope of the legal regimes applying to airspace and outer space.[132] In the Chicago Convention's silence on the matter, international space law may in the not-too-distant future require an implied vertical limitation to the interpretation of 'complete and exclusive sovereignty' under Article 1 of the Chicago Convention, as will be addressed in Section 2.2.4.

2.2.3 Horizontal Delimitation of Airspace

2.2.3.1 The Boundaries of the Territorial Sea

Adjacent to those States that happen to be coastal States, their territorial sea is defined under Article 3 of UNCLOS, which provides that a territorial sea may extend to 12 nm from the baseline of a State, where the baseline is generally the low-water line along the coast.[133] Within the bounds of this provision, States have the right to determine the extent of their territorial sea under their domestic laws.

Prior to UNCLOS, the breadth of the territorial sea was debated and as a corollary, the horizontal limits of national airspace under the Chicago Convention were also

wherever such aircraft may be, shall comply with the rules and regulations relating to the flight and maneuver of aircraft there in force' (Article 12). Further articles addressing matters such as the provision of air navigation facilities (Article 28) and interception under Article 3 *bis* provide States with rights and obligations aimed at helping to ensure the safety of international civil aviation over their territories.

129. This is provided in ASAs between States, including in the Transit Agreement (*see* Section 2.6.1).
130. Huang (n 127) 62.
131. *Ibid.* 42.
132. Committee on the Peaceful Uses of Outer Space, Promoting the discussion of the matters relating to the definition and delimitation of outer space with a view to elaborating a common position of States Members of the Committee on the Peaceful Uses of Outer Space: Working paper prepared by the Chair of the Working Group on the Definition and Delimitation of Outer Space of the Legal Subcommittee, 57th Session A/AC.105/C.2/L.302 (Vienna, 9-20 April 2018) 3.
133. UNCLOS, Articles 3 and 5. See the paragraph below on the determination of the baseline as to the inclusion here of the qualification 'generally'.

uncertain. UNCLOS entered into force thirty-seven years after the Chicago Convention and, although from the early twentieth century until UNCLOS the breadth of territorial sea was recognised in most parts of the world under customary international law as 3 nm, States had begun to make increasingly expansive claims from the mid-twentieth century.[134] UNCLOS confirmed the 12 nm territorial sea limit and this is now recognised as customary.[135] Most States declare their territorial sea to extend this distance from their baselines, including States that are not party to UNCLOS such as the US. However, some States – Jordan and Greece – claim less, and others – Benin, Ecuador, El Salvador, Liberia, Peru, and Somalia – claim up to 200 nm.[136] Claims extending beyond 12 nm remain controversial and 'call for careful assessment',[137] but they are overwhelmingly in the minority and, leaving aside these few outlying States, the airspace over which a State is permitted to exercise its sovereignty in terms of the horizontal extent of its territory is clearly defined under international law.

The determination of the baseline, from which the territorial sea is measured, depends on the specific features of a coastline (*see* Figure 2.1). For example, in the *Anglo-Norwegian Fisheries Case*,[138] the ICJ declared that straight baselines, as opposed to baselines strictly following the curvature of the land, are legitimate depending on the circumstances. In this case, the decision was made on the basis that the section of Norway's coastline in question contains deeply indented fjords, islands, islets, rocks and reefs. The ICJ's decision on the drawing of straight baselines for the types of coast as considered in the *Anglo-Norwegian Fishes* case is recognised as customary and is codified in Article 7 UNCLOS.[139] UNCLOS sets out methods for determining the territorial baseline with consideration to features including but not limited to reefs, deep indentations in the coastline or a fringe of islands off the coast, bays and ports.[140]

Baselines, and therefore the outermost limits of the territorial sea, can also be shifted seaward by permanent harbour works in accordance with Article 11 UNCLOS. Under this article, harbour works that 'form an integral part of the harbour system are

134. John Noyes, 'The Territorial Sea and Contiguous Zone' in Donald Rothwell, Alex G Oude Elferink, Karen N Scott and Tim Stephens (eds), *The Oxford Handbook of the Law of the Sea* (OUP 2015) 93.
135. *Territorial and Maritime Dispute (Nicaragua v. Colombia)*, Judgment, I.C.J. Rep. 2012 (19 November) p. 624, p. 690.
136. United Nations, 'Table of Claims to Maritime Jurisdiction (as at 15 July 2011)', available at www.un.org/Depts/los/LEGISLATIONANDTREATIES/PDFFILES/table_summary_of_claims.pdf accessed 1 May 2018.
137. Crawford (n 84) 246.
138. *Fisheries (United Kingdom v. Norway)*, Judgment, I.C.J. Rep. 1951 (18 December), p. 116.
139. Crawford (n 84) 244-245.
140. UNCLOS, Articles 6, 7(1), 10 and 11, respectively. An Arbitral Tribunal of the Permanent Court of Arbitration (PCA) recently considered the legal status and delimitation of the Bay of Savudrija/Piran (as it is known in Croatia)/the Bay of Piran (as it is known in Slovenia), among other maritime delimitations, in the case of *In the Matter of an Arbitration under the Arbitration Agreement between the Government of the Republic of Croatia and the Government of the Republic of Slovenia, Signed on 4 November 2009 (Croatia v. Slovenia)*, P.C.A. Case No. 2010-04, 29 June 2017. The Tribunal decided that the bay has the status of internal waters, divided between the States by a boundary line as determined by the Tribunal based on consideration of the *effectivités* invoked by the States, and that the bay is closed by a straight baseline from which Slovenia and Croatia's territorial seas are measured (pp. 243-292 paras 771-948 and pp. 370-371 VIII Dispositif, II A-C).

regarded as forming part of the coast'. Furthermore, State practice indicates that human-induced extension of the natural coastline, that is, land reclamation, can extend the baseline where the reclaimed land is 'an integral part of the mainland or island'.[141] This has occurred, for instance, in the Netherlands where land has been reclaimed along the coastline for the purpose of extending the Port of Rotterdam.[142] The implications of land reclamation for overflight will be addressed in Chapter 3.

To the landward side of the baseline sits a State's internal waters.[143] As part of the territory of a State, the airspace above internal waters is de facto closed to the aircraft of other States under international civil aviation law, just as the airspace over other sovereign territory.

Figure 2.1 Depiction of a Baseline Calculated in Consideration of Various Coastal Features[144]

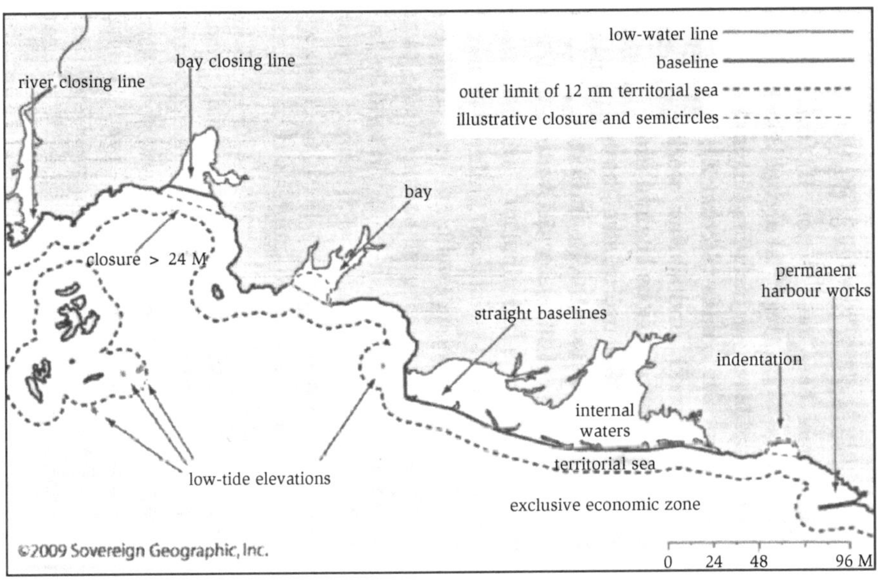

141. Coalter G Lathrop, J Ashley Roach and Donald R Rothwell, 'Baselines under the International Law of the Sea: Reports of the International Law Association Committee on Baselines under the International Law of the Sea' (2018) 2(1-2) The Law of the Sea 1, 52-53.
142. *Ibid.*
143. UNCLOS, Article 8(1).
144. *Source*: My Universities, 'Baselines', available at myuniversities.wordpress.com/2013/10/24/ baselines/ accessed 16 June 2018.

2.2.3.2 *Overflight Rights in Territorial Waters*

Just as States have sovereignty over the airspace above their territorial waters,[145] so too do they have sovereignty over the territory beneath: the sea itself[146] and the bed and subsoil.[147] Despite this, the implications of State sovereignty differ for overflight and navigation in respect of the territorial sea.

Sovereignty under international civil aviation law has resulted in a situation where transit through – or any other use of – a State's airspace, including its territorial seas, may only occur on the basis of permission from the State.[148] In contrast, under customary international law as recognised in Article 17 UNCLOS, ships have the right of innocent passage through another State's territorial sea. In other words, although the law of the sea recognises that the territorial sea of a State, and the State's exercise of sovereignty over it, extends from the subsoil up to and including the airspace, the privileges of other States differ depending on whether transit is on the sea or through airspace over the sea. Innocent passage is presumed to exist for the use of the sea but not, in accordance with international civil aviation law, for the use of its airspace.[149]

2.2.4 Vertical Delimitation of Airspace

The vertical limit of a State's territory is less clearly defined, or, more specifically, there is no internationally agreed altitude at which a State's sovereignty over its airspace ends. This is important because, while States enjoy sovereignty over their airspace, it does not extend to outer space. The non-appropriation by States of outer space is one of the founding principles of space law and is provided in Article 2 of the Treaty on Principles Governing the Activities of States in the Exploration and Use of Outer Space, including the Moon and Other Celestial Bodies ('Outer Space Treaty').[150] Article 2 reads:

> Outer space, including the Moon and other celestial bodies, is not subject to national appropriation by claim of sovereignty, by means of use or occupation, or by any other means.

In other words, while the foundation of international civil aviation law is State sovereignty over airspace, the basis of space law is that no State may claim sovereignty over outer space.

---

145. As recognised under Articles 1 and 2 of the Chicago Convention, and also by Article 2(2) UNCLOS. Article 2(2) UNCLOS in this sense refers not just to the territorial sea but also to internal waters and archipelagic waters.
146. UNCLOS, Article 2(1).
147. *Ibid.* Article 2(2).
148. Chicago Convention, Article 1 read together with Articles 3(c), 5, 6 and 8. *See* Sections 2.2.2.1, 2.3.3, 2.3.4 and 2.4.4.
149. In contrast to the territorial sea, the internal waters of a State are also closed to foreign ships.
150. Treaty on Principles Governing the Activities of States in the Exploration and Use of Outer Space, including the Moon and Other Celestial Bodies (London, Moscow, Washington, 27 January 1967) 610 U.N.T.S. 8843 *entered into force* 10 October 1967 ('Outer Space Treaty').

On the cusp of the adoption of the Outer Space Treaty, John Cobb Cooper, member of the US delegation at the Chicago Conference, recognised the necessity of 'defining airspace', as he termed the task. He saw it as a pressing concern as operations involving craft – whether they ultimately be defined as aircraft or spacecraft – become more commonly conducted by private enterprises in which case, at least part of the flight – that in airspace – may fall within the scope of the Chicago Convention:

> While it is true that most instrumentalities usable in outer space are not civil in character but are launched and controlled by a particular state, nevertheless this will not always be true.[151]

Indeed, today, commercial private activity in space is more common than State activity.[152]

Although the two principles – sovereignty over airspace and non-appropriation of outer space – require delimitation and although this has been acknowledged since the signing of the Outer Space Treaty, States have not agreed upon a fixed altitude that demarcates the two 'areas'.

The United Nations Committee on the Peaceful Uses of Outer Space (UNCOPUOS), which among other things was established for 'studying legal problems arising from the exploration of outer space',[153] recognises two main approaches in the debate surrounding the delimitation of airspace and outer space: the functionalist approach and the spatialist approach.[154] The spatialist approach supports delimitation and argues that the altitude should be determined by science, for example, by considering the aerodynamic characteristics of flight in accordance with the *von Kármán* line,[155] sitting at around 100 kilometres (km) above mean sea level where 'aerodynamic lift decreases to critical levels and the lowest perigees obtainable by space objects can be reasonably identified'.[156] The functionalist approach, on the other hand, argues that the applicable legal regime should be determined by the nature of the activity being conducted, including the vehicle, that is, an aircraft or a space object, and the objective of the activity, that is, for example, whether to transport people or cargo from one point on Earth to another or whether to orbit the Earth.[157] UNCOPUOS officially supports the spatialist approach, with delimitation based on the *von Kármán* line, a position 'based

151. John Cobb Cooper, 'The Chicago Convention – After Twenty Years' (1965) 19(3) U Miami L Rev 333, 343-344.
152. Paul Stephen Dempsey and Maria Manoli, *Suborbital Flights and the Delimitation of Air Space vis -à-vis Outer Space: Functionalism, Spatialism and State Sovereignty*, A submission by the Space Safety Law and Regulation Committee of the International Association for the Advancement of Space Safety to the Legal Subcommittee of the Committee on the Peaceful Uses of Outer Space, Vienna 9-20 April 2018, U.N. Doc. A/AC.105/C.2/2018/CRP.9 (29 March 2018) 13.
153. United Nations Office for Outer Space Affairs, 'Committee on the Peaceful Uses of Outer Space', www.unoosa.org/oosa/en/ourwork/copuos/index.html accessed 1 May 2018.
154. Working Paper of the Legal Subcommittee of the Committee on the Peaceful Uses of Outer Space, GOAR, 57th Session U.N. Doc. A/AC.105/C.2/L.302 (Vienna, 9-20 April 2018) 2.
155. Stephan Hobe, Nicolai Ruckteschell and David Heffernan, *Cologne Compendium on Air Law in Europe* (Carl Heymanns Verlag 2013) 206-207.
156. Working Paper of the Legal Subcommittee of UNCOPUOS (n 154) 3.
157. Dempsey and Manoli (n 152) 11.

on the opinion not only of academics but also delegations to [UNCOPUOS] and the Conference on Disarmament'.[158]

In the absence of an internationally agreed altitude for delimitation, national laws continue to define the vertical limits of the sovereignty of airspace, taking into account the national interests of the States implementing the legislation. For example, Denmark's legislation expressly defines outer space as the 'space above the altitude of 100km above mean sea level'.[159] This delimitation by Denmark has been described by Hulsroj and Pecujlic as 'a bold statement, indeed'.[160] In contrast, the UK's recently enacted *Space Industry Act 2018* refers to an altitude in order to establish the scope of the application of the legislation rather than to define outer space. Namely, the act refers to activities operating at or above the stratosphere,[161] which is understood to extend to an altitude of approximately 50 km above the Earth.[162] Similarly, Australia's national space legislation only applies to launches or attempted launches that go beyond 100km above mean sea level,[163] but the Australian government has made clear that this is not an attempt to define outer space[164] and that it is therefore not a recognition by Australia of an altitude at which its sovereignty over the airspace is extinguished.[165] While the legislation of these States is relatively consistent in terms of the altitude it applies to, not all national legislation follows the same trend: the

158. Working Paper of the Legal Subcommittee of UNCOPUOS (n 154) 3. The Conference on Disarmament is a multilateral forum that meets annually to address arms control and disarmament (United Nations, 'Conference on Disarmament: An Introduction to the Conference', available at www.unog.ch/80256EE600585943/(httpPages)/BF18ABFEFE5D344DC1256F3100311CE9?OpenDocument accessed 13 March 2019). The debate continues with momentum though: in November 2018, the Fédération Aéronautique Internationale (FAI) proposed to the International Astronautical Federation that a workshop be held to consider new scientific analyses which suggest that the *von Kármán* line should be reduced from 100 km to 80 km (Fédération Aéronautique Internationale (FAI), 'Statement about the Karman Line' (30 November 2018), available at www.fai.org/news/statement-about-karman-line accessed 4 August 2016).

159. The Danish Act on Activities on Outer Space, Act No. 409 of 11 May 2016, Article 4(4), translated from the original: 'Den del af rummet, der ligger over 100 km over havets overflade'.

160. Peter Hulsroj and Anja Nakarada Pecujlic, 'New in the Nest: The Danish Space Act' (2016) 41(3) A&SL 503, 504.

161. *Space Industry Act 2018* (UK), Article 5(a) and (b) read together with Article 4. More specifically, it refers to both 'space activity' and 'suborbital activity' as 'spaceflight activities', where 'suborbital activity' is that of a craft which operates above the stratosphere or of a balloon that is capable of reaching the stratosphere. 'Space activity' refers to 'any activity in outer space', among other things, where outer space is not further defined (Article 4). For further discussion on this aspect of the Act *see*, Thomas Cheney, UK Public Bill Committee Debate – Space Industry Bill (24 January 2018); Lesley Jane Smith and Ruairidh JM Leishman, 'Up, up and Away: An Update on the UK's Latest Plans for Space Activities' (2019) 44(1) A&SL 1, 14-15; Georgina Hutton, *The Space Industry Bill 2017-2019* (HC Briefing Paper, 2 February 2018) 5-6.

162. *Oxford English Dictionary*, available at www.oed.com/view/Entry/191344?redirectedFrom=stratosphere#eid accessed 17 April 2019.

163. *Space Activities Act 1998* (Cth) Section 8.

164. National Legislation and Practice Relating to Definition and Delimitation of Outer Space – Note by the Secretariat A/AC.105/865/Add.1 (20 March 2006); House of Representatives, Commonwealth of Australia, Space Activities Amendment Bill 2002, Explanatory Memorandum (20 February 2002) Item 2.

165. House of Representatives, Commonwealth of Australia, Space Activities Amendment Bill 2002, Explanatory Memorandum (20 February 2002) 4.

equatorial States that are signatories to the Bogotá Declaration claim sovereignty over the geostationary orbits above their territories, which is at an altitude of approximately 36,000 km above mean sea level.[166] The Bogotá Declaration does not purport to contribute to the discussion on the delimitation of airspace and outer space, but it demonstrates the vastly different approach States take in their application of the non-appropriation principle under Article 2 of the Outer Space Treaty in the absence of an internationally accepted altitude.

On an international level, the absence of an international delimitation is an 'important legal lacuna'[167] and, as mentioned above, one that will become increasingly so in light of growing private commercial space activities and rapid technological developments transforming space transportation.[168] This book is limited to considering navigation through airspace and will not further address the laws applying to outer space.

2.3 OVERFLIGHT RIGHTS FOR CIVIL AIRCRAFT IN NATIONAL AIRSPACE

2.3.1 The Different Legal Bases Stemming from the Chicago Convention

In addition to the territory being overflown – that is, whether it is national or international airspace – there are a number of relevant factors affecting the legal basis for overflight rights, as identified in Section 2.1. This section will examine those factors for the operation of civil aircraft and discuss the corresponding legal basis for each of them. It will first address the distinction between scheduled air services and non-scheduled flights. It will then set out the multilateral exchange of the right of overflight for non-scheduled flights under Article 5 of the Chicago Convention and the exchange of overflight rights for scheduled air services pursuant to Article 6. In order to address this latter point in context, the distinction between transit rights and traffic rights, as defined in Section 2.3.3.1 below, will be addressed. Finally, this part will discuss the legal basis for the exchange of overflight rights for unmanned aircraft. Figure 2.2 provides a diagrammatic representation of the relationship between these elements.

166. Declaration of the First Meeting of Equatorial Countries (Bogotá, 3 December 1976). The States are Brazil, Colombia, Congo, Ecuador, Indonesia, Kenya, Uganda and Zaire. Five of these States – Brazil, Ecuador, Indonesia, Kenya and Uganda – have ratified the Outer Space Treaty and Colombia is a signatory.
167. Working Paper of the Legal Subcommittee of UNCOPUOS (n 154) 4.
168. Dempsey and Manoli (n 152) 2.

Figure 2.2 Legal Basis for Overflight Rights in National Airspace[169]

2.3.2 Air Transport Outside the Normative Powers of ICAO

Under Article 44 of the Chicago Convention, ICAO's role is twofold: first, 'to develop the principles and techniques of international air *navigation*' and, second, 'to foster the planning and development of international air *transport*' (emphasis added).[170] International air navigation involves the non-commercial aspects of international civil aviation, while international air transport encompasses the commercial/business aspects.[171] Leclerc describes the division as follows:

> The first category relates to standards on air navigation. It is made up of technical and operational rules and includes regulations governing safety. The second category relates to standards on the economic and commercial aspects of international aviation. This specific branch of international civil aviation law is thus concerned with the economic regulation of international aviation, and at times comes down to the matter of traffic rights incorporating, in its broadest definition, the rules determining the allocation of routes, tariffs, capacity and frequency.[172]

169. *Source*: made by the author.
170. Chicago Convention, Article 44.
171. Havel and Sanchez (n 112) 69: '… there are parallel frameworks that organize international air services. One is the product of the Chicago Convention and focuses primarily on setting the terms of international technical cooperation and harmonization. The other is much more specific economic system that is based on bilateral exchange where two States negotiate an air service agreement (ASA) that grants each party's carriers the privilege to carry passengers, cargo or a combination of both to points to, from, over, or beyond their respective territories'.
172. Translated from the original: 'La première catégorie se rapporte aux normes relatives à la navigation aérienne. Elle se trouve constituée de règles techniques et opérationnelles et englobe une réglementation liée dès l'origine à l'exigence de sécurité. La seconde catégorie se rapporte quant à elle aux normes encadrant les aspects économiques et commerciaux de

This division is also reflected in the structure of the Chicago Convention itself: Part I addresses air navigation, while Part III addresses international air transport. It is in relation to the international air navigation aspects that the normative powers of ICAO sit, and consequently it is these aspects that the Chicago Convention annexes address. Normative powers here refer specifically to the competence of the ICAO Council to adopt Standards and Recommended Practices (SARPs) pursuant to Articles 54(l) and 90 of the Chicago Convention.

The Chicago Convention is an anomaly in public international law in the quasi-legislative function that it gives to the ICAO Council in relation to the adoption of SARPs for the air navigation aspects of international civil aviation. The SARPs comprise the annexes to the Convention and therefore become part of the rules that regulate international civil aviation, but they do not form part of the Convention itself. On whether SARPs have binding force, Milde has described the question as causing 'frequent misunderstandings', highlighting that some commentators consider Standards to have the same legal value as treaty provisions while others view SARPs as 'no more than guidance material or "soft law"'.[173] Cheng argues that the Standards are not binding, hence the term '*quasi*-legislative' to describe the Council.[174] States are mixed in their positions, some considering Standards to be a form of soft law and others considering them to be binding.[175]

l'activité aérienne internationale. Cette branche spécifique du droit international de l'aviation civile s'intéresse ainsi à la régulation économique de l'activité aérienne internationale, et se résume parfois à la question des droits de trafic intégrant, dans sa définition la plus large, les règles déterminant l'attribution des routes, des tarifs, des capacités et des fréquences' (Thomas Leclerc, Les mesures correctives des émissions aériennes de gaz à effet de serre. Contribution à l'étude des interactions entre les ordres juridiques en droit international public (Ph.D. thesis, E.M. Meijers Instituut, Leiden University, 2017) 65 67).

173. Michael Milde, 'Enforcement of Aviation Safety Standards: Problems of Safety Oversight' (1996) 45 ZLW 3, 4.
174. Cheng (n 90) 64.
175. For example, consider the contrast between France, on the one hand, and the US and the Netherlands, on the other, as to which *see*, Vincent Correia and Béatrice Trigeaud, 'Transport, Navigation et Sources du Droit International – Remarques Générales' in Saïda El Boudouhi (ed), *Les Transport au Prisme du Droit International Public* (Editions A Pedone 2019) 54-55: 'In France, the Council of State traditionally refuses to recognise the binding nature of the technical annexes of the Chicago Convention, which it considers to be mere recommendations, including with regard to standards', translated from the original: 'En France, le Conseil d'Etat refuse traditionnellement de reconnaître le caractère obligatoire des annexes techniques à la convention de Chicago, qui constituent selon lui de simples recommandations, y compris en ce qui concerne les norms'; the US and the Netherlands: 'In the United States, for example, the standards are enforced by the US Department of Transportation (DOT) and the Federal Aviation Authority (FAA) without prior approval from Congress. Likewise, in the Netherlands, the technical annexes published in the *Tractatenblad* acquire a force comparable to the Chicago Convention, without being subject to the control of the Dutch Parliament', translated from the original: 'Aux Etats-Unis, par exemple, les normes sont appliquées par *l'US Department of Transportation* (DOT) et la *Federal Aviation Authority* (FAA) sans approbation préalable du Congrès. De même, aux Pays-Bas, les annexes techniques publiées au *Tractatenblad* acquièrent une force comparable à la convention de Chicago, sans être soumises au contrôle du Parlement néerlandais'.

There is a clear distinction, however, between the contribution of Standards, on the one hand, and Recommended Practices, on the other, to international air navigation. 'Standards' and 'Recommended Practices' are defined, respectively, as:

> 'any specification for physical characteristics, configuration, matériel, performance, personnel or procedure ...',
>
> 'the uniform application of which is recognized as *necessary* for the safety or regularity of international air navigation and to which Contracting States *will conform* ...' (Standard; emphasis added), and 'the uniform application of which is recognized as *desirable* in the interest of safety, regularity or efficiency of international air navigation, and to which Contracting States *will endeavour to conform* ...' (Recommended Practice; emphasis added).[176]

Under Article 37 of the Chicago Convention, which applies to SARPs in general, each contracting State is required to 'undertake to collaborate in securing the highest practicable degree of uniformity' in regulations, standards, procedures and organisation. This is central to the aim of the Convention in ensuring the 'safe and orderly' development of civil aviation.[177] At the same time, national standards may be 'more stringent' than the SARPs[178] and States may also, under certain circumstances, deviate from them. In the case that a State deviates from a Standard – which, recalling the definition above, States 'will conform with' – it is required to file the difference with ICAO and immediately notify other States of the difference.[179] Article 38 of the Convention allows for the deviation from a Standard in the case that the State 'deems it necessary' to do so.[180] Where a State has filed a difference to an ICAO Standard, it is the responsibility of the aircraft of other States to ensure it meets the regulation of the State when within its territory.[181]

International air navigation, governed by these SARPs, includes both technical and operational aspects,[182] with most areas of international civil aviation law entailing elements of each.[183] Safety is a principal aspect of international air navigation and ensuring it is a primary objective of ICAO, as recognised in the Preamble and Article 44 of the Chicago Convention.[184] The Chicago Convention was originally silent on the

176. These definitions are in the Foreword to each annex to the Chicago Convention under the heading 'Status of Annex Components'.
177. Chicago Convention, Preamble and Article 44.
178. ICAO, 'The Convention on International Civil Aviation: Annexes 1 to 18', available at www.icao.int/safety/airnavigation/NationalityMarks/annexes_booklet_en.pdf accessed 19 September 2018, 10.
179. Chicago Convention, Article 38.
180. *Ibid.*
181. *Ibid.* Articles 11 and 12.
182. Ludwig Weber, *International Civil Aviation Organization* (Wolters Kluwer 2012) 19.
183. Annexes 9 and 17 though, addressing 'Facilitation' and 'Security' respectively, contain only operational aspects. The SARPs in Annex 9 outline, among other things, requirements for the entry and departure of aircraft, persons and baggage, and cargo, and Annex 17 provides measures to safeguard against acts of unlawful interference. Technical aspects on the other hand include, among numerous others, the technical airworthiness standards under Annex 8, pursuant to Article 33 of the Chicago Convention, and the specifications for the global navigation satellite system (GNSS), as used for aeronautical telecommunications under Annex 10, further to Article 37(a).
184. Specifically, Article 44 (a), (d) and (h).

matter of security but, as is evident from the adoption of Article 3 *bis* and Annex 17, 'Security', it sits within the scope of ICAO's normative powers by being, in the words of Huang, 'but one important aspect of aviation safety'.[185] This is clear when considering the subtitle of Annex 17, 'Safeguarding international civil aviation against acts of unlawful interference',[186] together with the fact that aviation safety is defined as 'the state of freedom from unacceptable risk of injury to persons or damage to aircraft and property';[187] necessarily, aviation security is required for aviation safety. Environmental matters may also, but more controversially, be listed among the normative powers of ICAO.[188]

ICAO's role in relation to international air *transport* is, in contrast, restricted to issuing guidance material, such as ICAO Documents and Assembly Resolutions, and States negotiate between themselves to facilitate this aspect of international civil aviation. Articles 5 and 6 of the Chicago Convention form the basis of this governance, but beyond this, transport aspects sit outside the normative framework of the Chicago Convention and its annexes.[189]

2.3.3 The Multilateral Exchange of Overflight Rights for Non-scheduled Flights and the Express Exclusion of the Exchange for Scheduled Air Services

Article 6 of the Chicago Convention, following from the basis of complete and exclusive sovereignty under Article 1, establishes the regime whereby the national airspace of a State is closed to the aircraft of other States operating scheduled air services until permission or authorisation to operate has been granted by the former State. More

185. Huang (n 127) 5.
186. Chicago Convention, Annex 17 (10th edn, April 2017).
187. Huang (n 127) 4, citing ICAO AN-WP/7699, *Determination of a Definition of Aviation Safety* (11 December 2001) 2.2.
188. Again, the Chicago Convention is silent on environmental regulation, which was not a concern at the time of the Convention's drafting. The argument that environmental matters are within ICAO's competence is based on the theory of implicit competence, as laid down by the ICJ in *Reparation for Injuries Suffered in the Service of the United Nations*, Advisory Opinion, I.C.J. Rep. 1949 (11 April), p. 174, p. 182: 'Under international law, the Organization must be deemed to have those powers which, though not expressly provided in the Charter, are conferred upon it by necessary implication as being essential to the performance of its duties.' On this basis, Leclerc argues that ICAO 'is … invested with a mission to remove obstacles to the development of international civil aviation, at least in its technical and operational aspects'. In this sense, '[the] appearance of environmental data could only be naturally understood within this multilateral forum', translated from the original: 'se trouve (…) investie d'une mission de suppression des obstacles au développement de l'aviation civile internationale, du moins dans ses aspects techniques et opérationnels'. In this sense, '[l]'apparition de la donnée environnementale ne pouvait donc qu'être naturellement appréhendée au sein de cette enceinte multilatérale' (Leclerc (n 172) 318). This argument is not without its critics however, for example, *see*, Andrew Macintosh, 'Overcoming the Barriers to International Aviation Greenhouse Gases Emissions Abatement' (2008) 33(6) A&SL 403, 411.
189. As noted briefly above in Section 2.2.2.3, Article 5 provides the legal basis for overflight rights for non-scheduled flights, while Article 6 expressly excludes from the Convention the exchange of the right of overflight for scheduled air services.

specifically, Article 6 expressly excludes the grant of access to airspace for scheduled international air services from the scope of the Convention:

> [n]o scheduled international air service may be operated over or into the territory of a contracting State, except with the special permission or other authorization of that State, and in accordance with the terms of such permission or authorization.

Bin Cheng, in 1962, framed this outcome as a failure of States and as a situation that was yet to be adequately dealt with:

> By far the most important sector of international civil aviation is scheduled international air transport, *a satisfactory multilateral solution for which has so far not been achieved*... [A]t the Chicago Conference 1944, it was decided that, at least for the moment, *the matter would have to be regulated by bilateral agreements between States* and this need was expressly recognised in Article 6 of the Chicago Convention 1944 (emphasis added).[190]

Given that today the Transit Agreement, as will be addressed in Section 2.3.3.1, has 133 State parties[191] – as opposed to 60 in 1962 – the statement is now less relevant concerning overflight rights. The global trend towards greater liberalisation of air services also reduces the relevance of the statement to the exercise of rights beyond the second freedom. Having said this, the core of the issue persists: there is still no global multilateral agreement regulating scheduled international air services as a whole.

The Chicago Convention does not provide a definition for 'scheduled international air service' but the ICAO Council later, in 1952, defined the term as: an air service that has all three of the following characteristics: (1) it passes through the airspace over the territory of more than one State; (2) it is performed by aircraft for the transport of passengers, mail or cargo for remuneration, in such a manner that each flight is open to use by members of the public; and (3) it is operated so as to serve traffic between the

190. Cheng (n 90) 229. The bilateral system was seen at the time of the drafting of the Convention as an interim arrangement though, pending a multilateral exchange of rights (Havel and Sanchez (n 112) 75-76). There are some instances today of a non-bilateral exchange of rights. For example, the exchange of all transit and traffic rights for EU Member States under the EU single aviation market (Regulation (EC) No. 1008/2008 of the European Parliament and of the Council of 24 September 2008 on common rules for the operation of air services in the Community (Recast) ('Regulation (EC) No. 1008/2008')). At the same time though, EU Member States' aviation relations with non-EU Member States continue to be governed through separate bilateral ASAs in most cases. Also, consider the Multilateral Agreement on the Liberalization of International Air Transport (MALIAT) between Brunei, Chile, the Cook Islands, Mongolia (cargo only), New Zealand, Samoa, Singapore, Tonga, and the US (Multilateral Agreement on the Liberalization of International Air Transportation (Washington DC, 1 May 2001) 2511 U.N.T.S. 33, *entered into force* 21 December 2001). Havel and Sanchez note though that MALIAT 'amounts to little more than a "pooled" open skies accord', in that it essentially just 'regulate[s] the bilateral aviation relations of its signatories' (Havel and Sanchez (n 112) 113).

191. State parties to the Transit Agreement as at July 2021. *See*, ICAO, 'Current Lists of Parties to Multilateral Air Law Treaties – International Air Services Transit Agreement', available at www.icao.int/secretariat/legal/List%20of%20Parties/Transit_EN.pdf accessed 13 November 2020.

same two or more points either according to a published timetable or with flights so regular or frequent that they constitute a recognisably systematic series.[192]

A non-scheduled flight is *a contrario* a flight that falls outside this definition,[193] but that is international; that is, it meets the first criterion. As for the second criterion, a non-scheduled flight may or may not be for remuneration; non-scheduled flights include both commercial and non-commercial operations. Many non-scheduled flights are clearly not open to members of the public or operated according to a published timetable or so regular or frequent that they constitute recognisably systematic series, but others fit less clearly into the mould, and so in practice, the distinction between scheduled air services and non-scheduled flights can be murky.[194]

States have exchanged the right of overflight for non-scheduled flights on a multilateral basis through Article 5 of the Chicago Convention. Under this article, each contracting State agrees that aircraft engaged in non-scheduled flights have the right to:

> make flights into or in transit non-stop across its territory and to make stops for non-traffic purposes without the necessity of obtaining prior permission.[195]

Article 5 clearly provides for the exchange of the right of overflight for non-scheduled flights, but this does not mean that there is freedom of overflight for aircraft operating these flights in the sense of freedom of overflight of the high seas. The article exempts such aircraft from having to obtain prior permission for overflight, which had typically been granted through diplomatic channels,[196] but they are still required to

192. ICAO Doc 7278-C/841, *Definition of Scheduled International Air Service* (1952). *See also*, more recently, ICAO WP/7, *Review of the Classification and Definitions Used for Civil Aviation Activities*, Presented by the Secretariat at the Statistics Division 10th Session, Montreal (16 October 2009), Appendix B; *see also*, ICAO Doc 9587, *Policy and Guidance Material on the Economic Regulation of International Air Transport* (4th edn, 2017) Appendix 4.
193. PPC Haanappel, *The Law and Policy of Air Space and Outer Space: A Comparative Approach* (Kluwer Law International 2003) 111.
194. *Ibid.*; Cheng (n 90) 173-177.
195. Chicago Convention, Article 5 (para. 1). In contrast, the second paragraph of Article 5 applies to non-scheduled services when taking on or discharging passengers, mail or cargo for remuneration, and provides a State with the right to impose 'regulations, conditions or limitations as it may consider desirable' to govern those commercial operations in its territory. These rules are usually governed unilaterally by States, under their national legislation (ICAO Doc 9060/5, *Reference Manual on the ICAO Statistics Programme* (5th edn, 2013) 1.3.2 fn 2). Specifically charter services though are governed under some States' ASAs, for example, those between the US and the UK and Canada and Russia (*Air Transport Agreement Between the Government of the United States of America and the Government of the United Kingdom of Great Britain and Northern Ireland*, 28 November 2018, Article 2(5); *Air Services Agreement Between the Government of Canada and the Government of the Russian Federation*, 18 December 2000, Annex II, A) 5). States have interpreted the second paragraph of Article 5 so broadly so as to include prior permission, that is, that States can require prior permission to be obtained for the operation of non-scheduled services, which effectively negates the purpose of Article 5 (Cheng (n 90) 197). Prior permission should not be required as a general standard as it could frustrate or make impossible the operation of non-scheduled services (Cobb Cooper (n 151) 340). For further discussion on the national regulation of the operation of non-scheduled services *see*, for example, Rigas Doganis, *Flying Off Course: Airline Economics and Marketing* (4th edn, Routledge 2010) 38-39.
196. Cheng (n 90) 195.

observe other entry requirements under the Chicago Convention and its annexes, including, for example, an approved flight plan.[197]

The State whose territory is being overflown can also require landing, and may, for safety purposes, require aircraft to 'follow prescribed routes or to obtain special permission' in the case that the aircraft wants to operate over a region that is 'inaccessible or without adequate air navigation facilities'.[198] The first of these – that the State being overflown can require landing – is unqualified under Article 5, but it must 'not be exercised in such a general way as to amount to a cancellation of the right granted to non-scheduled aircraft'.[199] The second right of the State – to require certain paths to be followed or for prior permission to be obtained – is again left to the discretion of the State, but if airspace is closed, it should be justified and consistent with the Chicago Convention and its annexes, for example, as a prohibited area under Article 9 of the Chicago Convention.[200]

The right of a State to designate the route to be followed over its territory is not restricted to non-scheduled flights: a State also holds this right under Article 68 of the Chicago Convention in respect of scheduled air services.[201] Unlike for non-scheduled flights, where the designation must be for safety purposes, under Article 68, a State is free to designate routes for scheduled services so long as it is in accordance with the Chicago Convention in general. As an illustration of the consequences of this right, on 1 July 2000, Canada and Russia began allowing commercial air transport to operate through routes over the North Pole, meaning that carriers would be able to operate direct services between certain Asian and North American cities for the first time. Nav Canada[202] estimated at the time that this would cut five hours of flight time between Hong Kong and New York which, for a carrier operating the route once a day, would amount to cost savings of USD 12 million per year.[203] The right of a carrier to operate on allocated routes in a foreign State relies on the fact that the State in which the aircraft is registered has already negotiated access to the airspace of the other State. The allocation of routes by Canada and Russia is, in this way, a secondary consideration to the discussion below in Section 2.3.3.1 regarding the exchange of overflight rights by these States on the basis that neither are party to the Transit Agreement.

When it comes to the operation of commercial non-scheduled services, the distinction between them and scheduled services is becoming less relevant both because non-scheduled services represent a diminishing proportion of overall international traffic and because the regulatory approaches to each are converging. Cheng, again writing in 1962, stated that 'non-scheduled international air transport has greatly

197. Milde (n 91) 110.
198. Chicago Convention, Article 5. *See* Proceedings to the Chicago Convention: Vol. I, Pt II 'Minutes of Meeting of Subcommittee 2 of Committee I, November 30' (Document 449) 687.
199. ICAO Doc 9587, *Policy and Guidance Material on the Economic Regulation of International Air Transport* (4th edn, 2017) Appendix 4.
200. *Ibid.*
201. Chicago Convention, Article 68.
202. The corporation that owns and operates Canada's civil air navigation system.
203. Joel Baglole, 'Canada, Russia's Decision to Permit Polar Routes Promises to Cut Hours' (The Wall Street Journal, 8 June 2000), available at www.wsj.com/articles/SB960415817821812909 accessed 4 March 2018.

increased in importance since the Chicago Conference', a statement that applied equally over the following decades.[204] In the 1970s, around 30 % of flights on North Atlantic routes were non-scheduled,[205] and in the early 1980s, approximately half of air passengers travelling within Europe made their journeys on non-scheduled services.[206] The growth in charter services, specifically, during this time was stimulated by the more liberal government regulation of them, particularly in the US and Europe, relative to the highly regulated market for scheduled air services.[207] Deregulation of scheduled services in the US marked the decline of charter services, the former consequently losing their competitive advantage.[208] The liberalisation of air services in the European Union (EU) has reduced the relevance of the distinction between scheduled and non-scheduled services from a regulatory perspective and may eventually lead it to it becoming obsolete.[209] As a result of the third package of air transport liberalisation measures, adopted in July 1991, there is no regulatory distinction between scheduled and non-scheduled services in that non-scheduled carriers are permitted to operate scheduled services and sell directly to the public.[210] Worldwide, non-scheduled services now play only a minor role in the delivery of air transport.[211] ICAO estimates from 2017 suggest that revenue from non-scheduled passenger traffic in that year made up just 4.1 % of the total revenue for international traffic,[212] representing a substantial decline even over the course of the preceding decade, from 8.1 % in 2007.[213]

---

204. Cheng (n 90) 27.
205. Haanappel (n 193) 111.
206. ICAO Doc 9060/5, *Reference Manual on the ICAO Statistics Programme* (5th edn, 2013) 1.3.2.
207. Doganis (n 195) 39.
208. *Ibid.*
209. Milde (n 91) 109.
210. The third liberalisation package was implemented through Regulation Nos 2407/92, 2408/92 and 2409/92, which have since been recast and consolidated into Regulation (EC) No. 1008/2008. For a discussion on the consequences of the third package of liberalisation *see*, Commission of the European Communities, 'Impact of the Third Package of Air Transport Liberalization Measures – Communication from the Commission to the Council and the European Parliament' (Brussels, 22 October 1996, COM(96) 514 final) 18. The distinction between scheduled and non-scheduled services has also become irrelevant to EU legislation governing other aspects of aviation: Regulation (EC) No. 261/2004 on compensation and assistance to passengers in the event of denied boarding and of cancellation or long delay of flights applies to both scheduled and non-scheduled services in contrast to the legislation it repealed, Council Regulation (EEC) No. 295/91 of 4 February 1991, which applied only to scheduled air transport. Recital 5 of Regulation (EC) No. 261/2004 acknowledges the decreasing relevance of the categorisation: 'Since the distinction between scheduled and non-scheduled air services is weakening, such protection should apply to passengers not only on scheduled but also on non-scheduled flights, including those forming part of package tours.'
211. Milde (n 91) 109 and 111.
212. ICAO, '2017 Air Transport Statistical Results', Table 7, available at www.icao.int/annual-report-2017/Documents/Annual.Report.2017_Air%20Transport%20Statistics.pdf accessed 12 March 2019. Non-scheduled traffic in these statistics covers both non-scheduled traffic of scheduled airlines and non-scheduled operators.
213. ICAO, '2016 Air Transport Statistical Results', Table 7, available at www.icao.int/annual-report-2016/documents/arc_2016_air%20transport%20statistics.pdf accessed 2 March 2019. Non-scheduled traffic in these statistics covers both non-scheduled traffic of scheduled airlines and non-scheduled operators.

2.3.3.1 *The Transit Agreement and the Value of Transit Rights*

Turning now to scheduled international air services, it is necessary at this point to draw a distinction between transit rights and traffic rights. While States did not exchange the rights of access to their airspace multilaterally for scheduled air services under the Chicago Convention, the 133 States that are parties to the Transit Agreement have exchanged the right of overflight on a multilateral basis.

At the Chicago Conference, two agreements were negotiated together with the adoption of the Convention to allow for the multilateral exchange of a limited number of so-called freedoms (*see* Figure 2.3), or rights for scheduled international air services to fly over, make technical stops in, and to operate to, from and within another State: the aforementioned Transit Agreement and the International Air Transport Agreement (Transport Agreement).[214] The Transit Agreement, also known as the 'two freedoms agreement', provides for the exchange of the first two freedoms of the air for State parties, while the Transport Agreement provides for the exchange of the first five freedoms of the air. In contrast to the Transit Agreement, the Transport Agreement has just eleven State parties.[215] A reason that States were, and remain, reluctant to sign the Transport Agreement is that the fifth freedom requires negotiation between two foreign States, in contrast to the first four freedoms which involve just one other State.[216]

214. International Air Transport Agreement (Chicago, 7 December 1944) 171 U.N.T.S. 387, *entered into force* 8 February 1945 ('Transport Agreement').
215. State parties to the Transport Agreement as at July 2021. *See*, ICAO, 'Current Lists of Parties to Multilateral Air Law Treaties – International Air Transport Agreement', available at www.icao .int/Secretariat/legal/List%20of%20Parties/Transport_EN.pdf accessed 13 November 2020.
216. Mendes de Leon (n 119) 59.

Figure 2.3 The Freedoms of the Air[217]

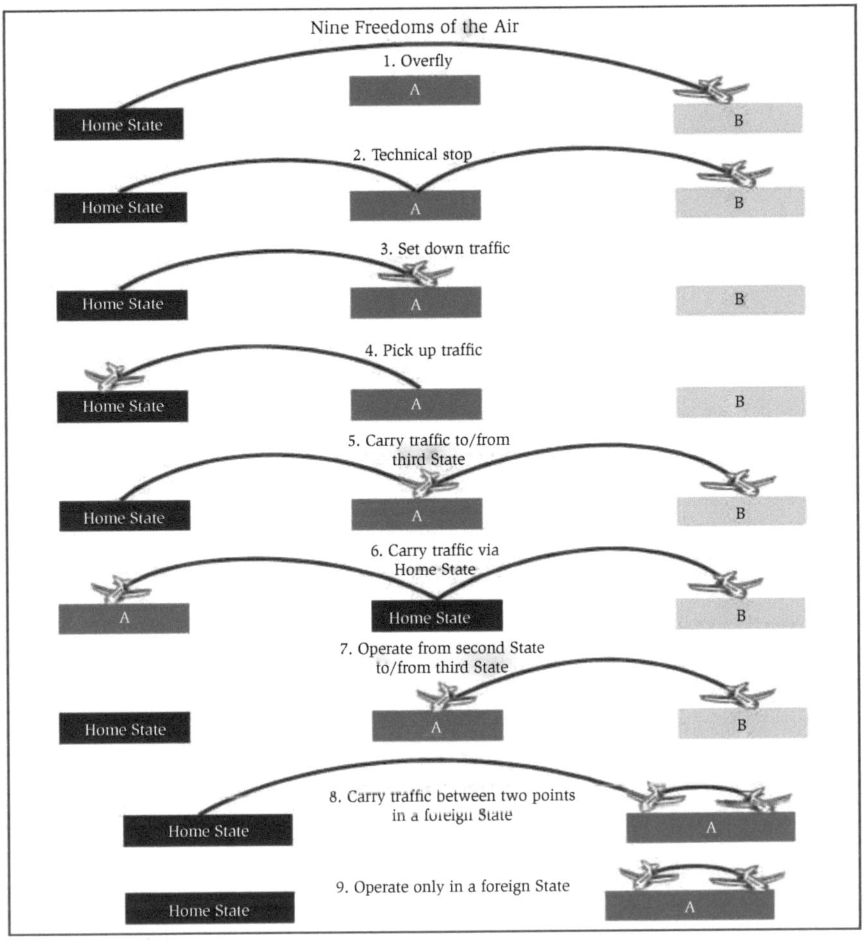

As mentioned above, the Transit Agreement provides for the first two freedoms of the air or more specifically, each State party grants to every other State party in respect of international air services: (1) the privilege to fly across its territory; and (2) the privilege to land for non-traffic purposes. The second freedom is in practice the right to make a technical stopover and is defined in the Chicago Convention as 'landing for any purpose other than taking on or discharging passengers, cargo or mail'.[218] It involves stops for, for example, refuelling and repairs.

217. *Source*: Air Cargo – How it Works, 'An Introduction to the Aircargo, Airfreight and Airmail Business', available at air-cargo-how-it-works.blogspot.com/p/interest-organisations.html accessed 12 July 2018.
218. Chicago Convention, Article 96(d).

The first and second freedoms together are known as 'technical freedoms' or 'transit rights' and can be distinguished from the remaining freedoms of the air on the basis that the former do not involve traffic that originates or terminates in the State granting the rights, while the latter do. In other words, the third to ninth freedoms establish market access for international civil air transport. Although the first and second freedoms do not provide market access in the sense of the other freedoms, 'it must not be assumed that [they] ... are of little economic value'.[219] Despite not being directly related to market access, the right of overflight has economic consequences.[220] This point was emphasised by the Representative of Canada during the Chicago Conference when he explained that 'the only bargaining power possessed by many countries in negotiating bilateral agreements is the possession of these two Freedoms'.[221] Mendes de Leon elaborates on this statement:

> [c]ountries with a big airspace including but not limited to the Russian Federation, Indonesia, Canada and Brazil prefer not to accede to the International ASA [referring to the Transit Agreement] *as they wish to keep their airspace as an asset in bilateral negotiations* (emphasis added).[222]

Canada was a party to the Transit Agreement but denounced it in November 1986.[223] It did so in response to a dispute with the UK in which the UK announced its intention to move Air Canada services from Heathrow to Gatwick.[224] As British carriers used Canadian airspace to fly to the west of the US, Canada's withdrawal was a way of exerting pressure on the UK.[225] Canada subsequently negotiated overflight rights for its territory with the signatories to the Transit Agreement by way of diplomatic notes and/or in its ASAs, including with the UK on the resolution of the dispute.[226]

The above provides an indication of how States can use not being a party to the Transit Agreement as leverage in negotiations as a result of the economic value of the right of overflight. The right of overflight is also economically significant by way of the imposition of overflight fees. As mentioned previously in Section 2.3.3, Canada and Russia opened up routes over the North Pole in 2000. In terms of the economic consequences of this, both countries stood to benefit from the collection of overflight fees from carriers for these routes, with Russia standing to attract an estimate at the time of up to USD 200 million per year.[227] States are entitled to charge for the provision of air navigation facilities under international civil aviation law for both scheduled and

219. Cheng (n 90) 25.
220. Havel and Sanchez (n 112) 76.
221. Proceedings to the Chicago Convention (Document 463) (n 125) 510.
222. Mendes de Leon (n 119) 57.
223. ICAO, 'Current Lists of Parties to Multilateral Air Law Treaties – International Air Services Transit Agreement', Note, p. 3, available at www.icao.int/secretariat/legal/List%20of%20Parties/Transit_EN.pdf accessed 1 May 2020.
224. Email from Roland Dorsay to Pablo Mendes de Leon (6 November 2003).
225. Haanappel (n 193) 121.
226. Email from Roland Dorsay to Pablo Mendes de Leon (6 November 2003).
227. Baglole (n 203).

non-scheduled services[228] but, in accordance with Article 15 of the Chicago Convention, they must not be higher for foreign aircraft than for national aircraft[229] and they must not be 'imposed by any contracting State in respect solely of the right of transit over … its territory'.[230] Put another way, the ICAO Council in its *Policies on Charges for Airport and Air Navigation Services* provides that they must be non-discriminatory and cost-related.[231] These policies, which were first published in 1974, direct States to impose fees only as part of a 'cost-recovery system' whereby 'the State may require the users of such services [air navigation services] to pay the portion of costs properly allocable to them' being 'the full cost of providing the service', as opposed to a greater cost.[232] This full cost includes the 'cost of capital and depreciation of assets, as well as the cost of maintenance, operation, management and administration'.[233]

2.3.3.2 *The Role of ASAs in the Exchange of Transit and Traffic Rights*

For those States that are not party to the Transit Agreement, the right of overflight for scheduled air services is provided along with the other freedoms through ASAs. Given that few States have signed the Transport Agreement, almost all States exchange the third to fifth freedoms through ASAs. The right of overflight (along with the second freedom) is also commonly included in the ASAs between States that have ratified the Transit Agreement.[234] For example, the ASA between Australia and New Zealand, both of whom are parties to the Transit Agreement, provides under Article 3(a) and (b) the right of overflight and the right to make a technical stopover.[235] This is done for the purpose of ensuring such rights continue in the case of a State or States withdrawing from the Transit Agreement.[236]

ASAs provide for the exchange of the rights and also establish the conditions under which the services between the States operate, including routes, designation[237] and the related ownership and control requirements, or equivalent, of carriers under

228. Chicago Convention, Article 15(a) and (b).
229. *Ibid.*
230. *Ibid.* Article 15 (final paragraph).
231. ICAO Doc 9082, *ICAO's Policies on Charges for Airports and Air Navigation Services* (9th edn, 2012) vii. The ICAO Council also highlights the importance of the charges being imposed in a transparent manner and in consultation with users.
232. *Ibid.* III-1.
233. *Ibid.* III-3.i. Although it is outside the scope of this research, Siberian overflight fees have been a source of conflict between Russia and the EU, with the latter claiming that the fees are not cost-related, transparent, or imposed non-discriminatorily ('Air Transport: Commission Welcomes Agreement on Siberian Overflights' (European Commission, Press Release, 1 December 2011), available at europa.eu/rapid/press-release_IP-11-1490_en.htm accessed 12 December 2018; Elena Carpanelli, 'The Siberian Overflights Issue' (2011) 11(23) Issues Aviation L & Pol'y 23).
234. Chicago Convention, Annex 2 (10th edn, 2005) Appendix 5 'ICAO Template Air Services Agreements', 8.
235. Agreement Between Australia and the Government of New Zealand Relating to Air Services, signed 8 August 2002 [2003] ATS 18 (entered into force 25 August 2003).
236. Chicago Convention, Annex 2, Appendix 5 'ICAO Template Air Services Agreements', 8.
237. That is, the carrier(s) permitted to exercise the rights that are exchanged under the ASA.

domestic law, capacity, change of gauge,[238] prices and safety, and security matters. As international air transport undergoes the process of liberalisation, the more restrictive aspects of ASAs are increasingly omitted.[239] The features of the more liberalised ASAs today include freedom with respect to pricing, no capacity restrictions, multiple designation, and in terms of route rights, the 6th freedom for passenger services and the option of the 7th freedom for all-cargo services.[240]

2.3.4 Pilotless Aircraft

The Chicago Convention imposes different requirements for admission to national airspace for pilotless aircraft.

In accordance with Article 8 of the Chicago Convention, special permission is required to operate pilotless aircraft over the territory of a contracting State:

> No aircraft capable of being flown without a pilot shall be flown without a pilot over the territory of a contracting State without special authorization by that State and in accordance with the terms of such authorization. Each contracting State undertakes to insure that the flight of such aircraft without a pilot in regions open to civil aircraft shall be so controlled as to obviate danger to civil aircraft.

This article was incorporated into the Chicago Convention from Article 15 of the Paris Convention, where it appeared in similar form, and ICAO has clarified that its scope extends to 'all unmanned aircraft, whether remotely piloted, fully autonomous or combinations thereof'.[241]

ICAO's regulation of unmanned aircraft has so far focused on remotely piloted aircraft (RPA), a subsection of the broader category of unmanned - pilotless - aircraft. An 'RPA' is defined in Annexes 2 and 7 of the Chicago Convention as 'an unmanned aircraft which is piloted from a remote pilot station'.[242] The decision to streamline the development of international civil aviation law applicable to unmanned aircraft to focus on RPA in these early stages of regulation was made by the Unmanned Aircraft Systems Study Group (UASSG), a body established to assist the ICAO Secretariat in its

238. That is, the 'transfer of passengers between aircraft at a foreign point for a through journey' (Paul Stephen Dempsey, 'Flights of Fancy and Fights of Fury: Arbitration and Adjudication of Commercial and Political Disputes in International Aviation' (2004) 32(2) Ga J Int'l & Comp L 231, 235). *See*, for example, *Air Service Agreement of 27 March 1946 between the United States of America and France (USA v. France)* (1978) XVIII R.I.A.A. 417, which involved change of gauge between London and Paris, and which will be discussed in Section 3.3.2.1.
239. Havel and Sanchez (n 112) 70-71.
240. *See*, for example, Air Transport Agreement between the European Union and the Unites States of America [2007] OJ L134/5; Multilateral Agreement on the Liberalization of International Air Transportation (Washington DC, 1 May 2001) 2511 U.N.T.S. 33, *entered into force* 21 December 2001; *Agreement Between Australia and the Government of New Zealand Relating to Air Services*, signed 8 August 2002 [2003] ATS 18 (entered into force 25 August 2003).
241. ICAO Doc 10019 AN/507, *Manual on Remotely Piloted Aircraft Systems* (2015) 1.1. 'RPAS' is the current term used by ICAO to refer to such aircraft, but accurately encompassing all aircraft without a pilot on board in a single term presents a definitional challenge. *See*, for example, Mikko Huttunen, 'Unmanned, Remotely Piloted, or Something Else? Analysing the Terminological Dogfight' (2017) 42(3) A&SL 349.
242. Chicago Convention, Annex 2, 1-8 and Annex 7 (6th edn, July 2012) 1.

work on integrating unmanned aircraft into airspace used by manned aircraft. The UASSG made this determination on the basis that only aircraft with some degree of control exercised over their operation – remotely piloted, as opposed to autonomous – could be safely integrated.[243] As a result, although Article 8 applies to pilotless aircraft more broadly, RPA will be the focus in this section.

The special permission under Article 8 is required regardless of whether the RPA is scheduled or non-scheduled, despite the apparent conflict with Article 5 in the case that the RPA aircraft is operating a non-scheduled flight. In other words, this aspect of Article 8 takes precedence over the conflicting element of Article 5 when both articles are applicable. The primacy of Article 8 is based on the principle of *lex specialis* and on the interpretation of the articles in accordance with their ordinary meaning.

The principle of *lex specialis* is not codified as a rule of treaty interpretation in the Vienna Convention on the Law of Treaties but it has been relied on a number of times by the ICJ.[244] Koskenniemi describes the principle as a 'pragmatic mechanism for dealing with situations where two rules of international law that are both valid and applicable deal with the same subject matter differently', as is the case regarding prior authorisation under Articles 5 and 8 in the event of an operation involving a non-scheduled flight conducted by an RPA.[245] In these cases, *lex specialis* dictates that 'if a matter is being regulated by a general standard as well as a more specific rule, then the latter should take precedence over the former'.[246] Article 5 of the Chicago Convention is the *lex generalis* in this context, in that it applies to all civil aircraft when conducting international non-scheduled flights. Article 8, in contrast, applies only to a subset of those aircraft: those that are RPA. Article 8 is thus the more specific rule that takes precedence.

The above interpretation is further supported by reading the two articles 'in accordance with the ordinary meaning to be given to the terms of the treaty in their context and in light of its object and purpose', as dictated by the general rules of treaty interpretation.[247] In its ordinary meaning, Article 5 provides that aircraft conducting non-scheduled flights do not require special authorisation or permission to overfly another State's territory, while Article 8 requires that they do if they are RPA. Considering the articles in the broader context of the treaty, it is clear that Article 8 necessarily has precedence over Article 5 in the interest of safety. One of the principal purposes of the Chicago Convention is to help ensure that 'international civil aviation

243. ICAO (n 241) 1.2.14.
244. *Accordance with International Law of the Unilateral Declaration of Independence in Respect of Kosovo*, Advisory Opinion, I.C.J. Rep. 2010 (22 July) p. 403, p. 438 para. 83; *Military and Paramilitary Activities in and Against Nicaragua (Nicaragua v. United States of America)*, Merits, I.C.J. Rep. 1986 (27 June) p. 14, p. 137 para. 274; *Case Concerning the Continental Shelf (Tunisia/Libyan Arab Jamahiriya)*, Judgment, I.C.J. Rep. 1982 (24 February), p. 18, p. 38 para. 24.
245. ILC (n 92) 30.
246. *Ibid.* 34-35.
247. Vienna Convention on the Law of Treaties, Article 31(1).

may be developed in a safe ... manner'.[248] RPA pose different risks to civil aviation and have different requirements than manned aircraft, for example, in terms of their detect and avoid capabilities and their detectability and conspicuity to other aircraft, as well their communication with ATS, among many other considerations.[249] It is through the request for authorisation that the State whose territory is to be overflown is able to ensure that the operation will be conducted safely,[250] and it is for this reason that special permission is required under Article 8, whether or not the RPA operates a scheduled air service or a non-scheduled flight. The obligation on States to ensure RPA are operated safely is found in Article 8 itself: States are required to undertake to ensure that RPA 'shall be so controlled as to obviate danger to civil aircraft'. While the Chicago Convention's primary focus is *international* civil aviation, this article requires that the safety of all civil aircraft – on international or domestic flights – is protected.[251]

The requirements for the special authorisation for overflight of an RPA through national airspace outside its State of registry are included in Annex 2, Appendix 4 to the Chicago Convention, with supporting guidelines in ICAO's 2015 *Manual on RPAS*.[252] From an operational perspective, the requirements include that the request for authorisation is made to 'the appropriate authorities of the State(s) in which the RPA will operate', which is usually the Civil Aviation Authority (CAA), and that the request is made at least seven days before the intended flight.[253] ICAO has issued a template form to submit the request,[254] in accordance with the criteria under Annex 2, which includes a request for information about, for example, the RPA operator and technical details of the RPA.[255]

Beyond the scope of Article 8 of the Chicago Convention, States are not bound by how they grant overflight rights for RPA and States are free to deviate from the ICAO specifications mentioned in the above paragraph. In pursuance of ICAO's objective that international civil aviation is 'developed in a safe and orderly manner' and that air transport services are operated 'soundly and economically',[256] it is in ICAO's interest that States eventually reach broader agreements facilitating the overflight of RPA, as has been achieved for manned aviation. For this purpose, ICAO emphasises that 'States may agree mutually upon simpler procedures through bilateral or multilateral agreements or arrangements for the operation of specific RPA or categories of RPA'.[257]

248. Chicago Convention, Preamble. This is reiterated in Article 44, where the aims and objectives of ICAO include ensuring: (a) '... the safe ... growth of international civil aviation throughout the world' and meeting (d) '... the needs of peoples of the world for safe ... air transport'.
249. As identified by ICAO, for example, when stating that '[s]afety analyses may be needed to establish RPAS capabilities to mitigate consequences of each specific hazard that may be encountered' (ICAO (n 241) 10.2.5).
250. *See* the template 'Request for Authorization Form' provided by ICAO for a more comprehensive list of the considerations (*Ibid.* Appendix A).
251. Cheng (n 90) 112.
252. ICAO (n 241) (2015).
253. Chicago Convention, Annex 2, Appendix 4, 3.1.
254. ICAO (n 241) Appendix A.
255. Chicago Convention, Annex 2, Appendix 4, 3.2.
256. *Ibid.* Preamble.
257. ICAO (n 241) 3.2.2. At the time of writing, the author is not aware of any such agreements or arrangements being in place.

The obvious benefit of these broader bilateral or multilateral arrangements in favour of ad hoc authorisation is that they reduce the burden on both RPA operators who have to submit the requests and on the State authorities responsible for processing them.[258] The operation of civil RPA is at present still predominantly restricted to national borders, although not exclusively. A 2016 ICAO survey found that, of the sixty-one Member States that responded, twenty-six had received requests in the last two years from foreign RPA operators, pursuant to Article 8 of the Chicago Convention, for 'special authorisation' to operate RPA in their territories.[259]

State aircraft, whether they are RPA or manned aircraft, fall outside the Chicago regime, that is, from the Chicago Convention and its annexes. Overflight rights for their operation stem from an entirely independent framework from that which has been set out above for civil aircraft, as will be addressed in the following section.

2.4 OVERFLIGHT RIGHTS FOR STATE AIRCRAFT IN NATIONAL AIRSPACE

2.4.1 Preliminary Matters

Under Article 3(b) of the Chicago Convention, 'aircraft *used* in military, customs and police services shall be deemed to be State aircraft' (emphasis added). In this sense, State aircraft are defined 'not by ownership or even control, but by a purely functional test'.[260] Whether an aircraft is a State aircraft or a civil aircraft is significant because State aircraft are expressly excluded from the scope of the Chicago Convention and its annexes.[261] The implications of this for national airspace will be addressed here below.

The focus in this section is on the consequences of the exclusion for the exchange of overflight rights but the impact is much greater, going beyond the scope of the Chicago Convention, the annexes attached to it, and the ASAs that flow from it, to the applicability of insurance policies and international air law instruments more broadly.[262] For example, the criminal law treaties in relation to international civil aviation do not apply to 'aircraft used in military, customs or police service'[263] and the Warsaw/Montreal regime is applicable to carriage performed by the State or by legally

258. ICAO (n 241) 3.2.2. At the time of writing, the author is not aware of any such agreements or arrangements being in place. 3.2.2.
259. ICAO Working Paper LC/37-WP/2-1, *Remotely Piloted Aircraft Systems Legal Survey* (26 July 2017) 4.4.1 and Appendix A-9.
260. Bin Cheng, 'The Destruction of KAL Flight KE007, and Article 3 *bis* of the Chicago Convention' in JWE Storm van 's Gravensande and A van der Veen Vonk (eds), *Air Worthy – Liber Amicorum Honouring Professor Dr IHPh Diederiks-Verschoor* (Kluwer 1985) 64.
261. Chicago Convention, Article 3(a).
262. Milde (n 91) 77.
263. Convention on Certain Other Acts Committed on Board Aircraft (1963) ICAO Doc 8364, Article 1(4) ('Tokyo Convention'); Convention for the Suppression of Unlawful Seizure of Aircraft (1970) ICAO Doc 8920, Article 3(2) ('Hague Convention'); and Convention for the Suppression of Unlawful Acts Against the Safety of Civil Aviation (1971) ICAO Doc 8966, Article 4(1) ('Montreal Convention 1971'). Neither does the Convention on Damage Caused by Foreign Aircraft to Third Parties on the Surface (1952) ICAO Doc 7364, Article 26 ('Rome Convention').

constituted public bodies, but States can make a reservation to exclude carriage performed directly by the State.[264]

Insofar as the exchange of overflight rights is concerned, in principle and without further negotiation between States, State aircraft are only permitted to fly above the territory of the State in which they are registered and over international airspace. In contrast to the regime for civil aircraft established through the Transit Agreement and ASAs, the framework that regulates the overflight of State aircraft is largely based on ad hoc arrangements between States.

The purpose of this section is first to briefly address the distinction between State aircraft and civil aircraft (Section 2.4.2) and, second, to set out the framework governing the grant of overflight rights in relation to the international operation of State aircraft (Section 2.4.4). The legal basis of overflight rights under the framework stems from clearances or authorisations, known as 'diplomatic clearances', granted to a State aircraft, in respect of a certain flight or flights or for a certain duration of time, by the relevant authority of the State whose territory is to be overflown, in response to an application made through diplomatic channels.

2.4.2 The Definition of State Aircraft

2.4.2.1 State Aircraft under the Paris Convention (1919) and the Chicago Convention (1944)

The Paris Convention distinguished between State aircraft and civil aircraft and, like the Chicago Convention, also excluded the former from its scope.[265] Under Article 30(a) and (b) of the Paris Convention, military aircraft together with 'aircraft exclusively employed in State service' were expressly considered State aircraft, where State service included 'posts, customs and police'. The Convention defined none of these terms although a definition of sorts was provided for military aircraft: '[e]very aircraft commanded by a person in military service detailed for the purpose shall be deemed to be a military aircraft'.[266] Goedhuis criticised this definition for the fact that it failed to take into account the characteristics of the aircraft itself, and his view that the article ought to be amended was shared by the International Commission for Air Navigation (ICAN) at the time.[267]

---

264. Convention for the Unification of Certain Rules for International Carriage by Air (1999) ICAO Doc 9740, Article 57 ('Montreal Convention 1999'); Convention for the Unification of Certain Rules Relating to International Carriage by Air (1929) Conférence Internationale de Droit Privé Aérien (Warsaw), Article 2(1) ('Warsaw Convention'). The inclusion of carriage performed by the State under the Warsaw/Montreal regime makes sense considering that at the time of the drafting of the Warsaw Convention 'in 1929 there were in fact no "private" carriers and, except in the USA and possibly Japan, the airlines were government owned and government controlled' (Milde (n 91) 69).
265. Paris Convention, Article 30.
266. *Ibid.* Article 31.
267. 'Tegen deze begripsformuleering vallen ernstige bezwaren in te brengen. Het is onjuist het militaire karakter van een luchtvaartuig uitsluitend door een persoonlijk criterium (een militair

Further ambiguity arose as a result of Article 30(b) providing that all other aircraft are 'private aircraft'[268] and therefore within the scope of the Convention, but then proceeding to state that '[a]ll State aircraft other than *military, customs and police aircraft* shall be treated as private aircraft' (emphasis added). This resulted in what has been described as a 'curious feature', whereby aircraft employed exclusively for postal services were initially included and then excluded from the definition of State aircraft.[269] The overall ambiguity of Article 30 was compounded by the initial reference to 'State service' in Article 30(a) which suggested, through the use of the words 'such as', that 'posts, customs, police' were examples, rather than constituting an exhaustive list, of State services. Considering that all aircraft had to fall into one of the two categories – State aircraft or private aircraft – it is not possible for all aircraft other than military, customs and police aircraft to be private aircraft if the term 'State aircraft' included aircraft used for military, customs, police and postal services, *among others*.

Article 3(b) of the Chicago Convention removes some of the confusion brought about by the Paris Convention, such as that regarding postal services, but it does not provide an unambiguous distinction between State and civil aircraft. The Chairman of the Drafting Committee of Article 3 of the Chicago Convention recognised in 1949 that the 'language used was understood to be vague' but that the final wording was preferable to an attempt to define aircraft in a fixed form, as opposed to by its use on a particular flight.[270] Regardless, international civil aviation law must contend with the questions that Article 3 raises, a task that the ICAO Legal Committee Secretariat undertook in a 1994 report, echoing the Chairman's words in its acknowledgement that 'there are no clear generally accepted international rules, whether conventional or customary, as to what constitute State aircraft and what constitute civil aircraft in the field of air law'.[271]

Article 3(b) states that aircraft that fall within the specified categories 'shall be deemed to be' State aircraft, but it does not define the term 'State aircraft'. Like the

als commandant) te doen bepalen, terwijl het objectieve criterium (de technische eigenschappen en de uitrusting van het toestel) buiten beschouwing blijft. Het feit, dat een militair luchtvaartuig niet onder militair commando wordt gevolgen, verandert niets aan het karakter van het luchtvaartuig' (Daniel Goedhuis, *Handboek voor het Luchtrecht* (Martinus Nijhoff 1943) 62), translated: 'There are serious objections to be raised regarding this method of interpretation. It is incorrect to determine the military character of an aircraft exclusively on the basis of the personality criterion (a military officer as commander), while disregarding the objective criterion (the technical characteristics and the equipment of the aircraft). The fact that the military aircraft is not under military command changes nothing of the character of the aircraft.' Goedhuis refers here to Resolution No. 1055 of the International Commission for Air Navigation (ICAN) (27th Meeting, Copenhagen 1939) 39.1, recognising that an attempt by the Commission to amend Article 30 had at that point not been successful. *See also*, discussion of this in JP Honig, *The Legal Status of Aircraft* (Martinus Nijhoff 1956) 38.

268. The term 'private aircraft' refers to what we now term 'civil aircraft'. This shift in language from the Paris Convention to the Chicago Convention took place as a result of a suggestion referred to the Drafting Committee of Subcommittee 2 on 10 November 1944 (ICAO WP/2-1, *Secretariat Study on 'Civil/State Aircraft'*, Presented by the Secretariat at the Legal Committee 29th Session, Montreal (3 March 1994) Attachment I at 2.2.1).
269. Honig (n 267) 37.
270. ICAO (n 268) Attachment I at 5.2.4.
271. *Ibid.* Attachment I at 1.1.

Paris Convention, 'military', 'customs' and 'police' are also not defined. As was the case with the Paris Convention, it is also unclear from the wording of the article whether the list is exhaustive, that is, whether State aircraft are exclusively those used for military, customs and police services or whether aircraft used for other State functions, such as post or search and rescue, are also classified as State aircraft. Furthermore, the article leaves open the question of whether aircraft used for the services listed can ever be considered civil, rather than State, aircraft.

2.4.2.2 Subsequent ICAO Consideration

The ICAO Legal Committee Secretariat ('the Secretariat') interprets Article 3(b) restrictively, concluding that aircraft used for military, customs and police services are necessarily State aircraft[272] and that no other aircraft are State aircraft for the purposes of the Chicago Convention.[273] In reaching this interpretation, the Secretariat considered, among other things, that the Chicago Convention does not explicitly deviate from the provision in the Paris Convention, which stated that all aircraft other than those listed as State aircraft were to be considered civil aircraft. Although this provision was omitted from Article 3 of the Chicago Convention, the fact that it did not expressly deviate from it is, according to the Secretariat, indicative that there was no intention to broaden the definition of State aircraft.[274]

Consistent with the ordinary meaning of Article 3(b) of the Chicago Convention, the Secretariat has furthermore emphasised that it is the *usage* that determines whether an aircraft is a State or civil aircraft and not 'other factors, such as aircraft registration ... ownership (public or private), type of operator (private/state), *except insofar as these criteria go towards showing the type of usage*' (emphasis added).[275] Other factors, including the technical specifications of the aircraft, such as its speed and capacity, may also contribute in this respect.[276]

2.4.2.3 Distinctions in Other Legal Frameworks Specific to Purpose

The ICAO Legal Committee Secretariat has also recognised that civil aircraft under the Chicago Convention may be treated as State aircraft in the context of other legal frameworks.[277] Where this occurs though, it is not indicative of the categorisation of the aircraft for the purposes of the Chicago Convention.

272. ICAO (n 268) Attachment I at 5.1.1.
273. *Ibid.* Attachment I at 5.2.3-5.2.4.
274. *Ibid.* Attachment I at 5.2.3.
275. *Ibid.* Attachment I at 1.3.
276. Milde (n 91) 74-75. *See also,* for a discussion on factors that are taken into account, Ruwantissa Abeyratne, 'Legal Issues of the Snowden Case: State Aircraft vs. Civil Aircraft' (2013) 62(4) ZLW 648, 652.
277. ICAO (n 268) Attachment I at 5.2.6.

As the ICAO Secretariat explains in the case of medical aircraft under the First Geneva Convention of 1949:[278]

> The fact that an aircraft is a medical aircraft under the Red Cross Conventions and the Protocol does not give it a special status vis-à-vis the Chicago Convention; an analysis will have to be made, as in the case of any other aircraft, to see if it falls under Article 3(b).[279]

Conversely, the Geneva Conventions:[280]

> do not link their own scopes of applicability to the determination under the Chicago Convention of the status of an aircraft. The Conventions of 1949 refer to civil and military aircraft, but not to these terms as 'defined' under Chicago. Consequently, the provisions of the Chicago Convention does [sic] not, and cannot, determine whether and to what extent the flight crew of an aircraft is given protection by these Conventions.[281]

This is also the case in EU aviation law. For example, Regulation (EU) 2018/1139 (European Union Aviation Safety Agency (EASA) Basic Regulation)[282] addresses regulatory matters, such as airworthiness, environmental certification and flight crew licensing, excludes from its scope 'aircraft ... while carrying out military, customs, police, search and rescue, fire fighting, border control, coastguard, or similar activities or services'.[283]

Eurocontrol, on the other hand, defines State aircraft and civil aircraft for ATM purposes using the terminology of the Chicago Convention. This position was clarified

278. Geneva Convention for the Amelioration of the Condition of the Wounded and Sick in Armed Forces in the Field (Geneva, 12 August 1949) 75 U.N.T.S. 31 *entered into force* 21 October 1950, Articles 36 and 37 ('First Geneva Convention').
279. ICAO (n 268) Attachment I at 4.6.1.
280. In addition to the First Geneva Convention: Geneva Convention for the Amelioration of the Condition of Wounded, Sick and Shipwrecked Members of Armed Forces at Sea (Geneva, 12 August 1949) 75 U.N.T.S. 85 287 *entered into force* 21 October 1950 ('Second Geneva Convention'); Geneva Convention Relative to the Treatment of Prisoners of War (Geneva, 12 August 1949) 75 U.N.T.S. 135 287 *entered into force* 21 October 1950 ('Third Geneva Convention'); Geneva Convention Relative to the Protection of Civilian Persons in Time of War (Geneva, 12 August 1949) 75 U.N.T.S. 287 *entered into force* 21 October 1950 ('Fourth Geneva Convention'); together with Protocol Additional to the Geneva Conventions of 12 August 1949, and relating to the Protection of Victims of International Armed Conflicts (Protocol I) (Geneva, 8 June 1977) 1125 U.N.T.S. 3 *entered into force* 7 December 1978 and Protocol Additional to the Geneva Convention of 12 August 1949 and relating to the Protection of Victims of Non-international Armed Conflicts (Protocol II) (Geneva, 8 June 1977) 1125 U.N.T.S. 609 *entered into force* 7 December 1978.
281. ICAO (n 268) Attachment I at 4.6.1-4.6.2.
282. Regulation (EU) 2018/1139 of the European Parliament and of the Council of 4 July 2018 on common rules in the field of civil aviation and establishing a European Union Aviation Safety Agency, and amending Regulations (EC) No. 2111/2005, (EC) No. 1008/2008, (EU) No. 996/2010, (EU) No. 376/2014 and Directives 2014/30/EU and 2014/53/EU of the European Parliament and of the Council, and repealing Regulations (EC) No. 552/2004 and (EC) No. 216/2008 of the European Parliament and of the Council and Council Regulation (EEC) No. 3922/91 ('EASA Basic Regulation').
283. EASA Basic Regulation, Article 2(3)(a).

by the Provisional Council for Eurocontrol[284] in 2001 when it issued a decision on the definition of State aircraft in which it stated that such aircraft are, 'with reference to article 3(b) of the Chicago Convention, only aircraft used in military, customs and police services' and that 'civil registered aircraft used by a State for other than military, customs and police service shall not qualify as State aircraft'.[285] The same definition is used in the EU in the framework regulation for the Single European Sky (SES),[286] and related legislation,[287] which was implemented to meet the safety and capacity needs of the European ATM network, of which Eurocontrol is the network manager.

Unlike EASA, Eurocontrol's ATM coordination division provides support to Member States for both civil aircraft and military aircraft and the distinction between the two is not for the purpose of excluding the latter but instead for ensuring an appropriate provision of ATM services based on the specifications of the aircraft involved. In the region under the management of Eurocontrol,[288] air traffic is divided into general air traffic (GAT) and operational air traffic (OAT), where GAT includes 'all movements of civil aircraft, as well as movements of State aircraft (including military, customs and police aircraft) when these movements are carried out in conformity with the procedures of ICAO'.[289] OAT is designed to facilitate flights involving aircraft that are not equipped to meet the requirements for GAT, such as those that lack certain communication or navigation tools or, particularly in the case of military aircraft, those that are expected to undertake activities that are not addressed by ICAO, such as airborne refuelling or formation flying.[290] Within a State, regulations applying to State aircraft, including military aircraft, may be a combination of OAT rules and rules determined through bilateral and regional arrangements.

284. This body is 'responsible for implementing Eurocontrol's general policy' and consists of representatives of the Member States of the Agency at the level of Director General of Civil Aviation (Eurocontrol, 'Governing Bodies', available at www.eurocontrol.int/info/governing-bodies accessed 1 August 2020).

285. Eurocontrol, 'Decision of the Provision al Council – Definition of State Aircraft' (Session 11, 12 July 2001) Principle 1.

286. Regulation (EC) No. 549/2004 of the European Parliament and of the Council of 10 March 2004 laying down the framework for the creation of the single European sky (the framework Regulation), Article 2(26).

287. Commission Regulation (EC) No. 29/2009 of 16 January 2009 laying down requirements on data link services for the single European sky, Article 2(6); Commission Implementing Regulation (EU) No. 1079/2012 of 16 November 2012 laying down requirements for voice channels spacing for the single European sky, Article 3(9). Although not related to the SES, also consider as an example of a piece of EU legislation that distinguishes between civil aircraft and State aircraft strictly in accordance with the terms of the Chicago Convention, Regulation (EC) No. 785/2004 of the European Parliament and of the Council of 21 April 2004 on insurance requirements for air carriers and aircraft operators, Article 2(2)(a).

288. Forty-one States including all EU Member States (as at July 2021).

289. Eurocontrol, 'General Air Traffic', available at ext.eurocontrol.int/lexicon/index.php/General_Air_Traffic accessed 20 February 2019.

290. Eurocontrol Specifications for Harmonized Rules for Operational Air Traffic (OAT) under Instrument Flight Rules (IFR) inside Controlled Airspace of the ECAC Area (EUROAT) (18 September 2016) 1.1.2. OAT applies to 'all flights which do not comply with the provisions stated for GAT and for which rules and procedures have been specified by appropriate national authorities' (Eurocontrol, 'Operational Air Traffic', available at ext.eurocontrol.int/lexicon/index.php/Operational_Air_Traffic accessed 20 February 2019). OAT follows ICAO rules as closely as possible and deviations from the rules are published by Eurocontrol.

2.4.2.4 *Ambiguity of Definition Not a Practical Concern for States*

Despite the ongoing lack of clarity in the distinction under the Chicago Convention, the question is, in recent years, no longer seen as a paramount concern to States. This is most evident in response to a 2016 ICAO questionnaire on the subject, which was distributed to ICAO Member States in response to a Working Paper that was submitted the year prior on behalf of ten Member States addressing what they described as 'an absence of clear and generally accepted international rules' regarding the distinction between State aircraft and civil aircraft.[291] Fifty-five States responded to the questionnaire, with only eight of those reporting any concern.[292] As a result, at the 37th Session of the Legal Committee in September 2018, the matter of the distinction between State aircraft and civil aircraft was removed from the Committee's General Work Programme.[293]

Of course, at the heart of the matter is the concept of State sovereignty, on which some States see a global, harmonised approach as an encroachment. Echoing the words of the Chairman of the Drafting Committee of Article 3, Ecuador, addressing the matter, spoke of 'the legal straightjacket interfering with the sovereignty of States' and emphasised that '[t]he breadth with which the Article [Article 3(b)] had been drafted had made it possible for Contracting States to maintain their sovereignty and classify their aircraft under their own legislation',[294] while Argentina likewise approved of the ambiguity of the article, which 'left it to the will of the States to determine whether an operation was "State" or "civil" in nature'.[295] At the very least, the pursuit of a definition may be viewed as a losing battle by other States, with India having declared, in relation to finding a clear definition, that 'international affairs would always be subject to the problem of conflicting interpretations and that no detail of clarification could resolve this problem completely'.[296]

2.4.3 State Aircraft Not Completely Excluded from the Chicago Convention and Its Annexes

Before turning to the framework governing the grant of overflight rights in relation to the international operation of State aircraft, the following section provides a brief qualification to the statement that State aircraft are excluded from the scope of the Chicago Convention. Despite the express exclusion of State aircraft from the Chicago

291. ICAO WP/2-6, *State/Civil Aircraft Definition and Its Impact on Aviation*, Presented by Poland, Bulgaria, the Czech Republic, Cyprus, Greece, Lithuania, Romania, Slovakia, Slovenia and Hungary at the Legal Committee 36th Session, Montreal (29 September 2015) 1.2.
292. ICAO WP/2, *Consideration of Other Items on the General Work Programme of the Legal Committee*, Presented by the Secretariat at the Legal Committee 37th Session, Montreal (12 July 2018) 4.4.
293. *Ibid.* 4.5 c).
294. ICAO (n 268) Attachment 2 (Extract of the Draft Summary Minutes of the Eighth Meeting of the 140th Session of the Council held on 22 November 1993) at 15.
295. *Ibid.* at 10.
296. *Ibid.* at 8.

Convention under its Article 3(a), some provisions of the Convention and its annexes apply, or may be applied, to State aircraft.

This begins in Article 3 itself where Article 3(c), regarding the requirement for State aircraft to receive special authorisation, in effect results in the same requirements as the first part of Article 8 applying to pilotless aircraft. Furthermore, under Article 3(d), in issuing regulations for their State aircraft, contracting States are required to undertake to have due regard for the safety of navigation of civil aircraft. This is, again, consistent with the obligation imposed on States under the second part of Article 8 in relation to pilotless aircraft.[297] ICAO also has a role in achieving coordination between military and civil aircraft pursuant to Article 3(d) of the Chicago Convention in order to help ensure that States exercise the required due regard under the article.

Huang has discussed this matter in relation to Article 3 *bis*,[298] which addresses the obligation of States to refrain from the use of weapons against civil aircraft in flight, concluding, with reference to Article 32 of the Vienna Convention on the Law of Treaties, that such an interpretation 'would lead to "a result which is manifestly absurd or unreasonable" if one were to conclude that [the article] is not applicable to state aircraft'.[299] In particular, Huang highlights the fact that interception of civil aircraft under the article would most likely be carried out by State aircraft and so the requirement under Article 3 *bis* (a) – that it be done without jeopardising the lives of persons on board and the safety of the aircraft – and the corresponding rules for the interception of civil aircraft in the Appendix to Annex 2 are directed to any aircraft performing the task, whether it be a State aircraft or a civil aircraft.[300] The willingness of States to provide ICAO with the power to legislate for State aircraft in this instance reflects the States' recognition of the potentially catastrophic consequences for civil aircraft involved in interception and the role that regulation can play in helping to avoid such consequences.[301]

Civil aviation rules have also been applied to State aircraft in the case of aircraft accident investigation. This occurred, for instance, after the 2010 aircraft accident in which the Polish President Lech Kaczyński, his wife, and a number of other Polish political and military leaders were killed, when the rules on aircraft accident and incident investigation under Annex 13 of the Chicago Convention were applied.[302]

The examples presented here are not comprehensive but are designed to demonstrate that, despite being explicitly excluded from the Chicago Convention, State aircraft remain subject to some of its provisions.

297. As such, while the provisions of Article 8 do not apply to RPAS employed for State purposes, similar considerations must be taken into account by contracting States that employ such RPAS, as a result of the general State aircraft provisions under the Convention.
298. *See also*, Section 2.3.2 in relation to Annex 17.
299. Huang (n 127) 111, in part quoting the Vienna Convention on the Law of Treaties, Article 31(3). *See also*, Cheng (n 260) 63.
300. Huang (n 127) 111.
301. The information contained in this sentence was provided by Professor Ludwig Weber (McGill University) through an interview with the author on 28 May 2019 at the Institute of Air and Space Law, McGill University, Montreal.
302. Piotr Kasprzyk, 'Legal Ramifications of the Investigations of the 2010 Polish President's Aircraft Accident' (2011) 36(3) A&SL 201.

2.4.4 The Framework for the Overflight of State Aircraft

State aircraft operate over the territory of other States on the basis of diplomatic clearances. There is no international practice for this and the operation of State aircraft is instead largely negotiated on a bilateral basis. The authority responsible for granting the clearance depends on the structural and procedural peculiarities of the State and may also differ based on the type of State aircraft involved, that is, whether it is used for police, customs or military services. For example, in the US, the clearances are granted by the Office of International Security Operations in coordination with the Department of Transportation (DOT), the Department of Homeland Security, the Department of Defense, US Secret Service and airport authorities, as relevant.[303] In Sweden, the government body responsible depends on the purpose of the operation: the Department of Defence (Regeringskansliet) grants the clearance for military aircraft, while police and customs aircraft are considered by the Swedish Maritime Administration (Sjöfartsverket).[304] In Singapore, the Ministry of Foreign Affairs is the responsible authority,[305] in Australia it is the Department of Defence,[306] and in Switzerland it is the Federal Office of Civil Aviation, in agreement with the Department of Foreign Affairs and the Swiss Air Force.[307] Upon issuing the diplomatic clearance, the granting State provides the aircraft with a diplomatic clearance number, which is then required to be submitted with the flight plan.

The length of prior notice required for obtaining the clearance differs between States, as does the information required by the State of overflight. The type of information may include the purpose of the mission, whether there are weapons or harmful substances on board, and whether there are photographic sensors or cameras attached to the aircraft.[308] The requirement for States to inform of and obtain permission for the carriage of weapons is an obligation that extends beyond bilateral diplomatic clearance arrangements for State aircraft to also include civil aircraft by way of Article 35 of the Chicago Convention. Under this article, States are prohibited from carrying 'munitions of war or implements of war in or above the territory of a State in aircraft engaged in international navigation, except by permission of such State'.

303. US Department of State, 'Diplomatic Aircraft Clearance Procedures for Foreign State Aircraft to Operate in United States National Airspace', available at www.state.gov/diplomatic-aircraft-clearance-procedures-for-foreign-state-aircraft-to-operate-in-united-states-national-airspace/ accessed 1 August 2020.
304. Swedish Armed Forces, 'Diplomatic Clearances', available at www.forsvarsmakten.se/en/about/diplomatic-clearances/ accessed 18 March 2019.
305. Aeronautical Information Publication Singapore, GEN 1.2 Entry, Transit and Departure of Aircraft – 3.1.1.3 Civil Non-scheduled Flights – Overflight (21 July 2016).
306. Australian Government, Department of Foreign Affairs and Trade, 'Diplomatic Clearances – Aircraft and Ships', available at www.dfat.gov.au/about-us/foreign-embassies/protocol/Pages/diplomatic-clearances-aircraft-and-ships accessed 5 January 2019.
307. Switzerland, Federal Office for Civil Aviation (FOCA), 'Diplomatic Clearances', available at www.bazl.admin.ch/diplomaticclearances accessed 1 August 2020.
308. *See*, for example, the EU Diplomatic Clearance Technical Arrangement (DIC TA) Form, available at dic.eda.europa.eu/ accessed 13 March 2020.

Clearances under specific circumstances are also governed at a multilateral level, such as those in the scope of the European Convention on Extradition.[309] Article 21(4) of this Convention requires notification of overflight and unscheduled landing and a request for transit in the case of intended landing, for flights within the scope of the Convention. Although the article does not mention the term 'State aircraft', the aircraft on these flights would likely be classified as State aircraft because, even without regard to other relevant factors, extradition is an act of the State.

The result of this system of bilateral agreements is that an international flight of a State aircraft involving the overflight of more than one State in addition to the State in which the aircraft is registered must generally be organised segment by segment. For example, a State aircraft flying from Romania to Spain will, in the absence of harmonised arrangements, as to which see below, need to obtain diplomatic clearances for each of the States whose airspace it operates over. In order to avoid the burden of having to obtain individual diplomatic clearances for each flight, or for each portion of territorial airspace for a flight where overflight of multiple countries is involved, some States and organisations have harmonised agreements in place. These agreements operate as a type of blanket arrangement for the operation of certain State aircraft, providing prior permission for the specified State aircraft of the participating States to operate in the airspace of the other participating States. For example, the European Union Defence Agency's (EDA) Diplomatic Clearance Technical Arrangement (DIC TA) facilitates the overflight of military transport aircraft of the States involved over the other States' territories.[310] Similarly, the North Atlantic Treaty Organization (NATO), which in peacetime uses bilateral agreements for the operation of its aircraft,[311] has also considered implementing harmonised arrangements between NATO Member States.[312]

2.5 IN SUMMARY: THE GRANT OF OVERFLIGHT RIGHTS IN NATIONAL AIRSPACE

The legal basis for the right of overflight depends on the airspace in question – national or international – as well as the type of aircraft involved. This chapter so far has established the legal bases for overflight rights in national airspace for civil aircraft,

309. European Convention on Extradition (Paris, 13 December 1957) ETS 24.
310. The DIC TA was first signed by eleven Member States on 19 November 2012 and now, in its current form as amended in 2017, it has seventeen Member State signatures (European Defence Agency, 'Diplomatic Clearances', available at dic.eda.europa.eu/ accessed 3 January 2019). *See also*, European Commission, 'Joint Communication to the European Parliament and the Council – Improving Military Mobility in the European Union' (Brussels, 10 November 2017, JOIN(2017) 41 final) 4.
311. 'NATO Policy for Civil/Military Aircraft Operating in Support of NATO or NATO-led Missions and Operations' (NATO, 2016) 8. *See also*, ICAO European and North Atlantic Office EUR Doc 032, *Interim Guidance Material on Civil/Military Cooperation in Air Traffic Management* (2nd edn, 2016) 30.
312. European Commission, 'Joint Communication to the European Parliament and the Council – Improving Military Mobility in the European Union' (Brussels, 10 November 2017, JOIN(2017) 41 final) 4.

taking into account whether the aircraft is manned or unmanned and whether the operation is a scheduled service or a non-scheduled flight, as well as for State aircraft, which fall outside the scope of the Chicago Convention.

Overflight rights are granted by a State in respect of the navigation of aircraft in the airspace over its territory. The first part of the chapter examined the relationship between sovereignty and territory in international civil aviation law and the interaction between this area of law and the law of the sea and space law in determining the limits of national airspace. While the horizontal limits are clear under international law, despite some disputed claims to an extended territorial sea, the vertical extent of national airspace is yet to be delimited.

Over national airspace, the grant of overflight rights for civil aircraft is conducted pursuant to Articles 5, 6 and 8 of the Chicago Convention. If the navigation involves manned aircraft on a non-scheduled flight, the grant of overflight rights is provided on a multilateral basis under Article 5 for aircraft of State parties to the Convention. Under Article 6, scheduled air services are permitted to fly over the territory of another State only with prior permission from that State. This provision forms the basis of the framework of ASAs that facilitate international air transport. For the right of overflight, however, the Transit Agreement provides for the exchange of the right on a multilateral basis. Despite this, the right of overflight, together with the right to make technical stopovers, is usually reiterated in the ASAs of States that are party to the Transit Agreement. For unmanned civil aircraft, special permission is required for operation over another State's territory. This is even in the case of unmanned aircraft conducting a non-scheduled flight because, in the case of Articles 5 and 8 applying, the latter, as *lex specialis*, takes precedence over the former.

State aircraft are explicitly excluded from the scope of the Chicago Convention and therefore from the legal framework that governs the overflight rights for civil aircraft. State aircraft are instead generally granted overflight rights through bilateral ad hoc arrangements. As with the grant of special permission to facilitate the overflight of civil unmanned aircraft, in some instances, arrangements have been put in place for a move towards a more harmonised approach to the grant of overflight rights for State aircraft, which would decrease the burden on both the granting and requesting States. In the case of State aircraft, the discussion surrounding a more harmonised approach is at present centred around the operation of aircraft within the activities of specific agencies (EDA) and organisations (NATO), rather than the international operation of State aircraft on a general basis.

The chapter up to this point has provided the foundation for the analysis in the remainder of the chapter which first examines the restriction of overflight rights over national airspace and, second, the basis for overflight rights in international airspace, where the interaction of the law of the sea with overflight is a central consideration.

2.6 RESTRICTION AND REGULATION OF OVERFLIGHT RIGHTS IN NATIONAL AIRSPACE

2.6.1 Withdrawal, Suspension and Revocation

The grant of the right of overflight by a State to the aircraft of another State is subject to compliance with applicable laws under both international law and the domestic law of the granting State. This section will consider the general circumstances giving rise to the withdrawal, suspension and revocation of overflight rights rather than look at specific ASAs or domestic laws. As such, reference to revocation under ASAs will be based on the template air services agreements (TASAs) provided by ICAO. In the words of ICAO, the TASAs 'include draft provisions on traditional, transitional and most liberal approaches to various elements in an air services agreement' representing 'a distillation of the most common and current usage by States'.[313] The TASAs have no legal value but are provided as guidance to States in drafting their ASAs.

As has been outlined above in Section 2.3.3.1, for international civil aviation, most States have exchanged overflight rights for scheduled air services in relation to their territory through the Transit Agreement, concluded in 1944 together with the Chicago Convention. For those States that are not party to the Transit Agreement, the exchange is made through ASAs on a bilateral basis, to be exercised by the designated carrier under the ASAs or, in the case of a more liberalised ASA, by all carriers of each State under the agreement.

Regardless of the source of the overflight right, in order for a carrier to exercise it, the granting State - or, more accurately, the aeronautical authority of the State - must have provided the carrier with operating authorisations and technical permissions based on a number of conditions, which are set out in the Transit Agreement and ASAs. The circumstances that are considered in the initial grant of the authorisation are in turn those that give rise to the right to withdraw, revoke or suspend a carrier's operating authorisation.[314] Of course, further to the right to retract overflight rights as a result of the circumstances that will be discussed in this section, States also reserve the right to denounce and withdraw from the Transit Agreement and the ASAs that they enter into, with the standard period of notice being twelve months.[315]

Two overarching scenarios provide a State with the right to withdraw, revoke or suspend overflight rights under both the Transit Agreement and ASAs: when the State granting the authorisation to the carrier is not satisfied that the ownership and control requirements, or equivalent, are met by the carrier; and, when the carrier has contravened the domestic law of the granting State.[316] The latter obligation, to operate in accordance with the domestic laws of the State whose territory is being overflown, reflects Article 11 of the Chicago Convention, which imposes an obligation on aircraft

313. Chicago Convention, Annex 2, Appendix 5 'ICAO Template Air Services Agreements', 1.
314. *Ibid.* 9 and 13.
315. This is provided in the Transit Agreement under Article III.
316. *Ibid.* Article 1, Section 5.

operating in the territory of another State to comply with the laws and regulations of that State regarding the operation and navigation of aircraft.

The ownership and control requirements on the other hand are imposed to determine which carriers are entitled to receive the special permission or authorisation referred to in Article 6 of the Chicago Convention, by way of allocation as a designated carrier under the ASA. The requirement that the carrier is substantially owned and effectively controlled by the State or nationals of the State in which it is registered is part of the traditional, restrictive approach to air transport governance and while the formula is gradually being replaced by more liberal requirements, it persists in a majority of ASAs.[317] The definitions of 'substantial ownership' and 'effective control' are subject to domestic law in the absence of internationally agreed definitions. In many cases though, such as for EU Member States under Regulation (EC) 1008/2008, a carrier meets the 'substantial ownership' criterion if more than 50 % of its equity is owned by the State or nationals of the State.[318] The US differs in this respect, requiring at least 75 % of the voting equity to be owned by the State or national of the State in order for the carrier to be able to be considered as an US designated carrier.[319] The approach to 'effective control' is more varied across jurisdictions and measuring it is more difficult. In the EU, for instance, again under Regulation (EC) 1008/2008, it involves consideration of 'the possibility of directly or indirectly exercising a decisive influence on an undertaking', including consideration of the right to use its assets and of involvement in decision-making regarding, for example, the composition, voting or running of the undertaking.[320] Once a carrier has been put forward as a designated carrier under an ASA by the State in which it is registered, it is then for the State granting the operating authorisation to determine whether the carrier meets the first State's ownership and control requirements. In other words, for the purpose of granting the authorisation, the granting State is 'the sole judge of whether the ownership and control criteria have been met'.[321]

More liberalised agreements typically omit the ownership restrictions and require effective *regulatory* control rather than effective control,[322] where effective regulatory control entails both safety and financial responsibility. As to the former, it involves the State ensuring that the carrier holds a valid operating licence or permit issued by the licensing authority, such as an air operator certificate (AOC), and for the latter, it includes considerations such as the carrier holding a valid air carrier licence and being

317. Chicago Convention, Annex 2, Appendix 5 (ICAO Template Air Services Agreements), 9.
318. Regulation (EC) No. 1008/2008, Article 4(f). The same hurdle applies under domestic law, for example, in Australia, although there it only applies to carriers flying international routes and there are no restrictions on foreign ownership for carriers operating purely domestic services.
319. US Department of Transportation, 'How to Become a Certified Air Carrier' (Information Packet, September 2012) 12-13. In Japan, foreign ownership is restricted for all carriers to 33 %. For a comparison of these rules, *see* 'Airline Ownership and Control Rules: At Once Both Irrelevant and Enduring' (CAPA – Centre for Aviation), available at centreforaviation.com/analysis/reports/airline-ownership-and-control-rules-at-once-both-irrelevant-and-enduring-345816 accessed 3 July 2017.
320. Regulation (EC) No. 1008/2008, Article 2(9).
321. Chicago Convention, Annex 2, Appendix 5 (ICAO Template Air Services Agreements), 9.
322. *Ibid.* 15-16.

of sound financial fitness. A transitional ASA – in between a traditional and fully liberalised ASA – may require, in addition to effective regulatory control, that the carrier's principal place of business is in the State of designation. This involves, for instance, that the carrier is established and incorporated in the State in accordance with its laws and regulations, that substantial operations and capital investment are in the State, and that it pays income tax in the State.

Although they will generally form part of a State's national laws and regulations, ASAs also expressly provide for withdrawal, revocation or suspension on the basis of failure to comply with the minimum ICAO Standards applying to safety and, more recently, security aspects.[323] Annex 17, 'Security', to the Chicago Convention was adopted in 1974, but it did not immediately become an express basis on which authorisation could be revoked under ASAs. For example, the Bermuda II agreement[324] between the UK and the US, which was adopted in 1977, referred to security in both its preamble and in a specifically dedicated article (Article 7), but it was not an express basis for revocation or suspension, in contrast to safety aspects (under Article 5). In today's ASAs, security and safety standards are expressly provided as bases for revocation.

Finally, under Article 1 of the Transit Agreement, overflight rights (along with second freedom rights) are suspended outside of peacetime:

> in areas of active hostilities or of military occupation, and in time of war along the supply routes leading to such areas, the exercise of such privileges shall be subject to the approval of the competent military authorities.[325]

This provision is consistent with the multilateral exchange of the right of overflight for non-scheduled flights under Article 5 of the Chicago Convention as a consequence of the fact that the Convention as a whole is suspended in case of war or national emergency as declared by a State, further to Article 89.[326] The distinction between war and national emergency is made in this article because, strictly speaking, a State is free to choose whether it suspends all or part of the Convention in the case of war, but in the case of a national emergency, it must first make a declaration to the ICAO Council notifying it of the intention to suspend the treaty.[327] ASAs traditionally contained a clause addressing the operation of services during armed conflict or a similar change of circumstances,[328] but States typically omit such a provision from

323. Chicago Convention, Annex 2, Appendix 5 (ICAO Template Air Services Agreements), 21 and 24.
324. United Kingdom of Great Britain and Northern Ireland and United States of America, Agreement Concerning Air Services (with Annexes, Exchange of Letters and Agreed Minute dated 22 June 1977) (Bermuda, 23 July 1977) 1079 U.N.T.S. 21 (No. 16509).
325. Transit Agreement, Article 1, Section 1.
326. Chicago Convention, Article 89. The full provision, titled 'War and emergency conditions', reads as follows: 'In case of war, the provisions of this Convention shall not affect the freedom of action of any of the contracting States affected, whether as belligerents or as neutrals. The same principle shall apply in the case of any contracting State which declares a state of national emergency and notifies the fact to the Council.'
327. Cheng (n 90) 113.
328. *See*, for example, Bermuda II, which provided that '[i]f, because of armed conflict, political disturbances or developments, or special and unusual circumstances, a designated airline of

their ASAs today. On this note, Cheng, speaking of Article 89 of the Chicago Convention, states that '[i]t is believed that such a provision is merely declaratory of international law',[329] in which case regardless of a treaty's silence on the matter, a State would have a right to terminate or suspend the treaty.[330]

States also have the right to restrict or prohibit access to their airspace under specific circumstances in accordance with Article 9, which will be addressed in the following section. The formalities under Article 89 are not required for the prohibition or restriction of airspace under Article 9.[331]

2.6.2 Prohibited and Restricted Areas

The terms 'prohibited area' and 'restricted area' are regulated in Article 9 of the Chicago Convention, as to which see below, and are defined in Annexes 2, 4 and 15. The terms refer to areas of 'defined dimensions, above the land areas or territorial waters of a State, within which the flight of aircraft is' prohibited or restricted 'in accordance with certain specified conditions'.[332]

A State can restrict or prohibit its airspace in accordance with two categories, depending on the situation in response to which the area has been established and each involves different conditions.

The first category, under Article 9(a) of the Chicago Convention, is 'for reasons of military necessity or public interest'[333] and the second, under Article 9(b), is 'in exceptional circumstances or during a period of emergency or in the interest of public safety'.[334]

In the first instance, certain areas of airspace may be restricted or prohibited if the restriction or prohibition applies in a uniform manner to all aircraft conducting international scheduled services, both of the State whose territory is concerned and the aircraft of other States. Differential treatment is permitted under this article though, between national and foreign aircraft engaged in non-scheduled flights. In terms of the size of the prohibition or restricted area, it must be of a 'reasonable extent and location

one Contracting Party is unable to operate a service on its normal routing, the other Contracting Party shall use its best efforts to facilitate the continued operation of such service ...' (United Kingdom of Great Britain and Northern Ireland and United States of America (n 324) Article 2(5)).

329. Cheng (n 90) 483.
330. The question of a treaty's status in the case of war is not as clear in other areas of international law though and it is a matter that remains heavily disputed. The ICJ has not delivered a judgment or advisory opinion to clarify the point the Vienna Convention on the Law of Treaties only states that it does not address such matters (Vienna Convention on the Law of Treaties, Article 73: 'The provisions of the present Convention shall not prejudge any question that may arise in regard to a treaty from a succession of States or from the international responsibility of a State or from the outbreak of hostilities between States'). State practice indicates that it depends on the object and purpose of the treaty as to whether it continues to apply between belligerent States during conflict (Silja Vöneky, 'Armed Conflict, Effect on Treaties' (Max Planck Encyclopedia of Public International Law 2011), 1, 3 and 5).
331. Cheng (n 90) 113.
332. Chicago Convention, Annex 2, Chapter 1, 1-7 and 1-8; Annex 4 (11th edn, July 2009) Chapter 1, 1-8; and, Annex 15 (16th edn, July 2018) Chapter 1, 1-8 and 1-9.
333. Chicago Convention, Article 9(a).
334. *Ibid.* Article 9(b).

so as not to interfere unnecessarily with air navigation'.[335] While this leaves the State with some discretion in establishing the physical and temporal limitations of the area, it is clear that they must be commensurate with the activity for which the area has been designated. States reserve significant portions of their airspace for military purposes under Article 9(a). For example, India allocates 35 % of its airspace for military use, while it is estimated that Thailand reserves up to 70 % of its airspace for these purposes,[336] as does China, where the situation creates delays to international civil aviation and has both economic and environmental consequences.[337] This has also been problematic in the past in Europe, although a focus on dual use - military/civil - airspace has improved the situation.[338]

Under the second category, in Article 9(b), the whole of the State's airspace may be restricted or prohibited and with immediate effect, but only temporarily.[339] The restriction or prohibition must be applied without distinction to the aircraft of other States[340] - both scheduled and non-scheduled services - however, 'national aircraft may be exempt from such restriction or prohibition'.[341] It is by way of their authority under this article that the US and Canada closed their airspace following the attack on the World Trade Centre and the Pentagon on 11 September 2001[342] and that parts of EU airspace were closed following the eruption of the Icelandic volcano, Eyjafjallajökull, in 2010.[343]

Under both Article 9(a) and Article 9(b), the State whose territory is concerned has a right to 'effect landing as soon as possible' of aircraft entering restricted or prohibited spaces,[344] with Annex 2 providing principles that States must observe and actions that intercepted aircraft are obliged to adhere to.[345]

2.6.3 ICAO Council Decisions Regarding Prohibition of Overflight

ICAO's dispute settlement mechanism under Chapter XVIII of the Chicago Convention tasks the ICAO Council with 'adjudicat[ing] legal disputes concerning the interpretation and application of the Chicago Convention and its Annexes'.[346] Out of the seven

335. Chicago Convention, Article 9(a).
336. ICAO WP/04 Secretariat, *Civil/Military Cooperation*, Presented by the Secretariat at the 1st Meeting of the ICAO Asia/Pacific Seamless ATM Planning Group, Bangkok (31 January-3 February 2012) 2.9 and 2.10.
337. Justin Bergman, 'This is Why China's Airports are a Nightmare' (BBC, 29 April 2016), available at www.bbc.com/capital/story/20160420-this-is-why-chinas-airports-are-a-nightmare accessed 8 May 2019.
338. Haanappel (n 193) 45.
339. Chicago Convention, Article 9(b).
340. *Ibid.*
341. Cheng (n 90) 124.
342. Haanappel (n 193) 45.
343. Havel and Sanchez (n 112) 43.
344. Chicago Convention, Article 9(c).
345. Chicago Convention, Annex 2, Chapter 3, 3.8 and Appendix 2.
346. Mathieu Vaugeois, 'Settlement of Disputes at ICAO and Sustainable Development' (McGill Centre for Research in Air and Space Law Occasional Paper Series No. IV, June 2016) 4. This dispute settlement mechanism is established by Article 84 of the Chicago Convention.

cases to have been brought before the ICAO Council, five have involved overflight rights, and two of those have specifically been in respect of Article 9 of the Chicago Convention. The first, brought by India in 1952, involved the closure of airspace by Pakistan on its western border, which prohibited Indian flights from operating from points in India to Kabul over Pakistan. At the same time, Iran's airline was permitted to continue operating over the airspace, and as a result, India submitted that Pakistan had violated Article 9 (in addition to Article 5 and the Transit Agreement). The second case was brought by the UK against Spain in 1967 as a result of a prohibited area established by Spain in the Bay of Algeciras, which the UK claimed compromised the safety of take-off and landing from its nearby airport in Gibraltar.[347] The most recent case to have been brought before the ICAO Council - the 2017 disagreement between Qatar and a number of Gulf States, as will be discussed in Chapter 4 - involved claims of violations of Article 9, but as part of a much broader series of claims relating to access to national airspace, including in respect of the Transit Agreement, relevant ASAs, and Articles 5 and 6 of the Chicago Convention.

Despite the India/Pakistan and UK/Spain cases directly addressing Article 9, they provide little in the way of legal analysis of the article, or further in respect of overflight rights more broadly, for two key reasons. *First*, as with the other cases that have been brought before the Council, including the 2017 Qatar case, neither resulted in a final decision based on the merits. The India-Pakistan case was resolved in a settlement between the two governments and the UK-Spain dispute was deferred *sine die* by the parties in 1969 and is therefore technically an ongoing dispute.[348] *Second*, the cases themselves and the dispute settlement process are inherently political. Cheng highlights the importance of the ICAO Council acting 'in an impartial and judicial capacity' in carrying out its functions as a dispute settlement body,[349] but in practice the ICAO Council, as an organ consisting of representatives of sovereign States following the instructions of their governments, is not able to act as an independent, unbiased judicial power.[350] Furthermore, the cases are founded on political disputes, with aviation reflecting just one element in a much wider web of implications. As Milde points out in reference to the overflight dispute between India and Pakistan in 1971,[351] but which applies equally to all of the overflight cases brought before the ICAO Council, 'it is apparent that the centre of gravity of the dispute was of a political nature and that

347. For a brief summary of these cases *see*, Milde (n 91) 204-208, in which the other two cases involving overflight are also discussed: (1) Pakistan brought a claim against India in 1971 for breach of Article 5 of the Chicago Convention and the Transit Agreement after India suspended the overflight rights of Indian carriers following hostilities between the two countries, including the hijacking of an Indian aircraft by pro-Pakistani Kashmiri nationalists; (2) Cuba brought a claim against the US after the US suspended the overflight rights of Cuban carriers in response to the shooting down of a US-registered aircraft by Cuban Air Force aircraft over the high seas. Cuba submitted that the suspension was a violation of Article 5 of the Chicago Convention and of the Transit Agreement.

348. *Ibid.* 205-206.

349. Cheng (n 90) 101.

350. Milde (n 91) 203. Bin Cheng also acknowledged these inherent challenges in the ICAO Council performing a judicial function (Cheng (n 90) 104).

351. *See* above n 347.

the "aviation" aspect could not be meaningfully addressed without a more general solution of the underlying political issues'.[352]

2.6.4 An Obligation to Close Airspace?

The restriction and prohibition of airspace under Article 9 of the Chicago Convention is a right and not an obligation.[353] According to the Dutch Safety Board in its 2015 report on the shooting down of MH17, which was published just over a year after the accident, it was not practice for States to close their airspace during armed conflict at that time[354] and this remains the case today.[355] After MH17, a group was formed by ICAO to review the application of international civil aviation law to conflict zones and as part of this review, the group considered whether Article 9 of the Chicago Convention should be amended to include an obligation to close airspace for safety reasons, finding that at this stage there is no need to do so.[356] This finding is consistent with the typical use by States of Article 9 'to maintain national interests in the use of their sovereign airspace'.[357]

2.6.5 Danger Areas

In addition to prohibited and restricted areas, ICAO provides procedures for the notification of 'danger areas'.[358] These are the only three terms that ICAO recognises as internationally agreed to denote areas for which States can provide warnings and/or

352. Milde (n 91) 207; *see also*, Vaugeois (n 346) 7.
353. This is clear from the wording of Article 9. *See also*, Marieke de Hoon, 'Navigating the Legal Horizon: Lawyering the MH17 Disaster' (2017) 33(84) Utrecht J Int'l and Eur L 90, 101-103; Wouter Oude Alink, 'How "Safe" Airspace Was Not Safe: The Downing of Flight MH17' (Leiden Law Blog, 9 September 2014), available at leidenlawblog.nl/articles/how-safe-airspace-was-not-safe-the-downing-of-flight-mh17 accessed 18 July 2019.
354. 'Crash of Malaysia Airlines Flight MH17 Hrabove, Ukraine, 17 July 2014' (Dutch Safety Board, October 2015) 204.
355. The Dutch Safety Board conducted a follow-up investigation to assess the implementation of the recommendations it made in its 2015 report on the MH17 crash. It published the results of this follow-up investigation in February 2019 and among them: '[t]he investigators found that very few changes relating to airspace management by nations dealing with armed conflict within their territories have been made' (Dutch Safety Board, 'More Attention Devoted to Overflying Conflict Zones', available at www.onderzoeksraad.nl/en/page/13613/more-attention-devoted-to-overflying-conflict-zones accessed 10 July 2019).
356. ICAO WP/14325, *Report on the Outcome of the Meeting of the Special Group to Review the Application of ICAO Treaties Relating to Conflict Zones (SGRAIT-CZ)*, Presented by the Secretariat at the Council 206th Session (20 October 2015) 2.2.
357. Stefan A Kaiser, 'Legal Considerations about the Loss of Malaysia Airlines Flight MH17 in Eastern Ukraine' (2015) 40(2) A&SL 107, 119.
358. Chicago Convention, Annex 4, 2.13, 7.9.2, 8.9.2, 9.9.2, 10.9.2, 11.10.3, 12.10.3 and 16.9.4, 17.9.4 and 18.8.3 *Recommendation* and 21.9.2, in relation to their inclusion on aeronautical charts; Annex 2, Chapter 3 3.8 and Appendix 2 Section 1.1, and Appendix 1 Section 3, respectively for interception and signalling protocol relating to danger areas; Annex 15, 6.3.2.3 (p), regarding the inclusion in NOTAMs of the establishment of or changes to a danger area. Danger areas are identified in Aeronautical Information Publications (AIPs) under ENR 5.1 (ICAO Doc 8126, *Aeronautical Information Services Manual* (6th edn, 2003) Chapter 5, Appendix, 5-A-24).

limit flight in a given airspace.[359] Unlike prohibited and restricted areas, the Chicago Convention does not mention the term 'danger area', which appears only in the annexes to the Convention, classified as 'an airspace of defined dimensions within which activities dangerous to the flight of aircraft may exist at specified times'.[360] ICAO has recognised that danger areas involve 'the least degree of restriction' towards other airspace users out of the three types of areas.[361] In accordance with its definition, the right to establish a danger area is limited in that it must be of defined dimensions, and only for a specified time, as opposed to for an indefinite or undefined period.[362] As also indicated by its definition, a State cannot physically prohibit or restrict the overflight of other States' aircraft through the imposition of a danger area but, in practice, the calculated risks in any given airspace will ultimately inform the decision of whether to operate an aircraft in the airspace.[363] In the past, pilots have avoided danger areas but under 'current safety management practices' certain aircraft may operate in danger areas according to 'appropriate risk assessment'.[364] A key difference of a danger area compared to restricted and prohibited areas, for the purpose of this book, is that it can be established by a State in international airspace.[365] In order to adequately present the concept of danger areas, this section will briefly consider their use in international airspace before continuing to address overflight in national airspace, as has been the focus of this book up to this point.

The annexes to the Chicago Convention do not provide examples of the circumstances in which danger areas may be established, but over the high seas, they are commonly implemented for the purpose of conducting military exercises.[366] The term is also used at ICAO in the context of risk management of flight operations in volcanic

359. ICAO SN/12, *Harmonised Notification of Areas of Volcanic Ash*, Presented by Steven Hill at the 5th Meeting of the Aeronautical Information Services – Aeronautical Information Management Study Group, Montreal (10 October 2011) 1.1: 'ICAO Annex 15 permits the notification by NOTAM of Prohibited, Restricted or Danger areas, which are the only three internationally-agreed terms that States can use to identify the presence of hazards which may affect air navigation or to limit access to a particular area.'
360. Chicago Convention, Annex 2, 1-5; Annex 4, 1-3; and, Annex 15, 1-4.
361. ICAO Doc 9426, *Air Traffic Services Planning Manual* (1992) 3.3.2.2.
362. This is despite the formal appearance of permanent danger areas on some aeronautical charts: 'The United States (and quite possibly most other major military users of international airspace) often establishes its version of warning areas on a continuous-use basis. The practical reason for not charting each area anew as it recurrently comes into use is that extensive, but interrupted, use justifies neither recharting for each exercise or series of activities conducted therein, nor even issuance of Notices to Airmen (NOTAMs). Unfortunately, the consequence of his practice is an uninterrupted depiction of these areas on charts, giving the questionable impression to other users and nations that the areas are under the constant use, domination, and control (i.e., de facto) of the United States' (George S Robinson, 'Military Requirements for International Airspace: Evolving Claims to Exclusive Use of a Res Communes Natural Resource' (1971) 11 Nat Resources J 162, 174-175).
363. *See* Section 3.3.3.3.
364. ICAO, *ATM Contingency Plan: Africa and Indian Ocean Region* (July 2019) 71.
365. ICAO (n 361) 3.3.2.2 and 3.3.2.4; ICAO European and North Atlantic Office IP/03, *ICAO Provisions Related to Access to the High Seas*, Presented by the Secretariat at the 3rd Meeting of the European Air Navigation Planning Group Flexible Use of Airspace Task Force, Paris (16 January 2009) 2.3.
366. John R Brock, 'Legality of Warning Areas as Used by the United States' (1966-1967) 21(3) The JAG J 69, 71; Pépin (n 90) 69.

ash, although this is in a slightly different sense from how it is used in its more general application.[367] All States have the right to use international airspace in a manner that requires the establishment of a danger area, regardless of which State is responsible for the FIR. Recalling Chapter 1, and as will be discussed in more detail below in Section 2.7.1, all States, both coastal and landlocked, enjoy the high seas freedoms set out in Article 87(1) UNCLOS, including freedom of overflight, which also applies in the EEZ.[368] The use of the high seas for military activities, while not explicitly mentioned in UNCLOS as a high seas freedom, is accepted as being encompassed by the freedom insofar as the purpose is peaceful.[369] Military activities are also legitimate in a State's EEZ, although this position is not universally accepted, as will be discussed in Section 4.3.3.2. Relevant to this book, military activities include those on the surface of the sea that may impact on the safety of overflight in the airspace above, as well as aerial military activities as part of the right to freedom of overflight.[370] Just as the principle of freedom of overflight means that a State responsible for an FIR cannot prohibit the aircraft registered in another State from operating within the FIR,[371] neither can it prevent the aircraft of another State from undertaking activities in international airspace within its FIR where those activities are accepted as being within the scope of the freedoms of the high seas.

This does not give a State an unfettered right to undertake activities requiring a danger area in all locations of international airspace, or to do so without coordination with the ATS authority in the FIR. Under Article 87(2) UNCLOS, freedoms of the high seas must be conducted with due regard for the interests of other States in the exercise of their freedoms, which includes the freedom of overflight of other States' aircraft.[372] Furthermore, recalling Section 2.4.3, contracting States are required to have due regard for the safety of navigation of civil aircraft in issuing regulations for their State aircraft.[373] Annex 11 of the Chicago Convention details the type of considerations to be made in respect of these due regard obligations. Standard 2.19.2 requires that the arrangements 'avoid hazards to civil aircraft and minimize interference with the normal operations of such aircraft', with the accompanying recommendations outlining that the location and duration should, for example, be 'selected to avoid closure or

367. ICAO Doc 9974, *Flight Safety and Volcanic Ash* (1st edn, 2012) (x) and 5.4 (d) 1); ICAO, *ATM Contingency Plan: Africa and Indian Ocean Region* (July 2019) 71.
368. UNCLOS, Article 58(1).
369. Myron H Nordquist, Neal R Grandy, Sataya N Nandan and Shabtai Rosenne (eds), *United Nations Convention on the Law of the Sea 1982: A Commentary – Volume II* (Martinus Nijhoff 1993) 85.
370. Kay Hailbronner, 'Freedom of the Air and the Convention on the Law of the Sea' (1983) 77 Am J Int'l L 490, 503: 'Freedom of the high seas includes, *inter alia*, use of the ocean space for military exercises, aerial reconnaissance, and all other activities of civil and military aircraft if due regard is paid to the rights and interests of third states'.
371. *See* Chapter 1. As also discussed in, ICAO European and North Atlantic Office IP/03, *ICAO Provisions Related to Access to the High Seas*, Presented by the Secretariat at the 3rd Meeting of the European Air Navigation Planning Group Flexible Use of Airspace Task Force, Paris (16 January 2009) 2.1.
372. In addition, and once again as will be addressed in Section 4.3.3.2, States must have due regard in carrying out their rights in an EEZ for the coastal State's EEZ rights.
373. Chicago Convention, Article 3(d).

realignment of established ATS routes, blocking of the most economic flight levels, or delays of scheduled aircraft operations, unless no other option exists'.[374] Where potential hazards to civil aviation exist, a State undertaking the activity is required under Annex 11 to coordinate the activity with the State responsible for the FIR. Specifically, Standard 2.19.1 provides that:

> The arrangements for activities potentially hazardous to civil aircraft, whether over the territory of a State or over the high seas, shall be coordinated with the appropriate air traffic services authorities. The coordination shall be effected early enough to permit timely promulgation of information regarding the activities in accordance with the provisions of Annex 15.[375]

The ATS authorities are then responsible for the promulgation of the information regarding the establishment of the danger area, including by way of the issuance of a Notice to Airmen (NOTAM).[376]

When aerial military activities are conducted by a State in international airspace under an FIR for which another State is responsible, prior notification and coordination are only required in the case that a defined airspace is necessary to protect civil aircraft navigating in the vicinity from potential safety hazards arising from the military activities. If the activities can be carried out without endangering civil aircraft, there is no obligation on the State to coordinate with the authorities of the State responsible for the FIR. Danger areas will be returned to throughout this book in both Chapters 3 and 4.

2.6.6 Closure of Airspace under Non-aviation Specific International Law

The ICAO Council dispute settlement mechanism discussed above in Section 2.6.3 includes, as a tool of aiming to ensure compliance, the enforcement of a prohibition of overflight for any airline that acts contrary to the terms of a final decision.[377] Another way in which overflight can be prohibited multilaterally under international law is through a United Nations Security Council (UNSC) resolution. In contrast to the enforcement of the prohibition of overflight for airlines under the Chicago Convention,

374. Chicago Convention, Annex 11 (15th edn, July 2018) 2.19.2 and 2.19.2.1 (a) *Recommendation*. 'Hazard' is defined by ICAO as 'a condition or an object with the potential to cause or contribute to an aircraft incident or accident' (ICAO Doc 10084, *Risk Assessment Manual for Civil Aircraft Operations Over or Near Conflict Zones* (2nd edn, 2018) xiii).
375. *Ibid.* 2.19.1, where Annex 15 addresses Aeronautical Information Services. *See also*, ICAO (n 371) 2.4.
376. *Ibid.* 2.18.3. *See* above n 358 for the specific requirements regarding the communication of danger areas under Annexes 2, 4 and 15. A NOTAM is defined as 'a notice distributed by means of telecommunication containing information concerning the establishment, condition or change in any aeronautical facility, service, procedure or hazard, the timely knowledge of which is essential to personnel concerned with flight operations' (Chicago Convention, Annex 11, 1-6).
377. Chicago Convention, Article 87: 'Each contracting States "undertakes not to allow the operation of an airline of a contracting State through the airspace above its territory."' Under Article 88, any contracting State that 'is found in default under the provisions' of the chapter will have its voting rights in the ICAO Assembly and Council suspended by the Assembly.

the sanctions under UNSC resolutions do not necessarily require there to have been a breach of international law, but rather they can be adopted when 'it appears conducive to the maintenance of international peace and security'.[378] Such resolutions are made by the UNSC pursuant to Articles 41 and 42 of the UN Charter. Under Article 41, the UNSC may take economic measures against a State, including the interruption of air services by way of a ban on flights. A UNSC resolution of this kind would require States to, for example, suspend the transit and traffic rights of aircraft registered in the sanctioned State. Article 42 provides that the UNSC may, if the measures under Article 41 are inadequate, 'take such action by air ... as may be necessary to maintain or restore international peace and security'. It is under this article that the UNSC imposes no-fly zones, which are established for humanitarian purposes, to facilitate humanitarian relief efforts and to prevent attacks on the civilian population from the air.[379] A no-fly zone achieves this goal by depriving the State of its effective control over its airspace, providing that control to another State or States, or an international organisation.[380] A UNSC resolution may include both a flight ban and a no-fly zone, as was the case in the 2011 Resolution applying to Libya.[381] Once adopted, it is widely accepted that the terms of the resolution are binding and that they override existing obligations of the States, for example, to permit overflight under the Transit Agreement.[382]

A State may also restrict or prohibit overflight of its territory by the aircraft of another State as a countermeasure under international law, in response to an internationally wrongful act committed by the second State. A countermeasure, as conduct which would otherwise be inconsistent with international law, may be legitimate when imposed in accordance with certain conditions, including that it is proportionate, temporary and reversible.[383] In relation to a countermeasure targeting aviation, a State could, for example, suspend another State's transit and/or traffic rights. In this case, the first State's responsibility to allow the transit/traffic rights to be exercised by the

378. UN Charter, Articles 39 and 41, as discussed in, Jeremy Farrall, 'Sanctions' in Jacob Katz Cogan, Ian Hurd and Ian Johnstone (eds), *The Oxford Handbook of International Organizations* (OUP 2016) 604. This is a feature of all measures under Chapter VII of the UN Charter, the chapter under which this mechanism falls.
379. Stefan A Kaiser, 'No-Fly Zones Established by the United Nations Security Council' (2011) 60 ZLW 402, 411. This article draws the distinction between, and discusses the implications of, UNSC measures applying to airspace taken under Articles 41 and 42 of the UN Charter (*see*, in particular, pp. 408-409).
380. *Ibid.* 402.
381. UNSC 1973 (17 March 2011) UN Doc S/RES/10200, paras 6-12 (no-fly zone) and paras 17-18 (ban on flights). Other UNSC Resolutions affecting overflight include UNSC Res 748 (31 March 1992) UN Doc S/RES/748, para. 4 (Libya); UNSC Res 917 (6 May 1994) UN Doc S/RES/917, para. 2 (Haiti); UNSC Res 1127 (28 August 1997) UN Doc S/RES/1127, para. 4 (Angola) (as discussed in, Nico Krisch, 'Ch. VII Action with Respect to Threats to the Peace, Breaches of the Peace, and Acts of Aggression, Article 41' in Bruno Simma, Daniel-Erasmus Khan, Georg Nolte, Andreas Paulus, Nikolai Wessendorf (eds), *The Charter of the United Nations: A Commentary, Volume II* (3rd edn, OUP 2012) 1313).
382. Nico Krisch, 'Ch. VII Action with Respect to Threats to the Peace, Breaches of the Peace, and Acts of Aggression, Article 41' in Bruno Simma, Daniel-Erasmus Khan, Georg Nolte, Andreas Paulus, Nikolai Wessendorf (eds), *The Charter of the United Nations: A Commentary, Volume II* (3rd edn, OUP 2012) 1310.
383. YILC (2001) Vol. II, Part 2, as corrected, 76.

second State in respect of its territory would not be terminated, but rather, the wrongfulness of the first State's conduct in prohibiting the exercise of those rights would be precluded.[384] In contrast to fulfilling an obligation under a UNSC resolution, determining the legality of a State restricting or prohibiting overflight through such sanctions involves consideration of the actions of and the relationship between the two States, including the terms of any treaty relevant to the dispute. It can be made more challenging when the decision-making process leading to the countermeasure is not fully transparent. This is the case in the ban on Qatari flights imposed by Bahrain, Egypt, Saudi Arabia and the United Arab Emirates (UAE) in June 2017, which will be addressed in Section 4.2.2.

2.6.7 In Summary: The Restriction and Regulation of Overflight in National Airspace

Sovereignty over national airspace, as recognised under Article 1 of the Chicago Convention, is the cornerstone of international civil aviation law. One of the defining features of a State is its capacity to enter into relations with other States and it is through this exercise of their sovereign rights that States negotiate the grant of access to their airspace for the aircraft of other States. The right of overflight and the other freedoms of the air are privileges and, as has been demonstrated in this chapter, there are various mechanisms through which States can retract or restrict these privileges as a result of the complete and exclusive sovereignty that they retain over their airspace.

Both the Transit Agreement and ASAs provide a State with the right to withdraw, suspend or revoke the rights granted to the carriers of another State where the domestic laws of the granting State have not been complied with, or where ownership and control requirements have not been satisfied. A State may also withdraw from the agreements entirely, in which case the rights granted under them also cease. States are also permitted under the Chicago Convention to establish prohibited and restricted areas in their airspace in certain circumstances and subject to specific requirements. This is not, however, an obligation. Finally, pursuant to UNSC resolutions, States may be obliged to prohibit the aircraft of another State from operating in their airspace. The obligation of States to adhere to the terms of the resolution overrides any existing treaty obligations that the States may have towards the State targeted by the sanctions. States may also prohibit overflight on the basis of countermeasures against a State. An example of this is the sanctions imposed on Qatar in 2017 by its neighbouring States, a situation that is complex and intrinsically political.

Having established the basis of overflight rights in national airspace in earlier sections of this chapter, for both civil aircraft and State aircraft, and the right of a State to close its airspace to the aircraft of other States in this section, the chapter will now address the legal basis of freedom of overflight, as codified in UNCLOS.

384. YILC (2001) Vol. II, Part 2, as corrected, 75 (Commentary para. 4 to Article 22).

2.7 OVERFLIGHT RIGHTS IN INTERNATIONAL AIRSPACE

This section will consider the legal basis of freedom of overflight and the provisions under UNCLOS and the Chicago Convention with implications for the right. It will set out the maritime areas over which freedom of overflight exists and establish the express rights of coastal States in these areas as provided under UNCLOS. The remainder of the book, in subsequent chapters, will build on this, examining the more ambiguous aspects of the rights of coastal States in respect of overflight in these maritime areas.

2.7.1 Freedom of Overflight

Outside national airspace there is so-called freedom of overflight. Freedom of overflight is founded on the concept of the broader principle of *mare liberum*, or freedom of the seas, as codified in UNCLOS.[385] The 1956 ILC commentary on the law of the sea recognised that the principle of freedom of the seas 'has governed maritime law since Grotius',[386] and the subsequent 1958 Convention on the High Seas - which recognises the principle of freedom of the high seas in Article 2, including freedom of overflight - states in its preamble that the provisions in the Convention are 'generally declaratory of established principles of international law'.[387] The principle means that 'no state may purport to subject any part of them [the high seas] to its territorial sovereignty'.[388] As a consequence of the principle of freedom of the seas, the law of the sea has developed on the basis that, outside the territorial sea, the sea is open to all users.[389] In addition to recognising the principle, UNCLOS stipulates specific freedoms that are entailed in such enjoyment, including the freedom of navigation and, closely tied to this, the freedom of overflight. The drafting history of the 1958 Convention on the High Seas considered and ultimately concluded that freedom of overflight in international airspace has customary status:

> During the discussions in the International Commission for Air Navigation at its extraordinary session of June 1929, the Commission 'recognized that flight over the sea, outside territorial waters, is free'.
>
> The minutes of the Chicago Conference contain no record of any discussion on this subject, but the representatives present seem to have regarded the principle as

385. UNCLOS, Articles 87(1) and 58(1).
386. YILC (1956) Vol. II, 266.
387. Convention on the High Seas (Geneva, 29 April 1958) 450 U.N.T.S. 11, *entered into force* 30 September 1962, Preamble ('Convention on the High Seas 1958'). The Convention on the High Seas 1958 was adopted at the First UN Conference on the Law of the Sea, together with three other conventions addressing: the territorial seas and the contiguous zone, the continental shelf, and fishing and the conservation of living resources of the high seas. The former three will be referred to at various stages throughout this research. Many UNCLOS articles are based on these conventions. The provisions in the 1958 conventions are in turn based on the ILC draft articles resulting from the ILC's 8th Session.
388. Jennings and Watts (n 72) 726.
389. Natalie Klein, *Maritime Security and the Law of the Sea* (OUP 2011) 2.

already established for; under Article 12 of the Convention, the right to make rules relating to the flight and manoeuvres of aircraft over the high seas is vested not in the contracting States but in ICAO; furthermore, the rules established by ICAO are binding on the said States.

Article 27 of the draft [of the 1958 Convention on the High Seas] contains in its second sentence the following statement: 'Freedom' of the high seas comprises, *inter alia*: '... "(4) Freedom to fly over the high seas." This provision confirms a principle of customary international law, which the Commission [the ILC] itself emphasizes in the first paragraph of its commentary to article 27: "Freedom to overfly the high seas is expressly mentioned in this article because the Commission considers that it follows directly from the principle of the freedom of the sea"'.[390]

Just as with freedom of navigation applying to vessels, freedom of overflight means that the aircraft of all States have the right to use the airspace within the bounds of international law and, as the reference to Article 12 of the Chicago Convention in the citation above indicates, the rules relating to the flight and manoeuvre of aircraft in international airspace are those established by ICAO, not by the contracting States. As to what these rules are, Section 2.7.2.2 discusses them in more detail.

The EEZ was formally recognised under international law in 1982, as to which *see* Section 2.7.3.1, which explains why it was not referred to in the above quotation. As of the adoption of UNCLOS, however, it is indisputable that freedom of overflight applies in both the high seas and the EEZ. This is codified under UNCLOS, which provides for the freedom of overflight in international airspace in two articles, Article 87(1)(b) and Article 58(1), reading, respectively:

> 'The high seas are open to all States, whether coastal or land-locked. ... It comprises ... (b) freedom of overflight'
>
> and,
>
> 'In the exclusive economic zone, all States, whether coastal or land-locked, enjoy ... the freedoms referred to in article 87 of navigation and overflight'.

ICAO recognition of freedom of overflight applying in the high seas and the EEZ can be seen, for example, in this discussion regarding the freedom applying in the EEZ, shortly after the adoption of UNCLOS:

> There is, your Rapporteur would suggest, no need for the Legal Committee to become involved in general questions of the status of the EEZ. It is sufficient to take note that, without ambiguity, the same right of freedom of navigation is enjoyed by aircraft over the EEZ as is enjoyed by aircraft over the high seas, which is the plain meaning of Articles 58 and 87 of UNCLOS.[391]

390. Pépin (n 90) 68; Nicholas Grief, *Public International Law in the Airspace of the High Seas* (Springer 1994) 2.
391. ICAO WP/5-41, *Report by the Rapporteur on Agenda Item 5: Consideration of the Report of the Rapporteur on 'United Nations Convention on the Law of the Sea – Implications, if any, for the Application of the Chicago Convention, its Annexes and other International Air Law Instruments'*, Presented at the Legal Committee 26th Session, Montreal (4 February 1987), reproduced in (1987) 3 Int'l Org & L Sea: Documentary YB 262, 269.

Figure 2.4 depicts the EEZ and the high seas. In this figure they appear to be overlapping, which they do not in practice; however, this depiction is representative of the fact that it is the prerogative of a coastal State to declare an EEZ and so, in the case it does not do so, the high seas meet the outer limit of the State's territorial sea.

Figure 2.4 Maritime Delimitations of the Sea and the Airspace above the Sea[392]

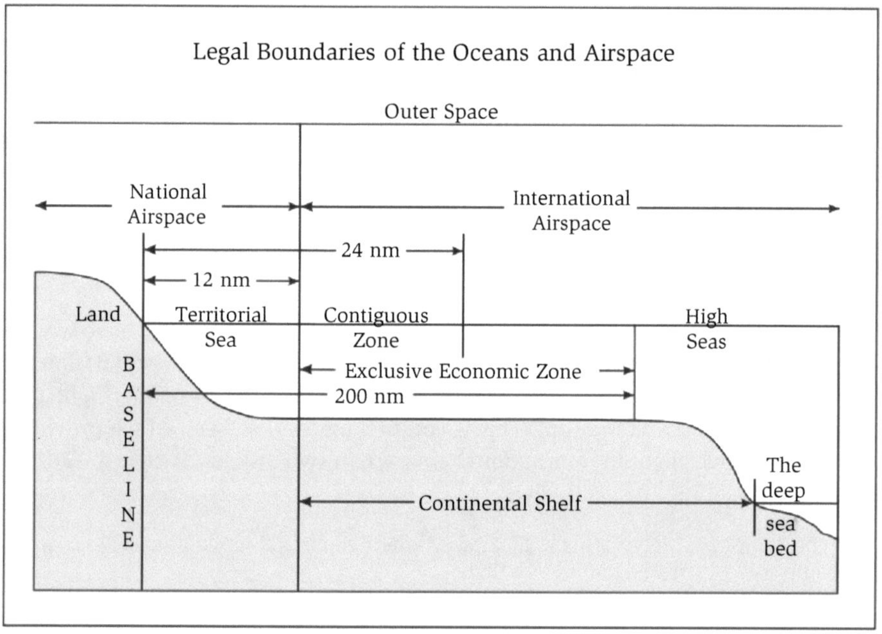

Freedom of overflight applies in international airspace independently of UNCLOS, on the basis of its customary status. This is relevant for those States that are not party to UNCLOS. Although UNCLOS is widely ratified,[393] around 15 % of States are not party to it, including the US, Turkey, Colombia, Israel, Peru and Venezuela. As a result, Treves emphasises that it is 'important to assess whether certain provisions of UNCLOS correspond to customary international law [because] [w]hen it is so, it may be held that the rules set out in UNCLOS are binding also for non-parties'.[394] Article

392. *Source*: The Commander's Handbook on the Law of Naval Operations (Department of the Navy – Department of Homeland Security and US Coast Guard, August 2017) 1-2.
393. 167 State parties and the EU as at July 2021 (United Nations Division for Ocean Affairs and the Law of the Sea, 'UNCLOS Status Table', available at www.un.org/Depts/los/reference_files/UNCLOS%20Status%20table_ENG.pdf accessed 13 November 2020).
394. Tullio Treves, 'UNCLOS and Non-party States Before the International Court of Justice' in Carlos Espósito, James Kraska, Harry N Scheiber and Moon-Sang Kwon (eds), *Ocean Law and Policy: Twenty Years of Development under the UNCLOS Regime* (Brill Nijhoff 2016) 367. Further to this though, the provisions under UNCLOS largely reflect customary international law, as to which *see*, for example, Maria Gavouneli, *Functional Jurisdiction in the Law of the Sea* (Brill Nijhoff 2007) 4: 'It is widely understood that the Law of the Sea Convention

311(1) of UNCLOS provides that the Convention prevails over the 1958 conventions between State parties. For those States that are not party to UNCLOS but are party to the 1958 conventions though, it is the latter conventions that continue to apply.[395] Considering this, this book will consider the customary status of UNCLOS provisions, as well as the 1958 conventions in relation to the subject matter being discussed, where relevant. The drafting histories of the 1958 conventions are also considered in examining the intentions of the drafters of UNCLOS, to examine why amendments were or were not made to those provisions in UNCLOS that have their basis in the earlier conventions.

Beyond providing for freedom of overflight, UNCLOS does not directly regulate it. It does though 'envisage the use of aircraft',[396] including in the case of piracy,[397] the hot pursuit of foreign ships[398] and the right of visit in certain instances.[399] Hot pursuit will briefly be addressed in Chapter 3 in establishing the jurisdiction of a coastal State in a safety zone around its maritime construction in its EEZ. However, beyond this, hot pursuit and the right of visit are outside the scope of this book as they do not provide coastal States with jurisdiction over the operation of foreign States' aircraft, either explicitly or tacitly, and nor have they been used by coastal States in an attempt to justify the exercise of jurisdiction over such aircraft.[400]

The piracy provisions under UNCLOS provide States with the right to seize an aircraft or vessel taken by piracy on the high seas or area outside the jurisdiction of a

---

constituted a codification of customary rules, existing at the time, and contained also instances of progressive development of international law, which have become in a very short period of time customary rules in their own right.'

395. These include the US, Venezuela and Israel (although Israel has signed but not ratified the Convention on Fishing and Conservation of the Living Resources of the High Seas 1958). Colombia has ratified the Convention on Fishing and Conservation of the Living Resources of the High Seas 1958 and the Convention on the Continental Shelf 1958 and signed but not ratified the Convention on the High Seas 1958 and the Convention on the Territorial Sea and the Contiguous Zone 1958 (United Nations Treaty Collection, 'Multilateral Treaties Deposited with the Secretary General – Chapter XXI: Law of the Sea', available at treaties.un.org/pages/Treaties.aspx?id = 21&subid = A&clang = _en accessed 13 November 2020).
396. Grief (n 390) 3.
397. UNCLOS, Articles 101-107. The definition of piracy is set out in Article 101: '(a) any illegal acts of violence or detention, or any act of depredation, committed for private ends by the crew or the passengers of a private ship or a private aircraft, and directed: (i) on the high seas against another ship or aircraft, or against persons or property on board such ship or aircraft; (ii) against a ship, aircraft, persons or property in a place outside the jurisdiction of any State; (b) any act of voluntary participation in the operation of a ship or of an aircraft with knowledge of facts making it a pirate ship or aircraft; (c) any act of inciting or of intentionally facilitating an act described in subparagraph (a) or (b)'.
398. *Ibid.* Article 111(5) and (6).
399. *Ibid.* Article 110(4).
400. Both the right of hot pursuit and the right of visit apply to measures against ships rather than aircraft. Insofar as which States have that right, there is a difference between the two. The right of visit is for 'a warship [as well as military aircraft and other duly authorized aircraft clearly marked and identifiable as being on government service (Articles 110(4) and (5)] which encounters on the high seas a foreign ship' (Article 110(1)) and so is not restricted to the coastal State. On the other hand, only the 'competent authorities of the coastal State' have the right to hot pursuit, 'by warships or military aircraft, or other ships or aircraft clearly marked and identifiable as being on government service and authorized to that effect' (Article 111(5)).

State and to arrest the persons and seize the property onboard.[401] As a threat to national security, an aircraft taken by piracy would be a threat that ADIZs are designed to address (Chapter 4), but as a specific crime, it will not be further discussed in the context of this book. This is because the provisions on piracy under UNCLOS, recognised as customary international law,[402] provide States with jurisdiction over aircraft taken by piracy, regardless of ADIZs. Furthermore, States have universal jurisdiction in respect of piracy,[403] and thus, it does not fit within the scope of this book which focuses on the balance between coastal State rights and freedom of overflight.

2.7.2 High Seas

2.7.2.1 Geographic Extent of the High Seas

The high seas constitute 64 % of the ocean's overall surface[404] and are defined under UNCLOS in terms of what they are not; that is, they include 'all parts of the sea that are not included in the exclusive economic zone, in the territorial sea or in the internal waters of a State, or in the archipelagic waters of an archipelagic State'.[405] In fact, this is the geographic scope of application of Part VII UNCLOS entitled 'High Seas', and is as close as UNCLOS comes to defining the area. These maritime zones that are excluded from Part VII are not addressed in the Chicago Convention: for the purpose of international civil aviation law, airspace is either under a State's sovereignty or it is international airspace, with the exception of the very small portion of the Earth that is of undetermined sovereignty.[406] No State may claim sovereignty over any part of the high seas.[407]

401. UNCLOS, Article 105.
402. Crawford (n 84) 286.
403. UNCLOS, Article 100. This is consistent with the fact that 'the principle of universal jurisdiction over piracy is well established under customary international law' (Ved P Nanda, 'Exercising Universal Jurisdiction over Piracy' in Michael P Scharf, Michael A Newton and Milena Sterio (eds), *Prosecuting Maritime Piracy: Domestic Solutions to International Crimes* (CUP 2015) 74).
404. Steven Katona, '2014 High Seas Regional Assessment' (Ocean Health Index, 2014), available at www.oceanhealthindex.org/news/2014_highseas_assessment accessed 12 May 2018.
405. UNCLOS, Article 86.
406. In areas of undetermined sovereignty, in accordance with the Chicago Convention, Annex 11, Chapter 2.1.2: 'Those portions of the airspace over the high seas *or in airspace of undetermined sovereignty* where air traffic services will be provided shall be determined on the basis of regional air navigation agreements.'
407. UNCLOS, Article 89.

Figure 2.5 Global Map Indicating EEZs (Green) and High Seas (Blue)[408]

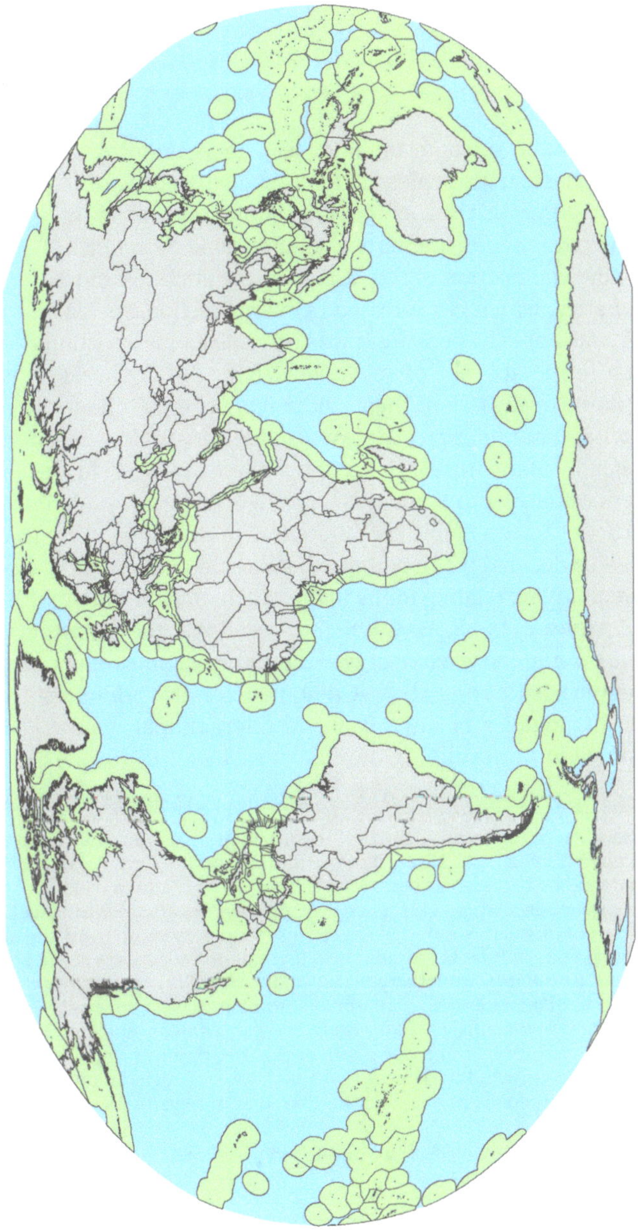

408. *Source:* Public Library of Science (PLOS), 'Close the High Seas to Fishing?', available at doi.org/10.1371/journal.pbio.1001826.g001 accessed 12 May 2020.

2.7.2.2 *Application of the Chicago Convention and Its Annexes to the High Seas*

2.7.2.2.1 *The Rules and Regulations Relating to the Flight and Manoeuvre of Aircraft*

The Chicago Convention refers to the high seas once, under Article 12, which states that 'over the high seas, the rules in force shall be those established under this Convention'. The term 'high seas' in this context is to be read as referring to 'international airspace' and is therefore also applicable in the EEZ.[409] Although this is now definitive, the codification of the EEZ upon the adoption of UNCLOS led to some debate on the matter, which is addressed below in Section 2.7.3.2.

Article 12 was adopted because it was recognised by the drafters of the Chicago Convention that in the absence of sovereignty over the high seas, it is necessary to ensure that aircraft, regardless of their nationality, operate under the same essential rules.[410] As to what these rules are, there was some debate after the adoption of Article 12: do they refer to Standards *and* Recommended Practices in the annexes to the Chicago Convention or just to Standards?; which Standards or SARPs are included in the scope of Article 12?; can States file differences to the rules? In terms of which rules are included, it was decided that it is those that Article 12 itself refers to in its opening: 'the rules and regulations relating to the flight and maneuver of aircraft'. At the time of the adoption of Annex 2, the ICAO Council resolved that the 'Annex constitutes *Rules relating to the flight and manoeuvre of aircraft* within the meaning of Article 12 of the Convention' (emphasis in original).[411] Other annexes also contain standards that are relevant to the manoeuvre of aircraft above international waters. Those rules are primarily contained in Annexes 6, 11 and 12[412] and also 10.[413] Annex 11 is particularly

409. This interpretation of the term 'high seas' is consistent across air law conventions, including the Rome Convention, Article 23(2): 'For the purpose of this Convention a ship or aircraft on the high seas shall be regarded as part of the territory of the State in which it is registered'; and, the Tokyo Convention, Article 1(2) 'Except as provided in Chapter III, this Convention shall apply in respect of offences committed or acts done by a person on board any aircraft registered in a Contracting State, while that aircraft is in flight or on the surface of the high seas or of any other area outside the territory of any State'; and Article 5(1) 'The provisions of this Chapter shall not apply to offences and acts committed or about to be committed by a person on board an aircraft in flight in the airspace of the State of registration or over the high seas or any other area outside the territory of any State unless the last point of takeoff or the next point of intended landing is situated in a State other than that of registration, or the aircraft subsequently flies in the airspace of a State other than that of registration with such person still on board.'
410. Jean Carroz, 'International Legislation on Air Navigation over the High Seas' (1959) 26 J Air L & Comm 158, 160.
411. Chicago Convention, Annex 2, (v).
412. Mendes de Leon (n 119) 14, addressing, respectively: Operation of Aircraft, Air Traffic Services, and Search and Rescue; Eugène Pépin, *The Law of the Air and the Draft Articles Concerning the Law of the Sea Adopted by the International Law Commission at Its Eighth Session* (A/CONF.13/4) – Extract from the *Official Records of the United Nations Conference on the Law of the Sea, Volume I* (Preparatory Documents), United Nations Conference on the Law of the Sea, Geneva, 24 February-27 April 1958, 68.
413. Grief (n 390) 62, addressing Aeronautical Telecommunications.

relevant to this book; however, Annexes 2 and 12 will also be revisited throughout the book.

2.7.2.2.1.1 Annex 2: Rules of the Air

Annex 2 'Rules of the Air' contains only Standards and, unlike the other annexes listed, it applies in its entirety over the high seas; that is, no State can derogate from it.[414] Some of the provisions in Annex 2 though 'implicitly require strict compliance with other rules of great importance to the safety of aircraft over the high seas'. So, while other annexes are not mandatory in their entirety, certain aspects of those mentioned in the previous paragraph are required to be followed.[415] Annex 2 establishes that the responsibility for the provision of ATS over the high seas rests with the appropriate ATS authority, as designated by the State responsible for ATS in the airspace, and it also sets out the rules for the interception of civil aircraft.[416] Both of these matters will be addressed further in Chapter 4, in relation to FIRs and ADIZs, respectively. Annex 2 also contains fundamental rules for the operation of aircraft from that the pilot-in-command has the final authority as to the disposition of the aircraft, to that distress signals are to be issued in accordance with established protocol.[417] Specific to the high seas, it sets out, for example, requirements that the lights on aircraft must be consistent with the rules established under the International Regulations for Preventing Collisions at Sea (COLREGs),[418] and that the 'appropriate authority' over the high seas for matters such as the dropping or spraying of anything from an aircraft is the State of registry of the aircraft.[419]

2.7.2.2.1.2 Annex 6: Operation of Aircraft

Annex 6 provides SARPs regarding the 'Operation of Aircraft'. In the words of the ICAO, 'the operation of aircraft engaged in international air transport must be as standardized as possible to ensure the highest levels of safety and efficiency' and the annex is designed to help achieve this aim.[420] Essentially, it provides rules and

414. Chicago Convention, Annex 2, (v). *See also*, Pépin (n 90) 68.
415. Pépin (n 90) 67-68; Grief (n 390) 62-63. For example, under Standard 2.2 of Annex 2, the operation of aircraft must be in compliance with the visual flight rules or instrument flight rules, whichever are relevant, the specifications of which are contained in Annex 11.
416. Chicago Convention, Annex 2, 2.1.2 and Appendix 2.
417. *Ibid.* Annex 2, 2.4, and Appendix 1, 1.1.
418. *Ibid.* 3.2.6.2 *Note 2*; the International Regulations for Preventing Collisions at Sea 1972 (COLREGs) are issued by the International Maritime Organization (IMO) and set out internationally agreed rules for navigation at sea: International Maritime Organization, 'Convention on the International Regulations for Preventing Collisions at Sea (COLREGs)', available at www.imo.org/en/About/Conventions/ListOfConventions/Pages/COLREG.aspx accessed 24 January 2018.
419. Chicago Convention, Annex 2, Chapter 1, definition of 'appropriate authority', read together with 3.1.4.
420. ICAO, 'The Convention on International Civil Aviation: Annexes 1 to 18', available at www.icao.int/safety/airnavigation/NationalityMarks/annexes_booklet_en.pdf accessed 11 November 2017.

regulations for the operation of all types of aircraft, from one-seat gliders to long-range jets, including a wide range of matters from maintenance to the responsibility of personnel.

2.7.2.2.1.3 Annexes 10 and 11: ATS and Aeronautical Telecommunications

Annex 11 of the Chicago Convention, 'Air Traffic Services', applies over the high seas although States may opt to file differences to the SARPs therein.[421] This decision was ultimately reached on the basis that States are able to file differences in relation to the provision of ATS over their territories. If it was not therefore also permitted over the high seas, it would result in an untenable situation where States responsible for the provision of ATS over parts of the high seas would be required to offer two sets of differing services: one over their territory and one over the portion of the high seas for which they are responsible.[422] The conclusion is reflected in the Foreword to Annex 11, in which a note was added indicating that a contracting State 'accepting such responsibility [for providing air traffic services over the high seas or in airspace of undetermined sovereignty] may apply the Standards and Recommended Practices in a manner consistent with that adopted for airspace under its jurisdiction'.[423] The same is also acknowledged in a note to Standard 2.1.2. This is not without restriction though. ICAO has stated that 'specific national provisions may only be applied to the extent that these are essential to permit the State the efficient discharge of the responsibilities it has assumed under the terms of the regional air navigation agreement'.[424] Schubert questions the legal basis of States providing ATS in international airspace in a manner that deviates from the multilaterally adopted SARPs in Annex 11 on the basis that these legal sources providing for the deviation – the Foreword to Annex 11 and a note following an ICAO Standard – do not carry any legal status.[425]

Finally, Annex 10, 'Aeronautical Telecommunications', is closely related to Annex 11 and, as the name suggests, contains technical and operational SARPs on aeronautical communication, navigation and surveillance systems.

421. Chicago Convention, Annex 11, (ix): 'The Standards and Recommended Practices contained in Annex 11 apply ... wherever a Contracting State accepts the responsibility of providing air traffic services over the high seas or in airspace of undetermined sovereignty. A Contracting State accepting such responsibility *may apply the Standards and Recommended Practices in a manner consistent with that adopted for airspace under its jurisdiction*' (emphasis added).
422. Carroz (n 410) 162. *See also*, Hailbronner (n 370) 491: 'It was feared that mandatory application of the ICAO standards might deter states from supplying air traffic control services over the high seas'.
423. Chicago Convention, Annex 11, (ix).
424. ICAO (n 361) 1.3.3. As referred to in, ICAO WP/02, *ICAO Provisions, Policy and Guidance Material on the Delegation of Airspace over the High Seas*, Presented by the Secretariat at the First Unassigned High Seas Airspace Special Coordination Meeting, Lima (22 June 2019) 2.6.
425. Francis Schubert, 'State Responsibilities for Air Navigation Facilities and Standards – Understanding Its Scope, Nature and Extent' (2010) J Aviat Manag 21, 29. This has also been questioned by Carroz who states, in relation to the comment in the above-mentioned Foreword to Annex 11: 'Insofar as these rules relate to the flight and maneuver of aircraft, it is questionable whether such a procedure is in conformity with Article 12' (Carroz (n 410) 162).

2.7.2.2.1.4 Annex 12: Search and Rescue

Annex 12, providing SARPs in relation to search and rescue, was adopted in response to an identified need to more quickly locate survivors of aviation accidents.[426] As the title suggests, the purpose of the annex is 'the establishment, maintenance and operation of search and rescue services ... [and the] coordination of such services between States', as delivered in both the territories of contracting States and over the high seas.[427] The SARPs in Annex 12 provide a general framework for search and rescue operations conducted by air. However, they are specifically targeted towards search and rescue of aircraft in distress and survivors of aircraft accidents. In terms of its application to the high seas, it provides that where search and rescue operations are conducted over the high seas or areas of undetermined sovereignty, the search and rescue services responsible will be determined by so-called regional air navigation agreements.[428] Annex 12 is supplemented by the International Aeronautical and Maritime Search and Rescue (IAMSAR) Manual,[429] which aims to, as one of its main objectives, 'foster cooperation' between aeronautical and maritime authorities in order to 'promote harmonization of aeronautical maritime services' in the provision of search and rescue services at sea.[430] Aeronautical search and rescue and the coordination of these services with maritime search and rescue, including the role of the IAMSAR Manual, will be addressed further in Chapter 4.

2.7.3 Exclusive Economic Zone

2.7.3.1 The Development of the EEZ as a Maritime Area and the General Rights Associated with It under UNCLOS

UNCLOS does not explicitly state that the EEZ is not part of the high seas, but given that the scope of Part VII 'High Seas' under Article 86 applies to 'all parts of the sea that are not included in the *exclusive economic zone* ...' (emphasis added), it is accepted as being separate from the high seas. A precise legal classification of the EEZ is elusive, but it 'appears a *sui generis* zone, as a transition zone between the territorial sea and the high seas'.[431]

426. ICAO, 'The Convention on International Civil Aviation: Annexes 1 to 18', available at www.icao.int/safety/airnavigation/NationalityMarks/annexes_booklet_en.pdf accessed 11 November 2017.
427. Chicago Convention, Annex 12 (8th edn, July 2004) (v).
428. *Ibid.* 2.1.1.1.
429. The IAMSAR Manual is jointly published by the International Maritime Organization (IMO) and ICAO and provides guidelines for the organisation of search and rescue services.
430. International Aeronautical and Maritime Search and Rescue (IAMSAR) Manual, Volume I: Organization and Management (2016) 1.1.3.
431. Umberto Leanza and Maria Cristina Caracciolo, 'The Exclusive Economic Zone' in David Attard, Malgosia Fitzmaurice and Norman A Martínez Gutiérrez (eds), *The IMLI Manual on International Maritime Law: Vol 1 – Law of the Sea* (OUP 2014) 185. Sui generis means 'of its own kind' and in the context of the EEZ, it refers to it having a distinct legal character from other maritime areas (*see* statement made by Chile upon signature of UNCLOS: United Nations

The EEZ extends the sovereign rights and jurisdiction of the coastal State in respect of certain matters, but not the territorial sovereignty, to a breadth of up to 200 nm from the baseline of the territorial sea of the State (*see* Figure 2.4 and Figure 2.5).[432] The ICJ recognised the customary status of the EEZ in 1982 in the *Case Concerning the Continental Shelf (Tunisia/Libyan Arab Jamahiriya)*, in which the Court stated that the concept of the EEZ 'may be regarded as part of modern international law'.[433] The Court reaffirmed the EEZ's customary status in its 1985 judgment of the *Case Concerning the Continental Shelf (Libyan Arab Jamahiriya/Malta)*: '[i]t is in the Court's view incontestable that ... the institution of the exclusive economic zone ... is shown by the practice of States to have become part of customary international law'.[434] Although the concept of the EEZ is customary, not all provisions relating to the EEZ in UNCLOS are recognised as such.

The concept of the EEZ was codified under UNCLOS largely in response to State claims, led by the US and soon after taken up by Iceland and a number of States in Latin America, for preferential fishing rights within the waters adjacent to their territorial sea.[435] These early claims resulted in fisheries zones, which very few States still possess as a result of the fact that the rights attributed to a State in their EEZ encompass fishing rights, together with rights in relation to all other natural resources. More specifically, in their EEZs, States have sovereign rights 'for the purpose of exploring and exploiting, conserving and managing the natural resources, whether living or non-living' as well as jurisdiction over marine scientific research and the protection and preservation of the marine environment.[436] Importantly for the purpose of this book, the coastal State also has the exclusive right in the EEZ to construct, operate and use artificial islands, as well as installations and structures in certain instances.[437] Third States making use of a coastal State's EEZ have a due regard obligation towards the rights and duties of the coastal State and an obligation to comply with the laws and regulations of the coastal State adopted in accordance with UNCLOS.[438] In exercising its rights in the EEZ, a coastal State in turn has an obligation to act with due regard for the rights and duties of other States in the zone and to act consistently with UNCLOS more broadly.[439] One of these rights of other States is the right to freedom of overflight.[440]

Treaty Collection, 'Chapter XXI: Law of the Sea, Declarations and Reservations - Chile', available at treaties.un.org/Pages/Declarations.aspx?index = Chile&lang = _en&chapter = 21&treaty = 463 accessed 3 February 2020).

432. UNCLOS, Article 57.
433. Judgment, I.C.J. Rep. 1982 (24 February), p. 18, p. 74 para. 100.
434. Judgment, I.C.J. Rep. 1985 (3 June), p. 13, p. 33 para. 34.
435. Crawford, *Brownlie's Principles* (n 84) 260-261.
436. UNCLOS, Article 56(1)(a) and (b)(ii) and (iii).
437. *See* Chapter 3.
438. UNCLOS, Article 58(3).
439. *Ibid.* Article 56(2).
440. *Ibid.* Article 58(1).

2.7.3.2 *The EEZ as Part of the High Seas for the Purpose of International Civil Aviation Law*

As mentioned above,[441] the codification of the EEZ in UNCLOS led to debate at ICAO, and among scholars, as to whether it formed part of the high seas for the purpose of international civil aviation law. Ultimately, this matter was concluded in the affirmative; however, the logic supporting the decision was varied.

Heller considered the consequences of the EEZ on freedom of overflight in the lead-up to the adoption of UNCLOS. One option he suggested was for the law applying to overflight in the EEZ to reflect that of the coastal State, that is, for it to be the rules of the air and 'all the regulations applying to operation and navigation, as they apply in the coastal State', including any differences to the rules of the air filed by that coastal State.[442] As for how that would work over artificial islands in the EEZ, he proposed that the provision that went on to become Article 60(2) UNCLOS, as to which *see* Section 3.2.3, could 'grant the coastal state further jurisdiction with regard to civil aviation regulation on artificial islands, installations and structures'.[443]

Hailbronner, considering the safety implications of Heller's approach, highlighted that the uniformity of the rules applying in international airspace is important for aviation safety and that this was in fact a driving factor in the decision to impose the mandatory uniform application of Annex 2 of the Chicago Convention. In the words of Hailbronner, '[b]y developing a uniform aviation code widely accepted by States, the Chicago system has made considerable progress in promoting safe and efficient international air transport'.[444] On this note, in respect of the impending developments prior to the adoption of UNCLOS, he questioned:

> whether or not a coastal State's regulatory authority extends to aircraft movements within the EEZ [considering that] [a]n affirmative answer to this question would … result in the possibility that coastal State's [sic] control over aircraft movement with respect to large areas of the airspace above the oceans might be established, differing from the legal regime of the ICAO Rules of the Air, mandatory for the airspace above the high seas.[445]

Hailbronner's interpretation ultimately prevailed although, as will be seen, safety was just one factor, along with the scope of coastal State rights in the EEZ and freedom of overflight, that contributed to the decision. The position as it is accepted today was proposed by the ICAO Secretariat and confirmed by the Rapporteur, AWG Kean, in 1987. The Secretariat reached the conclusion by consideration of the purpose of the EEZ and the specific rights it confers on a coastal State:

441. *See* Section 2.7.2.2.1.
442. Paul P Heller, 'Air Space over Extended Jurisdictional Zones' in John King Gamble (ed) *Law of the Sea: Neglected Issues* (Law of the Sea Institute, University of Hawaii 1979) 146.
443. *Ibid.*
444. Hailbronner (n 370) 491.
445. Kay Hailbronner, 'The Legal Regime of the Airspace Above the Exclusive Economic Zone' (1983) 8(1) Air Law 30, 35-36.

> the coastal States are not granted by the Convention any rights or jurisdiction over the airspace above the EEZ and no regulatory power with respect to flights over the EEZ. For all practical and legal purposes, the status of the airspace above the EEZ and the regime over the EEZ is the same as over the high seas and the coastal States are not granted any precedence or priority. Consequently, for the purposes of the Chicago Convention, its Annexes and other air law instruments, the EEZ should be deemed to have the same legal status as the high seas and any reference in these instruments to the high seas should be deemed to encompass the EEZ.[446]

The Rapporteur respected this line of reasoning, reiterating that:

> UNCLOS grants the coastal State only rights of economic exploration, exploitation, conservation and management of the resources of the waters and of the sea-bed, together with supporting jurisdiction; it grants no right to regulate air traffic over those waters. Your Rapporteur considers this a convincing argument.[447]

At the same time though, the Rapporteur reached his conclusion via a slightly different line of reasoning, that is, on there being freedom of overflight over the EEZ as over the high seas and therefore the Rules of the Air should equally apply over the former: '[i]t would follow that, as a consequence of Articles 58 and 87 of UNCLOS, the Rules of the Air applying over the EEZ are to be identical with those applying over the high seas'.[448]

Echoing the concerns of Hailbronner, the Rapporteur also recognised the validity of the arguments of safety, as put forward by International Federation of Air Line Pilots' Associations (IFALPA), which support the application of the rules of the air to the EEZ:

> Your Rapporteur [is] ... impressed by a further argument advanced by the International Federation of Airline Pilots' Associations (IFALPA), which makes a valid point of purposive interpretation: 'The Federation believes that, in the interests of international standardization of safety standards, the rules established under the Chicago Convention should be applicable not only in the airspace above the high seas but also in the airspace above any Exclusive Economic Zone (EEZ) which may have been established by a State either on the basis of UNCLOS or in any other manner.'[449]

It is now unambiguous that the 'high seas' as the term is used under international civil aviation law encompasses both the high seas and the EEZ. As can be seen from the above, this conclusion was reached as a result of the limited scope of a coastal State's rights and the application of freedom of overflight in the EEZ, and is supported by the implications for aviation safety.

446. ICAO WP/5-1, *Secretariat Study on Agenda Item 5: Consideration of the Report of the Rapporteur on 'United Nations Convention on the Law of the Sea – Implications, if any, for the Application of the Chicago Convention, its Annexes and other International Air Law Instruments'*, Presented at the Legal Committee 26th Session, Montreal (4 February 1987), reproduced in (1987) 3 Int'l Org & L Sea: Documentary YB 243, 256.
447. ICAO (n 391) 269.
448. *Ibid.*
449. *Ibid.*

2.7.4 Continental Shelf

The concept of the EEZ 'parallels that of the continental shelf in attributing certain limited rights to coastal States beyond the reach of the territorial sea'.[450] In the continental shelf, a coastal State 'exercises ... sovereign rights for the purpose of exploring it and exploiting its natural resources',[451] where the 'rights and the status of the continental shelf are distinct from the legal regime governing the water column'.[452] This latter point is reflected in the definition of the continental shelf: it 'comprises the seabed and subsoil of the *submarine areas* that extend beyond its territorial sea throughout the natural prolongation of its land territory' (emphasis added) (*see* Figure 2.6).[453]

UNCLOS explicitly provides that a coastal State's rights over the continental shelf 'do not affect the legal status of the superjacent waters' and that the exercise of the rights 'must not infringe on or result in any unjustifiable interference with navigation'.[454] Despite this, and despite being restricted to the submarine areas, the continental shelf is relevant to this book insofar as the regime applying to the EEZ in relation to artificial islands, installations and structures, applies *mutatis mutandis* to the continental shelf. So, although the continental shelf will not be directly addressed in this book, the implications for overflight rights in the EEZ in this context are equally applicable in the continental shelf. This is particularly relevant when a State's EEZ and continental shelf do not share an outer boundary, that is, when a coastal State has either not declared an EEZ or when the continental shelf extends beyond the outer limit of the EEZ. In this case, any portion of the waters above a continental shelf that does not intersect with an EEZ, if it exists, is considered part of the high seas.

450. Peter-Tobias Stoll, 'Continental Shelf' (Max Planck Encyclopedia of Public International Law 2008) 6.
451. UNCLOS, Article 77(1).
452. Stoll (n 450) 1.
453. UNCLOS, Article 76(1). The continental shelf extends to the outer edge of the continental margin, as defined in Article 76(3), or to a distance of 200 nautical miles from the territorial sea baseline in the case that the continental margin does not reach that distance (Article 76(1)).
454. *Ibid.* Article 78(1) and (2).

Figure 2.6 Cross Section Depiction of a Continental Shelf, Demonstrating the Essential Feature of the Shallow 'Natural Prolongation' of the Land Territory[455]

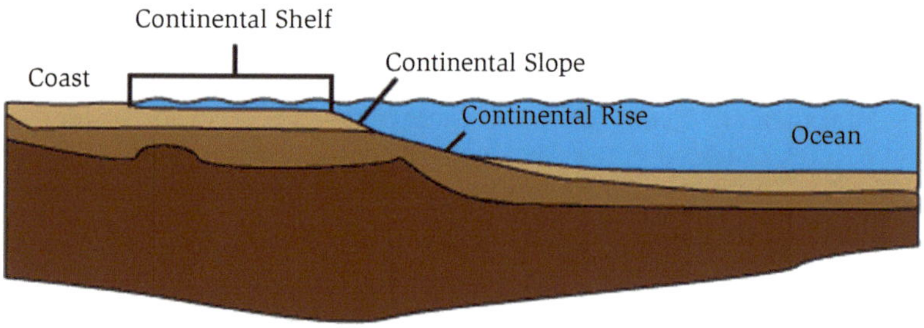

2.7.5 Contiguous Zone

A contiguous zone must be claimed by a coastal State[456] and if a State does so, it will either form part of that State's EEZ, if the State has also claimed an EEZ, and otherwise it will be part of the high seas (*see* Figure 2.4). The zone, which is simply described by UNCLOS as being, in relation to a State, 'a zone contiguous to its territorial sea',[457] extends beyond the territorial sea up to 24 nm from the territorial sea baseline. The contiguous zone is dependent upon the territorial sea; its sole purpose is to prevent and punish breaches of the law within the territorial sea, and it vests the coastal State with both prescriptive and enforcement jurisdiction in this capacity. Within its contiguous zone, a coastal State may exercise the control necessary to 'prevent infringement of its customs, fiscal, immigration or sanitary laws and regulations within its territory and territorial sea' and to 'punish infringement of the above laws and regulations committed within its territory or territorial sea'.[458] The distinction between 'prevent' and 'punish' may be seen as generally applying to incoming and outgoing ships, respectively.[459] Despite UNCLOS being silent on the matter, and the above provisions being exhaustive, some States also act in the contiguous zone on the basis of national security.[460] In 1956, the ILC considered the question of the inclusion of security within the scope of the provisions and concluded that it is 'unnecessary, and even undesirable' on the basis of two considerations: first, in most cases the customs head of power will suffice; and, second, States have an inherent right to self-defence, under which right they are able to act in the case of a threat to their security.[461]

455. *Source*: World Atlas, 'What Is a Continental Shelf?', available at www.worldatlas.com/articles/what-is-a-continental-shelf.html accessed 17 November 2016, originally sourced from the US Navy.
456. Kevin Aquilina, 'Territorial Sea and the Contiguous Zone' in David Attard, Malgosia Fitzmaurice and Norman A Martínez Gutiérrez (eds), *The Manual on International Maritime Law: Volume 1 – The Law of the Sea* (OUP 2014) 60.
457. UNCLOS, Article 33(1).
458. *Ibid.* Article 33(1)(a) and (b).
459. Aquilina (n 456) 64.
460. Crawford (n 84) 251.
461. YILC (1956) Vol. II, 5-6.

The *travaux préparatoires* of the 1958 UN law of the sea conventions identified a commentator who had described ADIZs as 'contiguous air space' zones.[462] The response to this, also recorded in the *travaux préparatoires*, was that ADIZs 'can hardly be regarded as airspaces connected with the sea areas which the Commission [the ILC] terms "contiguous zones"', based on the limited breadth of contiguous zones relative to ADIZs and the fact that in the contiguous zone, 'the coastal State may only exercise control ... for the purpose of preventing and punishing infringements of its customs, fiscal or sanitary regulations'.[463] Furthermore, given the silence of UNCLOS in this respect and the fact that other provisions of the Convention expressly include the airspace in their scope, the rights of the coastal State in the contiguous zone are understood to be restricted to the surface of the sea.[464] As a result, the contiguous zone will not be further discussed in the context of this book.

2.7.6 In Summary: Overflight Rights in International Airspace

In contrast to national airspace, there is freedom of overflight over international airspace. UNCLOS expressly provides for this right; however, it also codifies certain rights of coastal States in international waters. The rights of coastal States associated with the establishment of maritime constructions in the EEZ, applying *mutatis mutandis* to the continental shelf, form the basis of Chapter 3, the focus of which is an examination of whether the coastal State has the right to prohibit overflight on the basis of extending the safety zones around the construction to encompass the airspace above them. Furthermore, certain annexes to the Chicago Convention apply in international airspace pursuant to Article 12. The rules on ATS under Annex 11, which form the foundation of the provision of these services not just over national airspace but also over international airspace by way of FIRs, will be addressed in Chapter 4. Chapter 4 will also consider the establishment by some coastal States of ADIZs in international airspace, some of whom attempt to justify the zones on the basis of *inter alia* their rights and jurisdiction in their EEZs. Keeping in mind that freedom of overflight applies beyond national airspace, these subsequent chapters will examine how freedom of overflight applies in practice, in light of the rights and responsibilities of the coastal States under UNCLOS and the annexes of the Chicago Convention.

2.8 CONCLUSION TO CHAPTER

This chapter has introduced the concept of overflight, drawing the distinction between overflight of sovereign territory, as national airspace, and of the EEZ and the high seas as international airspace, the latter of which is the focus of this book. Overflight is regulated in national airspace through international treaties, with the Chicago Convention as the foundation of this regulatory framework. The basis of overflight rights

462. Pépin (n 90) 70 (the commentator was S/Ldr Murchison).
463. *Ibid.* 71.
464. Aquilina (n 456) 59.

differs depending on whether the overflight involves a scheduled service or a non-scheduled flight, a manned aircraft or an unmanned aircraft, and whether the aircraft is a State or civil aircraft.

In contrast, in international airspace, the above categories relevant to overflight in national airspace are irrelevant to freedom of overflight, which applies to all aircraft. As will be addressed in the following chapters, however, the reporting obligations of an aircraft in international airspace differ depending on whether it is a State aircraft or a civil aircraft, and the rules on interception apply differently depending on whether the intercepted aircraft is a State aircraft or a civil aircraft. Furthermore, recalling Chapter 1, coastal States attempt to regulate international airspace in the maritime areas adjoining their national airspace for, among other purposes, national security reasons. In these instances, although the distinction may not be drawn explicitly by the coastal State, State aircraft, usually perceived to pose a greater threat, are the key targets of the regulation.

CHAPTER 3

Overflight of Maritime Constructions in International Airspace

3.1 INTRODUCTION

Outside States' territorial seas, freedom of navigation and overflight exist, but this must be balanced by permitted maritime activities. As Mouton remarked, '[i]n pure theory and *ad absurdum* we could say that the freedom of navigation would only exist if but one ship sailed the oceans. As soon as a second appears, the first one might be hindered in its movement'.[465] This statement begs the question: *where is the balance between the freedom of overflight and jurisdiction over maritime constructions outside territorial sea?*

Representatives from ICAO did not play an active role in the negotiations during the drafting of UNCLOS, and little attention was paid to the rules applicable to the airspace in a State's EEZ.[466] Nevertheless, a number of developments in the law of the sea took place with consequences for overflight.[467] One of these was the codification of a legal regime for the construction, operation and use of artificial islands, installations and structures at sea. The UNCLOS provisions set out the right of the coastal State to construct artificial islands and installations or structures in its EEZ and continental

465. AMJ Heijmans, 'Artificial Islands and the Law of Nations' (1974) 21(2) Neth Int Law Rev 139, 145; citing MW Mouton, *The Continental Shelf* (Martinus Nijhoff 1952) 220.
466. ICAO WP/5-1, *Secretariat Study on Agenda Item 5: Consideration of the Report of the Rapporteur on 'United Nations Convention on the Law of the Sea – Implications, If any, for the Application of the Chicago Convention, Its Annexes and Other International Air Law Instruments'*, Presented at the Legal Committee 26th Session, Montreal (4 February 1987), reproduced in (1987) 3 Int'l Org & L Sea: Documentary YB 243, 244; Kay Hailbronner, 'The Legal Regime of the Airspace Above the Exclusive Economic Zone' (1983) 8(1) Air Law 30, 30.
467. For example, the extension of the territorial sea from 3 nm to 12 nm, which resulted in a number of straits becoming part of a State's territorial sea, as well as the development of the law which led to the recognition of archipelagic States. In response, the law codified transit passage and archipelagic sea lanes passage, respectively, to facilitate navigation and overflight (*see* Chapter 5).

shelf, a right that is exclusive in relation to artificial islands in all instances and to installations and structures in certain circumstances.[468] UNCLOS also provides that the right to construct artificial islands and installations for all States – coastal and landlocked – is one of the freedoms of the high seas.[469]

This chapter will examine jurisdiction in international airspace over maritime constructions – as artificial islands, installations and structures will be collectively referred to – beyond the territorial sea. The primary body of the book will consider the jurisdiction of coastal States over the airspace of such constructions in their EEZ through the imposition of so-called safety zones, as they are referred to under the law of the sea. Article 60(4) UNCLOS provides that a 'coastal State may, where necessary, establish reasonable safety zones around ... artificial islands, installations and structures'.[470] This article provides coastal States with the right to establish safety zones on the surface of the sea, in respect of vessels, but it is unclear whether it also includes the right to extend the zones to the airspace over the constructions.[471]

As a point of context, interference with overflight in relation to maritime constructions outside territorial seas is a corollary of the existence of the constructions, rather than a motivating factor for their construction. The reasons for the interference with airspace are varied, including for the safety of the constructions and aviation, for security, for political control, or for all these reasons.

Section 3.2.1 of this chapter will examine the definitions of 'artificial island', 'installation' and 'structure', as the terms are used in UNCLOS. Sections 3.2.2 and 3.2.3 will then consider the rights under UNCLOS for States, both coastal and landlocked, to build maritime constructions and their jurisdiction over them. These sections will introduce the concept of safety zones as the basis for examining the right of a State to prohibit overflight in the airspace based on that State's establishment of a maritime construction. Sections 3.2.4 and 3.2.5 will analyse the legal status and the associated rights of maritime constructions with natural features as their foundation, with reference to the discussion regarding the legal status of Mischief Reef in the *South China Sea Arbitration*. Section 3.3 forms the central study of the chapter and will attempt to determine whether States have a right to impose safety zones in international airspace on the basis of their maritime constructions, or whether a rule exists more generally under international law that could provide this right. In establishing whether this right exists, this section will examine the drafting history of UNCLOS; the practice of States; whether a legal basis exists under international civil aviation law, particularly with reference to Annexes 2 and 11 of the Chicago Convention; the context of UNCLOS more widely, analysing in particular how freedom of navigation and freedom of overflight are interpreted and applied; and the necessary elements for such

468. UNCLOS, Article 60(1)(a), (b) and(c), and Article 80. *See* Section 3.2.2.
469. *Ibid.* Article 87(1)(d).
470. This article will be discussed in further detail in Section 3.2.3.5, which will also briefly discuss (together with Sections 3.2.2 and 3.2.3.3) the other contexts in which UNCLOS addresses the establishment of safety zones around maritime constructions.
471. The PCA Arbitral Tribunal addressed the matter of a State's jurisdiction in its safety zones in, *In the Matter of the Arctic Sunrise Arbitration (Netherlands v. Russia)*, P.C.A. Case No. 2014-02, 14 August 2015, p. 49 para. 211, as to which *see* Section 3.2.3.2.

a right to arise under customary international law, with a focus on specific aspects that relate to safety zones in international airspace and the practice of States to date. Finally, in Section 3.4, this chapter will briefly consider jurisdiction over flights to and from a maritime construction, including in the case of an artificial island being constructed for the purposes of a civilian airport, and in Section 3.5, a related but ancillary matter will be addressed: the legal status of islands in the case of human modification in response to rising sea levels and erosion, as well as the redrawing of territorial baselines after the reclamation of land, both of which involve shifts in the delimitation of international airspace. Section 3.6 will draw together the findings and conclude the chapter.

This chapter contributes to the overarching analysis in this book of the right of a coastal State to prohibit or restrict the overflight of other States' aircraft by way of the coastal State's jurisdiction arising from its rights and responsibilities in the maritime areas off its coast. In the case of this chapter, the right being examined is the exclusive right of a coastal State in its EEZ and continental shelf to establish artificial islands, and to establish installations and structures for purposes related to exercising its EEZ rights and, more specifically, whether the corresponding right to establish safety zones in respect of those maritime constructions extends to a right to restrict or prohibit overflight.[472]

The impetus for this book was China's construction of artificial islands in the South China Sea. As the area stood in September 2018, *The New York Times* described it as one that 'presents a kaleidoscope of shifting variables ... a collection of Chinese fortresses', through which freedom of overflight has been curtailed on many occasions.[473] For example, in September 2018, a P-8A Poseidon US Navy reconnaissance plane flew low near Mischief Reef and was reported to have been met with the following radio response: 'US military aircraft ... [y]ou have violated our China sovereignty and infringed on our security and our rights. You need to leave immediately and keep far out.'[474] In December 2015, an American B-52 bomber flying over the South China Sea 'unintentionally flew within two nautical miles of an artificial island built by China ... exacerbating a hotly divisive issue for Washington and Beijing' and leading to a diplomatic protest being filed by China.[475] Concerns about infringements of freedoms under UNCLOS in the South China Sea led the UK, France and Germany to issue a joint statement in August 2019, in which they called for the respect of 'the freedom and rights of navigation in and overflight above the South China Sea'.[476]

472. These rights arise from UNCLOS, Article 60(1)(a) and (b), Article 56 and Article 60(4).
473. Hannah Beech, 'China's Sea Control Is a Done Deal, "Short of War with the US"' (The New York Times, 20 September 2018), available at www.nytimes.com/2018/09/20/world/asia/south-china-sea-navy.html accessed 10 October 2019.
474. *Ibid.*
475. Jeremy Page, 'US Bomber Flies over Waters Claimed by China' (The Wall Street Journal, 18 December 2015), available at www.wsj.com/articles/u-s-jet-flies-over-waters-claimed-by-china-1450466358 accessed 10 October 2019.
476. 'E3 Joint Statement on the Situation in the South China Sea' (Press Release, 29 August 2019), available at www.gov.uk/government/news/e3-joint-statement-on-the-situation-in-the-south-china-sea accessed 10 October 2019.

From the outset, it should be clearly stated that the Tribunal found that China did not have the right to build its maritime construction on Mischief Reef.[477] Thus, the discussion of China's jurisdiction over the airspace above the construction is a moot point. Rather, the situation is relevant in that it provides the set of circumstances that gave rise to the question instigating this book, of whether a State, in general, may exercise jurisdiction over international airspace on the basis of their constructions at sea. The book therefore takes the case of Mischief Reef and asks, hypothetically, if this situation were to occur in future within the EEZ or continental shelf of the State building the maritime construction, and if that construction was otherwise consistent with international law, would the State have the right to extend the safety zones around the construction to the airspace over it, thereby prohibiting the overflight of other States' aircraft? This question has broader resonance considering reports of interference with overflight in international airspace in the region beyond the South China Sea.[478] Mischief Reef is also useful for examining the application of the laws relating to maritime constructions in respect of, as will be explained in Section 3.2.5, the dual application of the legal regime applying to the reef in its natural form, and that applying to the maritime construction built over it.

3.2 THE LEGAL FRAMEWORK UNDER UNCLOS APPLYING TO SAFETY ZONES

3.2.1 Defining Artificial Islands, Installations and Structures

Purely in terms of purpose, and at the risk of oversimplification, installations and structures are most commonly built to explore and exploit natural resources in the sea. Most domestic law governing maritime constructions targets the offshore oil and gas industry and refers to 'installations and structures', or an equivalent, as opposed to 'artificial islands'. Artificial islands, in contrast, are constructed for myriad reasons such as building an offshore airport, either civil[479] or military,[480] for residential and

477. *See* Sections 3.2.2 and 3.2.4.
478. Nearby in the East China Sea, US military pilots were hit with lasers more than twenty times throughout 2018, although Chinese officials have not been definitively ruled as being behind the actions (Gordon Lubold and Jeremy Page, 'American Military Aircraft Targeted by Lasers in Pacific Ocean, US Officials Say' (The Wall Street Journal, 21 June 2018), available at www.wsj.com/articles/american-military-aircraft-targeted-by-lasers-in-pacific-ocean-u-s-officials-say-1529613999 accessed 10 October 2019); and, lasers were used against Australian Navy pilots in the region in May 2019 (Euan Graham, 'Australian Pilots Hit with Lasers During Indo-Pacific Exercise' (Australian Strategic Policy Institute, 28 May 2019), available at www.aspistrategist.org.au/australian-pilots-hit-with-lasers-during-indo-pacific-exercise/ accessed 10 October 2019).
479. For example, Kansai International Airport (Osaka, Japan), Hong Kong International Airport (Hong Kong), Macau International Airport (Macau), Chubu Centrair International Airport (Tokoname, Japan), Incheon International Airport (Seoul, South Korea). *See also*, the discussion surrounding the construction of an artificial island for the purpose of building an airport in the EEZ of the Netherlands, plans for which are currently on hold indefinitely.
480. For example, the construction of an airstrip by China on Fiery Cross Reef in the South China Sea.

agricultural purposes,[481] for commerce and tourism,[482] for military use,[483] and for environmental restoration,[484] and most are found off the coast of North America – both Canada and the US – and Asia, predominantly in Japan, Singapore and China.[485] Airports at sea outside territorial seas were discussed as early as the 1930s – so-called seadromes – to facilitate technical landings in the Atlantic Ocean, when technology in aviation did not allow engines to carry aircraft the distance in one leg.[486] It was not until the 1970s though that States began to plan the construction of large-scale projects for the purposes of natural resource exploitation, deepwater ports and airports.[487]

UNCLOS does not define artificial islands, installations, and structures, and in practice they are frequently conflated. This is despite the fact that 'the distinction is significant' because of the different legal regimes applying to each under UNCLOS. More specifically, a coastal State, and by extension other States in relation to that coastal State, has different rights vis-à-vis a maritime construction, depending on whether it is an artificial island, on the one hand, or an installation or structure on the other hand. These specific rights will be discussed in detail in Sections 3.2.2 and 3.2.3, but at this stage a few overarching points will be noted from those sections to establish the relevance of this current section.

First, Article 60 UNCLOS provides coastal States with the exclusive right to construct artificial islands in their EEZ, as well as the exclusive right to construct installations and structures, but only in certain circumstances.[488] *Second*, the article provides that the coastal States may then establish safety zones around 'such artificial islands, installations and structures' regardless of the type of maritime construction involved. That is, there is one legal framework for safety zones that applies without distinction to artificial islands, installations and structures. Finally, outside these exclusive rights of the coastal State, other States have the right to build maritime constructions and indeed, all States have the freedom to 'construct artificial islands and other installations' in the high seas in accordance with Article 87(1)(d). The matters discussed throughout this book in relation to safety zones are the same for these maritime constructions as for maritime constructions that apply to coastal States within the scope of Article 60. The rationale behind the extension of the safety zone provisions under Article 60 to other maritime constructions is provided in Section 3.2.3.5.

In consideration of the above points, the purpose of this section is twofold. First, it aims to provide a practical context in which to consider the legal framework under

481. For example, the Flevopolder, the Netherlands, and some new quarters of Singapore.
482. For example, the Palm Jumeirah and World Islands, United Arab Emirates. This land is also used for residential purposes.
483. For example, Willingdon Island, India.
484. For example, Poplar Island and Hart-Miller Island, US.
485. Iván Cáceres Rabionet, Vicente Gracia García and Montserrat Rubio Galindo, 'Indicators for Evaluating the Impact of Artificial Islands on Barcelona Coast' (2008) 36(3) Coastal Manage 254, 255. At the time of this article, the waters under the jurisdiction of these States contained over 80 % of the world's artificial islands.
486. Pablo Mendes de Leon and Erik Jaap Molenaar, 'Still a Mile Too Far? International Law Implications of the Location of an Airport in the Sea' (2001) 14 Leiden J Int Law 233, 235.
487. Heijmans (n 465) 140. These States included the US, Belgium, Germany, the UK and the Netherlands.
488. UNCLOS, Article 60(1)(a) and Article 60(1)(b) and (c). *See* Section 3.2.2.

which safety zones fall. Second, and more specifically, it endeavours to, together with Sections 3.2.2 and 3.2.3, demonstrate how the law applies in practice.

3.2.1.1 Artificial Islands

The term 'artificial island' was first included in international law in UNCLOS. There is no internationally agreed definition of the term under UNCLOS or in the wider body of public international law and it may be best defined in terms of what it is not. For this purpose, the definition of an 'island' under UNCLOS will be briefly discussed, as the starting point for defining an artificial island.

An island, as distinct from an artificial island, has its own territorial sea, EEZ and continental shelf.[489] The term 'island' is defined as 'a naturally formed area of land, surrounded by water, which is above water at high tide',[490] where the size of the area of land is irrelevant.[491] However, in accordance with Article 121(3) UNCLOS, 'rocks which cannot sustain human habitation or economic life of their own shall have no exclusive economic zone or continental shelf';[492] that is, they will only give rise to a territorial sea. The ICJ confirmed in its 2012 judgment of the *Territorial and Maritime Dispute (Nicaragua v. Colombia)* that the above definition of an island, its maritime zones and the exclusion of certain rocks as outlined are considered 'an indivisible regime, all of which ... has the status of customary international law'.[493]

While the definition of an island and the application of its maritime zones are generally clear, the determination of which rocks are excluded is less so. For example, to be excluded, must the rock be unable to *both* sustain human habitation *and* economic life, or just one or the other? Considering the phrase in its ordinary meaning (despite the use of 'or', the phrase is framed in the negative) and its teleological interpretation (the potentially low hurdle of fulfilling the requirement of 'human habitation' or 'economic life'), Franckx argues that both are required for a rock to be an island; that is, 'the absence of either of these two requirements is sufficient to deprive it of such maritime zones'.[494] In contrast, the Tribunal in the *South China Sea Arbitration* concluded that only one of the two elements is required, either human habitation or economic life. On this point, the Tribunal relied on a contextual and teleological interpretation of Article 121(3). Regarding the former, the contextual interpretation, the Tribunal noted that the second part of Article 121(3) – '... shall have

489. UNCLOS Article 121(2).
490. *Ibid.* Article 121(1).
491. *Case Concerning Maritime Delimitation and Territorial Questions (Qatar v. Bahrain)*, Merits, Judgment, I.C.J. Rep. 2001 (16 March), p. 40, p. 97 para. 185. Confirmed by the Court in the *Case Concerning Territorial and Maritime Dispute (Nicaragua v. Honduras)*, Reports of Judgments, Advisory Opinions and Orders, I.C.J. Rep. 2007 (8 October), p. 659, p. 696 para. 113; and in, *Territorial and Maritime Dispute (Nicaragua v. Colombia)*, Judgment, I.C.J. Rep. 2012 (19 November), p. 624, p. 645 para. 37.
492. UNCLOS, Article 121(3).
493. Judgment, I.C.J. Rep. 2012 (19 November), p. 624, p. 674 para. 139 .
494. Erik Franckx, 'The Regime of Islands and Rocks' in David Attard, Malgosia Fitzmaurice and Norman A Martínez Gutiérrez (eds), *The Manual on International Maritime Law: Volume 1 – The Law of the Sea* (OUP 2014) 116-117.

no exclusive economic zone or continental shelf' – also uses a negation of a disjunction. The Tribunal highlighted that it would lead to a manifestly absurd outcome if the 'or' in this second part was interpreted as meaning 'one or the other', and it would be implausible to consider that the drafters, employing the same construction in the first part of the provision, would have intended for it to have been interpreted differently.[495] Second, it considered that interpreting the provision too narrowly, thereby restricting the circumstances in which a rock will generate an EEZ and a continental shelf, 'could well deprive other populations, making use of islands ..., of the resources on which they have traditionally depended'.[496]

What can be concluded from the above is that an *artificial* island is 'an area of land that is above water at high tide that is not naturally formed'.[497] As Schofield explains:

> The 'naturally formed' requirement clearly serves to disqualify artificial islands such as platforms, for example, constructed on submerged shoals, low-tide elevations or reefs. Island-building activities on the part of states, in an effort to enhance their claims to maritime space by creating new islands, is therefore contrary to the Convention.[498]

Furthermore, we know that, as confirmed in the case of the *South China Sea Arbitration*, as to which *see* Section 3.2.4, construction on an area of land that is below sea level at high tide but above it at low tide – i.e., a low-tide elevation – that results in the feature remaining above the surface of the water at high tide is considered an artificial island.[499]

Beyond this though, precisely what 'not naturally formed' entails is not always clear, and UNCLOS does not explicitly provide for the situation in which an island 'originated partly from human activity and partly from natural processes'.[500] Consequently, '[t]he distinction between an island and an artificial island may require complex assessments of law and fact'.[501]

At the 1930 Hague Conference in early discussions on the legal status of artificial islands, the ambiguity led to proposals for the two – naturally formed islands and human-made islands – to be conflated. Gidel,[502] for example, argued that an artificial

495. *South China Sea Arbitration (Philippines v. China)*, pp. 209-210 paras. 495-496.
496. *Ibid.* p. 211 para. 497.
497. Alex G Oude Elferink, 'Artificial Islands, Installations and Structures' (Max Planck Encyclopedia of Public International Law 2013) 3.
498. Clive Schofield, 'The Trouble with Islands: The Definition and Role of Islands and Rocks in Maritime Boundary Delimitation' in Jon M van Dyke, Seoung-Yong Hong (eds), *Maritime Boundary Disputes, Settlement Processes and the Law of the Sea* (Brill Nijhoff 2009) 24.
499. *See* though Section 3.2.5.3 for the consequences of this in the case of the construction of a lighthouse or similar construction in the drawing of straight baselines.
500. Leendert Dorst, Alex G Oude Elferink and Thijs Ligteringen, 'Recent Changes in the Dutch Baseline: The Inseparable Connection of Human Activities and Natural Processes' (2012) 6, available at www.defensie.nl/downloads/brochures/2012/09/24/changes-dutch-baseline accessed 29 September 2018.
501. Oude Elferink (n 497) 4.
502. Described by the author of the quoted article as 'the French delegate at the conference [that is, The Hague Codification Conference in 1930] and the greatest living authority on the law of the sea' (DHN Johnson, 'Artificial Islands' (1951) 4(2) The Int'l L Q 203, 204).

island should be assimilated with a natural island so long as it fulfilled the conditions of being above the surface of the water at high tide and capable of effective occupation and use.[503] These discussions seem anachronistic today with the codification of the definition of a natural island under Article 121 of UNCLOS, but as will be seen in Section 3.2.5 and again in Section 3.5, the ambiguity between natural and man-made is a distinction that the law continues to grapple with.

3.2.1.2 Installations and Structures

The determination of the ordinary meaning of 'installation and structure' is necessarily tied to that of 'artificial island' and vice versa, although not all man-made objects at sea are an artificial island, installation or structure. Vessels, for instance, are clearly excluded;[504] however, even then, '[t]he distinction between ships and structures and installations in certain instances may be complex'.[505]

Before going into further detail, the terms 'installation' and 'structure' will be considered as a single term as there is no apparent relevant difference in the application of the legal regime between the two. Article 87(1)(d) UNCLOS, for example, refers only to 'artificial islands' and 'installations' in setting forth a State's right to construct on the high seas, but the author has been unable to find any evidence to suggest that this was intended to create a discrepancy in the scope of this article compared with Article 60 UNCLOS.[506] As a side note here, Article 87(1)(d) in fact refers to 'artificial islands and *other* installations' (emphasis added), suggesting that an artificial island is a type of installation. This does not detract from the fact that Article 60 explicitly requires that there is a distinction between the two and that they must necessarily therefore have defining features. The wording of Article 87(1)(d) may reflect the fact that no distinction between the two is necessary under international law in the high seas: all States have the same rights in relation to all maritime constructions.[507]

503. 'Une île est une élévation naturelle du sol maritime qui, entourée par l'eau, se trouve d'une manière permanente au-dessus de la marée haute et dont les conditions naturelles permettent la résidence stable de groupes humains organisés. Sont assimilées aux île naturelles les île artificielles satisfaisant aux mêmes conditions et dont la formation par l'action de phénomènes naturels a été provoquée ou accélérée au moyen de travaux' (Gidel, *Le Droit International Public de la Mer*, Vol. III, Paris, 1934 p. 700 n. 1, as cited in Johnson (n 502) 204), translated: 'An island is a natural elevation of the seabed which is surrounded by water and is permanently above the surface of the water at high tide and whose natural condition permits the stable habitation of organised human groups. Artificial islands satisfying the same conditions and whose creation has been formed or accelerated by means of human contribution also fall in this category.'
504. A clear distinction is made, for example, under Article 209 UNCLOS, which refers to 'vessels, installations and structures' in relation to pollution from activities in the Area.
505. Oude Elferink (n 497) 7.
506. In addition, Article 147 refers to only 'installations', Article 194(3)(c) and (d) to 'installations and devices', Article 209(2) to 'installations, structures and other devices', and Articles 258 and 262 to 'installations or equipment'. The Drafting Committee of UNCLOS noted these inconsistencies but ultimately no adjustments were made (Myron H Nordquist (ed), *United Nations Convention on the Law of the Sea 1982: A Commentary – Volume II* (Brill Nijhoff 2011) 584).
507. Except in those portions of where a State's continental self does not intersect with its EEZ, in which case that portion is part of the high seas but Article 60 UNCLOS applies *mutatis mutandis* in accordance with Article 80 UNCLOS. *See* Section 3.2.2.

Drawing on the extrapolated definition of artificial island as discussed in Section 3.2.1.1 – 'an area of land that is above water at high tide that is not naturally formed' – the logical distinction between it and an installation or structure is that the latter has some man-made foundation that does not mimic the seabed. Commentary supports this view, suggesting that it is the basis of the construction that is relevant:

> 'Installations and structures appear to differ from artificial islands in that the latter are built from man-made or natural materials that are piled on the seabed to form an area of land.'[508]
>
> And,
>
> 'The term "artificial island" refers to constructions which have been created by dumping of natural substances like sand, rocks and gravel', while '" installation" refers to constructions resting upon the seafloor by means of piles or tubes driven into the bottom, and to concrete structures'.[509]

Although taking a slightly different approach, the UK likewise defines an installation in relation to its foundation. Under the UK *Continental Shelf Act 1964*, an 'installation' refers to 'any floating structure or device maintained on a station by whatever means',[510] which is also the definition employed by the UK's *Petroleum Act 1987*.

Beyond UNCLOS, other international agreements and supporting material provide further guidance on the interpretation of installation and structures. For example, International Maritime Organization (IMO) Resolution A.671(16), entitled 'Safety Zones and Safety of Navigation Around Offshore Installations and Structures',[511] mentions artificial islands but suggests that they are a subset of installations and structures, at least for the purpose of the Resolution: '[b]eing aware that safety zone regulations are applied by coastal States to protect mobile offshore drilling units on stations, production platforms, *artificial islands ... referred to herein as installations or structures*' (emphasis added).[512] IMO Assembly Resolutions such as this are not binding, but the IMO has wide international acceptance, with 174 Member States and its resolutions 'are usually adopted by consensus or by a majority vote among IMO Members [and] may potentially be characterized as generally accepted to reach such status by widespread and representative practice'.[513]

The IMO Resolution echoes the US's proposal at the 1974 Caracas Conference, forming part of the Third UN Conference on the Law of the Sea, in conflating the terms by suggesting that the term 'artificial island' should include 'all offshore facilities, installations or devices other than those which are mobile in their normal mode of

508. Oude Elferink (n 497) 5.
509. Paul P Heller, 'Air Space over Extended Jurisdictional Zones' in John King Gamble (ed) *Law of the Sea: Neglected Issues* (Law of the Sea Institute, University of Hawaii 1979) 148.
510. *Continental Shelf Act 1964* (UK), section 11A.
511. IMO Resolution A.671(16) 'Safety Zones and Safety of Navigation Around Offshore Installations and Structures' (19 October 1989).
512. *Ibid.* 3.
513. Robert Beckman and Zhen Sun, 'The Relationship Between UNCLOS and IMO Instruments' (2017) 2 APOC 201, 226.

operations at sea', including also floating installations.[514] Presumably, the reference to mobility was designed to exclude ships which, as discussed, are not always clearly distinguishable even taking into account mobility, which itself can be difficult to define.[515] Heijmans, commenting at the time on the broad-sweeping US position compared to that of Belgium, described the latter State's proposal at the conference as limiting 'artificial islands' to 'to bottom-bearing islands', a view that is consistent with the commentary mentioned above, distinguishing between the two based on the construction's foundation.[516]

In 1989, the UN Office for Ocean Affairs and the Law of the Sea published a document examining the provisions of UNCLOS that are relevant to baselines, in which an 'installation (offshore)' is defined as a '[m]an-made structure in the territorial sea, exclusive economic zone or on the continental shelf usually built for the exploration or exploitation of marine resources. They may also be built for other purposes such as marine scientific research, tide observations, etc.'[517] This definition is unusual in its focus on the purpose of the structure, at the expense of any requirement regarding the structure itself, beyond that it be man-made. The reason for this becomes clear though when the definition is considered in the broader context of the document: under the definition of both 'artificial island' and 'structure', the reader is directed to the definition of 'installation'. Thus, the three terms are treated as one for the application of the law in accordance with this document.

Because of the different rights associated with installations and structures under Article 60 UNCLOS, they necessarily must be distinguished from artificial islands, but neither international law nor national law provides comprehensive definitions establishing the distinction. What can be drawn from the materials examined above is that the foundation of the maritime construction is generally the relevant factor to consider. Going further than this, although there is no uniformity in the approach, an artificial island is more likely to be a construction founded on an extension of the seabed, while an installation or structure remains distinct from the seabed. In any case, as explained at the beginning of this section, the purpose of establishing this distinction is to provide context to the legal framework under which safety zones fall and how it applies in practice. To reiterate, once a State has a right to build a maritime construction under UNCLOS, the type of maritime construction is irrelevant to the application of the legal regime on safety zones.

514. Heijmans (n 465) 155; citing, respectively, U.N. Doc. A/AC 138/91 dated 11 July 1973; and A/AC 138/SC II, L 35 Article 1,3 dated 16 July 1973 and Mr Stevenson, US Mission Press Release 18 July 1973, at p. 4.
515. Oude Elferink (n 497) 7.
516. Heijmans (n 465) 155; citing, respectively, U.N. Doc. A/AC 138/91 dated 11 July 1973; and, A/AC 138/SC II, L 35 Article 1,3 dated 16 July 1973 and Mr Stevenson, US Mission Press Release 18 July 1973, at p. 4.
517. United Nations Office for Ocean Affairs and the Law of the Sea, 'The Law of the Sea – Baselines: An Examination of the Relevant Provisions of the United Nations Convention on the Law of the Sea' (1989) Appendix I, 56.

3.2.2 The Right of States to Construct and Operate Maritime Constructions

Having determined, insofar as possible, what a maritime construction is, this section will examine the right of a State under UNCLOS to establish one. This provides the foundation for the following chapter, which sets out a State's jurisdiction in respect of their maritime constructions, including their right to establish safety zones.

A State's sovereignty over its territorial sea and archipelagic waters naturally encompasses any maritime constructions within these maritime zones and a State is only restricted in its construction, operation and use of them insofar as it is required to act in accordance with its international obligations.[518] On the high seas, the right of States to build maritime constructions, as one of the freedoms of the high seas, is governed only minimally by UNCLOS. The rules on installations established for carrying out activities in 'the Area' - i.e., the 'seabed and ocean floor and subsoil thereof, beyond the limits of national jurisdiction'[519] - are subject to the conditions under Article 147 UNCLOS, including that they are 'erected, emplaced and removed' in accordance with the relevant part of UNCLOS (Part XI) and with the rules of the International Seabed Authority.[520] Furthermore, Part XIII UNCLOS, 'Marine Scientific Research', provides rules for the establishment of installations for scientific research.[521] Each of these sets of rules applying to installations will be discussed further in Section 3.2.3.3, in respect of their provisions on safety zones. Finally, there are also a number of general provisions under UNCLOS relating to environmental protection and the management of maritime constructions, although these are not further relevant to this book.[522]

UNCLOS provides more detailed rules on the rights of coastal States in establishing and operating maritime constructions in their EEZ and on their continental shelf. The relevant provisions under UNCLOS regarding maritime constructions in the EEZ are found under Article 60 and apply *mutatis mutandis* to the continental shelf.[523] The application of the provisions to the continental shelf is relevant in the case that a coastal State has not declared an EEZ or if the continental shelf extends beyond the EEZ.[524] In each of these cases, the continental shelf forms part of the high seas. In this situation, therefore, elements of Article 60 are applicable to artificial islands, installations and structures on the high seas.[525] The freedom of the high seas to establish

518. Oude Elferink (n 497) 11. This includes the right of other States' vessels to innocent passage through the territorial sea of another State in accordance with Article 17 UNCLOS. At the same time, the coastal State may adopt laws to protect installations in its territorial sea in accordance with Article 21(1)(b) UNCLOS.
519. UNCLOS, Article 1(1)(1).
520. *Ibid.* Article 147(2)(a). Other conditions include that they 'may not be established where interference may be caused to the use of recognized sea lanes essential to international navigation or in areas of intense fishing activity' (Article 147(2)(b)), and they must be 'used exclusively for peaceful purposes' (Article 147(2)(d)).
521. *Ibid.* Articles 258-262.
522. *Ibid.* Articles 194(3)(c) and (d), 208, 209(2), 214 and 249(g).
523. *Ibid.* Article 80.
524. Under Article 76(1) UNCLOS.
525. Nordquist (ed), *UNCLOS: A Commentary – Volume II* (n 506) 83.

maritime constructions does not apply to these portions of the high seas that intersect with another State's continental shelf.

The legal regime of the EEZ (Part V UNCLOS) provides coastal States with, under Article 56, sovereign rights for the purpose of:

> exploring and exploiting, conserving and managing ... the natural resources ... and with regard to other activities for the economic exploitation and exploration of the zone, such as the production of energy from water, current and winds.[526]

It also provides the coastal State with jurisdiction over 'marine scientific research' and 'the protection and preservation of the marine environment'.[527]

Under Article 60(1) UNCLOS, a coastal State has 'the *exclusive* right to construct and to authorise and regulate the construction, operation and use of' (emphasis added) artificial islands[528] and of 'installations and structures for the purposes provided for in Article 56 and for other economic purposes'.[529] The lack of qualification for exclusive rights in respect of artificial islands suggests that coastal States have the exclusive right to construct them regardless of their purpose.[530] This interpretation is not uncontroversial though. For example, Vella argues that because Article 60 falls under Part V, it 'will only apply to the extent that such islands are used for economic purposes'.[531] While Vella's argument is logical, consideration of Article 60(1)(a) in relation to Article 60(1)(b) supports the former interpretation. Article 60(1)(b) provides States with the exclusive right to construct installations and structures, but *a contrario*, Article 60(1)(a) expressly restricts the exclusivity to instances in which the installation or structure is constructed for one of the purposes under Article 56.

In coastal areas in which a continental shelf does not coincide with an EEZ – either where a State has a continental shelf but has not declared an EEZ or where the continental shelf exceeds the EEZ – the coastal State's exclusive right to construct installations and structures in that area is restricted to purposes falling within the scope of Article 77, which sets out the sovereign rights of a coastal State in its continental shelf, rather than within the scope of Article 56, applying to the EEZ.[532] Article 77 provides that States have sovereign rights for the purpose of exploring and exploiting their natural resources where those resources consist of 'the mineral and other non-living resources of the seabed and subsoil together with living organisms belonging to sedentary species'.[533]

Installations and structures for purposes outside the categories under Articles 56 and 77 may be established and operated by a State in the EEZ or on the continental shelf

526. UNCLOS, Article 56(1)(a).
527. *Ibid.* Article 56(1)(b)(ii) and (iii).
528. *Ibid.* Article 60(1)(a).
529. *Ibid.* Article 60(1)(b).
530. *See also*, Tara Davenport, 'Island-Building in the South China Sea: Legality and Limits' (2018) 8 Asian J of Int'l Law 76, 86.
531. Ivan Vella, 'A New Advent for Renewable Offshore Resources' in Norman A Martínez Gutiérrez (ed), *Serving the Rules of International Maritime Law: Essays in Honour of Professor David Joseph Attard* (Routledge 2010) 146-147.
532. *Ibid.* 148.
533. UNCLOS, Article 77(1) and (4).

of another State, respectively, without the authority of the latter State[534] on the condition that they do not interfere with the rights of that State in the zone.[535] These include installations and structures for military purposes.[536] The freedom of all States to construct military installations and structures in the EEZ and on the continental shelf of any other State was a right that was closely protected during the drafting of UNCLOS. As Hailbronner explains:

> [p]roposals to cover *all* installations were rejected since a number of states were prepared to accept the EEZ concept only if military activities within the EEZ, including the movement of aircraft, were not subject to the coastal state's control (emphasis in original).[537]

At the same time, States have an obligation to use the sea for peaceful purposes and in exercising their rights must refrain from the threat or use of force against the territorial integrity or political independence of another State, as set forth in Article 2(4) of the UN Charter and as recognised in Article 301 UNLCOS.[538]

There are two restrictions to the right of a State, including the coastal State, to construct artificial islands, installations and structures in an EEZ or on a continental shelf. *First*, a State may not establish a maritime construction where it would interfere with recognised sea lanes essential to international navigation.[539] This restriction is not specifically provided for the exercise of the right on the high seas but, as with all freedoms of the high seas, it must be exercised with due regard for the interests of other States in their exercise of the freedoms of the high seas in accordance with Article 87(2) UNCLOS. The requirement to respect international sea lanes is not relevant in the case of constructions on natural features, including low-tide elevations, because sea lanes are established taking into account such features in any case.[540]

Second, States are obliged to ensure that the maritime construction does not interfere with their other obligations under public international law including the obligation to protect and preserve the maritime environment.[541] This was considered by the Tribunal in the *South China Sea Arbitration*, where it was found that, through its island-building activities, China had breached a number of environmental protection obligations under UNCLOS.[542] Furthermore, although a condition rather than a

534. James Kraska, 'Military Activities on the Continental Shelf' (Lawfare, 22 August 2016), available at www.lawfareblog.com/military-activities-continental-shelf accessed 10 October 2019.
535. UNCLOS, Article 60(1)(c).
536. Vella (n 531) 147.
537. Kay Hailbronner, 'Freedom of the Air and the Convention on the Law of the Sea' (1983) 77 Am J Int'l L 490, 203.
538. UN Charter, Article 2(4).
539. UNCLOS, Article 60(7).
540. Xinjun Zhang, 'The Latest Developments of the US Freedom of Navigation Programs in the South China Sea: Deregulation or Re-balance?' (2016) 1 J of East Asia & Int'l L 167, 179.
541. UNCLOS, Article 192. This provision is to be read together with other provisions under UNCLOS regarding the protection of the marine environment: Articles 123, 194, 197, 198, 200, 204, 205, 206 and 210.
542. *South China Sea Arbitration (Philippines v. China)*, p. 397 para. 993. China was found to have breached Articles 192, 194(1), 194(5), 197, 123 and 206 UNCLOS. For a discussion of these matter *see*, Yoshifumi Tanaka, 'The *South China Sea* Arbitration: Environmental Obligations

restriction, coastal States are also required to give due notice of the construction of an artificial island and to provide continual warning of their presence.[543]

In addition to the environmental concerns, the Tribunal in the *South China Sea Arbitration* concluded that the actions of China in respect of its construction on Mischief Reef are in breach of the above provisions based on the fact that the reef is situated in the EEZ of the Philippines. The Tribunal found that the early activities of China on the reef between 1995 and 2013,[544] which it considered construction of 'structures' for fishing purposes, were in violation of Article 60(1)(c) because they 'had the potential to interfere with the exercise by the Philippines of its rights' in the zone.[545] According to the Tribunal, from 2015, when the construction evolved into the creation of an artificial island, China was in violation of Article 60(1)(a) on the basis that the Philippines, as the coastal State, has the exclusive right to establish artificial islands in its EEZ.[546]

3.2.3 Jurisdiction over Maritime Constructions Including the Establishment of Safety Zones

3.2.3.1 A Coastal State's Exclusive Jurisdiction over Maritime Constructions

Having determined when States have the right to build a maritime construction, this section sets out the express provisions under UNCLOS in relation to the subsequent jurisdiction States have over them. This section introduces the concept of safety zones and enforcement powers within them as provided under UNCLOS.

Unlike islands, artificial islands, installations and structures do not generate a territorial sea and 'their presence does not affect the delimitation of the territorial sea, EEZ or continental shelf' of a coastal State.[547] In terms of the constructions themselves, a coastal State has 'exclusive jurisdiction' over the artificial islands, installations and structures it constructs in its EEZ and continental shelf under Article 60(2) UNCLOS. This encompasses both civil and criminal jurisdiction, including with respect to, but not limited to, 'customs, fiscal, health, safety and immigration laws and regulations'.[548]

---

under the Law of the Sea Convention' (2018) 27(1) RECIEL 90. *See also, Land Reclamation in and around the Straits of Johor (Malaysia v. Singapore), Provisional Measures, Order of October 2003, ITLOS Reports 2003*, p. 10, p. 28. In considering the impact of land reclamation on the marine environment, the International Tribunal for the Law of the Sea (ITLOS) issued a provisional measure under Article 290 UNCLOS directing Singapore 'not to conduct its land reclamation in ways that might cause … serious harm to the marine environment' in the Straits of Johor. In this case, the reclamation took place in Singapore's territorial sea, with Malaysia's rights and environment being affected due to the cross-border effects of the reclamation work. The case did not involve the construction of artificial islands but may be relevant in considering restrictions to the construction, operation and use of artificial islands where the rights of other States and the marine environment are affected.

543. UNCLOS, Article 60(3).
544. *South China Sea Arbitration (Philippines v. China)*, p. 402 para. 1004.
545. *Ibid.* p. 414 paras 1036-1037.
546. *Ibid.* pp. 414-415 paras 1036-1038.
547. UNCLOS, Article 60(8).
548. *Ibid.* Article 60(2).

3.2.3.2 *Right of the Coastal State to Establish Safety Zones and Its Jurisdiction Within Them*

Most importantly for the purposes of this book, under Article 60(4) a coastal State is permitted to establish safety zones around its maritime constructions. Specifically, the article reads:

> The coastal State may, where necessary, establish reasonable safety zones *around* such artificial islands, installations and structures in which it may take appropriate measures to ensure the safety both of navigation and of the artificial islands, installations and structures (emphasis added).

In the view of the PCA Arbitral Tribunal, henceforth referred to as 'the Tribunal', in the case of *In the Matter of the Arctic Sunrise Arbitration (Netherlands v. Russia)* ('*Arctic Sunrise Case*'), this provides the coastal State with the right to enact and enforce laws and regulations that 'go beyond its rights in the EEZ at large'.[549] More specifically, the Tribunal stated that Article 60(4) UNCLOS:

> allows the coastal State to take, in the safety zone, appropriate measures in the nature of the enactment of laws or regulations, and of the enforcement of such laws and regulations, provided that such measures are aimed at ensuring the safety of both navigation and the artificial islands, installations and structures.[550]

In this case, a number of inflatable boats were launched from a Greenpeace vessel, the Arctic Sunrise, registered as a Dutch vessel, and, while the Arctic Sunrise remained at a distance, the inflatable boats entered the safety zone around a Russian petroleum installation without authorisation. Upon reaching the installation, two people disembarked and attempted to scale it for the purpose of staging a protest. The question was whether the actions taken by Russian officials in response to this, including the subsequent boarding, seizure and detention of the Arctic Sunrise, were lawful.[551] The actions of the Russian authorities took place once the inflatable boats had returned to the Arctic Sunrise, which was outside the safety zone.[552] As a result of this, the question was whether the requirements of hot pursuit had been met, as to which *see* Section 3.2.3.6. The Tribunal did not consider in further detail the actions constituting a lawful response to breaches of domestic law within a safety zone.

As highlighted, Article 60(4) refers to safety zones *around* maritime constructions, as opposed to also *over* them, suggesting that the zones may be restricted to the surface of the sea. This is supported by the fact that Article 60(5) refers only to the *breadth* of the zones, with no mention of altitude, and to the obligation under Article 60(6) of *ships* to respect the zones and comply with generally accepted international navigation standards in their vicinity, with no mention of aircraft. This argument will be developed in Section 3.3.

549. P.C.A. Case No. 2014-02, 14 August 2015, p. 49 para. 211.
550. *In the Matter of the Arctic Sunrise Arbitration (Netherlands v. Russia)*, P.C.A. Case No. 2014-02, 14 August 2015, p. 49 para. 211.
551. It is worthy of note that Russia did not participate in the proceedings.
552. *Arctic Sunrise Arbitration (Netherlands v. Russia)*, p. 64 paras 262-263.

3.2.3.3 *Maximum Breadth of Safety Zones and Obligation of Vessels to Respect*

As with the maritime constructions themselves, safety zones must not interfere with recognised sea lanes essential to international navigation.[553] In accordance with Article 60(5) UNCLOS, the breadth of the safety zone may not exceed 500 metres from the outer edge of the artificial island unless 'authorized by generally accepted international standards' or 'recommended by the competent international organization', in this case the IMO.[554] As of 2012, the IMO had not authorised the extension of a safety zone beyond 500 metres.[555] In 2009, the IMO considered whether the maximum breadth of a safety zone should be extended, ultimately taking no further action on the basis that 'there are currently no international standards to assess such requests'.[556] It is for the State to determine the breadth of its safety zones within the 500-metre limit, and in doing so, it is required to consider the nature and function of the maritime construction.[557] In contrast to other maritime constructions, installations established for the purpose of scientific research under Article 260 UNCLOS do not appear to be entitled to a more expansive safety zone.[558] The provisions governing safety zones for installations built for the purpose of carrying out activities in the Area under Article 147 differ somewhat from those in Article 60 and, notably in the context of this discussion, there is no mention of any maximum breadth of such zones.[559]

While Article 60(6) provides that ships must respect safety zones around maritime constructions in the EEZ or continental shelf of a State, there is no mention in Article 147 of ships being required to comply with the safety zones. This says little about the intended physical scope of the safety zones though, in particular whether they can extend to the air, as no mention is made in Article 147 of any obligations of other States in respect of the installations and safety zones.

3.2.3.4 *Security as an Element of Safety in Establishing and Taking Measures Within Safety Zones*

At the First UN Conference on the Law of the Sea, in 1958,[560] the discussion on safety zones centred around the flammability of oil platforms and the need to keep vessels at

553. UNCLOS, Article 60(7).
554. Nordquist (ed), *UNCLOS: A Commentary – Volume II* (n 506) 586; Mikhail Kashubsky and Anthony Morrison, 'Security of Offshore Oil and Gas Facilities: Exclusion Zones and Ships' Routeing' (2013) 5(1) Aust J Marit Ocean Aff 1, 2.
555. Assaf Harel, 'Preventing Terrorist Attacks on Offshore Platforms: Do States Have Sufficient Legal Tools?' (2012) 4 Harv Natl Secur J 131, 152.
556. IMO, 'Sub-Committee on Safety of Navigation (NAV)' (55th Session, 27-31 July 2009), available at www.imo.org/en/MediaCentre/MeetingSummaries/NCSR/Pages/NAV-55th-session.aspx accessed 20 February 2020.
557. UNCLOS, Article 60(5).
558. Barbara Kwiatkowska, *The 200 Mile Exclusive Economic Zone in the New Law of the Sea* (Martinus Nijhoff 1989) 120.
559. UNCLOS, Article 147(2).
560. It was at this conference that the four 1958 law of the sea conventions were adopted, on which many UNCLOS articles are based. *See* Section 2.7.1 (n 387).

a safe distance. The representative of the Netherlands proposed a safety zone of a breadth of 50 metres, based on consultation with the oil industry, stating that this distance corresponded to the distance around oil installations on land within which a naked flame was forbidden.[561] The representative of Germany agreed with the Dutch proposal of the breadth of the zone, reiterating the Dutch view that 'the sole purpose of safety zones was to prevent fires'.[562] States present at the conference in 1958 then agreed on the greater maximum breadth of 500 metres, to provide an 'ample margin of safety'.[563] The specific focus of the drafters was based on the perceived threat to maritime constructions at that point:

> Drafters of the LOSC did not intend to address the threat of deliberate attacks, such as a deliberate ramming of a platform with a ship full of explosives, in the provisions pertaining to offshore platforms, as such attacks were not common at the time.[564]

During the 1960s and 1970s, there was a rapid rise in offshore oil and natural gas production,[565] and by 2016, it accounted for over 25 % of global supplies.[566] The significant role it plays in energy production as well as its economic value has led to offshore platforms involved in this production becoming a target for terrorists.[567] Recalling Section 2.3.2, security is a necessary consideration in meeting safety standards in international civil aviation. It is proposed here that security is likewise one of the elements a State must take into account in its safety zones in order to ensure the safety of its maritime constructions. In other words, as the threat to safety changes over time, so too does the focus in protecting that safety, within the limitations provided in Article 60, including the maximum breadth of the zone. States during the drafting[568] and since the adoption[569] of UNCLOS have argued that the 500-metre maximum breadth of safety zones is inadequate for protecting the security of maritime constructions, a view shared more recently by scholars.[570] O'Connell though, writing in 1989, emphasised that safety zones are just one method of protecting the safety of maritime constructions from threats to security, a recognition he explains also contributed to the

561. 'Summary Records of the 26th to 30th Meetings of the Fourth Committee – Extract from the Official Records of the United Nations Conference on the Law of the Sea' Vol. VI (Fourth Committee (Continental Shelf)) A/CONF.13/C.4/SR.26-30 (Geneva, 24 February-27 April 1958) 81.
562. *Ibid.* 85.
563. *Ibid.* 82. This was the wording of the representative of the United Kingdom, but other States supporting the extended breadth included Yugoslavia and Italy (*see* p. 87). This distance was first raised by the ILC: while the ILC draft articles did not specify a maximum breadth, 500 metres was provided as a reasonable consideration for States in the commentary to the articles (YILC (1956) Vol. II, 299).
564. Harel (n 555) 156; Stuart Kaye, 'International Measures to Protect Oil Platforms, Pipelines, and Submarine Cables from Attack' (2007) 31 Tul Mar LJ 377, 406.
565. Kaye (n 564) 384.
566. 'Offshore Energy Outlook' (International Energy Agency, 2018) 13.
567. Harel (n 555) 135.
568. DP O'Connell, *The International Law of the Sea – Vol I* (OUP 1982) 503. These States included the United States, Turkey and India (Harel (n 555) 148).
569. Harel (n 555) 150-151.
570. Kashubsky and Morrison (n 554) 3; Harel (n 555) 157; Kaye (n 564) 405.

retention of the 500-metre breadth during the drafting of UNCLOS.[571] In any case, States have the right to establish safety zones to protect the safety of their maritime constructions, where the considerations involved in that protection now involve risks stemming not just from fire or collision but also from security threats such as terrorism.

3.2.3.5 Safety Zones in Respect of Maritime Constructions Outside an EEZ

It is not clear under UNCLOS whether a State other than a coastal State constructing in an EEZ or on a continental shelf has jurisdiction over its maritime constructions or whether it has the right to establish safety zones in respect of those constructions. UNCLOS does not provide for jurisdiction over maritime constructions in another State's EEZ or on their continental shelf or for any State constructing on the high seas outside another State's continental shelf in accordance with Article 87(1)(d). Aside from coastal States under Article 60(4), and all States in relation to maritime constructions for the purposes in Articles 147 and 260, UNCLOS also provides no further mention of safety zones over maritime constructions. This is not necessarily indicative of an absence of such right though. Article 60 specifically addresses the rights of coastal States to construct and regulate maritime constructions in its EEZ, with the rights of other States to construct in the zone being residual.[572] In this way, it makes sense that the right to construct safety zones is granted to coastal States specifically. Article 87(1)(d), on the other hand, is general in nature, listing the broad freedoms of the sea, which must be read in the context of UNCLOS as a whole.

3.2.3.6 Enforcement Powers in Relation to Safety Zones under UNCLOS

The Tribunal in the *Arctic Sunrise Case* recognised the right of a coastal State to enforce its laws applying in its safety zone, as discussed in Section 3.2.3.2. This case furthermore considered the right of hot pursuit in connection with safety zones for the purpose of exercising these enforcement powers. Under UNCLOS, enforcement in relation to the breach of the law within a safety zone is explicitly addressed only in the context of hot pursuit. With reference to safety zones, this is relevant when the State which suspects its laws relating to the safety zone have been breached has been unable to stop the foreign vessel within the zone. The right of hot pursuit, which is accepted as customary international law,[573] is recognised under Article 111 UNCLOS:

571. O'Connell (n 568) 503: 'The mounting of armament on oil rigs would not be affected by limit of the safety zone because if it fired at an attacker beyond that distance, that would be in exercise of the right of self-defence. Nets and traps within the limit of the safety zone would be sufficient for protection against clandestine attachment of sabotage devices to the rig. In fact, neither expedient is necessary or likely, short of a major threat, because regular surveillance by suitable ships and aircraft suffices to ward off the mounting of terrorist attacks … .'
572. The title of Article 60 is 'Artificial islands, installations and structures in the Exclusive Economic Zone' and the article falls under Part V UNCLOS, 'Exclusive Economic Zone'.
573. Nicholas M Poulantzas, *The Right of International Pursuit in International Law* (2nd edn, Martinus Nijhoff 2002) 39.

> The hot pursuit of a foreign ship may be undertaken when the competent authorities of the coastal State have good reason to believe that the ship has violated the laws and regulations of that State.[574]

The rules of hot pursuit apply when the pursuit commences in waters over which a State has sovereignty – internal waters, archipelagic waters or the territorial sea – or in a contiguous zone,[575] and also, in accordance with Article 111(2):

> *mutatis mutandis* to violations in the exclusive economic zone or on the continental shelf, including safety zones around continental shelf installations, of the laws and regulations of the coastal State applicable in accordance with this Convention to the exclusive economic zone or the continental shelf, including such safety zones.

In addition to the coastal State having good reason to believe that there has been a violation of the laws and regulations applying in the safety zone and the pursuit having begun while the ship is still within the EEZ or the continental shelf, there are two other conditions for hot pursuit to be valid: (1) a signal to stop must have been issued to the ship prior to the pursuit commencing and (2) the pursuit may only be continued outside the EEZ or continental shelf provided that it is uninterrupted.[576] The International Tribunal for the Law of the Sea (ITLOS) confirmed in the case of *M/V 'Saiga' (No. 2)* that these conditions must be cumulatively met in order for a legitimate right of hot pursuit to exist.[577] Notably for the purpose of this book, although aircraft have the right to conduct hot pursuit, Article 111 provides no basis on which hot pursuit may be commenced against an aircraft violating the laws of a safety zone.

3.2.4 The South China Sea Arbitration

3.2.4.1 Relevant Facts of the Case

In the *South China Sea Arbitration*, the Tribunal addressed *inter alia* a claim by the Philippines that China had inflicted 'severe harm on the marine environment by *constructing artificial islands* and engaging in extensive land reclamation *at seven reefs in the Spratly Islands*' (emphasis added).[578] The Tribunal described the reefs as 'in their natural form ... largely submerged reefs, with small protrusions of coral that reach no more than a few metres above water at high tide'.[579] Four of those reefs – Cuarton Reef,

574. UNCLOS, Article 111(1). In accordance with Article 111(5), only warships, military aircraft or 'other ships and aircraft clearly marked and identifiable as being on government service and authorized to that effect' have the right of hot pursuit.
575. UNCLOS, Article 111(1) and (4).
576. *Ibid.* 111(4) and (1), respectively.
577. *M/V 'Saiga' (No. 2) (Saint Vincent and the Grenadines v. Guinea), Judgment, ITLOS Reports 1999*, p. 10, p. 59 para. 146; as restated in *Arctic Sunrise Arbitration (Netherlands v. Russia)*, p. 59 para. 246. For a discussion on why the hot pursuit regulations are impractical in the context of safety zones, *see*, Stuart Kaye, 'International Measures to Protect Oil Platforms, Pipelines, and Submarine Cables from Attack' (2007) 31 Tul Mar LJ 377, 406-408.
578. *South China Sea Arbitration (Philippines v. China)*, p. 3 para. 9.
579. *Ibid.* p. 179 para. 397.

Fiery Cross Reef, Johnson Reef and Graven Reef (North) - are rocks that are not capable of sustaining human habitation or economic life, and three - Hughes Reef, Subi Reef and Mischief Reef - are low-tide elevations, with the first two situated in the Philippines' territorial sea and the latter in the Philippines' EEZ.[580] As to the definitions and legal status of 'rocks' and 'low-tide elevations', *see* Section 3.2.4.2 and in particular, Table 3.1.

Construction on maritime features over which a State has sovereignty is not of interest to this book, as the airspace over them is national airspace. Therefore, rocks are not relevant to consider and nor are low-tide elevations in a State's territorial sea. The coastal State has sovereignty over the latter, including the airspace, and the former when they are situated in a State's territorial sea or when beyond the territorial sea in the case that they are subject to a valid claim to sovereignty.

Instead, this book is interested in Mischief Reef, as a natural feature - a low-tide elevation - outside the territorial sea of any State - in the Philippines' EEZ - which has been subject to human modification (*see* Figure 3.1 and Figure 3.2). As has been addressed in the introduction, this book does not set out to argue that China's actions in prohibiting overflight over Mischief Reef could have been justified through the imposition of safety zones in the airspace - they could not have - but rather it takes Mischief Reef as a starting point for examining whether the prohibition of overflight in international airspace over a maritime construction can ever be justified on the basis of that maritime construction. The construction on Mischief Reef brings with it interesting preliminary considerations regarding the legal status of a maritime construction built with an existing maritime feature, with its own legal status, as the foundation. In terms of the rights over natural maritime features, the UNCLOS framework is generally clear. In relation to Mischief Reef, as a low-tide elevation, it has certain rights associated with it (*see* Table 3.1), which vary according to the maritime zone in which the low-tide elevation is situated, but in any case, the rights do not extend to jurisdiction over the airspace. The question then is how these rights change when the low-tide elevation is subject to human modification.

The efficiency and vast expanse of the construction in the case of Mischief Reef were possible, at least in part, because of the use of the low-tide elevation as a pre-existing foundation for the construction. As the Tribunal described the activities:

> Intense land reclamation began at Mischief Reef in January 2015. Progress was rapid … . By November 2015, the total area of land created by China on Mischief Reef was approximately 5,558,000 square metres … . The massive scale of China's work at Mischief Reef and the transformation of nearly the entire atoll into an artificial island is apparent in satellite imagery[581] (*see* Figure 3.1 and Figure 3.2).

580. *South China Sea Arbitration (Philippines v. China)*, pp. 259-260 paras 643-645 and 647.
581. *South China Sea Arbitration (Philippines v. China)*, p. 397 paras 889-890.

Figure 3.1 Satellite Image of Mischief Reef in 2012[582]

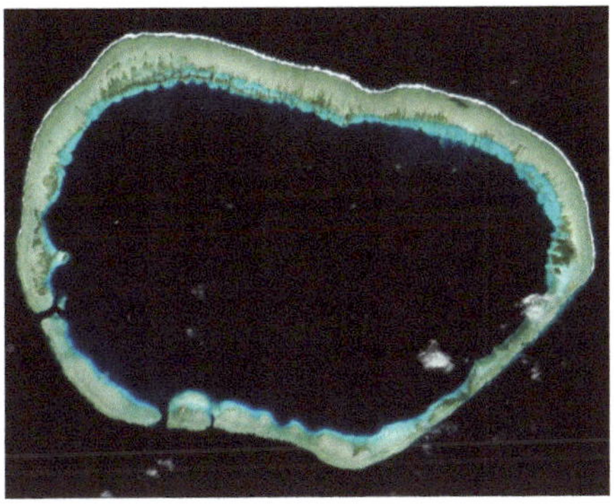

Figure 3.2 Satellite Image of Mischief Reef in 2019 (Google Maps)

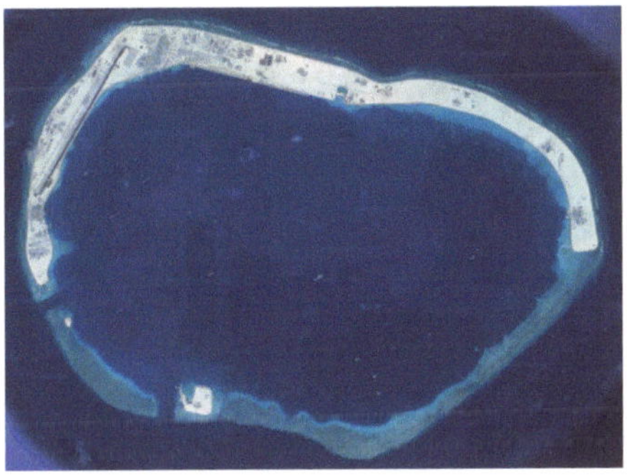

The fact that the destruction of the reef as a result of the construction atop it was in breach of environmental protection laws, as mentioned in Section 3.2.2, illustrates that States do not have an unfettered right to employ these construction methods. In this way, international airspace may be indirectly protected from jurisdictional claims by States in connection with this type of use of natural features – namely, that which is destructive to the natural environment and that is irreversible – by prohibiting the construction from the outset. This does not exclude construction on low-tide elevations in general though, for example, for use as a base for the construction of reversible artificial islands, i.e., with less environmental impact, or for installations or structures which are, as explained in Section 3.2.1.2, generally less invasive.

Three further clarifications on the *South China Sea Arbitration* are necessary in relation to its consideration in the context of this book. *First*, the Tribunal did not

582. *Source*: Matt Liddy and Ben Spraggon, 'Before and After: China Builds Artificial Island in South China Sea' (Australian Broadcasting Corporation, 22 September 2015), available at www.abc.net.au/news/2015-09-22/south-china-sea-islands-before-and-after/6794076 accessed 12 June 2018.

address overflight in its decision, which instead focused on 'the legal basis of maritime rights and entitlements in the South China Sea [and] the status of certain geographic features in the South China Sea'.[583] *Second*, there is no assertion that China has justified its practice of interfering with freedom of overflight over Mischief Reef on the basis of the human-modified elements of the reef. *Third*, the book does not consider the myriad other legal questions that construction on the reef raises, either those considered by the Tribunal, such as those pertaining to the protection of the environment, or those outside the scope of the Tribunal's decision, including questions of sovereignty and maritime delimitation.

These matters are beyond the scope of this book. Although there are disputes over sovereignty in the South China Sea, the Tribunal did not consider these matters because the arbitration claim was submitted under the dispute settlement mechanism set out in Part XV of UNCLOS and the Convention does not contain provisions on State sovereignty over land territory.[584] While UNCLOS does address maritime delimitation, it was not considered by the Tribunal because China has excluded maritime boundary delimitation from compulsory dispute settlement, as it is permitted to do under UNCLOS.[585]

On a final note, the Tribunal's decision has not been received without criticism. Tanaka has examined some of the primary arguments against the decision, which he characterises as 'reflecting the progressive development of the law of the sea towards universalism' as opposed to unilateralism.[586] These arguments include that the Tribunal was unable to rely on evidence of State practice or a body of jurisprudence to support its interpretation of Article 121(3) UNCLOS.

3.2.4.2 *No Sovereignty over Low-Tide Elevations or Subsequently over the Maritime Constructions Built Atop Them*

In the *South China Sea Arbitration*, the Tribunal considered whether low-tide elevations may be subject to claims of sovereignty. If low-tide elevations were subject to claims of territorial sovereignty, the 'artificial islands' created on them would also constitute the territory of the State and the regime applicable to artificial islands under UNCLOS would not be applicable. UNCLOS defines a low-tide elevation as 'a naturally formed area of land which is surrounded by and above water at low tide but submerged at high tide' and is silent on the matter of sovereignty regarding such features beyond unequivocally providing that they do not generate territorial sea.[587]

The ICJ considered the question of whether States have a right to claim sovereignty over low-tide elevations in its 2001 judgment on the *Case Concerning*

583. *South China Sea Arbitration (Philippines v. China)*, p. 1 para. 2.
584. *Ibid.* pp. 1-2 para. 5.
585. *Ibid.* p. 2 para. 6.
586. Yoshifumi Tanaka, 'Reflections on the Interpretation and Application of Article 121(3) in the *South China Sea Arbitration* (Merits)' (2017) 48(3-4) Ocean Dev & Int'l L 365, 378-339.
587. UNCLOS, Article 13(1) and (2).

Maritime Delimitation and Territorial Questions (Qatar v. Bahrain),[588] in which it acknowledged that the law did not provide an answer to the matter at that time. The Court stated that, if outside the territorial sea of a State, it is unclear whether a State may claim the land as part of its territory. In addition to recognising UNCLOS' silence on the matter, the Court acknowledged that State practice does not indicate a customary rule either way.[589] The ICJ again considered the legal status of low-tide elevations in 2012 in *Territorial and Maritime Dispute (Nicaragua v. Colombia)*, where it confirmed that they do not form part of the land territory of a State in a legal sense.[590]

This decision was affirmed by the Tribunal in the *South China Sea Arbitration*, which Guilfoyle has described as 'the equivalent of a major constitutional decision'.[591] On the matter, the Tribunal stated that:

> notwithstanding the use of the term 'land' in the physical description of a low-tide elevation, such low-tide elevations do not form part of the land territory of a State in the legal sense. Rather they form part of the submerged landmass of the State and fall within the legal regimes for the territorial sea or continental shelf, as the case may be. Accordingly, as distinct from land territory, the Tribunal subscribes to the view that 'low-tide elevations cannot be appropriated'.[592]

The Tribunal also clarified that what is relevant in determining the status of the feature is its 'natural condition, prior to the onset of significant human modification' and that in this sense, 'a low-tide elevation will remain a low-tide elevation under the Convention, regardless of the scale of the island or installation built atop it'.[593] Regarding the scale of construction in the *South China Sea Arbitration*, the Tribunal described it as being to such an extent that '[i]n some cases, it would likely no longer be possible to directly observe the original status of the feature, as the contours of the reef platform have been entirely buried by millions of tons of landfill and concrete' and that the actions of the State 'permanently destroyed ... evidence of the natural condition' of a number of the reefs in question.[594]

The above decisions clarify that construction on or around a natural feature does not alter the legal status of that natural feature, regardless of the physical alteration of its state. Following from this, such construction cannot give rise to a State's right to sovereignty *over the feature*. Given that sovereignty over airspace arises from sovereignty over territory, as recognised in Articles 1 and 2 of the Chicago Convention, this

588. Merits, Judgment, I.C.J. Rep. 2001 (16 March), p. 40.
589. *Ibid.* p. 40, pp. 101-102 paras 204-205. The question in this case was 'whether a State can acquire sovereignty by appropriation over a low-tide elevation situated within the breadth of its territorial sea when that same low-tide elevation lies also within the breadth of the territorial sea of another State' (p. 101 para. 204).
590. Judgment, I.C.J. Rep. 2012 (19 November), p. 624, p. 641 para. 26 ('*Territorial and Maritime Dispute (Nicaragua v. Colombia)*').
591. Australian Broadcasting Corporation (Radio National, Late Night Live), 'Who Owns the South China Sea?' – Interview with Douglas Guilfoyle (14 July 2016), available at www.abc.net.au/radionational/programs/latenightlive/who-owns-the-south-china-sea/7629968 at 8:09 minutes, accessed 8 June 2018.
592. *South China Sea Arbitration (Philippines v. China)*, p. 132 para. 309.
593. *Ibid.* pp. 131-132 paras 305-306 and pp. 214-215 para. 511.
594. *Ibid.* pp. 131-132 para. 306 and p. 476 para. 1203.

in turn means that such construction cannot give rise to a State's right to sovereignty *over the airspace* above the maritime construction.[595] As a result, it can be concluded that a State may have sovereignty over the airspace over a maritime construction, but only on the basis of existing sovereignty over that airspace, that is, where the maritime construction has been built atop a natural feature that can be appropriated and over which a State has sovereignty.

Table 3.1 Overview of Naturally Formed Areas of Land Surrounded by Water and Associated Sovereignty, Sovereign Rights and Jurisdiction

	Naturally Formed Areas of Land Surrounded by Water	
	Area of Land and Its Maritime Zones	*Subject to Claims of Territorial Sovereignty?*
Above water at high tide	- 'island' (Article 121(1)); - has a territorial sea, EEZ and continental shelf (Article 121(2)); - *but*, if the land is 'a rock that cannot sustain human habitation or economic life', it only has a territorial sea (Article 121(3)).	- If in the territorial sea, the coastal State has sovereignty over the area of land. - If outside the territorial sea of a State, territorial recognition is subject to public international law.
Above water at low tide (submerged at high tide)	- 'low tide elevation' (Article 13(1)); - has no maritime zones (Article 13(2)) but if within 12 nm of a State's coastline or an island may be used as a base point for extending the territorial sea (Article 13(1), Article 7(4) and Article 47(4)).	- A low-tide elevation cannot be appropriated.[596] If in the territorial sea though, the coastal State has sovereignty over the low-tide elevation, as it has sovereignty over the territorial sea itself. - If beyond the territorial sea of a State, but in the EEZ or continental shelf, the coastal State has sovereign rights and jurisdiction in accordance with the applicable regimes under Articles 56(3) and 77 UNCLOS, respectively. Again, the low-tide elevation cannot be appropriated. - If in the high seas beyond any State's EEZ or continental shelf, no State may claim any sovereign rights over the land. It is part of the deep seabed and subject to the applicable law under Pt XI UNCLOS.

595. *See* Section 2.2.2.1.
596. *Territorial and Maritime Dispute (Nicaragua v. Colombia)*, p. 641 para. 26.

	Naturally Formed Areas of Land Surrounded by Water	
	Area of Land and Its Maritime Zones	*Subject to Claims of Territorial Sovereignty?*
Below water at all times	- part of the bed and subsoil.	- If in the territorial sea, the coastal State has sovereignty over the feature as it has sovereignty over the territorial sea itself and the bed and subsoil. - If beyond the territorial sea of a State, but in the EEZ or continental shelf, the coastal State has sovereign rights and jurisdiction in accordance with the applicable regimes under Articles 56(3) and 77 UNCLOS, respectively. - If in the high seas beyond any State's EEZ or continental shelf, no State may claim any sovereign rights over the feature. It is part of the deep seabed and subject to the applicable law under Pt XI UNCLOS.[597]

3.2.5 The Dual Status of a Natural Feature/Maritime Construction

In confirming that a natural feature subject to human modification retains its prior legal status, the resulting land mass is both a natural feature and a maritime construction, with the legal regimes for each applying simultaneously. As outlined in Section 3.2.4, in relation to the relevance of Mischief Reef to this book to the exclusion of the other features in the *South China Sea Arbitration*, rocks and islands are subject to State sovereignty and construction over them does not generate new rights for the State. As such, when discussing changes to the rights of a State in relation to a natural feature as a result of maritime construction over that feature, it is low-tide elevations that are relevant, with the new rights being those under Article 60 UNCLOS.

Kohl argues that a natural feature's preservation of its original legal status upon human modification is inconsistent with the intention of the drafters of UNCLOS in that the drafters would not have created a specific legal regime for maritime constructions if those constructions were to retain their prior legal status:

> it would make little sense for the framers to create a rule for legal entitlements belonging to artificial islands, but nevertheless maintain a belief that entitlements of artificial islands would be defined by the rules attached to each separate island's underlying feature … . Moreover … the framers of UNCLOS likely did not intend the legal entitlements affecting artificial islands to be governed by some unrelated section of the Convention.[598]

597. *Territorial and Maritime Dispute (Nicaragua v. Colombia)*, p. 127 para. 291.
598. Adam W Kohl, 'China's Artificial Island Building Campaign in the South China Sea: Implications for the Reform of the United Nations Convention on the Law of the Sea' (2018) 122(3) Dickinson Law Rev 917, 930.

Counter to Kohl's view, the only logical interpretation of the relevant provisions of UNCLOS is that in the case of construction over a natural feature, that feature both retains its original legal status and takes on the legal status of an artificial island, installation or structure. This interpretation is supported by a number of considerations, outlined here below.

As discussed in Section 3.2.1, artificial islands are generally distinguished from installations and structures on the basis of the former involving an elevation of the seabed, where such construction has long been recognised in relation to man-made islands on coral reefs. In 1951, a hydrographer for the Admiralty in the UK who was asked to advise the Foreign Office on the legal status of artificial islands acknowledged the 'many forms of artificial islands in the Gulf built upon coral, which have a close assimilation to small, natural islands'.[599] Of course, artificial islands or maritime constructions more broadly built upon low-tide elevations are only a subset of what is within the scope of Article 60 UNCLOS in that maritime constructions exist independently of natural features. At the same time, there is nothing in the text of UNCLOS to suggest that this subset was intended to fall outside the scope of Article 60. Particularly considering the generally understood characteristic of an artificial island integrated into the natural seabed, the exclusion of construction on low-tide elevations would be an unusual omission, even more so given it is not expressly stated.

Furthermore, the provisions under Article 60 have been drafted in a manner consistent with the laws applying to the natural state of the feature. Of course, in the case of a maritime construction over a natural feature, certain provisions in Article 60 will not be applicable. These circumstances have been mentioned above, for example, in the case of a rock which is subject to a State's sovereignty, or in the case of a low-tide elevation where the requirement that the safety zone does not interfere with recognised sea lanes will not be relevant. In these circumstances, it is not that the natural feature is in conflict with the provisions, but that they are not relevant as a consequence of the natural feature already bringing about the result intended by the application of the provisions. Article 60 has been drafted to address maritime constructions in the EEZ as a whole, including those built on natural features, where those provisions are relevant. The broad scope of Article 60 reflects the fact that maritime constructions do not necessarily and in fact most often do not rely on natural features.

Reflecting the consistency between the two legal regimes is Article 60(8), which begins with the statement '[a]rtificial islands, installations and structures do not possess the status of islands' and goes on to provide that artificial islands, installations and structures '... have no territorial sea of their own, and *their presence does not affect the delimitation of the territorial sea, the exclusive economic zone or the continental shelf*' (emphasis added). Considered in context, this provision is clearly intended to ensure that a maritime construction does not generate maritime zones and is not used to extend a territorial sea baseline. At the same time though, it serves to ensure that a

599. Clive Schofield and Richard Schofield, 'Testing the Waters: Charting the Evolution of Claims to and from Low-Tide Elevations and Artificial Islands under the Law of the Sea' (2016) 1 Asia-Pacific J of Ocean L & P 37, 44.

natural feature that generates maritime zones - a rock or island - retains those zones regardless of any maritime construction that is built atop it.

A consequence of a feature retaining its prior legal status that is advantageous to high seas freedoms is that it may help to ensure that artificial islands do not end up being treated as natural islands over time and become subject to State sovereignty. Without the natural state of a feature being held as paramount, the passage of time may end up leading to it, in its modified form, being treated as a natural island. This new status may be de facto, or even de jure by way of the development of customary international law.

Despite the above arguments, the simultaneous application of two legal regimes to the one body of land in these situations does lead to some anomalous circumstances, which are addressed in the following sections in relation to rocks and low-tide elevations and lighthouses.

3.2.5.1 Consequences of a Natural Feature/Maritime Construction Dual Status

As explained in Section 3.2.4.1, the Tribunal in the *South China Sea Arbitration* made it clear that an artificial island built atop a natural feature retains its status as it was before human modification, meaning that the artificial island is at once an artificial island *and* a low-tide elevation or rock, as was the specific set of circumstances in this case. This raises questions in relation to the maritime zones pertaining to maritime constructions with these features as their foundations.

3.2.5.2 Rocks

As a conclusion extrapolated from Article 121(3) UNCLOS, we know that rocks that cannot sustain human habitation or economic life of their own generate territorial seas. The logical result under UNCLOS is that a maritime construction can be encircled by a territorial sea, by virtue of the rock on which it is constructed. At the same time, features permanently submerged and low-tide elevations with the exception of those discussed below in Section 3.2.5.3 'have no zone generative capacity even if a structure has been built on them, which is itself permanently above sea level'.[600] This makes sense given that neither the natural features themselves nor the maritime constructions generate maritime zones. As a result though, two identical maritime constructions in size and shape - one constructed over or around a rock and the other a low-tide elevation or an entirely submerged feature - may possess different maritime zones based on their, potentially now unrecognisable, original state. This in itself is logical considering the applicable law and the consequences of the alternative, as discussed in Section 3.2.5, and it is not necessarily problematic; however, it does require continuous recognition of the underlying form of the land mass as opposed to its existing and developing states.

600. Schofield (n 498) 27.

3.2.5.3 Low-Tide Elevations and Lighthouses

Lighthouses specifically, as a type of man-made structure, are a recurring theme in the records of the development of the law of the sea.[601] The basis for this is the *Fur Seal Arbitration Case* of 1893, in which Sir Charles Russell, the UK Attorney General at the time, argued that lighthouses should lead to the generation of a territorial sea: 'if a lighthouse is built upon a rock or upon piles driven into the bed of the sea, it becomes, as far as that lighthouse is concerned, part of the territory of the nation which has erected it, and ... it has ... all the rights that belong to the protection of territory'.[602]

In contrast, in 1912, in consideration of whether a lighthouse should be able to change a 'mere rock' into an island by virtue of having a lighthouse built upon it, Oppenheimer was unequivocal:

> 'If this assertion of Sir Charles Russell were correct', he said, 'it would be necessary to grant to any State which has built such a lighthouse a right of sovereignty over the territorial sea surrounding this lighthouse; but, in my opinion, this assertion is not justified. I believe that the assimilation of lighthouses and islands is misleading and that it would be better to treat lighthouses on the same footing as anchored flagships. Just as a state does not have the power to claim sovereignty over the territorial sea around an anchored flagship, so too does it have no power to claim sovereignty over a maritime area surrounding a lighthouse in the sea'.[603]

These discussions took place long before man-made structures and naturally formed islands were distinguished under international law, with only the latter ultimately entitled to maritime zones.[604] In this sense, these early discussions had

601. MW Mouton, *The Continental Shelf* (Martinus Nijhoff 1952) 233.
602. Oral Argument of Sir Charles Russell on Behalf of Great Britain (10 May 1893), Proceedings of the Tribunal of Arbitration, Convened at Paris Under the Treaty Between the United States of America and Great Britain, Concluded at Washington 29 February 1892 for the Determination of Questions Between the Two Governments Concerning the Jurisdictional Rights of the United States in the Waters of Bering Sea, Vol. XIII (US Government Printing Office 1895), 337; in the case of *Award between the United States and the United Kingdom relating to the rights of Jurisdiction of United States in the Bering's Sea and the Preservation of Fur* Seals (1893) XXVIII R.I.A.A. 263.
603. Johnson (n 502) 206-207; citing Oppenheim's report to the Institute of International Law for its Christiania session in 1912. Quote translated from the French: 'Si cette assertion de Sir Charles Russell était juste', he said, 'il serait nécessaire d'accorder à tout Etat qui a bâti un tel phare un droit de souveraineté sur la mer territoriale entourant ce phare; mais, à mon sens, cette assertion n'est pas justifiée. Je crois que l'assimilation des phares aux îles est de nature à induire en erreur et qu'il vaudrait mieux traiter les phares sur le même pied que les bateaux phares ancrés. De même qu'un Etat n'a pas le pouvoir de réclamer souveraineté sur une mer territoriale à l'entour d'un bateau-phare ancré, de même il n'a pas pouvoir de réclamer cette souveraineté sur une zone maritime à l'entour d'un phare dans la mer'. In 1951, Jessup echoed Oppenheim's sentiments: 'it would be a dangerous doctrine in many parts of the world to allow States to appropriate new areas of water by means of structures on hidden shoals' (PC Jessup, *The Law of Territorial Waters and Maritime Jurisdiction* (GA Jennings 1927) 69, as cited in, Johnson (n 502) 207).
604. YILC (1956) Vol. II, 270. Draft Article 10 read: 'Every island has its own territorial sea. An island is an area of land, surrounded by water, which in normal circumstances is permanently above high-water mark.' While it did not draw a distinction between naturally formed and man-made islands in the text of the article, the accompanying commentary clearly excludes from the scope of the article low-tide elevations that have lighthouses built upon them (as well as low-tide

added weight regarding claims of sovereignty over international waters compared with today, as it meant that a State would potentially be able to claim sovereignty over stretches of the high seas on the basis of small-scale constructions on tiny maritime features. The solution to this was to 'discover a more general principle of international law', which was 'to be found in the law relating to islands themselves'.[605] Thus, in relation to the above, the 'mere rock' referred to by Russell and Oppenheimer may today, if it is a 'rock' in the sense of Article 121(3) UNCLOS, generate a territorial sea regardless of the installation built upon it, as we have seen.

The development of the law through the three UN conferences on the law of the sea in the second half of the twentieth century focused on just that: the maritime feature as it exists naturally is generally the source of the rights associated with it. The condition 'generally' is used here because of: (1) the situation of low-tide elevations with lighthouses and similar constructions built upon them, which will be discussed directly below in this section; and (2) the rights attributed to a State on the basis of its maritime construction, under Article 60, considered in Sections 3.2.2 and 3.2.3, in particular in relation to the right to establish safety zones.

The *South China Sea Arbitration* unequivocally confirms the retention of the legal status of a natural feature in the case of construction. However, a construction over a low-tide elevation can, in specific circumstances, affect maritime zones. Under UNCLOS, a territorial sea baseline can be measured from a low-tide elevation where that low-tide elevation is wholly or partly within the territorial sea.[606] This is unremarkable and is consistent with other natural features, including reefs and bays, being used in such a manner.[607] However, under Article 7(4) UNCLOS, and in contrast to other instances of maritime construction, low-tide elevations that are beyond territorial sea may be used for the purpose of drawing straight baselines in the specific instance that 'lighthouses or similar installations which are permanently above the sea' are constructed on them.[608] Aside from off the coast of Norway, there is little in the way of State practice regarding the application of this provision.[609] The situation is significant though because, keeping in mind that a lighthouse or similar installation will not necessarily be a maritime construction for the purpose of Article 60, the provision

elevations in general) and 'technical installations'. These ILC draft articles formed the basis for the resulting four 1958 conventions on the law of the sea, including the Convention on the Territorial Sea and the Contiguous Zone, with its Article 10 as a revised form of the ILC draft Article 10 (Convention on the Territorial Sea and the Contiguous Zone (Geneva, 29 April 1958) 516 U.N.T.S. 205, *entered into force* 10 September 1964 ('Convention on the Territorial Sea and the Contiguous Zone 1958')). The final version of the article expressly provides that an island must be 'naturally-formed', as was carried over into Article 121 UNCLOS.

605. Johnson (n 502) 211.
606. UNCLOS, Article 13(1) or Article 47(4) in the case of archipelagic baselines.
607. *Ibid*. Articles 6 and 10.
608. Or Article 47(4), in the case of archipelagic baselines. The value of a low-tide elevation in generating maritime zones is restricted to this instance, i.e., when it is in sufficient proximity to the coast of a State. As a result, they are known as 'parasitic basepoints' (Schofield (n 498) 26, with reference to, Clive Symmons, 'Some Problems Relating to the Definition of "Insular Formations" in International Law: Islands and Low-Tide Elevations' (1995) 1(5) IBRU Marit Br 7).
609. International Law Association, 'Baselines under the International Law of the Sea', Final Report (2018) 29.

technically serves as an exception to maritime constructions being unable to generate maritime zones. It is only by way of the construction of the 'lighthouses or similar installations' resulting in the land mass of the low-tide elevation being permanently above the surface of the water that the mass is able to be used to draw the straight baseline. In essence, it is the human modification that extends the territorial sea, and in the case of that modification being a maritime construction, it is a case of a maritime construction doing so.

The provision leads to the unusual situation where a low-tide elevation with a lighthouse or similar installation may contribute to the delimitation of the territorial sea, but construction over the low-tide elevation to accommodate, for example, an airport, may not. Whether this is the case in practice will depend on the interpretation of the vague term 'similar installation' used in Article 7(4) UNCLOS, and whether airports would fall under it. Mendes de Leon and Molenaar explain that at the time of the seadromes in the 1930s, they were 'considered in the same fashion as beacons and lighthouses' insofar as they were 'instruments to bridge distances and to facilitate air navigation'.[610] The standard contemporaneous consideration for the construction of airports at sea is as a solution for lack of space rather than as an aid for navigation, in which case this comparison becomes more tenuous. Furthermore, due to advancements in navigation technology leading to increased reliance on tools such as the Global Position System (GPS), lighthouses are becoming obsolete and the provisions pertaining to lighthouses under UNCLOS are consequently losing their relevance.

As addressed in Section 2.2.3.1, natural features such as deep coastal indentations and fringes of islands,[611] as well as islets, rocks and reefs,[612] are legitimate basepoints for the drawing of a straight baseline, depending on the circumstances. The above case of construction on low-tide elevations is distinguished from these situations in that the defining factor is the human modification of the low-tide elevation. Finally, human modification can lead to the extension of the territorial sea baseline in one other case, although this time in the case of construction in territorial sea: coastal land reclamation. This will be considered in Section 3.5.

3.3 THE RIGHT TO EXTEND SAFETY ZONES TO ENCOMPASS AIRSPACE

3.3.1 Development of Treaty Law Applying to Safety Zones

The 'essential origins'[613] of safety zones is the recommendation by the ILC in 1953 of such areas around installations in the continental shelf.[614] The recommendation was part of a draft article that served as an early version of what went on to be accepted as

610. Mendes de Leon and Molenaar (n 486) 235.
611. UNCLOS, Article 7(1).
612. *Fisheries (United Kingdom v. Norway)*, Judgment, I.C.J. Rep. 1951 (18 December), p. 116.
613. Schofield and Schofield (n 599) 43.
614. YILC (1953) Vol. II, 213, as draft Article 6(2).

Article 5(2) of the 1958 Convention on the Continental Shelf,[615] which provides that 'the coastal State is entitled to ... establish safety zones around such installations and devices and to take in those zones measures necessary for their protection'. Article 5(3) further states that the zones may extend to a breadth of 500 metres and ships must respect them. The wording of this article in respect of safety zones is similar to that under Article 60 UNCLOS and provides no indication of whether safety zones were intended to extend also to the airspace in addition to the surface of the sea. The matter was, however, addressed during its drafting at the First UN Conference on the Law of the Sea in 1958.

The ILC's Report to the General Assembly in 1956, which included the draft articles on the law of the sea, was considered by the States present at the 1958 conference. A document forming part of the *travaux préparatoires* of the 1958 law of the sea conventions and addressing the relationship between international civil aviation law and the ILC draft articles reveals support for the position that the draft ILC articles should be interpreted as permitting the establishment of safety zones in the airspace over maritime constructions. The author of the document, Eugène Pépin, concludes:

> [n]either article 71 [the draft article on safety zones] nor its commentary ... refer to air traffic and, consequently, a safety zone established around installations situated on the surface of the sea can presumably include part of the superjacent airspace. Such a safety zone or space may thus be assimilated to a prohibited, restricted or danger area, depending on the regulations enacted by the State concerned, and may even have no upward limit.[616]

Section 3.3.3.2 will address the reason safety zones are different to these spaces - prohibited, restricted and danger areas - in international civil aviation law and therefore why the extension of safety zones to the airspace over maritime constructions cannot be justified on these grounds.

In contrast to Pépin's conclusion, the *travaux préparatoires* indicate that States present at the 1958 conference considered that safety zones were limited to the sea rather than extending to the airspace. On consideration of the draft article, the representative of Yugoslavia stated that the concept of 'safety zone' should expressly encompass the airspace: 'since installations could be endangered by aircraft even more than ships, the [Yugoslavian] proposal also provided for an air safety zone to a height of 1,000 metres'.[617] A vote on this proposal by States present was defeated eighteen

615. Convention on the Continental Shelf (Geneva, 29 April 1958) 499 U.N.T.S. 311, *entered into force* 10 June 1964 ('Continental Shelf Convention 1958').
616. Eugène Pépin, *The Law of the Air and the Draft Articles Concerning the Law of the Sea Adopted by the International Law Commission at Its Eighth Session* (A/CONF.13/4) - Extract from the *Official Records of the United Nations Conference on the Law of the Sea, Volume I* (Preparatory Documents), United Nations Conference on the Law of the Sea, Geneva, 24 February-27 April 1958, 73.
617. 'Summary Records of the 26th to 30th Meetings of the Fourth Committee - Extract from the Official Records of the United Nations Conference on the Law of the Sea' Vol. VI (Fourth Committee (Continental Shelf)) A/CONF.13/C.4/SR.26-30 (Geneva, 24 February-27 April 1958) 84.

votes to seventeen though, with twenty-one abstentions.[618] The reason for the defeat is unclear. Was it because States believed it should be left open for them to determine through their national law? Was it because States believed that safety zones should be restricted to the sea? Did States perhaps believe that safety zones could extend to the airspace but that a conference on the law of the sea was not the correct forum to do so and that this was instead the domain of ICAO?

Regarding the latter point, this was certainly the opinion of the UK, at least. The records of the conference state of the representative of the UK that 'she did not regard the question of air safety zones as falling within the competence of a conference on the law of the sea'.[619] Although definitive answers to these questions are elusive, the subsequent analysis in this chapter will reflect on them in attempting to determine what the legal status is today of establishing safety zones in the airspace over maritime constructions.

Following the adoption of UNCLOS, a 1987 ICAO Secretariat Study looking into the implications of UNCLOS for the application of the Chicago Convention found that 'since the Convention [referring to UNCLOS] refers to the "breadth" of the safety zone, no such restrictions would appear to be permitted over the airspace above such installations and the right of overflight cannot be, under the Convention, curtailed by the coastal State'.[620] It reiterated this view in respect of the continental shelf: '[t]he coastal State is not granted under the Convention [UNCLOS] any special rights or jurisdiction or precedence or priority with respect to the airspace above the waters superjacent to the continental shelf'.[621] Recalling Section 2.7.3.2, the ICAO Secretariat has also made its position clear that the EEZ provides the coastal State with no rights or jurisdiction in respect of airspace.

3.3.2 Practice Regarding Safety Zones Extending to Airspace

3.3.2.1 Support for the Extension of Safety Zones to Airspace

Despite the unambiguous statements of ICAO, the alternative position, that is, that safety zones may be extended to airspace, is supported by the domestic law of France and by commentary.

France extends its safety zones to airspace under its domestic law applying to installations in its oil and gas industry.[622] Under Article 29 of *Ordonnance n° 2016-1687 du 8 décembre 2016 relative aux espaces maritimes relevant de la souveraineté ou de la juridiction de la République française*:

618. 'Summary Records of the 26th to 30th Meetings of the Fourth Committee – Extract from the Official Records of the United Nations Conference on the Law of the Sea' Vol. VI (FourthCommittee (Continental Shelf)) A/CONF.13/C.4/SR.26-30 (Geneva, 24 February-27 April 1958) 90.
619. *Ibid.* 85.
620. ICAO (n 466) 255.
621. *Ibid.* 257.
622. Ordonnance n° 2016-1687 du 8 décembre 2016 relative aux espaces maritimes relevant de la souveraineté ou de la juridiction de la République française, Article 29 ('Ordonnance n° 2016-1687').

> The representative of the State at sea may establish a safety zone around artificial islands, installations, works and their related facilities on the continental shelf or in the exclusive economic zone, extending up to a distance of 500 metres.[623]

And in determining the extent of the safety zone:

> Restrictions may be imposed on the overflight of artificial islands, installations and works and their associated installations and safety zones, within the measure necessary for the protection of these artificial islands, installations and works and the safety of air navigation.[624]

Rothwell argues that the measures that a State may take in the safety zone include requesting prior overflight permission and altitude restrictions.[625] He argues that, despite the fact that Article 60 does not explicitly provide coastal States with the right to establish safety zones in the airspace above its maritime constructions, construing the provision as implicitly allowing for it is consistent with the intent of the article.[626]

This argument makes sense based on a teleological interpretation of Article 60 UNCLOS, a method of interpretation that involves consideration of the terms of the treaty in their context and of the treaty's object and purpose, as set out in Article 31(1) of the Vienna Convention on the Law of Treaties. This method of interpretation is increasingly relied upon by international courts and tribunals.[627] The provisions of Article 60 form part of the broader Part V of UNCLOS, which sets out the sovereign rights of the coastal State in the EEZ and establishes a framework for the State to effectively exercise those rights. Safety zones contribute to this aim by enabling the coastal State to exercise these rights safely, minimising the risk to the maritime construction itself and to other users of the maritime space. In terms of who these users are, the Preamble of UNCLOS highlights the danger of siloing the approach to managing activities at sea, emphasising that 'the problems of ocean space are closely interrelated and need to be considered as a whole', in this case the safety risks to and brought about by all users of the maritime space, including those in the airspace and on the surface of the water. Consideration of Article 60 in its wider context, acknowledging the 'interrelatedness' of activities at sea, and the purpose of the article in the legal

623. Translated from the original: 'Le représentant de l'Etat en mer peut créer une zone de sécurité autour des îles artificielles, installations, ouvrages et leurs installations connexes sur le plateau continental ou dans la zone économique exclusive, s'étendant jusqu'à une distance de 500 mètres'.
624. Ordonnance n° 2016-1687, Article 29 7°. Translated from the original in French: 'Des restrictions peuvent être apportées au survol des îles artificielles, installations et ouvrages et leurs installations connexes et des zones de sécurité, dans la mesure nécessaire à la protection de ces îles artificielles, installations et ouvrages et à la sécurité de la navigation aérienne'.
625. Donald R Rothwell, 'Artificial Islands and International Law' (Presentation delivered at ANU College of Law, Canberra, 28 July 2015) 23 and 27; Frank-Luke Attard Camilleri, *The Application of the High Seas Regime in the Exclusive Economic Zone* (Hamilton Books 2018) 31: 'coastal States may still require aircraft flying above artificial installations and structures to observe the coastal State's regulations regarding those structures'.
626. Correspondence from Donald Rothwell (Professor of International Law, Australian National University) to the author, dated 20 December 2019.
627. Irina Buga, *Modification of Treaties by Subsequent Practice* (OUP 2018) 81.

regime governing activities in the EEZ, therefore supports the interpretation that safety zones apply equally in the airspace as on the surface of the sea.

Rothwell further illustrates his argument through the example of a maritime construction extending far into the airspace. Inevitably, a maritime construction will occupy airspace and there are no provisions limiting the height of such constructions. Rothwell then poses the question: what is there to stop a State constructing a tower on an artificial island that would occupy considerable airspace? The answer to this is nothing, at least explicitly, in which case, he then reasons, 'an air exclusion zone would seem to be an appropriate response to deal with aircraft in the vicinity' of the maritime construction.[628] An argument against the right of a State to extend safety zones around its maritime constructions is that it is a violation of the right to freedom of overflight. This argument will be examined below, in Section 3.3.3.

Regardless of the method of interpretation favoured – as to which, *see* below in this section – a treaty is binding on all State parties to it, by application of the principle of *pacta sunt servanda*. This principle is customary international law,[629] and is codified under Article 26 of the Vienna Convention on the Law of Treaties. It states that a treaty that has entered into force is binding on the States that are party to it and that those States must perform their obligations under it in good faith (bona fides). The principle is closely linked to the interpretation of the provisions of a treaty given that the performance of the treaty 'presupposes the interpretation of the treaty'.[630] As such, rather than lending support to the interpretation of a treaty, Article 26 requires States to meet their obligations under that treaty and to do so in a manner that does not frustrate its object and purpose.

While State parties are bound by their obligations under a treaty, those obligations do not bind non-party States. The general principle of law[631] of *res inter alios acta (pacta tertiis nec nocet nec prodest)* refers to, in terms of international treaty law, the 'well-established' rule that 'a treaty cannot impose obligations upon a "third State"'.[632] This is relevant to the interpretation of Article 60 because if it is found that this article provides States with the right to impose safety zones in international airspace, and thereby prohibit other States' aircraft from operating in that airspace, it will not bind non-parties. This is so unless the right has also developed into customary international

628. Correspondence from Donald Rothwell (Professor of International Law, Australian National University) to the author, dated 20 December 2019.
629. Vienna Convention on the Law of Treaties, Preamble. The Preamble speaks of the principles of good faith and *pacta sunt servanda* as being 'universally recognised'; *see also*, Kirsten Schmalenbach, 'Pacta Sunt Servanda' in Oliver Dörr and Kirsten Schmalenbach (eds), *Vienna Convention on the Law of Treaties: A Commentary* (2nd edn, Springer 2018) 475; Mark Eugen Villiger, *Commentary on the 1969 Vienna Convention on the Law of Treaties* (Brill Nijhoff 2009) 368.
630. Mark Eugen Villiger, *Commentary on the 1969 Vienna Convention on the Law of Treaties* (Brill Nijhoff 2009) 366.
631. David J Bederman, 'Third Party Rights and Obligations in Treaties' in Duncan B Hollis (ed), *The Oxford Guide to Treaties* (OUP 2012) 328. As one of the sources of international law in accordance with Article 38(1)(c) of the Statute of the International Court of Justice (San Francisco, 26 June 1945) T.S. No. 993, *entered into force* 24 October 1945 ('ICJ Statute').
632. Lord McNair, *The Law of Treaties* (OUP 1986) 310.

law, as to which *see* Section 3.3.4. As established in Section 2.7.1, although UNCLOS is widely ratified, some key maritime States are not State parties to it.

In contrast to the teleological interpretation of Article 60, the textual interpretation does not support the extension of safety zones to airspace. Article 60 is not only silent on the establishment of safety zones in airspace but, in referring to the 'breadth' of the zones and the obligation for 'ships' to respect them, also indicates that they are restricted to the sea.[633] The textual interpretation is reflected in reference to the ordinary meaning of the text in Article 31(1) of the Vienna Convention on the Law of Treaties and gives less weight to subsequent practice in interpreting the provisions of a treaty.[634]

A treaty's silence on a point requires consideration of the nature of the treaty, and in the case that the treaty states broad principles, it will be more likely that implied terms will be accepted in interpreting it.[635] On this point, Gardiner highlights the decision of the Tribunal in *Air Services Agreement Case (USA v. France)*,[636] in which it was concluded that the prohibition on the change of gauge 'within the territory of the two parties' under the ASA between the USA and France meant that the agreement permitted the change of gauge in the territories of third States by airlines operating services under the agreement. In reaching its decision, the Tribunal considered the provision within the treaty as a whole and the context in which the treaty was negotiated,[637] stating that the treaty 'is silent concerning most of the major operational issues facing an air carrier' and that 'the Agreement leaves to the Parties ... the right to decide a wide range of key issues',[638] without amendment to the agreement having been considered necessary to achieve these objectives in the past. Thus, in this context, the Tribunal concluded that in interpreting the ASA, it was necessary to read into it an implied term permitting the change of gauge in the territory of a third State. At the same time, Gardiner emphasises, quoting Lord Sankey LC, that when interpreting the terms of a treaty, 'it is to be assumed that the parties have included the terms which they wished to include and on which they were able to agree'.[639] In contrast to the *Air Services Agreement Case,* Article 60 not only addresses a specific matter, rather than being general, but also, as mentioned above, includes specific terms that indicate that its application does not extend to the airspace.

The subjective method of interpretation of Article 60, reflected in Article 32 of the Vienna Convention on the Law of Treaties through its reference to the *travaux*

633. Section 3.2.3.2.
634. Buga (n 627) 79.
635. Richard Gardiner, *Treaty Interpretation* (OUP 2015) 165-166.
636. Air Service Agreement of 27 March 1946 between the United States of America and France (*USA v. France*) (1978) XVIII R.I.A.A. 417. As discussed in, Richard Gardiner, *Treaty Interpretation* (OUP 2015) 166.
637. *Ibid.* 435 and 440 (paras 48 and 66).
638. *Ibid.* 437-438 (para. 54).
639. Gardiner (n 635) 166, citing *Edwards v. Attorney General for Canada* [1930] AC 124, 136 per Lord Sankey LC.

préparatoires,[640] for example, lends further support to the textual interpretation. The subjective method aims to determine the intention of the drafters at the time of the treaty's conclusion.[641] As addressed in Section 3.3.1, the inclusion of airspace was discussed in the drafting process at the Geneva Conference and was rejected by those present. Recalling this discussion above, the article on safety zones accepted at the conclusion of this conference formed the basis for Article 60 UNCLOS, and despite the changes between the two articles, nothing further was added to suggest that they were to extend to the airspace. State practice generally reflects this interpretation, where the subsequent practice of States is relevant to the interpretation of the provisions of a treaty in terms of considering them in their context,[642] as will be explained in the following section.

3.3.2.2 Practice Supporting Restriction of Safety Zones to the Surface of the Sea

The subsequent practice of States in applying a treaty provision may be used as a tool for interpreting those terms of the treaty, pursuant to Articles 31(3)(b) and 32 of the Vienna Convention on the Law of Treaties.[643] The purpose of considering subsequent practice is to understand as accurately as possible the original intention of the drafters; however, State interpretation is a product of the context in which it takes place and so may shift over time.[644]

As indicated in Section 3.3.2.1, some States interpret Article 60 UNCLOS as providing the right to extend safety zones to include the airspace over maritime constructions. An overwhelming body of domestic legislation though, supported by IMO materials, strictly follows the text of Article 60 UNCLOS in omitting any reference to airspace, in accordance with what seems to have been the originally intended application of the provision, as discussed in Section 3.3.1.

In the UK, the *Petroleum Act 1987* states that:

> A safety zone ... shall extend to every point within 500 metres of any part of the installation (ignoring any moorings) and to every point in the water which is vertically above or below such point.[645]

640. Consideration of the *travaux préparatoires* is also viewed as part of teleological interpretation insofar as it contributes to establishing the original 'object and purpose' of the provisions of a treaty (Buga (n 627) 81).
641. Stefan Kadelbach, 'International Law Commission and Role of Subsequent Practice as a Means of Interpretation under Articles 31 and 32 VCLT' (2018) 46 QIL 5, 6.
642. Vienna Convention on the Law of Treaties, Article 31(3)(b).
643. Acknowledging the circumstances in which Article 32 applies, that is, 'when the interpretation according to article 31: (a) Leaves the meaning ambiguous or obscure; or (b) Leads to a result which is manifestly absurd or unreasonable'. *See also*, Georg Nolte, 'First Report on Subsequent Agreements and Subsequent Practice in Relation to Treaty Interpretation' (ILC 65th Session, 19 March 2013) 28.
644. Buga (n 627) 2.
645. *Petroleum Act 1987* (UK), Section 21(5).

Offences for entering the safety zone apply only to vessels, with no mention of aircraft.[646]

Under US federal law:

> A safety zone establishment ... may extend to a maximum distance of 500 meters around the OCS [outer continental shelf] facility measured from each point on its outer edge or from its construction site, but may not interfere with the use of recognized sea lanes essential to navigation.[647]

Keeping in mind that the US is not a party to UNCLOS, the source of its international rights and obligations in respect of safety zones outside territorial seas is Article 5 of the 1958 Convention on the Continental Shelf.

In Australia, under the *Offshore Petroleum and Greenhouse Gas Storage Act 2006* (Cth), the dimensions of a 'petroleum safety zone':

> may extend to a distance of 500 metres around the well, structure or equipment ... where that distance is measured from each point of the outer edge of the well, structure or equipment.[648]

As under UK legislation, the offences in relation to entering the zone are only applicable to vessels.[649]

The Russian Federal Law on the Continental Shelf of 25 October 1995 provides that:

> Safety zones extending for not more than 500 metres from each point on the outer edge of artificial islands, installations and structures shall be established around such islands, installations and structures.[650]

IMO Resolution A.671(16), referred to in Section 3.2.1.2,[651] provides no mention of airspace, suggesting an understanding that safety zones are restricted to the sea. This document is the 'principle IMO resolution dealing with safety zones around offshore oil and gas installations'[652] and the IMO is, as mentioned in Section 3.2.1.2, generally understood to be the 'competent international organization' responsible under Article 60(5) for providing recommendations on the extension of the breadth of a safety zone beyond 500 metres.

646. *Petroleum Act 1987* (UK), Section 23(1).
647. 33 C.F.R. 147 (2010) § 147.15.
648. *Offshore Petroleum and Greenhouse Gas Storage Act 2006* (Cth), Section 616(2).
649. *Ibid.* Section 616(1) and (3).
650. Federal Law on the Continental Shelf of the Russian Federation, adopted by the State Duma on 25 October 1995, Article 16. The above is an English translation, available at www.un.org/Depts/los/LEGISLATIONANDTREATIES/PDFFILES/RUS_1995_Law.pdf accessed 12 February 2019.
651. IMO Resolution A.671(16) (n 511).
652. Kashubsky and Morrison (n 554) 4.

Doctrine has also interpreted the silence as restrictive, declaring that '[t]he safety zone applies only to surface ship navigation';[653] 'the zone attracts no superjacent air rights as it is to be '*around* such installations';[654] and:

> [t]he right to establish safety zones around those structures is limited to navigations [sic]. Aerial safety zones in which freedom of overflight may be suspended or restricted are not mentioned in Article 60.[655]

In the absence of an express right to extend safety zones to the airspace over maritime structures, the following sections of this chapter will examine whether doing so is a breach of codified international law and whether the right exists or could develop as customary international law.

3.3.3 Is the Imposition of Safety Zones in the Airspace in Breach of International Law?

3.3.3.1 Interference with Overflight Does Not Necessarily Mean Violation of the Freedom

In accordance with Articles 58 and 87(1)(b) UNCLOS, freedom of overflight applies in the EEZ and on the high seas, respectively. This freedom 'follows directly from the principle of freedom of the sea', as explained in Chapter 1.[656] Returning to Mouton's statement at the start of the chapter, what exactly constitutes a violation of the freedom of overflight?

Taking an initial broad approach to answering this question, the relationship between the right of a State to build maritime constructions and the right of other States to freedom of navigation will briefly be examined. Lawrence, writing in the mid-1970s, was adamantly against the right to establish maritime constructions in the high seas due to his view that the physical space they possess and the jurisdiction over them means that they are prima facie in conflict with the freedom of the high seas.[657] In Lawrence's words, 'fixed installations on the high seas may offer numerous actual and potential benefits. At the same time, *their construction permanently precludes the utilization of the ocean space they occupy for other beneficial purposes*' (emphasis added).[658] Lawrence's views were shared by others, with a Rapporteur to the Council

653. Carlos Espósito, James Kraska, Harry N Scheiber and Moon-Sang Kwon (eds), *Ocean Law and Policy: Twenty Years of Development Under the UNCLOS Regime* (Brill Nijhoff 2016) 186.
654. Clive Symmons, *The Maritime Zones of Islands in International Law* (Martinus Nijhoff 1979) 106.
655. Hailbronner (n 537) 510.
656. Myron H Nordquist (ed), *United Nations Convention on the Law of the Sea 1982: A Commentary – Volume III* (Brill Nijhoff 2011) 81.
657. William H Lawrence, 'Superports, Airports and Other Fixed Installations on the High Seas' (1975) 6 J Mar L & Comm 575, 585-586.
658. *Ibid.* 591.

of Europe declaring that 'the creation of an artificial island amounts to exclusive occupancy of a maritime area'.[659]

These comments address the maritime constructions themselves, but the considerations apply equally to their safety zones and, more relevantly here, to their extension to airspace. In fact, they apply to the exercise of all activities of States and not exclusively in international waters. Even in its territorial sea, a coastal State is required to ensure that its actions, including the building of maritime constructions, do not interfere with innocent passage.[660]

Of course, as of the adoption of UNCLOS, there is no ambiguity that States have the right to establish maritime constructions in the high seas and in an EEZ, depending on the purpose of the construction. In exercising their freedom to build maritime constructions in the EEZ and on the high seas, States are required to have due regard for the interests of other States.[661] This due regard obligation acknowledges that in the exercise of their rights, States will, to some extent, limit the ability of other States to exercise their rights. For example, if State A builds an artificial island at certain coordinates on the high seas, State B does not have the right to do so at the same coordinates, despite having had the right prior to the construction of the artificial island by State A. As Mouton expressed, to interpret an action as being in breach of international law because it affects the ability of another State to exercise its rights would be absurd. Instead, the due regard obligation on States acknowledges that the matter is one of a balance between the 'exercise of high seas freedoms [and other rights] and the rights and interests of all States'.[662]

Given the above, is the argument that freedom of overflight exists in international airspace sufficient to deny States the right to extend safety zones to the airspace? In attempting to answer this question, the question of whether international civil aviation law provides any possible mechanisms through which safety zones could be justified will first be considered.

3.3.3.2 Consideration under International Civil Aviation Law

International civil aviation law contains SARPs to help ensure the safety of civil aircraft in the case of hazardous activities at sea. This section will examine whether any of these solutions could be interpreted in a manner so as to encompass safety zones over maritime constructions. In the alternative, it will consider whether these SARPs may serve to meet the requirements of a safety zone – to protect the safety of navigation and of the maritime construction – despite having a different intended purpose.

659. Nikos Papadakis, *The International Legal Regime of Artificial Islands* (Sijthoff 1977) 59, citing 'Report of the Legal Affairs Committee on the Legal Status of Artificial Islands Built on the High Seas' (Doc 3054), presented by Mr Margue, Rapporteur (Council of Europe Consultative Assembly, 9 December 1971) 7.

660. UNCLOS, Article 24(1). *See also*, the discussion on artificial islands and innocent passage in respect of the 1958 conventions in Papadakis (n 659) 53.

661. UNCLOS, Articles 56(2), 58(3) and 87(2). These articles apply respectively to the coastal State in the EEZ, other States in the EEZ and all States on the high seas.

662. Nordquist (ed), *UNCLOS: A Commentary – Volume III* (n 656) 73.

As mentioned in Section 2.6.5, ICAO provides procedures for States in relation to the establishment of danger areas in international airspace. Safety zones cannot be justified using the right to establish danger areas though because they do not bring with them a right to prohibit or restrict overflight; the areas instead designate spaces in which activities potentially dangerous to civil aviation take place. Danger areas are also insufficient because they must be temporary. This could possibly be suitable for installations and structures, which are usually established for a task with a fixed period, but artificial islands generally exist for a more sustained duration.

Section 2.6.5 discussed the requirement under Annex 11 that activities potentially hazardous to international civil aviation are coordinated with the responsible ATS provider,[663] where the purpose of this coordination is both to avoid hazards to civil aircraft and to minimise interference with their normal operations.[664] In the case that the State of the ATS authority is not the same as the State where the organisation planning the activities is located, '... initial coordination should be effected through the ATS authority responsible for the airspace over the State where the organization is located'.[665] As with the establishment of maritime constructions and their safety zones on the surface of the sea, Annex 11 regulates the location and duration of danger areas relative to the activities conducted.[666] As with safety zones on the surface of the sea, 'the size of the airspace designated for the conduct of [hazardous] activities should be kept as small as possible'.[667]

There is also in Annex 11 a Standard applicable to air traffic flow management (ATFM), in national or international airspace, in the situation where air traffic demand exceeds air traffic control (ATC) capacity, as determined by the ATC authority responsible for that airspace.[668] In the case of traffic over that which has been accepted in a given period of time or over a particular location, or where the rate of traffic needs to be managed, ATC is required to notify certain parties of the restrictions, including flight crews operating in the airspace.[669] It is recommended that ATFM be implemented through regional air navigation agreements or multilateral agreements.[670] These ATC provisions are designed to allow coastal States to restrict overflight in international airspace and may possibly be used to restrict overflight over maritime constructions. The purpose of the SARPs in relation to this matter though is to enable ATC to maintain safe airspace, and it only applies in the case of airspace demand that exceeds the accepted traffic, when that situation arises. In this respect, it requires an initial accepted capacity and thus necessarily presupposes that the coastal State has not prohibited all flights in the airspace. Where these SARPs might be particularly relevant to coastal States in restricting overflight over maritime constructions is in the case of

663. Chicago Convention, Annex 11 (15th edn, July 2018) 2.19.1.
664. *Ibid.* 2.19.2.
665. *Ibid.* 2.19.1.1 *Recommendation.*
666. *Ibid.* 2.19.2.1 (a). The location and duration of an activity should be no greater than necessary for the activity.
667. *Ibid.* 2.19.2.1 (b).
668. *Ibid.* 3.7.5.1 and *Note. See* Section 4.2.1.1 for the definition of ATC and the relationship between it and other aspects of airspace management.
669. *Ibid.* 3.7.5.3.
670. *Ibid.* 3.7.5.2 *Recommendation.*

the construction of an airport at sea, as to which *see* Section 3.4. In this case, overflight restrictions are likely necessary in order for ATC to safely coordinate take-offs and landings.

The ICAO Procedures for air navigation services (PANS) in Doc 4444 (PANS-ATM) complement Annexes 2 and 11 and contain further guidance on ATM in international airspace, including in relation to the coordination of military aeronautical operations with civil aviation operations.[671] The material in the PANS-ATM does not have the same legal status as SARPs, but upon reaching a sufficient level of acceptance among the international community, provisions within it may eventually become SARPs.[672] Prior to or in the absence of this occurring, the material serves to 'assist the user in the application of those SARPs'.[673] The relevant SARPs and accompanying PANS-ATM are solely designed to facilitate the safe and efficient operation of civil aviation as opposed to also ensuring the safety of the activities in response to which they apply. In contrast, the purpose of safety zones under UNCLOS is the safety of both navigation and of the maritime construction. The provisions under international civil aviation law would at most consequentially fulfil this latter element.

3.3.3.3 Prohibition of Overflight in International Airspace Inconsistent with Freedom of Overflight

SARPs and PANS for ATS regarding activities in international airspace are designed to address the safety and efficiency of international civil aviation. Where activities dangerous to aviation are conducted in international airspace, as an exercise of freedom of overflight, the State undertaking the activity is not permitted to prohibit other aircraft from the airspace, but instead has an obligation to warn of the danger. As such, the rules 'are predicated on the principle of voluntary compliance'[674] rather than, in the words of Lawrence, being 'assertions of a claim to exclusive use or control over an area'.[675] Ultimately, as Standard 2.4 of Annex 2 dictates, the final authority on the disposition of the aircraft, including whether to enter such airspace, rests with the pilot-in-command.

In practice though, hazardous activities conducted in international airspace will often result in the exclusive use of the airspace by the State conducting the activities on the basis that the pilot-in-command also has an obligation, under Standard 3.1.1 of Annex 2, not to operate an aircraft in a negligent or reckless manner. Flying through airspace that has a NOTAM[676] issued in relation to it on the basis of the operation of military exercises, for example, could constitute negligent or reckless operation of an

671. ICAO Doc 4444, *ICAO Procedures for Air Navigation Services on Air Traffic Management* (16th edn, 2016) 16.1.
672. *Ibid.* 3.2.
673. *Ibid.*
674. Lawrence (n 657) 587; citing, *Legality of Using the High Seas in Connection with Nuclear Weapons Tests in the Pacific Ocean*, US Delegation Paper, UN Conference on the Law of the Sea, 1958, US/CLS/Pos/48(2)-(3), Annex II, 20 February 1958.
675. *Ibid.* 586.
676. *See* Section 2.6.5 (n 376) for the definition of 'NOTAM'.

aircraft, depending on the circumstances. Therefore, although the airspace is not closed de jure, it is closed de facto, in that it is unlikely that aircraft will operate in the area due to the risks to safety being too great.

As on the sea, every use of international airspace involves a balance between States' freedom of overflight. Mouton's single ship example can equally be extended to international airspace in relation to aircraft, but considering the balance more meaningfully, the legitimate impingement of a State's freedom of overflight as a result of the exercise of another State's exercise of the freedom can be illustrated through the use of airspace for military exercises. For example, en route air navigation warnings issued by the Netherlands in March 2019 included that in danger areas in international airspace en route instrument flight rules (IFR) and visual flight rules (VFR) GAT 'shall remain clear of the areas' and that authorisation for the use of the areas will only be granted to pre-scheduled OAT and/or special test flights.[677] This prohibition is on the basis of military aeronautical operations in the airspace or, more specifically, 'certain flying activities [that] are not readily adaptable to air traffic control, since specific aircraft – during at least part of their flight – cannot maintain a constant profile, heading and speed (e.g. test flights, air combat training manoeuvres)'.[678]

The peaceful use of international airspace for military activities falls within the freedom of overflight and in this respect, like all freedoms, its lawfulness depends on the balance between the right to exercise the freedom and the rights of other States to exercise their rights and freedoms.[679] Provided that the activities in the area of international airspace meet the prerequisite of being temporary, whether this balance has been achieved rests on a consideration of the reasonableness of the impact of the activities. Activities that limit the operation of other States' aircraft 'in large areas of airspace and/or over an excessively long period of time can probably no longer be regarded as a reasonable enjoyment of a State's freedom of overflight'.[680]

The above serves to illustrate that although international civil aviation law does not expressly permit a State to prohibit the operation of another State's aircraft in international airspace, the activities of States in carrying out their freedoms of the high seas can in practice lead to the closure of airspace to other States' aircraft. Furthermore, this situation is generally accepted by States, provided it is temporary and that the restrictions are commensurate to the needs of the activities carried out.

Based on the above, there appears to be a discrepancy in the interpretation of freedom of navigation and freedom of overflight in international law. Under the law of the sea, States are expressly permitted to exclude other States' vessels from certain areas of international waters, in pursuit of the exercise of their rights in the area, and violations of the exclusion can be enforced by the State imposing the exclusion. Under international civil aviation law, no State has the right to prohibit use of the airspace by another State's aircraft. In practice, as we have seen, the use of airspace by one State's

677. Aeronautical Information Publication Netherlands, ENR 5 Navigation Warnings – ENR 5.1 Prohibited, Restricted and Danger Areas (28 March 2019) 1.1.
678. *Ibid.*
679. As addressed in Section 3.3.3.1.
680. Hailbronner (n 466) 42.

aircraft may de facto result in the airspace being avoided by the aircraft of other States, but even when this occurs, there are strict requirements on the extent of the operations that impact freedom of overflight.

3.3.4 Provision for the Right to Establish Safety Zones in Airspace Through the Development of Customary International Law

3.3.4.1 Relevance and Approach to Section

The US's action in overflying China's artificial islands in the South China Sea was an explicit message to China and to the international community that the US did not accept China's proclaimed right to prohibit the operation of its aircraft in a portion of international airspace. Such actions, when undertaken by a sufficient number of States, can inhibit the development of customary international law or, in the case of emerging customary law, make clear a State's intention not to be bound by that law in the case it crystallises. The first of these results is part of the consideration of what constitutes State practice in the case of customary international law and the second is an example of a State acting as a persistent objector. Both of these matters will be considered in this section.

As has been established so far in this chapter, there is an absence of an express right under international treaty law to extend safety zones to airspace. There is also currently no evidence that the right exists under customary international law. In light of these two positions, could the right to do so emerge under customary international law? This section will first address the elements of customary international law, including so-called particular custom, also known as 'special' or 'local' custom. It will then examine the role of the persistent objector in the case of general customary law and finally the emergence of customary international law in violation of codified law. This will be considered in light of the argument that the extension of safety zones to airspace is a violation of the freedom of overflight.

3.3.4.2 The Elements of Customary International Law

Customary international law, as set out in Article 38(1)(b) of the ICJ Statute, is 'evidence of a general practice as accepted as law' or, in the words of the ILC, it 'means those rules of international law that derive from and reflect a general practice accepted as law'.[681] For a customary international law to exist two elements must be satisfied.[682] First, the custom must be a general practice of States and, second, there must be *opinio juris*, or a belief by States that they are bound by the practice. The division of customary

681. Michael Wood, 'Second Report on Identification of Customary International Law' (ILC 66th Session, 22 May 2014) 7.
682. *Continental Shelf (Libyan Arab Jamahiriya/Malta)*, Judgment, I.C.J. Rep. 1985 (3 June), p. 13, p. 29 para. 27. In this case, the ICJ stated: '[i]t is of course axiomatic that the material of customary international law is to be looked for primarily in the actual practice and *opinio juris* of States'.

law into these two elements is widely accepted, including by the ICJ, other international courts and tribunals, and in academic literature,[683] but differentiating between the two can be difficult as they are 'closely, if not often impossibly, entangled'.[684]

Sources serving as evidence of State practice are various and include, among many others, the physical actions of States, acts of the executive, and diplomatic acts and correspondence.[685] However, the fact that 'relatively few States compile and publish their practice'[686] adds to the challenge in determining when a practice becomes general practice. The duration can be significant in helping to determine the existence of practice; however, it need not necessarily be long-standing.[687] The practice must be uniform and consistent, but uniformity does not require all States to adopt the practice.[688] In the *North Sea Continental Shelf Cases*, the ICJ stated that the practice should be 'extensive and virtually uniform'[689] but subsequently, in the *Military and Paramilitary Activities Case*, that it 'does not consider that ... practice must be in absolutely rigorous conformity'.[690] The Court also highlighted in the *North Sea Continental Shelf Cases* the importance of considering the practice of 'States whose interests are specially affected'.[691] This matter is also central to the concept of local custom, as to which *see* the following section.

The determination of *opinio juris*, or a State's acceptance of a practice as law, marks the distinction between practice as common usage – for example, salute at sea[692] – and as custom.[693] Evidence of its existence depends on the type of practice involved; for example, it may differ 'between cases involving the assertion of a legal right and those acknowledging a legal obligation'.[694] While general practice may serve to indicate the presence of *opinio juris*,[695] it is not determinative of its existence.[696]

683. Wood (n 681) 7.
684. Buga (n 627) 202-203. The ILC also recognised this, stating that it would cover them together in the same report 'given the close relationship between the two' (Wood (n 681) 4).
685. James Crawford, *Brownlie's Principles of Public International Law* (9th edn, OUP 2019) 21-22; Wood (n 681) 22-23.
686. Wood (n 681) 3.
687. *North Sea Continental Shelf (Federal Republic of Germany/Netherlands; Federal Republic of Germany/Denmark)*, Judgment, I.C.J. Rep. 1969 (20 February), p. 3, p. 43 para. 74: 'the passage of only a short period of time is not necessarily, or of itself, a bar to the formation of a new rule of customary international law'.
688. Crawford (n 685) 22.
689. *North Sea Continental Shelf (Federal Republic of Germany/Netherlands; Federal Republic of Germany/Denmark)*, Judgment, I.C.J. Rep. 1969 (20 February), p. 3, p. 43 para. 74 ('*North Sea Continental Shelf Cases*').
690. *Military and Paramilitary Activities in and Against Nicaragua (Nicaragua v. United States of America)*, Merits, I.C.J. Rep. 1986 (27 June), p. 14, p. 98 para. 186. *See* Section 4.3.3.4 for further discussion on the distinction between the standards in these two cases.
691. *North Sea Continental Shelf Cases*, p. 43 para. 74.
692. Dear Kemp and Peter Kemp (eds), *The Oxford Companion to Ships and the Sea* (2nd edn, OUP 2006), available at www.oxfordreference.com accessed 20 November 2019.
693. Wood (n 681) 56.
694. *Ibid.* 58.
695. Crawford (n 685) 24-25.
696. For example, *see*, *Legality of the Threat or Use of Nuclear Weapons*, Advisory Opinion, I.C.J. Rep. 1996 (8 July), p. 226, p. 32 para. 67.

3.3.4.3 Local Custom

The weight given to interested States for the purpose of identifying customary law has been the subject of ICJ cases involving practice between a small number of States.[697] Through these cases, the ICJ has repeatedly declared that customary international law can exist locally and even bilaterally, binding only on those States involved. This is relevant in the case that overflight restrictions emerge as common practice in a specific region, in which those States could be bound by the actions through the development of it into local customary international law. The 1960 case, *Right of Passage over Indian Territory*, involved transit by Portugal through Indian territory to Portuguese territory enclaved by the aforementioned Indian territory, without which passage Portugal was unable to exercise its sovereignty over the enclaves. The case was brought before the ICJ after India prevented Portugal from transiting through its territory 'contrary to the practice hitherto followed'.[698] The Court considered whether, as Portugal claimed, a local custom had arisen by way of the 'practice hitherto'. India on the other hand argued that 'no local customs could be established between only two States'.[699] The Court ultimately found in favour of Portugal stating that '[i]t is difficult to see why the number of States between which a local custom may be established on the basis of long practice must necessarily be larger than two'.[700] The Court reached its decision considering that India had both permitted the actions of Portugal and failed to express any objection to it.[701]

3.3.4.4 The Persistent Objector Rule

Once a customary international law has crystallised, a State may not withdraw from being bound by it.[702] That is, unless a State is a persistent objector, in which case the persistent objector rule exempts the State from being bound by the law if it has consistently objected to it during the process of its formation,[703] the onus of proof in relation to which is on that State.[704] The ICJ has supported the persistent objector rule in its judgments in the *Asylum Case*, the *Anglo-Norwegian Fisheries Case* and the *North Sea Continental Shelf Cases*,[705] although the Court has not used the rule in its *ratio decidendi*. In both the *Asylum Case* and the *Anglo-Norwegian Fisheries Case*, the rule

697. Michael Wood, 'Third Report on Identification of Customary International Law' (ILC 67th Session, 27 March 2015) 54.
698. *Case Concerning Right of Passage over Indian Territory (Portugal v. India)*, Merits, I.C.J. Rep. 1960 (12 April), p. 6, p. 27.
699. *Ibid.* p. 39.
700. *Ibid.*
701. *Ibid.* p. 40.
702. Elias Olufemi, 'Persistent Objector' (Max Planck Encyclopedia of Public International Law 2006) 1.
703. *Ibid.* 2.
704. James A Green, *The Persistent Objector Rule in International Law* (OUP 2016) 66.
705. *Asylum Case (Colombia/Peru)*, Judgment, I.C.J. Rep. 1950 (20 November), p. 266 ('*Asylum Case (Colombia/Peru)*'); *Fisheries (United Kingdom v. Norway)*, Judgment, I.C.J. Rep. 1951 (18 December), p. 116; *North Sea Continental Shelf Cases*.

was discussed in obiter dictum, and in the *North Sea Continental Shelf Cases*, it was indirectly mentioned in that the Court acknowledged the importance of State objection.[706] It is generally accepted that the persistent objector rule applies only in the case of general customary law and not also to that of local custom.[707] Exactly how the objection must be issued in order to fulfil the elements of a persistent objector is unclear,[708] but certain elements are accepted as a minimum: the objection must be expressed, be made known internationally, and be maintained.[709] Some publicists have argued that an objection may be either verbal or through actions.[710] Others, in contrast, are of the opinion that actions are required to demonstrate persistent objection in addition to verbal opposition, which brings with it practical challenges, such as that States may not be presented with the opportunity to act or that doing so could be costly.[711] These factors potentially present impediments to States functioning in the international legal order on the basis of the principle of the sovereign equality of States, as recognised in Article 2(1) of the UN Charter. Finally, whether a persistent objector objects to being bound by the emerging law or to the emergence of the law per se is not necessary for the application of the persistent objector rule and in practice, States may expressly do both.[712]

The US overflight over China's artificial islands in the South China Sea demonstrates that it does not recognise the right of China to impose prohibitions in the airspace. Likewise, the statements from the governments of the UK, France and Germany, as discussed in the introduction, demonstrate these States' explicit objection to China's actions. If the prohibition of airspace over maritime constructions was to develop into general customary international law, these States could potentially stand as persistent objectors and therefore be exempt from the law. From this point, the States would have to maintain their persistent objection to the law in order for the exemption to continue to apply.[713] At the same time, on the basis of their objections, these States may be estopped from imposing their own safety zones above maritime constructions in future. The doctrine of estoppel prevents – or estops – a representing party 'from successfully adopting different, subsequent statements on the same

706. Holning Lau, 'Rethinking the Persistent Objector Doctrine in International Human Rights Law' (2005) 6(1) Chic J Int Law 495, 499-500.
707. Olufemi (n 702) 10. As the author explains on this point, however, the ICJ in the *Asylum Case (Colombia/Peru)*, pp. 276-277, applied Article 38 of the ICJ Statute which relates to general practice, despite the case involving regional custom: 'the ICJ did not base its ruling on a typological distinction between general and regional custom – if such difference can be said to exist'.
708. Green (n 704) 66; Olufemi (n 702) 15.
709. Olufemi (n 702) 16.
710. *Ibid.*
711. Both the initial claim and the tensions that arise as a result are identified in Green (n 704) 76.
712. Green (n 704) 75. As discussed by the author, this was so, for example, with Turkey in the case of the extension of the territorial sea to 12 nm. During the drafting of UNCLOS, Turkey argued that this rule had not achieved the status of customary international law and then afterwards stated that if it had indeed developed into customary law, Turkey was not bound by it on the basis of its persistent objection.
713. Green (n 704) 80.

issue'.[714] International law is dynamic though, and so subsequent actions would be considered in the context at the time. Furthermore, the complications of the situation in the South China Sea – the consideration that China in fact declares the artificial islands as sovereign territory and bases the prohibition of its airspace on that – could be used to the advantage of these States if they were to be estopped in the case that they could sufficiently distinguish the future situation from the current situation by way of these specificities.

3.3.4.5 *Customary International Law as International Law Applicable in the Relations Between the Parties*

In the case that the right to establish a safety zone in the airspace above a maritime construction existed in the form of customary international law, it could either exist independently from Article 60, operating in parallel to it, or alternatively demonstrate the application of Article 60. It is the latter that will be examined here. Taking into account Rothwell's interpretation of Article 60 UNCLOS, the practice of States in establishing safety zones over maritime constructions involves the application of Article 60.

As mentioned in Section 3.3.2.2, subsequent practice in the application of a treaty is relevant to the interpretation of those terms of the treaty in accordance with Article 31(3)(b) and Article 32 of the Vienna Convention on the Law of Treaties. The ICJ recognised in its *Namibia Advisory Opinion* that customary international law, where it is a relevant rule of international law applicable in the relations between the parties, is also to be taken into account, in accordance with Article 31(3)(c) of the Vienna Convention on the Law of Treaties. This is a form of systemic integration, as mentioned in Section 2.2.2.1.[715] Customary international law is relevant in this respect whether it is 'general, regional or local customary rules'[716] provided it is relevant to the subject matter of the treaty.[717]

The Court in the *Namibia Advisory Opinion*, discussing the interpretation of the Mandate for German South West Africa, found that it:

> must take into consideration the changes which have occurred in the supervening half-century, and its interpretation cannot remain unaffected by the subsequent development of law, through the Charter of the United Nations *and by way of customary law*. Moreover, an inter-national instrument has to be interpreted and

714. Thomas Cottier and Jörg Paul Müller, 'Estoppel' (Max Planck Encyclopedia of International Law 2007) 1. Estoppel does not fit neatly within one of the sources of international law under Article 38 of the ICJ Statute. As the authors explain, 'it is more suitable to base it upon a combination of general principles of law, precedent, and doctrine, resulting in a norm of customary international law' (para. 10).
715. *Legal Consequences for States of the Continued Presence of South Africa in Namibia (South West Africa) notwithstanding Security Council Resolution 276 (1970)*, Advisory Opinion, I.C.J. Rep. 1971 (21 June), p. 16, p. 31 para. 53 ('*Namibia Advisory Opinion*').
716. Villiger (n 630) 433.
717. Mark Eugen Villiger, 'The Rules on Interpretation: Misgivings, Misunderstandings, Miscarriage? The "Crucible" Intended by the International Law Commission' in Enzo Cannizzaro (ed), *The Law of Treaties beyond the Vienna Convention* (OUP 2011) 112.

> applied within the frame-work of the entire legal system prevailing at the time of the interpretation (emphasis added).[718]

In the context of this book, customary international law, if it were found to exist and had formed through the application of Article 60 UNCLOS, is taken into account in accordance with Article 31(3)(c) as a tool for interpretation more directly than the Court's consideration of it in the *Namibia Advisory Opinion*. The question before the Court was what the consequences were for States involved of the continued presence of South Africa in Namibia[719] and the development of law included the demise of the League of Nations and the enshrinement of the principle of self-determination in the subsequent UN Charter.[720] In the present case, the development of the law is the hypothetical crystallisation of customary international law supporting the, in this case, teleological interpretation of Article 60 which provides States with the right to impose safety zones in the airspace over maritime constructions. It is recognised that this argument has a circularity to it - State practice in interpreting and applying the law in turn feeds back into determining how that law is to be interpreted - and, while not ideal, the circularity of treaty interpretation has been recognised on numerous occasions.[721]

A final point to note on Article 31(3)(c) is that the principle of systemic integration is solely 'to further the process of interpretation, not to displace the treaty',[722] and once the practice constituting the customary law can no longer be considered to be an interpretation of the terms of the treaty - in the case that it modifies the provision, for instance - the practice no longer falls within the scope of Article 31(3)(c).[723]

3.3.4.6 Customary International Law in Violation of Treaty Law

Customary international law can develop in conflict with treaty law,[724] which is relevant in light of the argument that the establishment of safety zones in international airspace is a breach of freedom of overflight.[725] The ability for customary international

718. *Namibia Advisory Opinion*, p. 31 para. 53.
719. *Ibid.* p. 27 para. 42.
720. *Ibid.* pp. 28 and 31 paras 44 and 52.
721. *See*, for example, Michael Beyers, *Custom, Power and the Power of Rules* (CUP 1999) 130-131. In this instance, Beyers discusses 'the chronological paradox' in relation to customary international law: 'States creating new customary rules must believe that those rules already exist, and that their practice, therefore, *is* in accordance with the law.' *See also*, 'Report of the Study Group on Fragmentation of International Law: Difficulties arising from the Diversification and Expansion of International Law', finalised by Martti Koskenniemi (ILC 58th Session, 13 April 2006) 190, which addresses the 'disturbing circularity' of the formulation of Article 53 of the Vienna Convention on the Law of Treaties, specifically the conflict between *jus cogens* limiting what can be agreed upon by States under treaty law and what States agree upon in a treaty possibly being indicative of the content of *jus cogens*.
722. Gardiner (n 635) 291.
723. Buga (n 627) 219.
724. *Ibid.*
725. Acknowledging that UNCLOS merely recognises the freedoms of navigation and overflight, which exist independently of the Convention (*see* Section 2.7.1).

law to modify treaty law is a result of there being no hierarchy between the two sources under Article 38(1) of the ICJ Statute; they are both primary sources of international law.[726] The order in which the sources are listed under this article reflects 'the degree of certainty with which their existence can be discerned' as opposed to their authority, and in the case of conflict between a customary rule and a treaty norm, 'the norm that will prevail in a given case will depend on their normative content, context, and the parties bound by them'.[727] The determination of customary international law that has developed in conflict with a treaty obligation is the same as with other rules of customary law, however given that it is created *contra legem*, or against the existing law, the existence of *opinio juris* may be more difficult to prove. In contrast to the emergence of customary international law in general though, customary international law modifying treaty law 'requires the intention of all of [the parties]' rather than just a general practice,[728] providing a significant hurdle to its crystallisation.

A well-known example of customary international law developing in conflict with treaty law is the emergence of the EEZ, which had developed as a form of customary international law at the time it was codified in UNCLOS.[729] The EEZ reserved sovereign rights for the coastal State that were in direct conflict with certain freedoms of the high seas codified under the 1958 Convention on the High Seas, such as freedom of fishing.[730]

Another example is the launch of the Sputnik 1 satellite in 1957. This launch occurred well prior to the existence of the Outer Space Treaty, which codified that outer space is not subject to State sovereignty, but after the entry into force of the Chicago Convention, which makes clear that a State has sovereignty over the airspace over its territory.[731] Despite this, no objections were raised to the orbit of Sputnik 1, which passed over the territories of numerous States.[732] The absence of opposition is seen as evidence that States viewed outer space as having a different legal character to airspace, where in outer space States are free to undertake activities without the permission of the underlying State[733] or, in other words, that 'customary international law did not extend claims of sovereignty into outer space'.[734] Just as the demarcation of the airspace and outer space is still not defined, nor is the altitude at which States are permitted to undertake space activities over the territories of other States. The Manual of International Law Applicable to Military Uses of Outer Space (MILAMOS) excluded

726. *Jus cogens* norms are an exception to this, as recognised under Articles 53 and 64 of the Vienna Convention on the Law of Treaties.
727. Buga (n 627) 213.
728. *Ibid.* 198.
729. *See* Section 2.7.3.1 for the recognition by the ICJ of the customary status of the EEZ in 1982, which occurred prior to the adoption of UNCLOS.
730. Convention on the High Seas 1958, Articles 1 and 2.
731. Outer Space Treaty, Article 2 and Chicago Convention, Article 1. *See* Section 2.2.4 for discussion of these treaty provisions.
732. John Cobb Cooper, 'Flight-Space and the Satellites' (1958) 7(1) The International and Comparative Law Quarterly 82, 88.
733. Steven Freeland, 'Fly Me to the Moon: How Will International Law Cope with Commercial Space Tourism?' (2010) 11 Melb J Int'l L 1, 10.
734. Michael G Gallagher, 'Legal Aspects of the Strategic Defense Initiative' (1986) 111 US Mil Law Rev 11, 20.

the issue of the use of airspace at lower altitudes over other States for launches on the basis that there was insufficient acceptance by States to consider it as an emerging customary international law.[735]

The determination between subsequent practice demonstrating the application of a treaty provision or modifying the terms requires interpretation itself,[736] and States are reluctant to recognise that subsequent practice modifies a treaty provision, in part because it is seen as a departure from the principle of *pacta sunt servanda*.[737] As a result, it is generally a last resort, when there is 'genuine incompatibility' that is 'irreconcilable through interpretation'.[738] On this point, a parallel may be drawn between the cases of Sputnik 1 and safety zones. Rather than resulting in a modification of Article 1 of the Chicago Convention in relation to the former, and the principle of freedom of overflight as it is recognised under Article 87(1)(b) UNCLOS in relation to the latter, these cases involve interpretation of the law. For Article 1 of the Chicago Convention, the new customary international law meant that 'airspace above its territory' now had a maximum altitude, albeit undefined. Similarly, in the case of safety zones, they could be understood not to involve a violation of the principle of freedom of overflight but to bring about a shift in the interpretation of it, consistent with the relationship between the corresponding freedom of navigation and the right to construct safety zones on the surface of the sea.

3.3.4.7 *Customary International Law Supporting the Restriction of Safety Zones to the Surface of the Sea*

Taking a contrasting view, and merely as a point to note, it could instead be argued, considering the wide body of domestic law implementing Article 60 UNCLOS only on the surface of the sea, that there is State practice – and possibly also *opinio juris* – to suggest that general customary international law could develop or even exist in support of the opposite proposition, that is, that a State's right to establish safety zones around its maritime constructions in international waters is restricted to vessels.

3.4 ARTIFICIAL ISLANDS FACILITATING AIRCRAFT OPERATIONS

3.4.1 Jurisdiction in Airspace over Artificial Islands Facilitating Aircraft Operations

This section will consider the rights of States to manage the airspace over maritime constructions in international waters when those structures facilitate the take-off and

735. McGill University, 'MILAMOS Project', available at mcgill.ca/milamos/ accessed 3 November 2019.
736. Buga (n 627) 2.
737. '38th Meeting of the Committee of the Whole – Extract from the Official Records of the United Nations Conference on the Law of Treaties, First Session (Summary Records of the Plenary Meetings and the Meetings of the Committee of the Whole)' A/CONF.39/C.1/SR.38 (Vienna, 26 March-24 May 1968) 210-213. States raising this concern included Chile, Russia, Guinea, Uruguay, Cuba, Portugal and the Netherlands.
738. Buga (n 627) 219.

landing of aircraft. This is the case, for example, for offshore petroleum installations, which rely on helicopter operations as part of their activities. It is also the case for artificial islands built for the purpose of facilitating airports at sea in international waters. China's military airport on Fiery Cross Reef is one example of this but airports for international civil aviation are also likely in future. To date artificial islands with civil international airports have been constructed and are operating in territorial seas,[739] but plans for airports in international waters have not yet come to fruition.

In 1979, Heller stated that:

> [i]t appears to be doubtful (and consequently should be clarified) whether the right granted to the coastal state in Article 60(1) to regulate the operation and use of artificial islands, installations and structures includes the right to regulate and exercise jurisdiction with regard to aviation, because of the reference to particular governmental interests (customs, fiscal, health, safety, immigration) only in Article 60(2).[740]

Forty years later, this point seems today to be clarified, at least to an extent. Article 60(2), as discussed in Section 3.2.3.1, provides the coastal State with *exclusive jurisdiction* over those maritime constructions that it has the exclusive right to construct under Article 60(1) and that exclusive jurisdiction *includes* jurisdiction with regard to customs, fiscal, health, safety and immigration laws and regulations. The wording in this provision 'includes jurisdiction with regard to ...' suggests that the list is indicative rather than exclusive. This is consistent with Article 60(1), which provides that, in respect of the relevant maritime constructions, the coastal State 'shall have the exclusive right to ... regulate .... the operation and use of ...'. This interpretation is also consistent with the purpose of the provision in its broader context. It is included to enable coastal States to effectively exercise their rights in the zone which, given the nature of the activities and the distances involved from the shore, were logically intended to encompass air transport. In fact, to deny States the right to regulate air traffic to and from their maritime constructions would not only be illogical but also have adverse safety consequences. This view is supported by Hailbronner who, in 1983, observed that '[j]urisdiction in respect of flights to and from those structures and islands is inseparably interconnected with the coastal state's exclusive rights to construct and use the installations'.[741] Finally, although in practice unlikely to be relevant, the provision addresses the 'exclusive jurisdiction' of the coastal State. Even if the regulation of aviation operations was to fall outside its scope, it does not preclude the coastal State from exercising jurisdiction over it.

As mentioned in the previous paragraph, the exclusive jurisdiction under Article 60(2) is only over the maritime constructions that the coastal State has the exclusive right to construct. Recalling Section 3.2.3.1, those maritime constructions are: artificial islands, regardless of their purpose, installations and structures for the purposes under Articles 56 and 77 – that is, for carrying out their rights in the EEZ or on the continental shelf, whichever the case may be – and *other economic purposes*, as well as installations

739. *See* above n 479.
740. Heller (n 509) 149.
741. Hailbronner (n 537) 509.

and structures which may interfere with the exercise of the rights of the coastal State in the zone. This leaves other States unable to construct artificial islands in the EEZ or on continental shelf of that coastal State and with little incentive to construct an installation or structure. Going further than this, considering Article 60(1)(c), the coastal State arguably even has the exclusive right to construct airport facilities in its EEZ and continental shelf as any construction and operation of an installation or structure by another State would be likely to interfere with the rights of the coastal State.[742]

The argument put forward here is that together these provisions are so broad that coastal States will almost always have exclusive jurisdiction over aviation on maritime constructions in their EEZ and on their continental shelf. This position is supported by a 1987 ICAO Secretariat Study, which stated that 'the interpretation of the text leads to a conclusion that the coastal State would have the exclusive jurisdiction over any airports or heliports constructed on installations in the EEZ'.[743] State practice supports this interpretation and the legislation of coastal States worldwide indicates that States assume jurisdiction over flights to and from structures on the continental shelf, including in terms of licensing, insurance, liability, safety regulations and traffic rules.[744] For example, through various structures and to varying degrees, the US, Norway, the UK, Canada and Australia have legislation or memoranda of understanding between departments governing the operation of helicopters to and from their offshore petroleum facilities.[745]

As demonstrated above, the legal basis for the regulation of aviation on maritime constructions does not involve safety zones, but instead centres on the scope of Article 60(1) and 60(2) UNCLOS. Again returning to Hailbronner, '... the exercise of jurisdiction under Article 60(2) does not justify general restrictions on the freedom of overflight over those installations'.[746] The operation of air services to and from a maritime construction does involve risks for airspace users though, and air traffic must be managed to mitigate those risks. This is achieved in the same way as in relation to any other risks in the airspace, as managed by the responsible authority pursuant to arrangements specific to that FIR.

3.4.2 Rights of the State in the Operation of an Airport for International Civil Aviation Outside Territory

If a coastal State were to establish a maritime construction beyond its territorial sea – in its EEZ or on its continental shelf – for the purpose of establishing a civil international airport, there are a number of considerations additional to the above that have to be taken into account under international civil aviation law.

742. Camilleri (n 625) 31, with reference to Soons (1974).
743. ICAO (n 466) 255. This also extends to those constructed on the continental shelf, through Article 80 UNCLOS.
744. Hailbronner (n 537) 510.
745. 'Review of Selected Offshore Petroleum Regulatory Regimes: Offshore Helicopter Safety Inquiry' (Aerosafe Risk Management, Canada, 2010).
746. Hailbronner (n 537) 510.

First, as outlined in the previous section, it is indisputable under Article 60(1) and (2) UNCLOS that the coastal State has jurisdiction over the airport. *Second*, the negotiation of traffic rights in ASAs is based on each State in the ASA designating a location to and from which the rights may be exercised, that is, the defined territory of the State. If a State constructs an airport on a maritime construction that sits beyond its territorial sea, the State would have to demonstrate that it has the right to grant traffic rights in its EEZ and the other State or States in the ASA would have to be prepared to accept this.[747] In addition, and further to the statement of ICAO mentioned in Section 3.3.1 that a State does not have jurisdiction over the airspace over artificial islands beyond its territorial sea, the State would have to negotiate the exclusive use of the airspace above the airport and in the approach and take-off corridors with the other States that use the airspace, which could be achieved through amendments to the relevant regional air navigation agreements, upon approval by the ICAO Council.[748] Recalling Section 3.3.3.3, it would be difficult to see how exclusive use of the airspace in this case would be accepted by other States considering freedom of overflight. This would most likely require lawmaking by concluding a new international agreement. The above matters, among other relevant considerations, have been addressed thoroughly in previous academic publications[749] and this book will not delve further into them here.

3.5 CHANGES TO INTERNATIONAL AIRSPACE DELIMITATION AS A RESULT OF LAND FORTIFICATION AND RECLAMATION

The last section of this chapter will highlight some final, ancillary, matters with implications for overflight in international airspace. The aim of this section is not so much to analyse and find answers to these issues, but to draw attention to them as matters that will, in future, need to be addressed to ensure clear delimitation of international airspace.

3.5.1 The Legal Status of Islands in the Face of Submersion and Erosion

This section will address a number of related issues on the legal status of islands and their maritime zones in light of human modification in response to rising sea levels and coastal erosion. These issues have implications for the delimitation of national airspace and correspondingly consequences for international airspace and freedom of overflight.

747. Mendes de Leon and Molenaar (n 486) 240-241.
748. *Ibid.* 243.
749. PPC Haanappel, *The Law and Policy of Air Space and Outer Space: A Comparative Approach* (Kluwer Law International 2003) 23; Niels van Antwerpen, *Cross-Border Provision of Air Navigation Services with Specific Reference to Europe: Safeguarding Transparent Lines of Responsibility and Liability* (Kluwer Law International 2008) 160; Lawrence (n 657); Hailbronner (n 537); Mendes de Leon and Molenaar (n 486).

The first of these is related to the discussion going back to the early twentieth century on whether international law should draw a distinction between natural and man-made islands, as addressed in Section 3.2.1.1. Of course, this is now well settled in international law under Article 121 UNCLOS, but part of the debate questioned where the demarcation lies between natural and man-made islands, a matter that has not been resolved but which has new significance today in light of rising sea levels and erosion due to climate change.[750]

Recalling Section 3.2.4.2, the Tribunal in the *South China Sea Arbitration* provided some clarity, confirming that the relevant consideration is the *natural* state prior to human modification. But the question then is what exactly constitutes 'human modification' and subsequently, 'whether an island of mixed natural and human origin should fall under Article 121'[751] under certain circumstances. This seems to be prima facie a simple matter, but there are circumstances with no clear classification. For example, if an island has been submerged and is then built back up is it an artificial island? What if an island has been eroded so significantly or submerged to the point that it can no longer sustain human habitation or economic life and it is then rebuilt – will it be an artificial island built on a rock or a natural island as it was prior to erosion/submersion? And, what would the status be of a low-tide elevation in the case of 'an artificial construction near [that] low-tide elevation that leads to the accumulation of materials that change the feature into an island'?[752] Answers to these questions are not provided under Article 121 in relation to naturally formed islands.

These questions were similarly posed by Johnson in 1951, with reference to the 1805 case, *The Anna*:

> If a natural island is in the process of gradually disappearing beneath the waves and it is decided to erect earthworks so as to keep the island above the level of the sea, is that island natural or artificial? Again, if, in the well-known case of *The Anna*, the 'little mud islands composed of earth and trees drifted down by the river', which were the subject of Lord Stowell's judgment, had been 'embanked and fortified', would they then have been natural or artificial?.[753]

Evidently, neither Lord Stowell nor Johnson was considering the impact of climate change, but their words have a new resonance reflecting on these challenges today, as States rely on human modification to protect their land. The example that Johnson describes may also impact territorial boundaries and therefore airspace

750. 'Regional patterns of sea-level rise have been observed from satellites since 1993 and are associated with increased coastal impacts in many regions. It is unknown whether such patterns will be transient, arising from natural climate variations, or persistent, driven by external climate forcing. Here, using climate model ensembles, we demonstrate that forced changes are likely to have contributed significantly to observed altimeter-era patterns of rise and that these patterns may persist for decades to come, with increased intensity as climate change progresses' (John T Fasullo and R Steven Neren, 'Altimeter-Era Emergence of the Patterns of Forced Sea-Level Rise in Climate Models and Implications for the Future' (2018) 115(51), Proc Natl Acad Sci USA 12944, 12944).
751. Dorst, Oude Elferink and Ligteringen (n 500).
752. *Ibid.*
753. Johnson (n 502) 212; in part quoting, *The Anna* (1805) 5 C.Rob. 373.

division when it occurs on a State's coastline, in an area within its sovereignty. This is discussed below in Section 3.5.2.

Second, if a natural island becomes submerged due to rising sea levels or erosion, does the State also lose the maritime zones that the island generated? At its most extreme, this may be applied to the case of an entire island State becoming submerged, in which case that State would either lose its territorial sea and other maritime zones or, which is not envisaged by UNCLOS, retain its maritime zones despite them being generated by a land mass that no longer exists. This matter does not directly involve maritime constructions, but closely related is the question of whether artificial islands can amount to a 'defined territory' for the purpose of statehood in these circumstances, the answer to which is unclear.[754] For example, the Maldives has built an artificial island, Hulhumalé, next to its capital, Malé, for the purpose of relocating its population.[755] In instances such as this, the question of whether an artificial island can constitute territory is relevant in order to determine whether a submerged State is able to relocate to an artificial island and maintain its statehood.[756] Hulhumalé was constructed in the territorial sea of the Maldives, so it is clearly under the sovereignty of the Maldives and thus its construction has no implications for overflight rights. However, if artificial islands constructed in territorial seas could be considered territory – presumably without maritime zones, in accordance with UNCLOS, but this too stands to be debated[757] – and this recognition then became practice in the high seas, it would significantly impact overflight rights. Having said this, it is difficult to see how sovereignty over artificial islands could be extended to those in the high seas given that no State may claim sovereignty over the high seas.[758] Once again, this has a direct impact on freedom of overflight as, if a State has the right to declare sovereignty over an artificial island beyond its territorial sea, the airspace over it will correspondingly be considered national airspace.

Without intervention, submerged features have in the past resulted in the loss of rights associated with the land mass that had comprised the feature and the maritime zones it generated. For example:

> [I]n the course of negotiation of the maritime boundary between Belgium and the United Kingdom, the United Kingdom was forced to abandon one of its key basepoints, a drying bank called the Shipwash, when a new hydrographic survey revealed that the feature had eroded to the extent that it no longer dried and could no longer be regarded as a low-tide elevation.[759]

These issues as legal issues, and their significant implications in practice, are recognised by the international community. At its 75th Conference of the International

754. *See*, for example, discussion in, Jenny Grote Stoutenburg, *Disappearing Island States in International Law* (Brill Nijhoff 2015) 169-173.
755. Michael Gagain, 'Climate Change, Sea Level Rise, and Artificial Islands: Saving the Maldives' Statehood and Maritime Claims Through the "Constitution of the Oceans"' (2012) 23(1) Colo J Int'l Envtl L & Pol'y 77, 81-82.
756. A defined territory is one of the four necessary elements of a State, as discussed in Section 2.2.1.
757. *See*, for example, discussion in, Grote Stoutenburg (n 754) 173.
758. UNCLOS, Article 89.
759. Schofield and Schofield (n 599) 65.

Law Association (ILA), two resolutions were adopted on the impact of rising sea levels on territorial baselines, reflecting the broad topics on which the need for future work was acknowledged during the conference:

> 6. The implications of the existing law of the normal baseline in situations of territorial loss resulting from sea-level rise;
>
> 7. The recognition that substantial territorial loss resulting from sea-level rise is an issue that extends beyond baselines and the law of the sea, and encompasses consideration at a junction of several parts of international law, including such fundamental aspects as elements of statehood under international law, human rights, refugee law, and access to resources, as well as broader issues of international peace and security.[760]

So far, these issues are rarely considered in terms of their impact on international airspace and overflight, despite each of them resulting in the redrawing of international airspace.

3.5.2 Reclaimed Land and the Effect on the Delimitation of International Airspace

This section will discuss changes to the delimitation of international airspace as a result of the redrawing of territorial baselines after the reclamation of land. While maritime constructions do not generate maritime zones, State practice indicates that coastal land reclamation does generally lead to changes in the delimitation of the territorial sea. This is certainly so in the case of reclaimed land attached to the mainland. As such, this is an example, in contrast to artificial islands, installations and structures, of constructions at sea bringing – albeit indirectly – international airspace under coastal State sovereignty. For reclaimed land not connected to the mainland, it is not generally accepted as being considered for the purpose of redefining the baseline of the territorial sea.

The starting point for discussing the legal basis of land reclamation for the drawing of territorial sea baselines is Articles 11 and 5 UNCLOS, read together.

Article 11 UNCLOS, titled 'Ports', states that:

> For the purpose of delimiting the territorial sea, the outermost permanent harbour works which form an integral part of the harbour system are regarded as forming part of the coast. Off-shore installations and artificial islands shall not be considered as permanent harbour works.

Article 5 UNCLOS, titled 'Normal baseline' reads:

> Except where otherwise provided in this Convention, the normal baseline for measuring the breadth of the territorial sea is the low-water line along the coast as marked on large-scale charts officially recognized by the coastal State.

760. Resolution No. 1/2012 on Baselines under the International Law of the Sea, adopted at the 75th Conference of the International Law Association (Sofia, 26-30 August 2012).

Considering these two together, if construction, including reclaimed land, 'forms an integral part of the harbour system', it will be part of the coast and will therefore, in accordance with Article 5, be able to be used as a point from which to draw the territorial sea baseline.

Article 11 makes clear that the body must be connected to the coast in that 'offshore' constructions are excluded, but beyond this, UNCLOS is silent on the definition of 'harbour works' and of what will 'form an integral part of the harbour system'. The term 'harbour works' has been defined by the International Hydrographic Organization (IHO), a body that surveys and charts the world's oceans. It defines the term as:

> 'permanent manmade structures built along the coast which form an integral part of the harbor system such as ... sea walls, etc.', where 'harbour' is defined as 'a natural or artificially improved body of water providing protection for vessels, and generally anchorage and docking facilities'.[761]

Reclaimed coastal land tends to be within enclosed waters, in which case it has no impact on territorial sea delimitation,[762] and there is relatively little State practice on the use of reclaimed land for the drawing of baselines. There are sufficient instances to conclude though that reclaimed land that does not contribute to harbour works is accepted under customary international law as forming part of the coast and may therefore be used as a base point for measuring the territorial sea baseline.[763] This has been recognised by the ILA:

> existing international law recognizes harbor works ..., *any coast protective work which extends above the chart datum, and any human-induced extension of the natural coast,* as part of the coast for the purpose of Article 5. As such, the normal baseline moves, sometimes seaward, with the resulting changes in coastal configuration (emphasis added).[764]

Huge land reclamation projects have taken place in Singapore since the 1970s, with Changi Airport, Sentosa, Jurong Island and Tuas South, all resting on reclaimed land, but it is not known whether this land is used to measure its territorial sea baseline.[765] The Netherlands relies heavily on reinforcing its coastline, including through many man-made structures. Hoek van Holland, for example, which consists almost entirely of man-made land, extended the coastline by around five and a half miles and has been used to measure the territorial baseline 'with no objection from the international community'.[766]

761. International Hydrographic Organization, *Hydrographic Dictionary*, available at hd.iho.int/en accessed 2 February 2018.
762. Chris Carleton, 'Problems Relating to Non-Natural and Man-Made Basepoints under UNCLOS' in Clive Ralph Symmons (ed), *Selected Contemporary Issues in the Law of the Sea* (Martinus Nijhoff Publishers 2011) 53.
763. Oude Elferink (n 497) 9.
764. International Law Association, 'Baselines under the International Law of the Sea', Final Report (2012) 28.
765. Carleton (n 762) 53.
766. *Ibid.* 52.

Under Article 11 UNCLOS, land that is reclaimed to form part of the coastline but is later detached, intentionally or through erosion, will not continue to be able to be taken into account in determining the territorial sea baseline. This occurred in the UAE with the construction of Palm Jumeirah. At the completion of its construction, it was attached to the coast but was subsequently severed and connected by bridges.[767] A similar situation exists in the Netherlands, where part of the Rotterdam harbour known as the Zandmotor, which is an artificial extension of the coast, was designed with the intention of it becoming separated.[768] Whereas the Zandmotor is considered coastline for the purposes of the territorial sea baseline,[769] in accordance with Article 11, it would no longer be able to serve as a baseline point after it separates from the coastline. Some commentators have questioned whether the fact that its breakaway from the coast involves natural erosion might mean that it could continue to be considered as a base point for the territorial sea baseline;[770] however, there is no international practice to support this claim. In any case, it is the nautical charts that provide the definitive judgment on States' territorial sea baselines and so until they are revised to take into account the change in conditions, they will continue to reflect the extended baselines. In the case of the Zandmotor, although the territorial baseline was extended as a result of it, the continental shelf and the EEZ boundaries remained unchanged as they have been settled by the Netherlands and its neighbouring sea States through treaties.[771]

Although land reclamation is accepted under customary international law as contributing to the measurement of a State's baseline, it is not always uncontroversial when a State does so.[772] As with the issues raised in Section 3.5.1, the ILA also recognised the relevance of this matter at its 75th Conference, listing as one its significant issues: '[t]he implications of the existing law of the normal baseline in situations of territorial gain resulting from human-made structures and the artificial conservation or extension of existing coasts'.[773]

Again, as with the issues raised above in Section 3.5.1, the reclamation of land along coastline is rarely considered from the perspective of international civil aviation law, despite the impact it has on the redrawing of international airspace boundaries.

3.6 CONCLUSION TO CHAPTER

This chapter began by outlining the distinction between artificial islands, on the one hand, and installations and structures, on the other, as the constructed bodies – maritime constructions – that are the subject of Article 60 UNCLOS. It demonstrated that there are some obstacles to definitively classifying them in certain circumstances, notwithstanding the importance of the distinction to the application of Article 60. A

767. Carleton (n 762) 57.
768. Dorst, Oude Elferink and Ligteringen (n 500).
769. *Ibid.*
770. *Ibid.*
771. Including between the Netherlands and Germany (1964 and 1971), the United Kingdom and Northern Ireland (1965) and Belgium (1996) (*Ibid.*).
772. Oude Elferink (n 497) 9.
773. Resolution No. 1/2012 on Baselines (n 760).

coastal State has the exclusive right in its EEZ and on its continental shelf to construct artificial islands and to construct installations and structures for purposes relating to its specific rights and jurisdiction within those maritime areas. In order to ensure both the safety of navigation and of the constructions themselves, the State also has the right to establish a safety zone around the construction. This safety zone may extend to a maximum breadth of 500 metres from the outer edge of the maritime construction and, as confirmed by the Tribunal in the case of the *Arctic Sunrise Case*, the jurisdiction a State may exercise in the zone for the protection of the construction and of navigation in its vicinity, goes beyond the rights and jurisdiction the State has within the EEZ or the continental shelf more broadly. The provisions explicitly provide that the safety zones apply to the sea and restrict navigation, but as to whether they may also be applied in the airspace over the construction, and therefore prohibit overflight, UNCLOS provides no indication.

A legal matter that has, until relatively recently, lacked clarification is that of the legal status of a natural feature combined with a maritime construction. This matter was addressed by the Tribunal in the *South China Sea Arbitration*, in which it was confirmed that, where a construction uses an existing maritime feature as its foundation, the maritime feature retains its legal status as per its original form. This was an important clarification for the law of the sea, and for this book, because it confirmed that the maritime construction over a low-tide elevation, or a rock, cannot change the legal status of that low-tide elevation or rock. For a low-tide elevation, this means that any maritime construction on or around it cannot result in it being a rock or an island and thereby forming the basis for territorial claims, leading to international airspace becoming national airspace. The Tribunal also confirmed that no State may appropriate a low-tide elevation outside its territorial waters, and thus, once again, the question of sovereignty over a maritime construction built atop such feature or over the airspace above it is not relevant. Finally, in relation to maritime constructions over natural features, the chapter explained that, as a result of the foundations of maritime constructions retaining the legal status of their original form, the dual nature of these natural features/maritime constructions may result in a situation that appears to conflict with Article 60(8) UNCLOS, particularly that maritime constructions do not possess a territorial sea or affect the delimitation of the territorial sea, both situations with implications for the delimitation of national and international airspace.

Having established when a maritime construction necessarily falls outside the sovereignty of a coastal State, this chapter then turned to examine whether a coastal State has the right to extend the safety zone of such maritime construction to the airspace above it, thereby providing the State with the right to prohibit the overflight of other States' aircraft above the construction. International law indicates that safety zones are restricted to the surface of the sea. This is supported by a number of factors including the ordinary meaning of Article 60(4) and (5); the drafting history of the 1958 Convention on the Continental Shelf and the fact that no significant amendments were made to the articles as adopted in UNCLOS; the subsequent interpretation of the articles by ICAO and subsequent materials published by the IMO; and State practice.

The principle of freedom of overflight also supports the argument that safety zones are limited to the sea itself. The coastal State does have the option, however, of establishing danger areas in the airspace, as does any other State in international airspace. A State using international airspace to the exclusion of other States does not necessarily violate freedom of overflight, just as a State using the ocean – e.g., through a maritime construction – is not violating freedom of navigation. Considering other acceptable uses of international airspace though, there are specific limitations on the way in which a State's activities is able to legitimately restrict the overflight of other States' aircraft whenever necessary and proportionate. The danger area over the maritime construction would need to be temporary, rather than a permanent measure, and it would not provide the State establishing it with the right to prohibit the aircraft of other States.

In the absence of an explicit right under UNCLOS to extend safety zones to the airspace over maritime constructions, the right to do so may still crystallise into customary international law, although there is insufficient State practice to suggest the emergence of any such customary law. If the right were to emerge as customary international law, its conflict with freedom of overflight would not necessarily stand as an obstacle to this, as discussed.

It is proposed here that the solution to meeting the safety risks presented both by maritime constructions to aircraft and by aircraft to maritime constructions, just as with any other safety risk regarding overflight, should be managed by the ATS provider responsible for the FIR within which the maritime construction is located. This management would involve coordination of the traffic and perhaps a reasonable restriction of altitude to avoid collision with the maritime construction, but nothing beyond this. This conclusion is also consistent with the management of air traffic to and from a maritime construction, where that forms part of the activities on the construction. While a State does not have jurisdiction over international airspace above its maritime construction, in the case of aviation operations to and from a maritime construction, Article 60(1) and (2) UNCLOS makes it clear that the coastal State has jurisdiction over those operations insofar as matters such as licensing, insurance, liability, safety regulations and traffic rules are concerned. In the case of a maritime construction built for the purpose of an airport for international civil aviation, the exclusive use of international airspace over the maritime construction would need to be negotiated with other States and, considering the principle of freedom of overflight, it is difficult to see how this will be accepted as a permanent measure.

Finally, this chapter briefly raised some ancillary matters regarding maritime constructions with implications for overflight in international airspace. The purpose of this section was not to attempt to find solutions but to raise the issues as ones of significance that require attention going forward, particularly given their link to climate change which is affecting island States, and indeed coastal areas in general, to an increasing extent worldwide.

CHAPTER 4

Flight Information Regions and Air Defence Identification Zones

4.1 INTRODUCTION

This chapter addresses two areas in international airspace that do not arise from the law of the sea. The first, FIRs, have their basis in international civil aviation law, while the second, ADIZs, have no foundation in international law but are imposed by a number of States, with various requirements and corresponding legal justifications.[774]

FIRs are established for the purpose of the provision of ATS, which is solely a technical and operational function. They are generally not controversial but where a State's FIR encompasses a neighbouring State's territory, there can be practical challenges and disputes involving the exercise of the ATS responsibility.[775] This chapter examines an aspect of one of these scenarios, specifically the ban imposed by the Gulf States on Qatar in mid-2017. Although this case involved both national and international airspace, it is the prohibition as it applied to Qatari-registered aircraft in international airspace within these States' FIRs, as applied early on and for a short period of time, that will form the foundation for the analysis in this chapter. On the basis of freedom of overflight, the ban as it applied to international airspace was a violation of international law, as to which *see* the discussion on what the concept of freedom of overflight entails in Sections 2.7.1 and 2.7.3.2. This chapter instead will step aside from freedom of overflight to examine whether there is also a prohibition independently under international civil aviation law. From this perspective, the first part of the chapter will examine whether a State is prohibited under international civil aviation law from discriminating against a foreign aircraft in international airspace within the first State's FIR based on the State of registration, i.e., the nationality, of the

774. The States and basic requirements are set out in Section 4.3.2 and the legal bases relied on in Section 4.3.3.

775. *See*, for instance, those addressed in Section 4.2.1.2.

aircraft. The principle of non-discrimination does not apply expressly to the provision of ATS in international airspace under international civil aviation law, and so this examination will involve determining whether an implicit prohibition exists.

In contrast to FIRs, there is no clear legal basis for the establishment of ADIZs in international airspace, and the legality of these unilaterally declared zones will be the focus of the book in the second part of this chapter. ADIZs have received significant attention in the media and in academia, both examining their origin and their possible legal basis in international law. This chapter will consider the main arguments used to justify them, before turning to examine whether the zones are, on the contrary, prohibited under international law. Certain features of ADIZ, such as military authorities having the right to issue instructions in addition to ATS authorities, arguably pose safety risks to international civil aviation. This chapter will explore whether ADIZs are in breach of international civil aviation law on this basis,[776] before finally turning to the matter of whether ADIZs are consistent with the principle of freedom of overflight.

Section 4.2 will address the basis of FIRs in international law and ultimately the scope of a coastal State's responsibility within the region. This section will first set out the legal framework for the establishment of an FIR over international airspace and the allocation of responsibility for ATS provision within it (Section 4.2.1.1). Closely linked to this, Section 4.2.1.2 will make clear that the responsibility for an FIR does not confer sovereignty, notwithstanding the association States continue to make between the two. The chapter will then discuss the prohibition on Qatari-registered flights as an example of States discriminating against aircraft in international airspace within their FIRs based on the State of registration of the aircraft. These sections will outline the facts of the case, its relevance to this book and Qatar's arguments for the discrimination amounting to a violation of international law (Sections 4.2.2.1-4.2.2.3). At this point, the chapter will turn to the central research question regarding FIRs: does the principle of non-discrimination apply under international civil aviation law to prohibit a State from discriminating against a foreign aircraft in international airspace within the first State's FIR based on the State of registration of the aircraft? This section sets aside the law of the sea to first set out the narrow scope of the authority of coastal States within their FIRs over international airspace, as prescribed by Annex 11 (Section 4.2.3). The chapter will then turn to consider the context of Annex 11 within the Chicago Convention more broadly, under Section 4.2.4, to examine whether it is possible to argue that there is an implicit application of the principle of non-discrimination in the provision of ATS over international airspace. This section will consider the integral role that the principle of non-discrimination plays in international civil aviation law (Section 4.2.4.1), including the relationship of the principle with State sovereignty (Section 4.2.4.2) and its purpose in national airspace (Section 4.2.4.3). It will then turn to consider whether, based on the foregoing sections, it is possible to interpret an overarching implied principle of non-discrimination applying to navigation in international airspace (Section 4.2.4.4) and the implications of the principle of

776. As will be discussed in Section 4.3.6.1.

non-discrimination in the broader Chicago Convention framework on the interpretation of Annex 11 (Section 4.2.4.5).

Section 4.3 will examine the legality of ADIZ under international law. It will begin by discussing the most recent significant developments regarding ADIZ, illustrating the relevance of the topic as well as the discrepancies in the regulations that apply to the zones (Section 4.3.1). Section 4.3.2 will outline the origins and definition of ADIZ before revisiting the main legal bases used to justify them, examining whether these bases are legitimate. The justifications that will be addressed in these sections (Sections 4.3.3.1-4.3.3.4) are a State's laws and regulations relating to admission to territory, restricting military activities in the EEZ, the right to self-defence, and customary international law. Section 4.3.4 will address the *Lotus Case*, examining the contemporary approach towards the *Lotus* principle and thereby considering whether the determination of extraterritorial prescriptive jurisdiction involves demonstrating a legal basis for the exercise of the jurisdiction or merely the absence of a prohibition. In either case, the PCIJ made clear in *Lotus* that a State is not permitted to enforce its laws outside its territory. This will be addressed in Section 4.3.5, which will demonstrate that the actions a coastal State may take against an aircraft in international airspace are the same regardless of whether or not the State has established an ADIZ over that airspace. Finally, the chapter will examine whether in establishing and maintaining ADIZs coastal States are violating their obligations under international law, considering both the safety obligations of States under international civil aviation law (Section 4.3.6.1) and the right to freedom of overflight (Section 4.3.6.2).

4.2 FLIGHT INFORMATION REGIONS

4.2.1 Legal Framework Governing the Provision of ATS in International Airspace

4.2.1.1 Definition of and General Responsibility for FIRs[777]

The world's airspace is divided into FIRs for the purpose of the provision of ATS.[778] Over territory, FIRs generally follow territorial borders. International airspace, on the other hand, is divided and allocated to coastal States on the basis of those coastal States having accepted responsibility for the regions (*see* Figure 4.1).[779] Annex 11, Standard 2.1.2 outlines this arrangement:

777. The information in this section builds on that in Section 2.7.2.2.1, particularly Section 2.7.2.2.1.3, addressing the application of Annex 11 to international airspace.
778. Both 'FIR' and 'ATS' are defined below.
779. This is with the exception of one FIR that has not yet been allocated to a State. The FIR sits off the west coast of central America, and a number of States – Chile, Ecuador, France Peru and the US – have put forward their interest in it before ICAO, which is in the process of hosting discussions to allocate it (ICAO Summary of Discussions, *First Unassigned High Seas Airspace*, Special Coordination Meeting, Lima (24 July 2019)).

> Those portions of the airspace over the high seas or in airspace of undetermined sovereignty where air traffic services will be provided shall be determined on the basis of regional air navigation agreements. A contracting State having accepted the responsibility to provide air traffic services in such portions of airspace shall thereafter arrange for the services to be established and provided in accordance with the provisions of this Annex.

An FIR is defined by ICAO in Annexes 2 and 11 to the Chicago Convention as 'an airspace of defined dimensions within which flight information service and alerting service are provided'.[780] While the definition of FIR refers to 'flight information service' and 'alerting service', Standard 2.1.2 noticeably instead refers to ATS, also the title of Annex 11, where ATS consists of[781] not only flight information service[782] and alerting service[783] but also air traffic advisory service,[784] and ATC.[785] The definition of FIR does not refer to ATS as a whole because ATC is not or cannot be provided in all airspace, i.e., in uncontrolled airspace.

The regional air navigation agreements, or plans (RANPs), referred to in Standard 2.1.2 are further defined in the Annex as 'the agreements approved by the Council of ICAO normally on the advice of Regional Air Navigation Meetings'.[786] Thus, States agree at a regional level[787] on the responsibilities for the provision of air navigation services in international airspace, as published in the RANPs, which are finally approved by ICAO.

780. Chicago Convention, Annex 2 (10th edn, July 2005), 1-5; Annex 11 (15th edn, July 2018) 1-8.
781. In accordance with the Chicago Convention, Annex 11, 1-3.
782. Flight information service is 'a service provided for the purpose of giving advice and information useful for the safe and efficient conduct of flights' (Annex 11, 1-8) and includes information on, for example, 'meteorological conditions, volcanic activity, the release into the atmosphere of radioactive materials or toxic chemicals, and changes in the serviceability of navigation aids' (Francis Schubert, 'Air Navigation' in Paul Stephen Dempsey and Ram S Jakhu (eds), *Routledge Handbook of Public Aviation Law* (Routledge 2017) 92).
783. Alerting service is 'a service provided to notify appropriate organizations regarding aircraft in need of search and rescue aid, and assist such organizations as required' (Annex 11, 1-4).
784. Air traffic advisory service is 'a service provided within advisory airspace to ensure separation, in so far as practicable, between aircraft which are operating on IFR flight plans' (Annex 11, 1-3). This service is typically employed as a temporary measure in a portion of airspace where the flight information service is not sufficient but where the responsible State does not have the means to provide ATC in the portion of airspace (ICAO Doc 4444, *ICAO Procedures for Air Navigation Services on Air Traffic Management* (16th edn, 2016) 9.1.4.1.2).
785. ATC service is 'a service provided for the purpose of preventing collisions between aircraft … and expediting and maintaining an orderly flow of air traffic' (Chicago Convention, Annex 11, 1-3).
786. Chicago Convention, Annex 11, 2.1.2 *Note 1*.
787. There are nine ICAO Air Navigation Regions: the Asia (ASIA) and Pacific (PAC) region, the Middle East (MID) region, the African-Indian Ocean (AFI) region, North American (NAM) and Caribbean (CAR) region, the South American (SAM) region, the European (EUR) and North Atlantic (NAT) region (ICAO, 'Global Air Navigation Strategy', available at www4.icao.int/ganpportal/GanpDocument#/?_k=d978it accessed 4 August 2019).

Figure 4.1 Map of the World's Airspace Divided into Its FIRs[788]

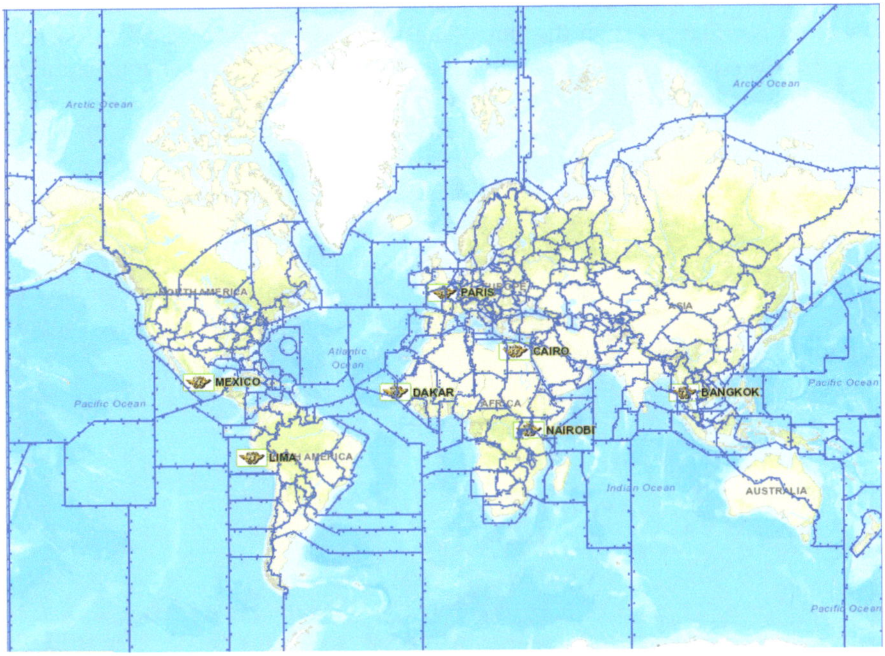

The ATS provider in an FIR also plays a role in search and rescue. It is responsible for collecting and distributing information about aviation emergencies, as well as coordinating search and rescue aircraft.[789] These are the functions that fall within the 'alerting service' responsibilities of an ATS provider. The ATS provider feeds into the search and rescue function through the provision of alerting services but search and rescue does not further fall within the scope of the activities of an ATS provider.

For the purpose of search and rescue services at sea, international airspace – together with national airspace over maritime areas – is divided into aeronautical search and rescue regions (SRRs) pursuant to international civil aviation law.[790] Like FIRs, the provision of aeronautical SRRs[791] in international airspace is determined on

788. *Source*: Created using ICAO GIS, available at gis.icao.int/ accessed 14 July 2019.
789. Chicago Convention, Annex 11 (15th edn, July 2018) 2.2 e).
790. Annex 12 establishes the SARPs applying specifically to aeronautical search and rescue; however, other annexes also contain provisions contributing to search and rescue operations. These include Annex 11, which sets out the responsibility of ATS in the context of search and rescue operations, as well as Annex 10 (Vol. III, 2nd edn, July 2007), which provides technical standards for communication systems in search and rescue operations, and Annex 15, which details the search and rescue arrangements that are required for the purpose of aeronautical information services.
791. SRR is defined as 'an area of defined dimensions, associated with a rescue coordination centre, within which search and rescue services are provided', where 'search and rescue service' is defined as 'the performance of distress monitoring, communication, coordination and search and rescue functions, initial medical assistance or medical evacuation, through the use of

the basis of the RANPs.[792] Also like FIRs, the boundaries of SRRs should be determined solely on the basis of technical and operational considerations[793] and States are directed to ensure that, 'in so far as practicable', SRR boundaries align with FIR boundaries (*see* Figure 4.2 for the global division of airspace for each).[794] Considering the role of the ATS provider in search and rescue operations, the general alignment of the two regions is operationally beneficial.[795]

Maritime SRRs, governed by the Search and Rescue Convention of 1979 (Search and Rescue Convention),[796] partition the sea itself for the purpose of carrying out search and rescue operations, where the sea and air regions are closely coordinated.[797] Maritime SRRs are not aligned with either FIR or aeronautical SRRs, but many are similar to the latter (compare Figure 4.3 in relation to the north of the Pacific Ocean). As with FIRs and aeronautical SRRs, it is desirable to align aeronautical and maritime SRRs as much as possible, at the most basic level to ensure that the responsible authority is easily identifiable in the case of an emergency.[798]

public and private resources, including cooperating aircraft, vessels and other craft and installations' (Chicago Convention, Annex 12 (8th edn, July 2004) 1-2).

792. Chicago Convention, Annex 12, 2.1.1.1.
793. *Ibid.* Annex 12, 2.2.1 *Note 2.*
794. *Ibid.* 2.2.1.1 *Recommendation.*
795. International Aeronautical and Maritime Search and Rescue (IAMSAR) Manual, Volume I: Organization and Management (2016) 2.3.15 (b) ('IAMSAR Manual – Volume 1').
796. International Convention on Maritime Search and Rescue (Hamburg, 27 April 1979) 1405 U.N.T.S. 118, *entered into force* 22 June 1985 ('Search and Rescue Convention').
797. The IAMSAR Manual provides guidelines to achieve a common search and rescue approach. Article 98(2) UNCLOS includes a general statement on the role of all coastal States in search and rescue: 'Every coastal State shall promote the establishment, operation and maintenance of an adequate and effective search and rescue service regarding safety on or over the sea and, where circumstances so require, by way of mutual regional arrangements cooperate with neighbouring States for this purpose.'
798. IAMSAR Manual – Volume I, 2.3.15 (d).

Figure 4.2 FIRs (Blue) and Aeronautical SRRs (Other Colours)[799]

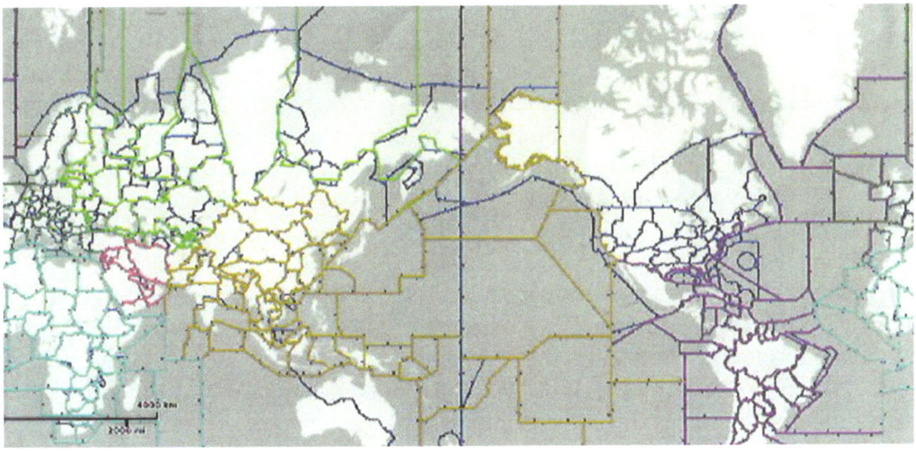

Figure 4.3 Maritime Search and Rescue Regions in the Pacific Ocean[800]

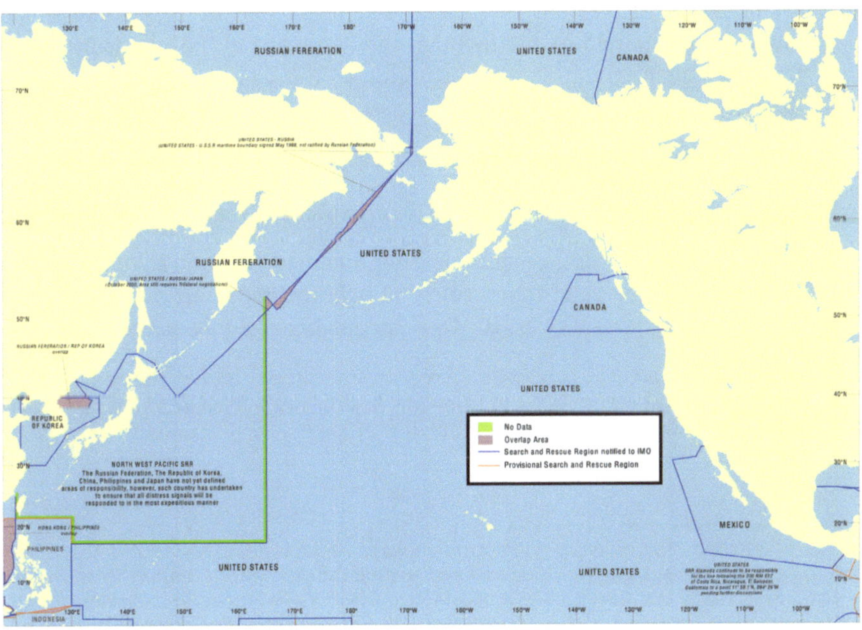

799. *Source*: Created using ICAO GIS, available at gis.icao.int/ accessed 2 July 2019.
800. *Source*: Compiled from individual maps obtained from US Coast Guard, 'IMO Maritime SAR Regions', available at www.dco.uscg.mil/Portals/9/CG-5R/nsarc/IMO%20Maritime%20SAR%20Regions.pdf accessed 25 October 2019.

4.2.1.2 *FIR Allocation Does Not Confer Sovereignty over Airspace*

The general alignment of FIR and State territory borders reflects the overarching principle in international civil aviation law of sovereignty over airspace. As acknowledged in Section 2.2.2.3, national security was a paramount concern in the drafting of the Chicago Convention. This is illustrated in the Preamble to the Convention: 'the future development of international civil aviation can greatly help to create and preserve friendship and understanding ... yet its abuse can become a threat to the general security' and, 'it is desirable to avoid friction and to promote that cooperation between nations and peoples upon which the peace of the world depends'. With sovereignty as the cornerstone of international civil aviation, it is not surprising that the delineation of FIR boundaries in the years following the conclusion of the Chicago Convention followed national borders.[801]

However, FIRs do not give rise to sovereignty and nor are they intended to be aligned geographically with sovereign airspace.

As to the former, for national airspace, Article 1 of the Chicago Convention recognises that a State has sovereignty over its territory, as defined in Article 2. No additional grounds for sovereignty over airspace are provided in the Chicago Convention or further under international law. The only airspace over which a State has sovereignty in its FIR therefore is that which also forms part of its national airspace. This conclusion is supported by the fact that the definition of 'FIR' indicates that the regions are established strictly for the provision of ATS. For international airspace, beyond the narrow purpose for which FIRs are established, ICAO has emphasised that:

> [t]he approval by the Council of regional air navigation agreements relating to the provision by a State of air traffic services within airspace over the high seas does not imply recognition of sovereignty of that State over the airspace concerned.[802]

Regarding the latter point, geographical alignment of FIRs and sovereign borders, FIR boundaries should be determined solely to achieve the safest and most efficient provision of air navigation services. ICAO is unequivocal on this matter:

> The limits of ATS airspaces, whether over States' territories or over the high seas, shall be established on the basis of technical and operational considerations with the aim of ensuring safety and optimizing efficiency and economy for both providers and users of the services.[803]

801. Francis Schubert, 'Limits in the Sky: Sovereignty and Air Navigation Services' in Pablo Mendes de Leon and Niall Buissing (eds), *Behind and Beyond the Chicago Convention: The Evolution of Aerial Sovereignty* (Wolters Kluwer 2019) 148; Niels van Antwerpen, *Cross-Border Provision of Air Navigation Services with Specific Reference to Europe: Safeguarding Transparent Lines of Responsibility and Liability* (Kluwer Law International 2008) 151.
802. ICAO Assembly Resolution A38-12, Consolidation Statement of Continuing ICAO Policies and Associated Practices Related Specifically to Air Navigation (4 October 2013), Appendix G, 7.
803. *Ibid.* Appendix G, 1. Consider also, Chicago Convention, Annex 11, 2.11.1 *Recommendation*: 'The delineation of airspace, wherein air traffic services are to be provided, should be related to the nature of the route structure and the need for efficient service rather than to national boundaries'; ICAO Assembly Resolution A38-12 (n 802): 'Member States should seek the most

Despite this, States continue to pursue the alignment of their FIRs with their territorial borders and in some instances, the pursuit has become more pronounced.

Nationalist sentiment has resulted in an increased interest in aligning FIR and territorial boundaries in Indonesia, where the national airspace is partially encompassed by Singapore's FIR (*see* Figure 4.4).[804] The leaders of each State are in the process of negotiating a revised framework for the FIR boundaries. A media report following discussions between Prime Minister Lee Hsien Loong and Indonesian President Joko Widodo in October 2019 declared that:

> Indonesia wants Singapore to respect 'Indonesia's sovereignty over its territory, including its territorial waters, archipelagic waters and its airspace' and 'to understand Indonesia's strong desire to align the FIR in a timely manner which corresponds to its territorial sovereignty'.[805]

efficient and economic delineation of ATS airspaces, the optimum location of points for transfer of responsibility and the most efficient coordination procedures in cooperation with the other States concerned and with ICAO' (Appendix G, Associated Practices – 1); 'Established ATS airspaces should not be segmented for reasons other than technical, operational, safety and efficiency considerations' (Appendix G, 2).

804. Ida Bagus Rahmadi Supancana, 'Realignment of FIR from Singapore to Indonesia' in Pablo Mendes de Leon and Niall Buissing (eds), *Behind and Beyond the Chicago Convention: The Evolution of Aerial Sovereignty* (Wolters Kluwer 2019) 171: '[i]t is clear that the realignment of the FIR is not only a purely technical and operational measure designed to promote the safety of international civil aviation but also it affects Indonesian sovereignty and even dignity'; Chappy Hakim, 'A Strange Anomaly in Management of Airspace' (The Straits Times, 21 March 2016), available at www.straitstimes.com/opinion/a-strange-anomaly-in-management-of-airspace accessed 13 May 2019: 'This is a problem of dignity! The problem of national awareness, the awareness of the dignified attitude of a nation! The pride that I Am An Indonesian!'; Chappy Hakim, *FIR di Kepulauan Riau Wilayah Udara Kedaulatan NKRI* (Penerbit Buku Kompas 2019) 43-45.

805. 'Leaders' Retreat: Singapore and Indonesia Agree on Framework to Discuss Airspace Management, Military Training' (The Straits Times, 8 October 2019), available at www.straitstimes.com/politics/leaders-retreat-singapore-and-indonesia-agree-on-framework-to-discuss-airspace-management accessed 28 December 2019, citing The Jakarta Post.

Figure 4.4 Singapore's FIR, Spanning Part of Indonesian Territory in the South West[806]

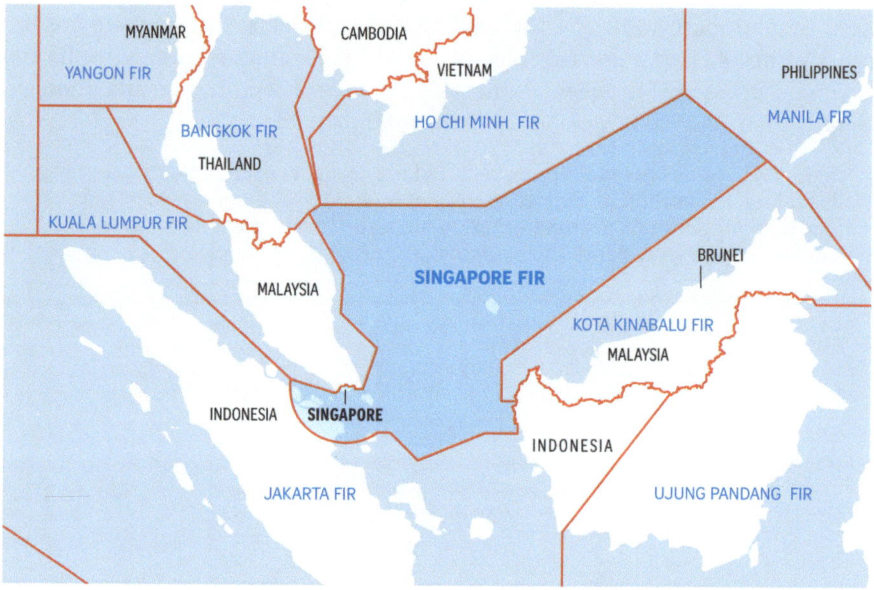

At the same time, Indonesia's FIR covers East Timor's territory, as well as Australia's over Christmas Island.[807]

There are also practical reasons for the recent shift in focus towards an alignment of FIR and territorial boundaries. As Boyd explains:

> it is anticipated that a need for precise geofencing for drone operations may increase the desire to align an FIR 'perfectly' with national borders.[808]

For instance, he points out that, in reference to Figure 4.5, 'a drone programmed to operate within the NIAMY [sic] FIR [Burkina Faso] will be in and out of Burkina Faso and Côte d'Ivoire numerous times as it moves along the south western FIR boundary'.[809]

806. *Source*: Karamjit Kaur, 'Aviation's Shifting Centre of Gravity' (The Straits Times, 4 June 2016), available at www.straitstimes.com/singapore/aviations-shifting-centre-of-gravity accessed 16 March 2020, originally sourced from the Civil Aviation Authority of Singapore (CAAS).
807. Hakim (n 804).
808. Correspondence from Mike Boyd (Technical Officer, ICAO) to the author, dated 3 December 2019.
809. Correspondence from Mike Boyd (Technical Officer, ICAO) to the author, dated 3 December 2019.

Figure 4.5 Map Showing the Discordant Territorial and FIR Borders Between Burkina Faso and Côte d'Ivoire (And Between Burkina Faso and Mali)[810]

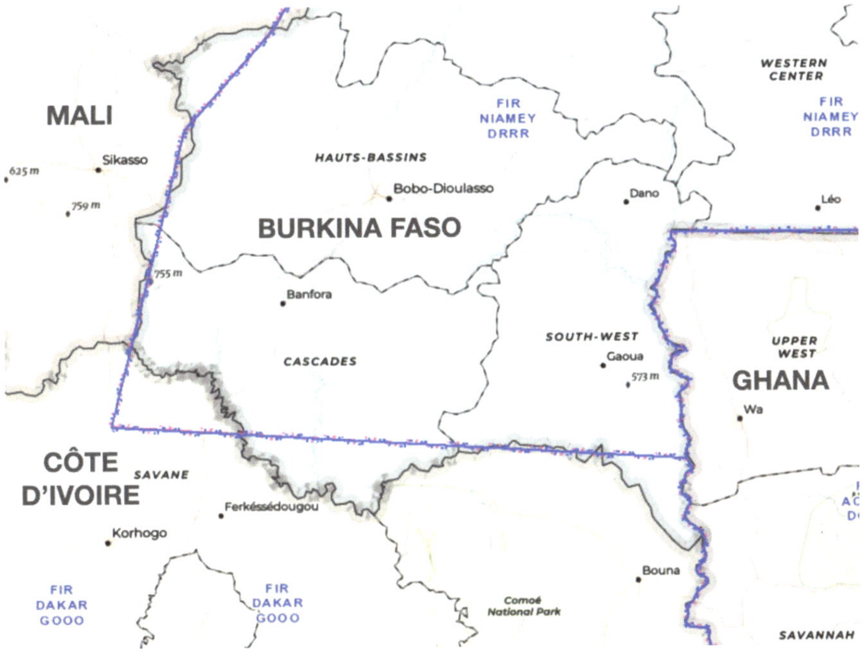

The above situations demonstrate that, despite ICAO materials reiterating otherwise, States continue to associate FIRs with national airspace, whether as a matter of perceived national pride as in the case of Indonesia or because of practical implications arising from their interaction, as in the case of Burkina Faso and Côte d'Ivoire.

Regardless of the association, there is no support in international law for any claim to sovereignty arising from a State's administration of an FIR, whether over national or international airspace.

4.2.1.3 *Jurisdiction in FIRs*

While a State administering an FIR that encompasses international airspace does not have sovereignty over that airspace, it does have jurisdiction in the airspace to the extent necessary to carry out the services it is responsible for. This is functional jurisdiction: jurisdiction in a defined geographical area that is for the sole purpose of carrying out a particular right or obligation. Csabafi, addressing the concept of functional jurisdiction in the context of activities in outer space, highlights that 'claims to this kind of jurisdiction must be founded on the requirements of and contained by

810. Created using ICAO GIS, available at gis.icao.int/ accessed 11 September 2021.

the inherent nature of a specific activity', and he furthermore emphasises the essential element of a 'close link' between the defined geographical space and the activity.[811]

Recalling Section 2.7.2.2.1.3, a State that accepts to provide ATS 'over the high seas or in areas of undetermined sovereignty' may apply the SARPs in Annex 11 'in a manner consistent with that adopted for airspace *under its jurisdiction*',[812] that is, subject to differences to the relevant SARPs having been filed by the State responsible for the provision of services in the FIR. The use of the term 'jurisdiction' considers the situation of delegation: national airspace of another State in which the provision of air navigation services has been delegated to another State comes under the jurisdiction of the latter State to the extent necessary for the provision of those services. The Foreword to Annex 11 also uses this terminology, stating that the SARPs in Annex 11 'apply in those parts of the *airspace under the jurisdiction* of a contracting State wherein air traffic services are provided' (emphasis added).

The wording in Annex 11 is ambiguous though. By providing that a State is permitted to deliver ATS over the high seas in a manner consistent with that in airspace under its jurisdiction suggests that high seas airspace is not under the providing State's jurisdiction. Furthermore, the section of the Foreword referred to above continues, '... *and also* wherever a State accepts the responsibility ... over the high seas' (emphasis added),[813] suggesting the same.

Interestingly, the US Federal Aviation Administration (FAA) has rephrased the statement in the Foreword to Annex 11 in its Federal Register to assume that the coastal State responsible for an FIR exercises jurisdiction in that airspace:

> [t]he SARPs in Annex 11, apply to airspace under the jurisdiction of a Contracting State that has accepted the responsibility of providing air traffic services over the high seas (oceanic airspace), or in airspace of undetermined sovereignty.[814]

In this respect, an analogy can be drawn between the provision of air navigation services in FIRs and the provision of search and rescue services at sea. Article 2(1) of the Search and Rescue Convention sets out that the treaty does not prejudice the development of the law of the sea or of coastal or flag State jurisdiction. Furthermore, like the boundaries of FIRs, those of SRRs have no impact on national borders, but are purely designated as areas 'of defined dimensions in which search and rescue services are provided'.[815] Trevisanut describes the relationship between these areas and the jurisdiction of the States providing the services as follows:

> SAR regions [SRRs] are non-jurisdictional areas, that is to say in those regions states have obligations but not rights. States are thus deemed to be responsible for

811. Imre Anthony Csabafi, *The Concept of State Jurisdiction in International Space Law: A Study in the Progressive Development of Space Law in the United Nations* (Martinus Nijhoff 1971) 131.
812. Chicago Convention, Annex 11, (ix) and 2.1.2 *Note 2*.
813. *Ibid.* (ix).
814. US Federal Register, Department of Transportation – FAA, 'Designation of Oceanic Airspace: Notice of Provision of Air Traffic Services in Oceanic Airspace' (Volume 80-No. 126, 1 July 2015) 37711.
815. Search and Rescue Convention, Annex 12, 2.1.7 and 1.3.1, respectively.

> the SAR regions and to exercise a limited jurisdiction, which is exclusively functional to the performance of SAR services.[816]

The above passage stands equally true for ATS provision in FIRs: if 'SAR regions' was substituted for 'FIRs' and 'SAR services' for 'ATS', they would hold. The limited jurisdiction referred to here is restricted to prescriptive jurisdiction, and an FIR does not provide the coastal State with any corresponding enforcement jurisdiction. The distinction between these types of jurisdiction will be addressed in Section 4.3.4.

4.2.2 Gulf States' Prohibition of Qatari-Registered Aircraft in Their FIRs

4.2.2.1 Relevant Facts of the Case

On 5 June 2017, a number of Gulf States - Bahrain, Egypt, Saudi Arabia and the UAE - issued NOTAMs that imposed a ban on Qatari flights in their airspace, as part of a broader severance of diplomatic relations with Qatar.[817] The ban denied Qatari-registered aircraft entry to the national airspace of the States and to international airspace within those States' FIRs. The States also imposed restrictions on non-Qatari-registered aircraft using their airspace when operating to and from Qatar.[818]

To the extent that the ban applied to Qatari-registered aircraft, Qatar brought the matter before the ICAO Council, invoking the dispute settlement mechanism in Article 84 of the Chicago Convention. In its application, Qatar submitted that the prohibition was imposed when the States:

> announced, with immediate effect and without any previous negotiation or warning, that Qatari registered aircraft are not permitted to fly to or from the airports within their territories and would be banned not only from their respective national air spaces, but also from their Flight Information Regions (FIRs) extending beyond their national airspace even over the high seas.[819]

Figure 4.6 and Figure 4.7 depict the peninsula of Qatar and its surroundings. Figure 4.6 shows, in blue, the boundaries of the FIRs administered by Saudi Arabia, Bahrain, the UAE and Iran, as well as the delimitation of national airspace at the outer edge of the territorial sea, in green. As is evident from this image, the territory of Qatar sits wholly within Bahrain's FIR. This heightened the consequences of the ban in that Qatar relies on access to Bahrain's FIR to operate flights in and out of its territory via its coast. In announcing its restrictions, Bahrain maintained two entry and exit points

816. Seline Trevisanut, 'Is There a Right to Be Rescued at Sea? A Constructive View' (2014) 4 QIL 3, 12.
817. Memorial Presented by the State of Qatar to the Application (a) of the State of Qatar – Disagreement on the Interpretation and Application of the Convention on International Civil Aviation (Chicago 1944) and of its Annexes (30 October 2017), c).
818. *Ibid.*
819. Application (A) of the State of Qatar – Disagreement on the Interpretation and Application of the Convention on International Civil Aviation (Chicago 1944) and of its Annexes, Submitted on behalf of the State of Qatar by its Agent, Essa Abdulla Almalki, Qatar Civil Aviation Authority Permanent Representative to ICAO (30 October 2017).

through its FIR to Qatar's airspace (Figure 4.8),[820] in contrast to the thirteen that were in operation prior to the ban (Figure 4.9).

Figure 4.6 Delimitation of FIRs and Territorial Seas in the Area[821]

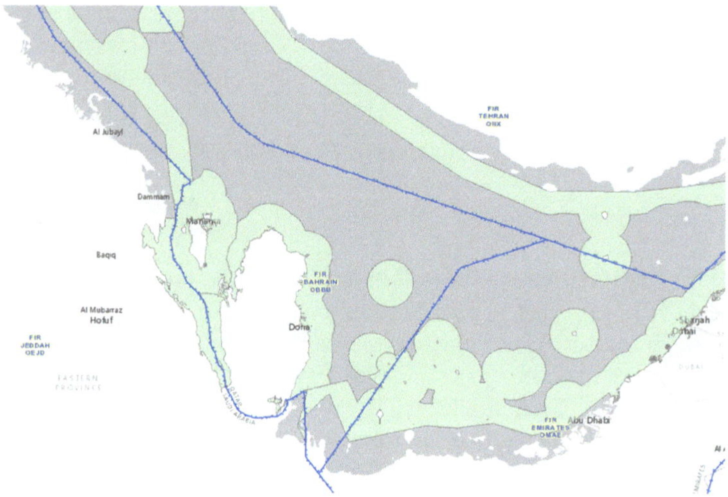

Figure 4.7 FIRs in the Region More Broadly[822]

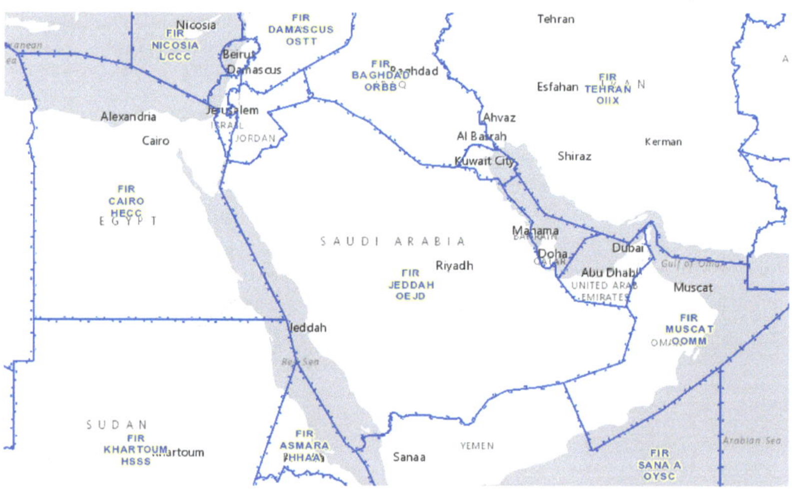

820. Appeal Relating to the Jurisdiction of the ICAO Council under Article 84 of the Convention on Civil Aviation (*Bahrain, Egypt, Saudi Arabia and United Arab Emirates v. Qatar*) I.C.J. Counter-Memorial of the State of Qatar – Vol. I (filed 25 February 2019) 2.9.
821. *Source*: Created using ICAO GIS, available at gis.icao.int/ accessed 14 July 2019.
822. *Source*: Created using ICAO GIS, available at gis.icao.int/ accessed 14 July 2019.

Figure 4.8 Thirteen Routes Available to/from Qatari Airspace Prior to 5 June 2017[823]

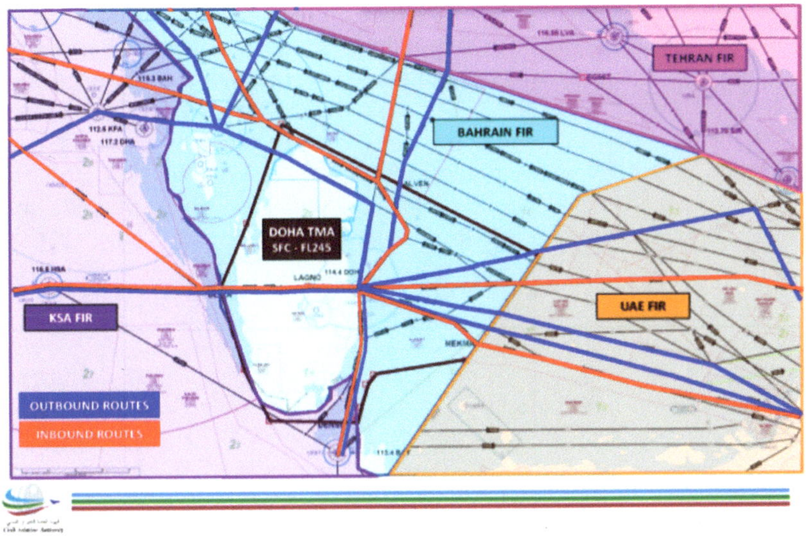

Figure 4.9 Two ATS Routes Available as at 6 June 2017[824]

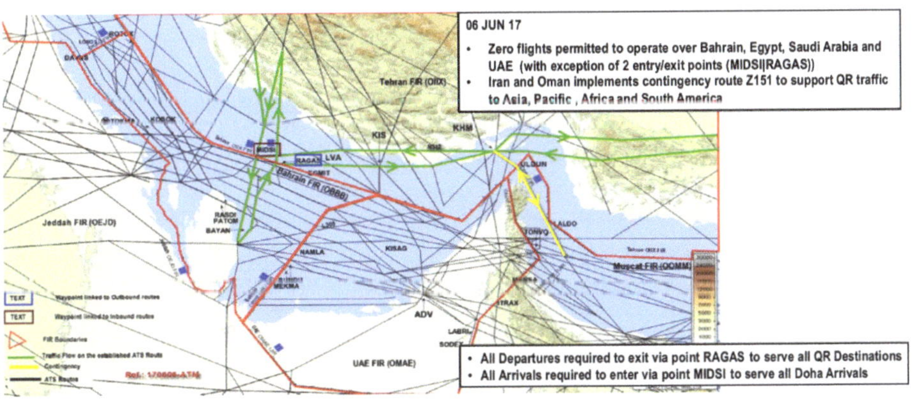

---

823. *Source*: Appeal Relating to the Jurisdiction of the ICAO Council under Article 84 of the Convention on Civil Aviation (*Bahrain, Egypt, Saudi Arabia and United Arab Emirates v. Qatar*) I.C.J. Counter-Memorial of the State of Qatar – Vol. I (filed 25 February 2019) Figure 1. Originally sourced from Qatar Civil Aviation Authority.
824. *Source*: Appeal Relating to the Jurisdiction of the ICAO Council under Article 84 of the Convention on Civil Aviation (*Bahrain, Egypt, Saudi Arabia and United Arab Emirates v. Qatar*) I.C.J. Counter-Memorial of the State of Qatar – Vol. I (filed 25 February 2019) Figure 2. Originally sourced from Qatar Airways.

That Qatar is contained within Bahrain's FIR reflects the fact that both States were protectorates of Britain until their independence in 1971 and that the FIR was established prior to this date, based on where the radars had been installed.[825] The FIR arrangement was maintained following independence for reasons of safety and efficiency, with the alternative requiring multiple ATC handovers/takeovers for aircraft in a short space of time.[826] Since the 2017 blockade, Qatar has requested an amendment to the RANP for the establishment of its own FIR.[827] The amendment process involves addressing any objections to the proposal from affected provider and user States and international organisations,[828] which could be a lengthy process: in the past, amending RANPs has sometimes taken up to thirty years.[829]

4.2.2.2 Relevance of the Case to This Research

This book is concerned only with the prohibition imposed on: (1) Qatari-registered aircraft;[830] and (2) in international airspace, that is, in the States' FIRs in the areas outside their national airspace. The purpose of this book is to examine what, under international civil aviation law, if anything, prevents a State from discriminating against foreign aircraft in international airspace within its FIR based on the State of registration of the aircraft.

There are three preliminary matters to address in order to establish the context in which this matter is being examined.

First, as of early January 2021, the restrictions are no longer in place.[831] Up to this point, Qatari-registered aircraft were forbidden to operate in the national airspace of the four States, but access to international airspace within the FIRs had been reinstated earlier. In fact, this access was reinstated relatively quickly, approximately a week after the first NOTAMs were issued, when, following closed negotiations at the ICAO

825. Alex Macheras, 'Here for the Long Haul: How Qatar Is Overcoming the Aviation Blockade' (The New Arab, 8 January 2018), available at english.alaraby.co.uk/english/comment/2018/1/8/how-qatar-is-overcoming-the-aviation-blockade accessed 12 April 2019.
826. *Ibid.*
827. CAA (Qatar), Request of the State of Qatar for Consideration by the ICAO Council under Article 54(n) of the Chicago Convention: Supplement to our letter reference no. 2017/15995, dated 15 June 2017, 10: '... the State of Qatar urges the ICAO Council to take immediate steps for the establishment of a distinct Qatari Flight Information Region (FIR), encompassing the area over the exclusive economic zone and contiguous with the Tehran FIR'.
828. ICAO Council, Procedure for the Amendment of Regional Air Navigation Plans (18 June 2014) 5.5.
829. Correspondence from Mike Boyd (Technical Officer, ICAO) to the author, dated 3 December 2019, in which he also explains that, in previous situations, a vertical separation of the airspace has provided a workable solution. This model is currently applied between Rwanda and Tanzania where the Kigali FIR extends to 24,500 feet in altitude and then above that the Dar es Salaam FIR covers Rwandan territory.
830. Non-Qatari-registered aircraft operating to and from Qatar were not physically prohibited from operating in the States' airspace but were required to obtain prior approval from the CAAs of the States to overfly their airspace (Counter-Memorial of the State of Qatar (n 820) 2.6-2.10).
831. 'ICAO Welcomes Resolution of Gulf Airspace Restrictions' (ICAO, 7 January 2021), www.icao.int/Newsroom/Pages/ICAO-welcomes-resolution-of-Gulf-airspace-restrictions.aspx accessed 21 January 2021.

Council, Bahrain, Egypt and the UAE issued revised NOTAMs which limited the prohibitions only to their national airspace.[832] As such, this research does not apply to the current scenario but is instead an examination of the situation during that limited period of time. In this way, this research is relevant in the case of discrimination arising in future rather than to this specific case.

Second, as mentioned in Section 4.1, this research begins from the position that a State is not permitted to prohibit the overflight of aircraft registered in a particular State from international airspace within its FIR because doing so is a violation of the customary international law principle of freedom of overflight, as recognised under UNCLOS. Akbar al-Baker, the CEO of Qatar Airways, alluded to this in an interview with Al Jazeera in the days following the sanctions, stating that, 'Bahrain and the UAE have illegally blocked that airspace. The airspace that they have blocked does not belong to them. It belongs to the international community.'[833] The almost immediate reinstatement of access to the international airspace within the States' FIRs suggests that this was also the advice of the ICAO Council. The following sections will instead take a step back from the interaction between the law of the sea and international civil aviation law to examine whether the application of the principle of non-discrimination under international civil aviation law is implicit in international airspace, as the framework of law that is the foundation for FIRs and which subsequently forms the basis for the governance of the responsibility of coastal States in international airspace.

Third and finally, the States implementing the ban relied on non-aviation laws[834] to support its legality, claiming that it is a response to Qatar allegedly breaching the so-called Riyadh Agreements,[835] by sponsoring terrorism.[836] They argued that the

832. Counter Memorial of the State of Qatar (n 820) 2.16; 'UAE and Bahrain Grant Qatar Airways New Routes' (Reuters, 9 August 2017), available at www.aljazeera.com/news/2017/08/uae-bahrain-grant-qatar-airwaysroutes170808161602538.html accessed 26 August 2019.

833. 'Akbar al-Baker on the Gulf Crisis and Qatar Airways' (Al Jazeera, 14 June 2017), available at www.aljazeera.com/programmes/talktojazeera/2017/06/akbar-al-baker-qatar-airways170613020759574.html accessed 27 August 2018.

834. Although the basis of these prohibitions is based on the customary international law principle, recognised in Article 1 of the Chicago Convention, of sovereignty over national airspace.

835. These agreements are between the States making up the Gulf Cooperation Council (GCC) and contain measures addressing antiterrorism and non-interference. The First Riyadh Agreement was signed on 23 November 2013 by Kuwait, Qatar and Saudi Arabia and, a day later, by Bahrain, Oman and the UAE. The second Riyadh Agreement, known as the Mechanism Implementing the Riyadh Agreement, was signed by the GCC States on 17 April 2014, in an attempt to 'strengthen the obligations in the First Riyadh Agreement'. Finally, the Supplementary Riyadh Agreement was concluded on 16 November 2014 by all GCC States but Oman, and was 'intended to reinforce the obligations in the earlier Agreements' (Opening Statement of the Agent of the Kingdom of Bahrain, Public sitting held on Monday 2 December 2019 – Verbatim Record in the case concerning, Appeal Relating to the Jurisdiction of the ICAO Council under Article 84 of the Convention on Civil Aviation (*Bahrain, Egypt, Saudi Arabia and United Arab Emirates v. Qatar*) I.C.J. Joint Application Instituting Proceedings (filed 4 July 2018), pp. 20-21 paras 5, 6 9 and 10).

836. For example, the States allege that '[i]n April 2017, Qatar paid a sum of hundreds of millions of US dollars to terrorist groups, on the pretext that it was a ransom' (Opening Statement of the Agent of the Kingdom of Bahrain (n 835) p. 21 para. 11). *See also*, 'Update 2 – Saudi Arabia says Airspace Ban on Qatari Flights to Protect Citizens' (Reuters, 13 June 2017), available at

sanctions were 'lawful counter-measures authorized by general international law'.[837] Further to this, the States brought the matter before the ICJ, contesting the ICAO Council's rejection of the States' objections to the Council's competence to hear the matter, the objections in part resting on the argument that the subject matter is not within the Council's competence.[838] The ICJ rejected the States' arguments, leaving the matter open to be decided by the ICAO Council.[839] A discussion of these arguments is outside the scope of this research, as is the legality of the bans in general under international civil aviation law, which largely focuses on the prohibition of the aircraft from national airspace. Other authors have addressed these points though, considering the Chicago Convention, the Transit Agreement and the relevant ASAs, and seem to conclude that there is little support for the ban.[840]

---

www.reuters.com/article/gulf-qatar-flightsidUSL8N1JA1FK accessed 7 May 2019, which describes the States as accusing Qatar of 'fomenting regional unrest, supporting terrorism and getting too close to Iran', adding: 'all of which Doha denies'.

837. Appeal Relating to the Jurisdiction of the ICAO Council under Article 84 of the Convention on Civil Aviation (*Bahrain, Egypt, Saudi Arabia and United Arab Emirates v. Qatar*) I.C.J. Joint Application Instituting Proceedings (filed 4 July 2018) p. 8 para. 9. *See* Section 2.6.6.
838. The States brought the matter before the ICJ in two separate cases, which were considered jointly by the Court. One related to the ICAO Council's jurisdiction to hear the matter under Article 84 of the Chicago Convention and the other to its jurisdiction under Article II, Section 2 of the Transit Agreement: Appeal Relating to the Jurisdiction of the ICAO Council under Article 84 of the Convention on Civil Aviation (*Bahrain, Egypt, Saudi Arabia and United Arab Emirates v. Qatar*) I.C.J. Joint Application Instituting Proceedings (filed 4 July 2018); Appeal Relating to the Jurisdiction of the ICAO Council under Article II, Section 2, of the 1944 International Air Services Transit Agreement (*Bahrain, Egypt and United Arab Emirates v. Qatar*) I.C.J. Joint Application Instituting Proceedings (filed 4 July 2018). Saudi Arabia is not a State party to the Transit Agreement and so was not involved in the second proceedings. The States brought the matter before the ICJ also on two other grounds that: (1) the Council 'erred in fact and in law' in its rejection of the States' objection to the Council's competence which was based on the argument that Qatar had not met the precondition of sufficiently attempting to resolve the dispute through prior negotiations; (2) the Council's decision in rejecting the States' objections to its competence on the two grounds mentioned should be set aside because the procedure adopted by the Council in reaching its decision was 'manifestly flawed and in violation of fundamental principles of due process and the right to be heard' (Appeal Relating to the Jurisdiction of the ICAO Council under Article 84 of the Convention on Civil Aviation (*Bahrain, Egypt, Saudi Arabia and United Arab Emirates v. Qatar*) I.C.J. Joint Application Instituting Proceedings (filed 4 July 2018); Appeal Relating to the Jurisdiction of the ICAO Council under Article II, Section 2, of the 1944 International Air Services Transit Agreement (*Bahrain, Egypt and United Arab Emirates v. Qatar*) I.C.J. Joint Application Instituting Proceedings (filed 4 July 2018) p. 14 paras 32 and 30, respectively; Appeal Relating to the Jurisdiction of the ICAO Council under Article 84 of the Convention on Civil Aviation (*Bahrain, Egypt, Saudi Arabia and United Arab Emirates v. Qatar*) I.C.J. Joint Application Instituting Proceedings (filed 4 July 2018) p. 14 paras 31 and 29, respectively).
839. Appeal Relating to the Jurisdiction of the ICAO Council under Article 84 of the Convention on Civil Aviation (*Bahrain, Egypt, Saudi Arabia and United Arab Emirates v. Qatar*), Judgment, I.C.J. 2020 (14 July); Appeal Relating to the Jurisdiction of the ICAO Council under Article II, Section 2, of the 1944 International Air Services Transit Agreement (Bahrain, Egypt and United Arab Emirates v. Qatar), Judgment, I.C.J. 2020 (14 July).
840. *See*, for example, SJ Sreejith, 'Legality of the Gulf Ban on Qatari Flights: State Sovereignty at Crossroads' (2018) 43(2) A&SL 191; Elena Carpanelli, 'To Overfly or Not to Overfly ... ? Autonomous Sanction in International Civil aviation Amidst the Recent "Gulf Crisis" – Part II' (Blog of Groningen Journal of International Law, 25 September 2017), available at grojil.org/2017/09/25/to-overfly-or-not-to-overfly-autonomous-sanctions-in-international-civil-aviation-amidst-the-recent-gulf-crisis-pt2/ accessed 2 June 2018.

4.2.2.3 Qatar's Arguments for the Discrimination as a Violation of International Law

Further to its primary argument of the ban amounting to a violation of the principle of freedom of overflight, Qatar also invoked the principle of non-discrimination in its Memorial to the ICAO Council. Qatar stated on this point that the respondent States had:

> pursuant to a regional air navigation agreement and as a matter of international trust, the responsibility of providing air traffic services within their FIRs and that function must be performed without discrimination.[841]

In national airspace, the Chicago Convention expressly prohibits States from discriminating against aircraft on the basis of their State of registry in aspects of air navigation.[842] However, whether the same principle of non-discrimination applies to the provision of ATS in international airspace is less clear. At the same time, nothing in the Chicago Convention or its annexes provides a State with the right to discriminate against aircraft in international airspace within its FIR based on the State of registry of that aircraft.

In its Counter-Memorial to the ICJ, Qatar presented the matter as a breach of Article 12 of the Chicago Convention:

> Qatar challenges the aviation prohibitions as violations of multiple provisions of the Chicago Convention and its Annexes, including ... Article 12 by discriminatory treatment over the high seas within Joint Appellants' FIRs.[843]

Specifically, Qatar relies on the Article 12 stipulation that '[o]ver the high seas the rules in force shall be those established under this Convention' and that pursuant to this, the Standards in Annex 2 apply without exception.[844] As discussed in Section 2.7.2.2.1, the rules referred to in Article 12 go beyond the Rules of the Air in Annex 2 and also include Annexes 6, 10, 11 and 12. Annex 2 establishes that the appropriate ATS authority over a portion of the high seas will be the authority designated by the State that has accepted responsibility for the provision of the services pursuant to a RANP, and then the provision of those services is governed by the SARPs in Annex 11. The Foreword to Annex 11 sets out the relationship between the two annexes in stating that:

> [i]ts [Annex 11's] purpose, together with Annex 2, is to ensure that flying on international air routes is carried out under uniform conditions designed to improve the safety and efficiency of air operation.[845]

Beyond this aspect of Annex 2's relationship with Annex 11, it is difficult to see further relevance of Annex 2, or Article 12, in relation to Qatar's claim. The analysis

841. Memorial Presented by the State of Qatar (n 817) (e) 3 and 4.
842. *See* Section 4.2.4.1.
843. Counter-Memorial of the State of Qatar (n 820) 2.22.
844. Memorial Presented by the State of Qatar (n 817) (e) 4.
845. Chicago Convention, Annex 11, (ix).

from here will therefore focus on the SARPs in Annex 11 and their context within the Chicago Convention legal framework more broadly in examining Qatar's statement, quoted above in this section, that 'the responsibility of providing air traffic services ... must be performed without discrimination'.

The fact that the States restricted the prohibition to international airspace (and national airspace) *within their FIRs* leads to the conclusion that there was an attempt by them to justify the prohibition on the basis of their responsibility for the FIRs.

4.2.3 The Scope of Responsibility over International Airspace in an FIR under Annex 11

ATS is provided in international airspace in accordance with Annex 11 and is consistent with any differences to Standards that have been filed by the State responsible for the FIR, where it is essential to the efficient discharge of responsibilities under the RANP for those differences to apply also in international airspace.[846]

Standard 2.2 of Annex 11 sets out the objectives of ATS, which are as follows:

> to prevent collisions between aircraft; to prevent collisions between aircraft on the manoeuvring area and obstructions on that area; to expedite and maintain an orderly flow of air traffic; to provide advice and information useful for the safe and efficient conduct of flights; to notify appropriate organizations regarding aircraft in need of search and rescue aid, and assist such organizations as required.[847]

These objectives are solely related to safety and efficiency. As discussed in Section 4.2.1.2, safety and efficiency are correspondingly the only two considerations involved in the delimitation of ATS airspace. Consistent with this, ICAO has clarified that the extent of responsibility in international airspace in an FIR is likewise restricted to the safety and regularity of operations in the airspace:

> any assignment of responsibility over the high seas shall be limited to technical and operational functions pertaining to the safety and regularity of the air traffic operating in the airspace concerned.[848]

The limitation of the assignment does not mean that an ATS authority does not have the right to restrict the overflight of aircraft in international airspace. In fact, on the contrary, in order to adequately deliver ATS, restrictions may be required. Schubert indicates the conditions under which such restrictions will be consistent with international civil aviation law:

> For the purpose of maintaining a safe and an orderly flow of air traffic, a State providing ATS in a part of its FIR that extends over the high seas would be entitled to declare some restrictions (e.g. increased separation) on a specific trajectory, including one feeding a particular State. However:

846. *See* Section 2.7.2.2.1.3.
847. Chicago Convention, Annex 11, 2.2 (a)-(d).
848. ICAO Assembly Resolution A38-12 (n 802) Appendix G, 5.

- the provider State must be able to demonstrate that the restrictions serve a safety or operational efficiency purpose and are dictated by objective reasons;
- the restriction must apply to all aircraft operating along that trajectory, regardless of their nationality.[849]

The ICAO PANS-ATM, referred to in Section 3.3.3.2, which complements Annex 11, provides technical and operational procedures, including for instances in which ATS authorities may be required to restrict overflight.[850] The provisions in this document recognise the necessary discretion that the ATS authority has in carrying out the services, but in each case, the discretion is limited to safety and efficiency considerations. Two examples are provided here to illustrate this point, the first in relation to capacity management and the second regarding separation methods. The former is addressed under Chapter 3 which provides that:

> to ensure that safety is not compromised whenever the traffic demand in an airspace or at an aerodrome is forecast to exceed the available ATC capacity, measures shall be implemented to regulate traffic volumes accordingly.[851]

These measures include rerouting and rescheduling,[852] in relation to which the ATC authority is directed to implement 'larger separations than the specified minima ... whenever exceptional circumstances such as unlawful interference or navigational difficulties call for extra precautions', with the stipulation that '[t]his should be done with due regard to all relevant factors so as to avoid impeding the flow of air traffic by the application of excessive separations'.[853] On this basis, an aircraft or a number of aircraft registered in a particular State may temporarily be restricted due to specific circumstances that require the restriction on the basis of safety and efficiency considerations, but where this occurs, the sole consideration must be safety and/or efficiency, and the restriction must be imposed only to the extent necessary to ensure those objectives.

Thus, the measures taken by a State in its FIR in the course of carrying out the provision of ATS, including in the exercise of ATC discretion, are only justified if they are designed to address the safety and efficiency of international civil aviation. Furthermore, considering that the sole function of a coastal State in international airspace within an FIR for which that State has accepted responsibility is the provision of ATS, there is no other legal basis that can serve as a justification for a measure that does not fulfil at least one of these two purposes.

The narrow scope of responsibility for an FIR set out under Annex 11 therefore supports Qatar's statement that 'the responsibility of providing air traffic services ... must be performed without discrimination', at least insofar as the discrimination is not

849. Correspondence from Francis Schubert (Chief Corporate Officer and Deputy CEO, Skyguide, Adjunct Professor, Institute of Air & Space Law, McGill University) to the author, dated 19 February 2020.
850. *ICAO Procedures for Air Navigation Services* (n 784) 16.1. This document also complements Annex 2.
851. *Ibid.* 3.1.3.3.
852. *ICAO Procedures for Air Navigation Services* (n 784) 3.2.3.1 (b) and (c).
853. *Ibid.* 5.2.1.3.

the result of technical or operational functions with a safety and/or efficiency purpose. With this as a foundation, this research aims to go further and examine whether it can be argued that there is, in addition, an implied principle of non-discrimination applicable to the provision of ATS in international airspace, on the basis of the role the principle plays in international civil aviation law more broadly.

4.2.4 The Principle of Non-discrimination under International Civil Aviation Law

4.2.4.1 The Development and Application of the Principle of Non-discrimination in International Civil Aviation Law

At the Chicago Conference, the UK emphasised the importance of 'the great principle of non-discrimination' to the development of international civil aviation law.[854] The UK delegate said of the principle:

> Everybody has always paid lip service to it and many indeed have paid more, but nobody can pretend that in the past that concept has been of universal application. What a great advance it would be if we could all agree, one with the other, that there shall be no discrimination in our own practices.[855]

The principle of non-discrimination, with its basis in the principle of the sovereign equality of States,[856] has since been referred to as a 'cornerstone of international civil aviation'[857] but, as will be considered here below, the principle has been adopted only in certain aspects. The term 'discrimination' is only explicitly referred to once in the Chicago Convention, in Article 44(g), as one of the objectives of ICAO. Specifically, Article 44 provides that ICAO, in developing principles for air navigation and in fostering the development of air transport, aims to achieve a number of objectives, including 'avoid[ing] discrimination between contracting States'.[858] More broadly speaking, the principle of non-discrimination has recently been at the forefront of discussions in international civil aviation law in respect of ICAO's adoption

854. Proceedings to the Chicago Convention: Vol. I, Pt II 'Verbatim Minutes of Joint Plenary Meeting of Committees I, III, and IV, November 22' (Document 372) 451.
855. *Ibid.* At the outbreak of WWII just thirty-three States had ratified the Paris Convention (Proceedings to the Chicago Convention: Vol. I, Pt II 'Delegation Proposals: United Kingdom Proposal on International Air Transport' (Document 48) 567).
856. Vincent Correia, 'The Legacy of the 1919 Paris Convention Relating to the Regulation of Aerial Navigation' in Pablo Mendes de Leon and Niall Buissing (eds), *Behind and Beyond the Chicago Convention: The Evolution of Aerial Sovereignty* (Wolters Kluwer 2019) 19. *See* Section 3.3.4.4.
857. Alejandro Piera, *Greenhouse Gas Emissions from International Aviation: Legal and Policy Changes* (Eleven International Publishing 2015) 51; Benoit Mayer, *The International Law on Climate Change* (CUP 2018) 106.
858. Chicago Convention, Article 44(g).

of its Carbon Offsetting and Reduction Scheme for International Civil Aviation (CORSIA) in 2016. Alongside the principle of non-discrimination,[859] ICAO has accepted the principle of common but differentiated responsibilities and respective capabilities (CBDRRC) in the implementation of these market-based measures (MBMs),[860] with the process and ultimate decision involving debate on the consistency between non-discrimination and CBDRRC.[861]

Further to being recognised among ICAO's objectives, the principle of non-discrimination is implemented in the Chicago Convention a number of times: Article 7, prohibiting States from granting exclusive cabotage rights to a State or airline of a particular State; Article 9, in relation to prohibited and restricted areas in national airspace, as discussed in Section 2.6.2; Article 11, setting out the applicability of air regulations for entry and departure of national airspace and while operating and navigating therein; Article 12, regarding the application of the Rules of the Air; Article 15, governing the use of airports and air navigation facilities, and charges for such use; and Article 35(b), in relation to a State's right to regulate the carriage of articles above its territory. The principle of 'national treatment', as a subset of non-discrimination,[862] is furthermore reflected in Article 9(a), for scheduled services, Article 11, Article 15 and Article 35(b), requiring that the law must be applied equally to national aircraft and the aircraft registered in other States.[863] Article 9(a) though does not apply the national treatment principle to non-scheduled flights; i.e., the article leaves States with the right to treat aircraft registered in other States engaged in non-scheduled flights differently to their national aircraft likewise engaged. It has also been argued that the national

859. ICAO Assembly Resolution A39-2, Consolidated Statement of Continuing ICAO Policies and Practices Related to environmental Protection – Climate Change (27 September-6 October 2016) 2 and 9.
860. *Ibid.* 9.
861. Alejandro Piera, 'Reconciling CBDR with Non-discrimination: A Fundamental Requirement for ICAO's Global MBM Success' (Green Air, 23 September 2014), available at www.greenaironline.com/news.php?viewStory=1983 accessed 3 November 2019: 'CBDR must be reconciled with non-discrimination in a manner compatible with the international aviation environment. This is necessary to enhance political acceptance and ensure that the system is widely implemented.' On the other hand, Leclerc argues that the scope of non-discrimination in international civil aviation law is limited to the legal regime of air navigation and, as MBMs come under the distinct legal regime of air transport, there is in fact no conflict between the principle of non-discrimination and the principle of CBDRRC (Thomas Leclerc, *Les mesures correctives des émissions aériennes de gaz à effet de serre. Contribution à l'étude des interactions entre les ordres juridiques en droit international public* (Ph.D. thesis, E.M. Meijers Instituut, Leiden University, 2017) 235-269).
862. National treatment is a general notion of legal theory in that it is found across different fields of international law. It is particularly prominent in the law and policy of the World Trade Organization (WTO) where the non-discrimination obligation is understood to consist of two main elements: the national treatment obligation and the most favoured nations (MFN) treatment obligation (Peter Van den Bossche and Werner Zdouc, *The Law and Policy of the World Trade Organization* (4th edn, CUP 2017) 342). National treatment is also prominent in foreign investment treaty law, where it is 'designed to complete non-discrimination goals derived from the MFN treatment' (Raúl Emilio Vinuesa, 'National Treatment, Principle' (Max Planck Encyclopedia of International Law 2011) 55).
863. YILC (1970) Vol. II, Part 2, 215.

treatment principle applies under Article 9(b)[864] but, in contrast, this article states only that it is 'applicable without distinction of nationality to aircraft of all *other* States' (emphasis added), thereby allowing for aircraft of the State whose territory is involved to be treated differently.[865]

Finally, the Preamble to the Convention recognises that the States agree that 'international air transport services may be established on the basis of equality of opportunity'. Equality of opportunity, as the reference to international air *transport* indicates, involves the economic aspects of international civil aviation, addressing, among other things, market access and barriers to entry. Wassenbergh describes the principle as implying 'an equal freedom for every State to build up a civil aviation of its own, i.e. not a *right* to a civil aviation' (original emphasis).[866] Equality of opportunity is not the same as non-discrimination, but the principle of non-discrimination contributes to achieving it, for example, in the context of the allocation of airport slots pursuant to Article 15 of the Chicago Convention.[867] The role of the principle of non-discrimination in contributing to the economic aspects of international civil aviation will be discussed in Section 4.2.4.3.

4.2.4.2 Interaction Between Sovereignty and the Principle of Non-discrimination in National Airspace

The specific references to the non-discrimination principle in the Chicago Convention only apply in the case that the State of registry has negotiated access for its aircraft to the territory of a particular State. This is a direct consequence of the 'complete and exclusive sovereignty' that sits at the heart of international civil aviation law. Non-discrimination in national airspace applies subject to the sovereign power of a State to decide who it admits to its territory and the terms on which it does so. Once this access has been granted, however, the principle of non-discrimination under each of the articles means that a State cannot provide different treatment to aircraft navigating or operating within its territory under these articles. This resulting situation, of the simultaneous centrality of non-discrimination to international civil aviation law and the requirement that States separately negotiate the terms of access to each other's national airspace, can be understood in the context of the distinction between air

864. Pablo Mendes de Leon, Vincent Correia, Uwe Erling and Thomas Leclerc, 'Possible Legal Arrangements to Implement a Global Market Based Measure for International Aviation Emissions' (Study for the Directorate General Climate Action of the EU Commission, 2 December 2015) 11.
865. Bin Cheng, *Law of International Air Transport* (Stevens & Sons 1962) 124.
866. Henry Abraham Wassenbergh, *Post-war International Civil Aviation Policy and the Law of the Air* (Springer 1957) 137.
867. ICAO WP/64, *Fair and Equal Opportunities to Access the International Air Transport Market and the Problem of Airports' Congestion*, Presented by Bahrain, Egypt, Iraq, Jordan, Lebanon, Libyan Arab Jamahiriya, Morocco, Oman, Qatar, Saudi Arabia, Sudan, Syria, Tunisia, United Arab Emirates, Yemen and the Observer from Palestine at the 5th Air Transport Conference, Montreal (17 March 2003) 3.4, 4.1 and 5.1 a); Peter PC Haanappel, *The Law and Policy of Air Space and Outer Space: A Comparative Approach* (Kluwer Law International 2003) 45.

transport and air navigation, recalling Section 2.3.2. This is the approach taken by Leclerc, who argues that:

> a close reading of the Chicago Convention provides the observation that the explicit presence of the principle of non-discrimination is limited to the provisions relating to the law of navigation. This does not mean that the application of the principle is definitively restricted to the field of air navigation, but at present it seems largely premature to assert the widespread application of this principle to international air transport.[868]

As addressed in Sections 2.3.2 and 2.3.3, international air transport is based on the exchange of traffic rights, which is still predominantly undertaken through bilateral ASAs under which the conditions attached to the exercise of those rights are also negotiated.[869] While States are increasingly adopting more liberal provisions in their ASAs, and negotiating them on a multilateral or regional basis,[870] the system establishes a framework that necessarily results in discrimination.

The interaction of the non-discrimination principle under Article 15 with Article 68 of the Chicago Convention provides an example of the application of the non-discrimination principle subject to the exception of the conditions on which the exercise of the rights has been granted. While the non-discrimination principle in Article 15 applies to all aircraft, the exception to the principle in Article 68 applies only to scheduled services, a matter that will be addressed below. Article 15 of the Chicago Convention applies the non-discrimination principle to the use of airports and air navigation service facilities, and charges for such use. Regarding the former, the article requires that 'every airport in a contracting State which is open to public use by its national aircraft shall likewise ... be open under uniform conditions to the aircraft of all the other contracting States'.[871] The exception under Article 68 at the same time

868. Leclerc (n 861) 243, translated from the original: '... une lecture attentive de la convention de Chicago permet d'observer que la présence explicite du principe de non-discrimination se trouve limitée aux dispositions relatives au droit de la navigation aérienne. Cela ne signifie pas que l'application du principe soit définitivement restreinte au champ de la navigation aérienne, mais il apparait aujourd'hui largement prématuré d'affirmer l'application étendue de ce principe en matière de transport aérien international'.
869. *See* Section 2.3.3 (n 195), for the exchange of traffic rights in relation to non-scheduled services. As mentioned, States usually regulate the operation of these services unilaterally under their national legislation, but some include charter services in their ASAs, leading inevitably to different conditions for services between States.
870. *See* Section 2.3.3 (n 190) on the EU single aviation market and MALIAT, and Section 2.3.3.2 for a brief discussion on the liberalisation of ASA provisions.
871. For example, the procedures for the approach and departure sequence of aircraft clearly exclude the option to discriminate between aircraft in these decisions, making clear that in the case of arrival the sequence is to be determined so as to 'facilitate arrival of the maximum number of aircraft with the least average delay' and in the case of departure, aircraft 'shall normally be cleared in the order in which they are ready for take-off', but that this can be adjusted to, as with arrivals, maximise the number of aircraft that can take off with the least delay (ICAO (n 784) 6.5.6.1.1 and 7.9.1).
As a side note here, given that this article specifically applies to airports in a State's territory, an airport constructed in a State's EEZ is not within its scope. If, or perhaps when, the construction of international civil airports in EEZs and even on the high seas becomes commonplace, it will be interesting to see how international civil aviation law adapts to meet these lacunas.

reserves States the right to 'designate the route to be followed within its territory by *any international service* and the airports which *such service* may use' (emphasis added). So, although a State cannot provide use of its airports in a discriminatory manner to those aircraft that have access to the airport, the State has the right to provide access to the airport to only certain services and in this respect may distinguish between aircraft based on their State of registry. This is consistent with route schedules in ASAs sometimes specifying routes in terms of not only the city-to-city points but also the airports within those cities. For example, Bermuda II provided that '[n]onstop services by a United States airline or airlines between Atlanta and London and between Houston and London will serve London-Gatwick Airport'.[872]

In addressing route designation, Article 68, as cited above, allows a State to designate the routes both for aircraft engaged in services to or from its territory and for those exercising the first freedom. As a result, the exercise of the first freedom, i.e., overflight, is also subject to the conditions under which it was negotiated in terms of the route to be followed, which may differ depending on the State of registration. In essence, there is no non-discrimination principle applying to overflight insofar as the route to be followed is concerned. In discussing Article 68, Bin Cheng stated that the regulation of routes is 'one of the most potent instruments in the bargaining of *transit and traffic rights* in bilateral air services agreements' (emphasis added).[873] The implications of this in the case of Canada and Russia designating North Pole routes over their territories were seen in Section 2.3.3. *The Wall Street Journal*, reporting at the time, addressed the need for States to negotiate access to the routes independently with the two States:

> 'airlines must seek Russian permission to fly over northern Siberia from Canada, and some have done so on a month-by-month basis. Even after July 1, permission can be denied at anytime [sic]. Canada, with an open-skies policy, would be unlikely to deny access'. And, '... snags in getting airlines access to them [the routes] could still develop. Bilateral overflight agreements with Russia will have to be negotiated on a country-by-country basis. Even Canada needs an overflight agreement with Russia. However, State Department officials in Washington say they're optimistic that once talks begin, they will be easy to conclude'.[874]

While States might be able to use route designation as a bargaining chip in negotiating an ASA, those States that have multilaterally exchanged the right of overflight over their territories under the Transit Agreement equally have the right to

872. United Kingdom of Great Britain and Northern Ireland and United States of America, Agreement Concerning Air Services (with Annexes, Exchange of Letters and Agreed Minute dated 22 June 1977) (Bermuda, 23 July 1977) 1079 U.N.T.S. 21 (No. 16509), Annex 1. More liberal ASAs do not determine routes so precisely, instead only naming cities or, in the case of the particularly liberal ASA between Australia and New Zealand, only that it applies to 'points' in each country (Agreement between the Government of Australia and the Government of New Zealand Relating to Air Services Auckland, Australia-New Zealand, signed 8 August 2002, [2003] ATS 18 (entered into force 25 August 2003), Annex Section 1).
873. Cheng (n 865) 124.
874. Joel Baglole, 'Canada, Russia's Decision to Permit Polar Routes Promises to Cut Hours' (The Wall Street Journal, 8 June 2000), available at www.wsj.com/articles/SB960415817821812909 accessed 4 March 2018.

subsequently designate the route to be followed by aircraft engaged in scheduled services in their airspace.[875] The inclusion of this provision in the Transit Agreement, which is a restatement, in part, of Article 68 of the Chicago Convention, was pursuant to a proposal from the UK during the Chicago Conference.[876] The case is different for overflight for non-scheduled flights for which, under Article 5 of the Chicago Convention, States may require aircraft to follow prescribed routes over their territories only 'for reasons of safety' when the aircraft wishes to operate over 'regions which are inaccessible or without adequate air navigation facilities'.[877] Despite the exchange of overflight rights for non-scheduled services under Article 5 of the Chicago Convention, not all States act consistently with the provision: the ASA between Canada and Russia provides that '[a]uthorization of overflights for air carriers of either Contracting Party operating charter services shall be considered on the basis of comity and reciprocity'.[878]

These provisions indicate that sovereignty over national airspace governs when, and in some respects how, the aircraft of certain States are permitted to access the airspace and facilities of that State. The principle of non-discrimination then applies further to these considerations.

4.2.4.3 *Purpose of the Non-discrimination Principle in National Airspace*

The safety objectives of international civil aviation law have been emphasised in Section 2.3.2, which also addressed the central role of SARPs in facilitating the safety of civil aviation through the harmonisation of regulation. The non-discrimination principle in the Chicago Convention contributes to the safety of international civil aviation law by requiring that all aircraft are subject to the same rules - for example, under Articles 11 and 12 - and by ensuring that all aircraft have access to air navigation facilities - Article 15 - a significant part of the role of which is to ensure the safety of aircraft.

The non-discrimination principle also has an economic purpose. For example, under Article 7 of the Chicago Convention, a State cannot grant cabotage rights to another State on an 'exclusive basis'. The non-discrimination principle in this article does not prohibit a State from granting cabotage rights to one State and not to another, but specifically from granting the right to the *exclusion* of other States. Considering that cabotage stems from the 'mercantilist purpose of protecting domestic commerce from foreign competition', Havel and Sanchez have described the non-discrimination clause under Article 7 as 'a restraint on the degree of sovereignty the Convention's State parties can trade away'.[879] For a weaker aviation State, they explain, this prevents it from being pressured by stronger States in the exchange of these rights, to the

875. Transit Agreement, Section 4(1).
876. Proceedings to the Chicago Convention: Vol. I, Pt II 'Minutes of Meeting of Subcommittees 1 and 2 of Committee I, December 2' (Document 465) 653.
877. Chicago Convention, Article 5. As discussed in Section 2.3.3.
878. Air Services Agreement Between the Government of Canada and the Government of the Russian Federation, 18 December 2000, Annex II, (A) (5).
879. Brian Havel and Gabriel Sanchez, *The Principles and Practice of International Aviation Law* (CUP 2014) 50-51.

detriment of the domestic market of the former State and, for a stronger State, the article alleviates it from the concern that other strong aviation States are granted cabotage rights in a State to its exclusion.[880]

The non-discrimination principle as an expression of protectionism, as it applies in Article 7, is in contrast to the role that the US delegation envisioned the principle playing in the Chicago Convention. The US delegate at the Chicago Conference, arguing for a highly liberalised multilateral exchange of privileges under the Chicago Convention, as discussed in Section 2.2.2.3, compared the need to avoid discrimination in the operation of international air services over national airspace to the significance of access to the high seas for economic purposes:

> You will recall that for a time nations forgot the famous Roman observation, I think it was the Emperor Gaius, that the law was lord of the sea, and endeavored to establish great closed zones from which they attempted to exclude all intercourse except through their own ships, or to place any other nation permitted to enter these zones at a discriminatory disadvantage ... . These zones became fertile breeding grounds for great commercial monopolies, which sought to levy tribute on the commerce of the world or to exclude or discriminate against the trade of other nations ... . The dangers of closed air, where it lies across established or logical routes of commerce, are not dissimilar from the dangers which arose through the closing of sea lanes.[881]

Leaving aside Article 7, the non-discrimination principle in other articles under the Convention serves to restrict the sovereignty of a State by preventing it from imposing regulations to the detriment of the air services of a particular State or States. This economic focus of Article 9(a), for instance, is demonstrated by the fact that national treatment applies specifically to scheduled services, with the commercial potential of non-scheduled services considered to be minimal at the time of the drafting of the Convention.[882] Other instances of non-discrimination in the Convention that apply to air navigation matters but which have economic consequences, in protecting the air services of other States by allowing them to exercise their transit and traffic rights unimpeded by discriminatory regulations of the State whose territory is involved, are found under Articles 9(b), 11, 12 and 15.

Equally in international airspace, there are both safety and economic arguments to be made for the application of the law in a non-discriminatory manner. Qatar's claims in relation to the prohibitions imposed by the Gulf States reflect this:

> The blocked FIRs forced the Qatar Airways to use limited airways, leading to danger of congestion. The safety, security, regularity and economy of civil aviation have been seriously compromised.[883]

880. Havel and Sanchez (n 879) 51.
881. Proceedings to the Chicago Convention: Vol. I, Pt I 'Verbatim Minutes of Second Plenary Session, November 2' (Document 42) 56-57.
882. Rigas Doganis, *Flying Off Course: Airline Economics and* Marketing (4th edn, Routledge 2010) 38.
883. Memorial Presented by the State of Qatar (n 817) (c).

There is no doubting the economic importance of access to international airspace to airlines operating international air services. Without access to international airspace, the non-discrimination principle as it applies in the Chicago Convention would be of little value to many airlines which rely on services that operate across the oceans. McDougal and Burke wrote, in reference to the period in the late 1950s and early 1960s:

> '[t]he oceans have perhaps been most efficiently employed as an avenue of transport ...' and, 'travel in space above many parts of the ocean has quickly become highly intense, especially in the movement of people'.[884]

Since this time, international civil aviation has grown exponentially, as has the corresponding economic importance of the use of international airspace.

The non-discrimination principle has been adopted in the Chicago Convention for economic and safety purposes. These objectives are equally important in international airspace in the sense that international civil aviation relies on a global network where the segments of operation over international airspace are indivisible from those over national airspace for the purpose of delivering services that span the two.

4.2.4.4 *Non-discrimination Principle in International Airspace on the Basis of Its Application in National Airspace*

Based on the above, is it possible to interpret an overarching implied principle of non-discrimination applying to navigation in international airspace, including the right to access the airspace? One way of approaching this would be to consider the contrast between access to national airspace and international airspace, in terms of the fact that no State has sovereignty over the latter and that the baseline principle is freedom of overflight, thereby resulting in a situation where the preliminary negotiations over access to airspace, and conditions attached to such rights, are irrelevant and therefore that the principle of non-discrimination applies without preconditions. The logic of this argument is flawed, however.

First, while it is a central aspect, the non-discrimination principle is not a blanket principle in international civil aviation law. The principle of non-discrimination in national airspace does not apply to the right to *access* national airspace, or operate routes to and from it, which are governed by the States externally to the Chicago Convention. Therefore, there seems little basis to subsequently interpret that the non-discrimination principle can be implied as applying in international airspace to prohibit States from banning the aircraft of other States from accessing their FIRs. The Convention also reserves States the right to determine the routes that any air service may operate on; i.e., the non-discrimination principle does not apply to the designation of routes in national airspace. Further to this, the non-discrimination principle in Article 9(a) in relation to prohibited areas applies only to scheduled services as opposed to aircraft in general. It would, as a result, be illogical then to rely on the non-discrimination principle in the Chicago Convention to argue that a State

884. Myres S McDougal and William T Burke, *The Public Order of the Oceans: A Contemporary International Law of the Sea* (New Haven Press 1987) 732-733.

administering an FIR is restricted from discriminating in these aspects against an aircraft navigating in international airspace within its responsibility.

Furthermore, the principle of non-discrimination in national airspace has both safety and economic purposes. These objectives are equally important in international airspace, but the principle of non-discrimination is not necessarily needed to achieve these aims. State sovereignty over national airspace entails the corresponding legal competence of the State in respect of that airspace, including jurisdiction over the operation and navigation of aircraft within its territory to the extent that the laws and regulations are consistent with international law. It is for this reason that the non-discrimination principle is expressly required in the Chicago Convention in respect of national airspace. In contrast, no State has sovereignty over international airspace, and the jurisdiction of a coastal State over international airspace within its FIR is found solely in its responsibilities based in Annex 11 as developed and agreed upon under the relevant RANP.

As a result, it is both unhelpful and misguided to consider whether, on the basis of the principle of non-discrimination applying to national airspace, there may be an implied principle of non-discrimination in Annex 11 of the Chicago Convention that prohibits discrimination in international airspace. This does not mean though that a State has the right to discriminate against aircraft in international airspace within its FIR. Rather, as was demonstrated above in Section 4.2.3, the narrow scope of FIR responsibilities under Annex 11 provides a State with no legitimate grounds on which to discriminate against aircraft on the basis of the State of registry of the aircraft. This position is supported by the discussion in the following section, which addresses the principle of good faith in interpreting the responsibilities set forth in Annex 11.

4.2.4.5 Interpretation of Annex 11 Consistent with Non-discrimination in International Airspace

As mentioned in Section 4.2.4.1, one of the objectives of ICAO is 'to develop the principles and techniques of international air navigation ... so as to ... avoid discrimination between contracting States'.[885] ICAO's normative powers within the development of principles and techniques for international air navigation include 'air traffic control practices'[886] for which it is responsible for adopting SARPs. Annex 11 is adopted pursuant to this article.[887]

The provision of ATS in a discriminatory manner based on the State of registration of an aircraft, with no legitimate basis in safety and efficiency objectives, not only goes beyond the provision of the services that the State accepting responsibility is tasked with delivering but also goes against the non-discriminatory context of the legal framework that the SARPs fall within. To read into the provisions any right to

885. With specific reference to Article 44(g).
886. Chicago Convention, Article 37(c).
887. Annex 11 used to be titled, 'Air Traffic Control', which is now considered an element of ATS, as described in Section 4.2.1.1.

discriminate would be a violation of the principle of *pacta sunt servanda*,[888] which applies to every treaty, including its annexes.[889] The main element of *pacta sunt servanda* is good faith[890] and in accordance with good faith, '[p]arties are required to the best of their abilities to observe the treaty stipulations in their spirit …'.[891] The ICJ, in its *Nuclear Tests Case*, addressed the concept of good faith:

> One of the basic principles governing the creation and performance of legal obligations, whatever their source, is the principle of good faith. Trust and confidence are inherent in international co-operation, in particular in an age when this co-operation in many fields is becoming increasingly essential. Just as the very rule of *pacta sunt servanda* in the law of treaties is based on good faith, so also is the binding character of an international obligation assumed by unilateral declaration. Thus interested States may take cognizance of unilateral declarations and place confidence in them, and are entitled to require that the obligation thus created be respected.[892]

The Chicago Convention and its annexes, Annex 11 being most relevant to this research, together with the RANPs that are developed pursuant to the Convention, set out the legal framework governing the establishment of FIRs and the responsibilities for the provision of ATS within them. Although the framework does not reference the principle of non-discrimination in setting out its rules for ATS over international airspace, the principle underpins ICAO's lawmaking capacity, and in establishing the responsibilities for the provision of ATS, ICAO has accordingly so narrowly defined the role so as to leave no right for discrimination based on the State of registry of an aircraft.

4.2.4.6 Overflight Fees in International Airspace

Although outside the scope of this research – which focuses on prohibition or restrictions on the operation of an aircraft in international airspace – the charging of air navigation fees for services provided in international airspace cannot be considered alongside the provision of those services when it comes to non-discrimination.

In its Policies on Charges for Air Navigation Services, ICAO has stated that:

> [t]he system of charges must not discriminate between foreign users and those having the nationality of the State or States responsible for providing the air navigation services and engaged in similar international operations, or between two or more foreign users.[893]

For charges for services used by aircraft when not over the provider State, however, including in international airspace, ICAO is less prescriptive. Recognising

888. *See also* Section 3.3.2.1.
889. Mark Eugen Villiger, *Commentary on the 1969 Vienna Convention on the Law of Treaties* (Brill Nijhoff 2009) 365.
890. *Ibid.*
891. *Ibid.* 367.
892. *Nuclear Tests Case (Australia v. France)*, Judgment, I.C.J. Rep. 1974 (20 December), p. 253, p. 268 para. 46.
893. ICAO Doc 9082, *ICAO's Policies on Charges for Airports and Air Navigation Services* (9th edn, 2012) 6 iv).

that the collection of such fees in this case 'poses difficult and complex problems', ICAO provides that 'it is for the States to find the appropriate kind of machinery on a bilateral or regional basis' to facilitate the rates and method of collection.[894] In this respect, the provision of ATS is distinguishable from the imposition of the fees for those services, in the degree to which it is regulated by ICAO and also, it appears, in the right to discriminate.

4.2.5 In Summary: Non-discrimination in International Airspace

International airspace is divided into FIRs for the purpose of ATS provision. A State that accepts responsibility for an FIR over international airspace, pursuant to a RANP, provides those services consistently with the SARPs under Annex 11. A State's acceptance of responsibility for an FIR confers no sovereignty on that State over the airspace within the FIR and, while FIR boundaries over national territory often follow State borders, the intention is that they are delimited based only on technical and operational considerations, and it is not uncommon for the FIR of one State to encompass the territory of another. In the case of Qatar, its territory is entirely encompassed by Bahrain's FIR, and so when Bahrain, together with other Gulf States, prohibited Qatari-registered aircraft from the FIRs, including in international airspace, the consequences were particularly severe for the operation of flights to and from Qatar.

Prohibiting an aircraft from international airspace on the basis of the State of registration of the aircraft is indisputably a violation of freedom of overflight. Leaving this freedom aside, Section 4.2 set out to determine whether there is a prohibition on doing so specifically under international civil aviation law, as the body of law under which FIRs and the responsibility for ATS within them is established. While the principle of non-discrimination applies in the Chicago Convention, the application is to specific aspects, to the exclusion of others, rather than being a cornerstone principle. Furthermore, while the safety and economic goals that non-discrimination helps to meet in national airspace are important in international airspace, the principle is not necessary to meet these goals in international airspace on the basis that, cumulatively, no State exercises sovereignty over the airspace and that the terms of Annex 11 provide the State responsible for an FIR with a limited scope of jurisdiction in its provision of ATS. State responsibility for the provision of ATS services, as set out in Annex 11 and the corresponding PANS-ATM are narrow - purely for safety and efficiency - and all decisions must be justifiable on one of these two bases. Supporting this is the consideration that the SARPs in Annex 11 of the Chicago Convention are legislated by ICAO and one of its main objectives in developing its principles for international air navigation is to avoid discrimination between States. To interpret the SARPs as permitting discrimination in the absence of an express permission to do so would be a breach of good faith.

894. ICAO Doc 9082 (n 893) 11.

4.3 AIR DEFENCE IDENTIFICATION ZONES

4.3.1 Recent Developments Shed Light on Inconsistent Approach to ADIZ

In November 2013 China announced[895] that it had established an ADIZ, reaching more than 300 miles off its coast.[896] The announcement was met with opposition from a number of States, including the US, Japan, South Korea, Australia, Canada and the UK.[897] Despite this, China's actions within its ADIZ are 'largely in line with international norms regarding ADIZs'.[898]

Some of the most vehement opposition to China's ADIZ stemmed from consequences beyond the restrictions that the ADIZ places on aviation.[899] The airspace within China's ADIZ controversially includes disputed territory: the Senkaku/Diaoyu/Tiaoyutai Islands, which are claimed by Japan, China and Taiwan;[900] and the Ieodo/Suyan Reef, claimed by South Korea and China.[901] This issue contributes to demonstrating the political nature of ADIZs, but the territorial disputes themselves are outside the scope of this research.

The dimensions of the ADIZ are also problematic in that the zone overlaps with the ADIZs of Japan, South Korea and Taiwan.[902] It is not exceptional in this respect

895. Announcement of the Aircraft Identification Rules for the East China Sea Air Defense Identification Zone of the People's Republic of China', issued by the Ministry of National Defense, China (23 November 2013).
896. Roncevert Almond, 'Clearing the Air above the East China Sea: The Primary Elements of Aircraft Defense Identification Zones' (2016) 7 NSJ 126, 129.
897. *See* respectively, 'Statement on the East China Sea Air Defense Identification Zone' (John Kerry, Secretary of State – Press Statement, 23 November 2013), available at 2009-2017.state.gov/secretary/remarks/2013/11/218013.htm accessed 3 November 2019; United States of America Congressional Record, Proceedings and Debates of the 113th Congress – Second Session (Volume 160-Part 8, 20 June-15 July 2014) 11803; 'China's Air Defense Identification Zone: Impact on Regional Security' (Centre for Strategic and International Studies, 26 November 2013), available at www.csis.org/analysis/chinas-air-defense-identification-zone-impact-regional-security accessed 3 November 2019; 'China's Announcement of an Air-Defence Identification Over the East China Sea' (Minister for Foreign Affairs, Julie Bishop, Press Release, 26 November 2013), available at www.foreignminister.gov.au/minister/julie-bishop/media-release/chinas-announcement-air-defence-identification-zone-over-east-china-sea accessed 3 November 2019; 'Baird Concerned over China's Announcement of Air Defence Identification Zone' (Foreign Affairs, Trade and Development Canada, News Release, 2 December 2013), available at www.canada.ca/en/news/archive/2013/12/baird-concerned-china-announcement-air-defence-identification-zone.html accessed 3 November 2019; HL Deb 16 January 2014, Vol. 751, col 444.
898. Ian E Rinehart and Bart Elias, 'China's Air Defense Identification Zone (ADIZ)' (Congressional Research Service Report, 31 January 2015) 10. Notwithstanding the significant variation in practice in the establishment of ADIZ, as will be demonstrated throughout Section 4.3.
899. 'China Establishes "Air Defence Zone" over East China Sea' (BBC, 23 November 2013), available at www.bbc.com/news/world-asia-25062525 accessed 5 May 2018.
900. Almond (n 896) 129; Susan V Lawrence et al., 'US-China Relations' (Congressional Research Service Report, 3 September 2019) 29.
901. Christopher K Lamont, 'Conflict in the Skies: The Law of Air Defence Identification Zones' (2014) 39(3) A&SL 187, 188.
902. Lawrence et al. (n 900) 29.

though: the extension of Japan's ADIZ in 2010 resulted in overlap with Taiwan's,[903] while the extension of South Korea's in 2015 led to overlap with Japan's.[904] Necessarily, overlapping ADIZs also involve ADIZs crossing FIR boundaries. In addition to the overlapping ADIZs of China, Japan, South Korea and Taiwan, ICAO has referred to an unnamed ADIZ established in 2018, which crossed over into two adjacent FIRs,[905] and Canada's ADIZ crosses very slightly into the FIRs of Greenland and the US, as does Thailand's ADIZ with FIRs under the responsibility of Malaysia and Vietnam.[906] The consequences of ADIZs that result in an overlap in responsibilities or authority in airspace will be addressed in relation to the safety implications of ADIZs in Section 4.3.6.1.

The element of China's ADIZ that caused particular concern among States[907] when it was announced was that the State would be prepared to use force in the case that its ADIZ requirements are not complied with. The announcement specifically stated on this matter that 'China's armed forces will adopt defensive emergency measures to respond to aircraft that do not cooperate in the identification or refuse to follow the instructions'.[908] As will be discussed in Section 4.3.5, a coastal State has very limited powers to enforce non-compliance of its ADIZ within international airspace. Despite China's claim, however, it has so far not resorted to taking defensive measures against non-complying aircraft, although whether this is a calculated decision is unclear.[909]

A key criticism of the US of China's ADIZ is the fact that it applies to all aircraft in the zone, including those that remain in international airspace.[910] As will be demonstrated in Section 4.3.3.1, there is no legal basis to suggest that the territorial

903. 'Japan Extends Air Defence Identification Zone into Taiwan Space' (BBC Monitoring Asia Pacific, 26 June 2010), text of report in English by Shih Hsiu-chuan on Taiwanese newspaper *Taipei Times* website on 26 June 2010 written, available at www.taipeitimes.com/News/front/archives/2010/06/26/2003476438 accessed 3 November 2019; Christopher K Lamont, 'Conflict in the Skies: The Law of Air Defence Identification Zones' (2014) 39(3) A&SL 187, 191.
904. Chang-Hoon Shin, 'South Korea's Inevitable Expansion of Its ADIZ' (Asian Maritime Transparency Initiative 8 December 2014), available at amti.csis.org/south-koreas-inevitable-expansion-of-its-adiz/ accessed 19 August 2019.
905. ICAO WP/295, *Establishment of Military Requirements and Restrictions on International Civil Aviation*, Presented by IATA and IFALPA at the 13th Air Navigation Conference, Montreal (28 September 2018) 2.3.
906. Jinyuan Su, 'The Practice of States on Air Defense Identification Zones: Geographical Scope, Object of Identification, and Identification Measures' (2019) 18 Chinese JIL 811, 829.
907. *See*, for example, 'Declaration by the High Representative Catherine Ashton on behalf of the European Union on the establishment by China of an "East China Sea Air Defence Identification Zone"' (European Union, Press Release, 28 November 2013), available at www.consilium.europa.eu/uedocs/cms_Data/docs/pressdata/EN/foraff/139752.pdf accessed 13 February 2016.
908. Announcement issued by the Ministry of National Defense, China (n 895).
909. Edmund J Burke and Astrid Stuth Cevallos, 'In Line or Out of Order? China's Approach to ADIZ in Theory and Practice' (RAND Project AIR FORCE Strategy and Doctrine Program, 2017) 1: 'whether the lack of enforcement is an operational choice or the result of insufficient capabilities is an open question'.
910. Announcement issued by the Ministry of National Defense, China (n 895). The US voiced its concern immediately upon China's announcement: 'We don't support efforts by any State to apply its ADIZ procedures to foreign aircraft not intending to enter its national airspace' (Statement on the East China Sea ADIZ – US Secretary of State (n 897)).

connection claimed by the US legitimises ADIZ. Furthermore, China is once again not unusual in requiring all aircraft to comply with its ADIZ requirements; Su's comparative research on national regulations in ADIZs found that many States that have imposed ADIZs in international airspace have required aircraft transiting the airspace without entering national airspace to comply with the regulations.[911]

The above comments on the characteristics of China's ADIZ are not statements on the legality of its ADIZ. The comments here are instead included to: (1) address the inconsistencies in the approach States take to ADIZs, which is relevant to the discussion in Section 4.3.3.4 on the lack of clear State practice for the purpose of establishing customary international law; and (2) bring attention to the political motivations surrounding ADIZs. These political incentives underlie the basis on which States justify and distinguish ADIZ practices. In the words of the South China Morning Post, in part quoting Alan Tan, 'politics, nationalism and sovereignty "lurk in the background, and that reality simply has to be acknowledged"'.[912] While in reality the political and legal aspects of ADIZs are inextricable, this research aims to set to one side the political considerations to undertake an – insofar as possible – objective legal analysis of the legality of the zones under international law.

4.3.2 Defining ADIZ

In 1950,[913] the US was the first State to claim an ADIZ,[914] which extended, and still does, up to 400 miles off its coast in parts.[915] Canada established its ADIZ soon after, in 1951,[916] while in the same year, the US established Japan's during its administration of

911. Su (n 906) 820-822. Su identified the following States as falling within this category: Argentina, Australia, Bangladesh, Canada, China, Taiwan, India, Iran, South Korea, Myanmar, Pakistan and Thailand.
912. Toh Ee Ming, 'Explained: What's Behind Indonesia's Move to Reclaim Control of Riau Islands Airspace from Singapore?' (South China Morning Post, 22 August 2019), available at www.scmp.com/week-asia/explained/article/3023918/whats-behind-indonesias-move-reclaim-control-riau-islands accessed 30 September 2019. Alan Tan is Professor at the National University of Singapore Law School, specialising in, among other areas, aviation law.
913. Elizabeth Cuadra, 'Air Defense Identification Zones: Creeping Jurisdiction in the Airspace' (1978) 18 Va J Int'l L 485, 492; Pratik Jakhar, 'Analysis: Why Is Airspace in East Asia Becoming Contentious?' (BBC Monitoring, 31 July 2019), available at monitoring.bbc.co.uk/product/c200zen7 accessed 14 November 2019.
914. 'US ADIZ' will be used throughout this chapter as a collective term for the four ADIZs that surround US territory: Contiguous US ADIZ, Alaska ADIZ, Guam ADIZ, and Hawaii ADIZ.
915. Rinehart and Elias (n 898) 5. The breadth of ADIZ apparently developed to mirror the contiguous zone for vessels. The distance of 400 miles represented the approximate distance an aircraft could travel over the duration of one hour in the 1950s when ADIZ was first implemented. At the time, the concept of a contiguous zone was beginning to emerge – although was far from being customary international law – and the breadth of it was in general the distance a vessel could travel in one hour (Ivan L Head, 'ADIZ, International Law, and Contiguous Airspace' (1964) 3 Alta L Rev 182, 188).
916. Pai Zheng, 'Justifications and Limits of ADIZs under Public International Law' (2015) 14(2) Issues Aviation L & Pol'y 183, 197.

the country following World War II, and South Korea's during the Korean War.[917] Towards the end of the 1970s, around twelve States had declared ADIZs[918] and this number was maintained through to the end of the twentieth century.[919] There has been a renewed focus on ADIZs since the events of 11 September 2001[920] and to date approximately thirty States[921] have imposed an ADIZ off their coasts at some point.[922] Some States, such as Sri Lanka and Turkey, have restricted their ADIZs to territorial sea.[923] These ADIZs, along with those that are restricted to national airspace over land,[924] are not relevant to this research, which is interested in ADIZs in international airspace. A number of States have also recently extended their ADIZs. In addition to the extensions of Japan and South Korea's ADIZs, as mentioned in Section 4.3.1, Canada extended its ADIZ in 2018 to encompass Ellesmere Island.[925]

ICAO defines an ADIZ as a 'special designated airspace of defined dimensions within which aircraft are required to comply with special identification and/or reporting procedures additional to those related to the provision of air traffic services'.[926] Little else is provided by ICAO on ADIZs but for requirements that States identify them in their aeronautical charts and aeronautical information publications

917. Kimberly Hsu, 'Air Defense Identification Zone Intended to Provide China Greater Flexibility to Enforce East China Sea Claims' (US-China Economic and Security Review Commission, 14 January 2014) 3.
918. Cuadra (n 913) 495 and 507.
919. Michel Bourbonniere and Louis Haeck, 'Military Aircraft and International Law: Chicago Opus 3' (2001) 66(3) J Air L&C 885, 954, *Note 255* (citing, Barry E Carter and Phillip R Trimble, *International Law* (3rd edn, Wolters Kluwer 1999) 1028).
920. Natalie Klein, *Maritime Security and the Law of the Sea* (OUP 2011) 60; Pratik Jakhar, 'Analysis: Why Is Airspace in East Asia Becoming Contentious?' (BBC Monitoring, 31 July 2019), available at monitoring.bbc.co.uk/product/c200zen7 accessed 14 November 2019, quoting a Russian newspaper *Izvestiya* from 25 July 2019: 'The trend of "self-appointed seizure" of international airspace and the expansion of identification zones has become apparent in the past decade.'
921. These include Australia, Argentina, Bangladesh, Canada, China, Cuba, France, Iceland, India, Indonesia, Iran, Italy, Japan, Myanmar, Norway, Oman, Pakistan, Panama, the Philippines, Russia, South Korea, Sri Lanka, Sweden, Taiwan, Thailand, Turkey, United Kingdom, United States and Vietnam, as to which *see*, variously, Su (n 906) 814-819; Cuadra (n 913) 495 and 507; J Ashley Roach, 'Air Defence Identification Zones' (Max Planck Encyclopedia of Public International Law 2017) 6 and 14; Zoltán Papp, 'Air Defense Identification Zone (ADIZ) in the light of Public International Law' (2015) 2 Pecs J Int Eur Law 28, 33.
922. ADIZ may be temporary, such as when they are imposed for security purposes for a certain event. *See*, for example, the two ADIZs established off the coast of Brisbane, Australia, during the 2018 Commonwealth Games: Australia Aeronautical Information Service – AIP Supplement (SUP), XXI Commonwealth Games, Gold Coast, 2-18 April 2018, 7.2; Airservices Australia, 'Commonwealth Games Airspace Procedure Guide', available at www.airservicesaustralia.com/wp-content/uploads/17-0067-BRO-Commonwealth-Games-airspace-new.pdf accessed 23 May 2019.
923. Su (n 906) 814.
924. *Ibid.* Such as Poland, Finland, Libya, Peru and Brazil.
925. 'Canadian Air Defence Identification Zone Now Aligned with Canada's Sovereign Airspace' (Canada National Defence, News Release, 24 May 2018), available at www.canada.ca/en/department-national-defence/news/2018/05/canadian-air-defence-identification-zone-now-aligned-with-canadas-sovereign-airspace.html accessed 26 June 2018.
926. Chicago Convention, Annex 4 (11th edn, July 2009) 1-1 and Annex 15 (16th edn, July 2018) 1-2. The inclusion of the definition is a recognition of the potential safety implications for international civil aviation as opposed to being a statement on their legality (Papp (n 921) 37).

(AIPs).[927] The broad definition provided by ICAO is indicative of the variation in practices associated with the imposition and administration of the zones. The purpose of ADIZs is generally to enhance national security,[928] but they are also arguably used in an attempt to bolster territorial claims through the exertion of control over an area of international airspace.[929] Considering ICAO's role is to ensure the safety of international civil aviation, it is perhaps not surprising that it has not adopted further SARPs in the area. ADIZs do, however, have safety implications for international civil aviation, as will be addressed in Section 4.3.6.1.

As an indication of the types of procedures that apply in an ADIZ, China and the US both require that in order to operate an aircraft within the zone, a pilot must file a flight plan,[930] and maintain a two-way radio connection[931] and an operating radar transponder.[932] The definition of a flight plan according to ICAO is a '[s]pecified information *provided to air traffic services units*, relative to an intended flight or portion of a flight of an aircraft' (emphasis added);[933] however, in the case of China's ADIZ, the flight plan is to be submitted to the CAA *or* the Ministry of Foreign Affairs.[934] No further direction is provided in the announcement as to which body applies to which flight, but it is logical to assume that flight plans for civil aircraft are required to be submitted to the CAA while the Ministry of Foreign Affairs applies in the case of State aircraft. The US regulations state that the flight plan must be filed with 'an appropriate aeronautical facility'.[935] It defines this body as 'a communications facility where flight plans or position reports *are normally filed* during flight operations', suggesting that it refers to the ATC unit applicable in the airspace (emphasis added).[936]

---

927. *Ibid.* Annex 4, 7.9.3.1.1 (l), 16.9.5.2, 17.9.5.2, 18.8.4.2, and Annex 15, 6.2.1 (a) (6). An aeronautical information publication (AIP) is 'a publication issued by or with the authority of a State and containing aeronautical information of a lasting character essential to air navigation' (Chicago Convention, Annex 15, 1-2).
928. ICAO WP/295, *Establishment of Military Requirements and Restrictions on International Civil Aviation*, Presented by IATA and IFALPA at the 13th Air Navigation Conference, Montreal (28 September 2018) 1.3: 'IATA and IFALPA ... recognise that, often the establishment of an ADIZ is driven by military or political sensitivities attributed to national security'; *see also*, in relation to the US and Canada ADIZs, Head (n 915) 183.
929. *See*, for example, in the East Asia maritime region, Rinehart and Elias (n 898) 12: 'The ECS ADIZ did not involve aggressive actions by the PLA in the initial phase, but some observers view the declaration of the ADIZ as another of the PRC's incremental law-enforcement and military actions, especially since 2005, to advance its national interests'; 'Military Experts Explain China's Air Defense Identification Zone' (People's Daily Online, 24 November 2013), available at en.people.cn/90786/8464466.html accessed 15 March 2019: 'Military expert Yin Zhuo said that China's establishment of the zone is based on the need to tackle a more complex security environment, and the move is a justified act to maintain the sovereignty and security of the country's territory and airspace'; Lamont (n 901) 191 and 200.
930. 14 C.F.R. §99.11 (2015); Announcement issued by the Ministry of National Defense, China (n 895).
931. 14 C.F.R. §99.9; Announcement issued by the Ministry of National Defense, China (n 895).
932. 14 C.F.R. §99.13, referring to a 'coded radar beacon transponder'; Announcement issued by the Ministry of National Defense, China (n 895): 'if equipped with the secondary radar transponder'.
933. Chicago Convention, Annex 2 (10th edn, 2005) 1-6.
934. Announcement issued by the Ministry of National Defense, China (n 895).
935. 14 C.F.R. §99.11.
936. 14 C.F.R. §99.3.

Pilots must also comply with the instructions of the relevant authorities in each State's ADIZ. In China's ADIZ that authority is the Ministry of National Defence.[937] In the case of the US, these 'special security instructions', as they are termed, are issued by 'the Administrator'.[938] The US ADIZ, together with the Canadian ADIZ, is jointly administered by the ATC authorities and militaries of each State, through a body known as the North American Aerospace Defense Command (NORAD).[939] In both cases, failure to comply with these instructions, or failure to comply with the ADIZ requirements in general, may result in action being taken against the aircraft in international airspace. As mentioned in Section 4.3.1, China's ADIZ announcement stated that its armed forces would be prepared to adopt defence measures, and the US AIP on interception of aircraft states that:

> [p]ilots of aircraft that do not adhere to the procedures [which include ADIZ procedures][940] ... may be intercepted, and/or detained and interviewed by federal, state, or local law enforcement or other government personnel.[941]

These requirements, and their deviation from standard ATC procedures, will be discussed further in Section 4.3.6.2, but at this point, they serve to demonstrate that ADIZs impose additional obligations on pilots operating in the airspace, and that these obligations can be issued by defence, who may also enforce them if they are not complied with.

4.3.3 Examination of International Law Used to Support Establishment of ADIZ

Both in terms of State response to ADIZs and academic argument, Cuadra notes that '[t]here is considerable weight of opinion on both sides of the question whether ADIZ's [sic] are legitimate under international law', while concluding that '[i]nternational law provides no support for such coastal-State jurisdiction'.[942] Conversely, States that impose ADIZs not surprisingly argue that there is no prohibition on doing so under international law.[943] Both of these arguments may be correct and the first does not necessarily mean that ADIZs are prohibited, while the second does not necessarily legitimise them, as will be explained in Section 4.3.4. In light of this complexity,

937. Announcement issued by the Ministry of National Defense, China (n 895).
938. 14 C.F.R. §99.7.
939. Rinehart and Elias (n 898) 3. There is no ADIZ between the US and Canada (US FAA, 'Entering, Exiting and Flying in United States Airspace', available at www.faa.gov/air_traffic/publications/us_restrictions/airspace/ accessed 14 February 2020).
940. 'ENR 1.12 National Security and Interception Procedures – National Security', 1.4, available at www.faa.gov/air_traffic/publications/atpubs/aip_html/part2_enr_section_1.12.html#Para_1_8_4 accessed 2 July 2019.
941. *Ibid.* 1.2.5.
942. Cuadra (n 913) 505 and 507.
943. *See*, for example, the US: The Commander's Handbook on the Law of Naval Operations (Department of the Navy – Department of Homeland Security and US Coast Guard, August 2017) 2.7.2.3: 'International law does not prohibit States from establishing air defense identification zones (ADIZs) in the international airspace adjacent to their territorial airspace.'

Haanappel describes ADIZs as being 'on the margin of unilateral illegality'.[944] Consistent with the diversity in the procedures adopted in ADIZs, States use various arguments to justify the zones.

4.3.3.1 A State's Laws and Regulations Relating to Admission to Territory

As mentioned in Section 4.3.1, the US only applies its ADIZ requirements to aircraft – both State and civil – that are entering or departing its national airspace. That is, the ADIZ regulations do not apply to aircraft operating in the ADIZ without the intention of entering US national airspace, or without having departed US national airspace. This is stipulated in the Code of Federal Regulations that sets the rules for the US ADIZ (14 C.F.R. §99), which states that it 'prescribes rules for operating all aircraft ... *into, within, or out of the United States* through an Air Defense Identification Zone' (emphasis added).[945]

Secretary of State John Kerry, in his statement on the denouncement of the US of China's ADIZ, clarified the State's position: '[t]he United States does not apply its ADIZ procedures to foreign aircraft not intending to enter U.S. national airspace'.[946] Furthermore, the *Commander's Handbook on the Law of Naval Operations* confirms that the legal basis of the US ADIZ regulations rests on this territorial connection:

> The legal basis for ADIZ regulations is the right of a State to establish reasonable conditions of entry into its territory. Accordingly, an aircraft approaching national airspace can be required to identify itself while in international airspace as a condition of entry approval.[947]

This includes State aircraft, on which the US government has explicitly stated its position:

> in accordance with the norm of airborne innocent passage [sic],[948] the United States does not recognize the right of a coastal nation to apply its ADIZ procedures to foreign state aircraft not intending to enter national airspace nor does the United States apply its ADIZ procedures to foreign state aircraft not intending to enter United States airspace.[949]

---

944. Peter Haanappel, 'Aerial Sovereignty: from Paris 1919, Through Chicago 1944, to Today' in Pablo Mendes de Leon and Niall Buissing (eds), *Behind and Beyond the Chicago Convention: The Evolution of Aerial Sovereignty* (Wolters Kluwer 2019) 28.
945. 14 C.F.R. §99.1(a). At the same time, Su questions the wording of §§99.9(a), 99.11(a) and 99.15(a) (2015), which seem to require all aircraft in the ADIZ, regardless of any connection of their operation to US national airspace, to maintain a two-way radio connection, to have submitted a flight plan and to submit position reports.
946. Statement on the East China Sea ADIZ – US Secretary of State (n 897).
947. The Commander's Handbook (n 943) 2.7.2.3.
948. The use of this term is peculiar given that States have freedom of overflight outside national airspace. Under international law there is no 'airborne innocent passage' and innocent passage applies only to vessels and only in territorial seas.
949. United States of America Congressional Record, Proceedings and Debates of the 113th Congress – Second Session (Volume 160-Part 8, 20 June-15 July 2014) 11803.

Based on this, the *Commander's Handbook* directs US military aircraft not intending to enter another State's national airspace to 'not identify themselves or otherwise comply with ADIZ procedures established by other States, unless the United States has specifically agreed to do so'.[950]

In practice though, the US does not necessarily adhere to the exclusion of State aircraft from its ADIZ procedures. For instance, in March 2020, Russian fighter jets were intercepted and 'escorted' through the US ADIZ off the coast of Alaska for the duration of their four-hour flight.[951] This response is difficult to reconcile with the US's stated exemption of foreign State aircraft from its ADIZ procedures. It indicates that while the US does not expressly impose its ADIZ procedures on State aircraft that do not intend to enter national airspace, practice – at least on this occasion – suggests that it acts towards such aircraft in the same manner as if it would in the case that the ADIZ procedures did apply to them and had been breached. Having said this, and as will be discussed in Section 4.3.5, there is no express prohibition under international law on intercepting State aircraft in international airspace, or rules regulating the action.

The US[952] and some academics[953] have referred to the Chicago Convention as providing a legal basis for ADIZs in the case that a State only applies the procedures to aircraft bound for, or exiting, national airspace.

For civil aircraft, Article 11, 'Applicability of air regulations', reads:

> the laws and regulations of a contracting State relating to the admission to or departure from its territory of aircraft engaged in international air navigation, ... shall be complied with by such aircraft upon entering or departing from ... the territory of that State.

The US legitimises the application of ADIZs to State aircraft through Article 3(c) of the Chicago Convention.[954] Although State aircraft are excluded from the scope of the Chicago Convention, Article 3(c) requires 'authorization by special agreement' to have been obtained for a State aircraft to operate a flight over the territory of another State.[955] The argument proceeds that the coastal State may impose the ADIZ requirements through the terms of the diplomatic arrangements that have been made between the States pursuant to Article 3(c) of the Chicago Convention. Given that States decide on the terms of these agreements bilaterally, this section will instead focus on the scope of application of Article 11.

950. The Commander's Handbook (n 943) 2.7.2.3; Peter A Dutton, 'Caelum Liberum: Air Defense Identification Zones Outside Sovereign Airspace' (2009) 103 Am J Int'l L 691, 700.
951. 'US and Canadian Jets Intercepted Russian Reconnaissance Planes near Alaska' (Business Insider, 10 March 2020), available at www.businessinsider.com/us-canadian-jets-intercept-russian-reconnaissance-planes-near-alaska-2020-3?international = true&r = US&IR = T accessed 11 March 2020.
952. Stefan A Kaiser, 'The Legal Status of Air Defense Identification Zones: Tensions over the East China Sea' (2014) 63 ZWL 527, 538.
953. Roach (n 921) para. 7: the author argues that a State does not have the right to require aircraft to comply with ADIZ requirements if they are not intending to enter national airspace; Head (n 915) 189-190.
954. Kaiser (n 952) 538.
955. *See* Section 2.4 for discussion on Article 3(c).

Kaiser[956] and Papp[957] argue that, while Article 11 is to be interpreted literally, it does not extend to providing a legal basis for ADIZs. The grounds on which Kaiser and Papp reach this conclusion are different, however.

Kaiser argues that Article 11 'expressly permits national identification procedures which bind aircraft ... in international airspace, provided they are entering or departing national airspace' but that ADIZs go beyond this and cannot therefore be justified under this article.[958] He points out, in support of this line of reasoning, that it is standard practice in international civil aviation to require identification and reporting of aircraft at certain locations and that there is no need to establish a zone to do so.[959]

Papp argues that Article 11 does not provide 'explicit legal grounds for regulating acts/events occurring abroad' and that it therefore cannot serve as an express rule permitting ADIZs. Papp's initial statement is accurate; however, the conclusion is non sequitur. Article 11, when considered in the context of the Chicago Convention as a whole, implicitly includes laws and regulations that make entry conditional upon obligations fulfilled abroad. For example, Annex 9 of the Chicago Convention, 'Facilitation', which mentions Article 11, among others, as having 'special pertinence' to the SARPs it contains, includes provisions recognising that States may establish prior obligations for flights to be permitted to enter their territory.[960]

The above arguments cannot be used by States with an ADIZ that also applies to aircraft not intending to enter national airspace. There are two main, more general, arguments that are relied upon to support a State's right to establish an ADIZ in this case. First, that coastal States have the right to restrict the military activities of other States in their EEZs and, second, the right of self-defence, as to which *see* the discussion in the following sections.

4.3.3.2 Restricting Military Activities in the EEZ

China is one of approximately twenty States asserting what it claims as its right as a coastal State, to regulate or prohibit military activities in its EEZ,[961] a position which

956. Kaiser (n 952) 529.
957. Zoltán Papp, 'Air Defense Identification Zone (ADIZ) in the light of Public International Law' (2015) 2 Pecs J Int Eur Law 28, 38-39.
958. Kaiser (n 952) 530 and 542.
959. *Ibid.* 530. *See also*, Su (n 906) 824: 'Under international law, a State need not establish an ADIZ so as to require identification of entering aircraft.'
960. Chicago Convention, Annex 9 (15th edn, October 2017) Foreword (ix) and 2.33, respectively.
961. States include Bangladesh, Brazil, Burma, Cape Verde, Guyana, India, Indonesia, Iran, Kenya, Malaysia, the Maldives, Mauritius, Pakistan, Peru, Portugal, North Korea, and Uruguay. *See*, variously: Stuart Kaye, Freedom of Navigation in the Indo-Pacific Region (Papers in Australian Maritime Affairs No. 22, Sea Power Centre Australia, 2008) 8-12; Euan Graham, 'Southeast Asia's Neglected Navigational and Overflight Challenges' (The Interpreter, 27 February 2017), available at www.lowyinstitute.org/the-interpreter/southeast-asia-s-neglected-navigational-and-overflight-challenges accessed 13 August 2018; Dutton (n 950) 696-697; Raul Pedrozo, 'Military Activities in the Exclusive Economic Zone: East Asia Focus' (2014) 90 Int'l L Stud 514, 521-522.

objection to has resulted in serious consequences.[962] In practice, the conflict that has arisen in relation to China's ADIZ has centred on the restrictions it places on foreign military aircraft.[963] China's establishment of its ADIZ is possibly in pursuance of this interpretation of coastal State power in the EEZ to restrict the operation of foreign military aircraft in the zone. Burke and Cevallos present this view more bluntly, stating that the Chinese government saw the establishment of its ADIZ as 'a means to legitimize and promote this interpretation and limit US and other foreign and military surveillance activities above the EEZ'.[964] In 2018, Bangladesh, another State declaring the right of a coastal State to control foreign military activity in its EEZ, established an ADIZ that coincided with the dimensions of its EEZ. In commenting on this feature, the ICAO Secretariat reiterated that the EEZ has no effect on airspace.[965]

The interpretation of coastal State powers to include the right to regulate military activities in the EEZ is problematic as a justification for ADIZs on a practical level for two reasons. First, it fails to legitimise the application of the zones to civil aircraft and, second, even if the ADIZ procedures were applied solely to military air operations, the argument still does not hold for those States whose ADIZs extend beyond their EEZs, which is the case for China.[966]

Beyond these practical reasons, the interpretation is, more crucially, problematic because there is no legal basis for restricting military operations in the EEZ, provided they do not interfere with the coastal State's exercise of its EEZ rights and jurisdiction. UNCLOS regulates military activities of foreign States in the territorial seas, but it provides little in the way of further regulation.[967] In the high seas, military activities are accepted as a high seas freedom[968] provided that they are conducted for peaceful

962. In 2001 a mid-air collision between an F-8-II fighter aircraft from China and an EP-3E Aries aircraft from the US led to the death of the pilot of the Chinese aircraft. China intercepted the US aircraft on the basis that it was an intelligence gathering flight in its EEZ, which China views as being a violation of international law. For a discussion of this case *see*, Stuart Kaye, 'Freedom of Navigation, Surveillance and Security: Legal Issues Surrounding the Collection of Intelligence from Beyond the Littoral' (2005) 24 Aust YBIL 93, 102-104.
963. Burke and Cevallos (n 909) 8.
964. *Ibid.* 11.
965. ICAO WP/29, *Civil/Military Cooperation Update*, Presented by the Secretariat, 9th Meeting of the South Asia/Indian Ocean ATM Coordination Group, Bangkok (26-29 March 2019) 2.15. *See also*, Section 2.7.3.2.
966. China's ADIZ extends more than 300 miles from its coast (Section 4.3.1), which amounts to more than 260 nm and therefore exceeds China's EEZ by more than 60 nm.
967. Making clear that innocent passage does not include: research or survey activities, which is understood to include military surveillance; the launching, landing or taking on board of any military device; interference with systems of communication or other facilities or installations; or, 'any other activity not having a direct bearing on passage' (UNCLOS, Article 19(j), (f), (k) and (l)). In addition, submarines and other underwater vehicles are required to surface when navigating in territorial seas (UNCLOS, Article 20. This applies to all underwater vehicles, military and non-military alike). Finally, Article 30 provides that a coastal State may require a warship to leave its territorial sea in the case that the warship 'does not comply with the laws and regulations of the coastal State concerning passage though the territorial sea and disregards any request for compliance'.
968. Myron H Nordquist, Neal R Grandy, Sataya N Nandan and Shabtai Rosenne (eds), *United Nations Convention on the Law of the Sea 1982: A Commentary – Volume II* (Martinus Nijhoff 1993) 85.

purposes.[969] In the EEZ, both the explicit, limited sovereign rights and jurisdiction of the coastal State and the freedoms enjoyed by other States in the zone, including freedom of overflight, support the conclusion that the coastal State does not have the right to interfere with peaceful military activities.[970] The purpose of the EEZ is, as the name indicates, for the economic benefit of the coastal State through the State's protection and exploitation of the natural resources in the area and beyond this, it does not have a national security purpose. From the perspective of the rights of the other States in the zone, UNCLOS stipulates that freedom of overflight applies in the EEZ which, as mentioned previously, applies to both State and civil aircraft and includes the right to conduct aerial military activities.[971] The only exception to this is that freedom of overflight in the EEZ, as with the rights and freedoms of other States in general in the EEZ, must be exercised with due regard to the coastal State's rights and duties in the zone.[972] It is in this limited context that the coastal State has the right under UNCLOS to regulate activities, including military activities, in its EEZ. While it is perhaps more relevant to vessels rather than aircraft, considering that interference with EEZ rights is more likely to occur from activities on or under the surface of the sea, it applies equally to aircraft. It is unclear to what extent coastal States are permitted to regulate activities, including whether certain activities, such as the use of weapons, are per se prohibited.[973] The beginning of this section noted that there are a number of States who claim a right, to varying extents, to regulate military activities in their EEZs. Some practices of these States may be justified as regulations to protect their coastal State EEZ rights and obligations; however, other practice goes beyond the scope of this right, for example, to serve purely national security interests, which is considered by Klein as a position that 'at present ... could well be construed as in violation of international law'.[974] The establishment of ADIZs is not justified as a measure to protect the limited EEZ rights and jurisdiction provided to the coastal State under UNCLOS and would instead need to be justified on the basis of a customary international law right to regulate military activities beyond the scope of UNCLOS, the formation of which, as suggested here, there is currently insufficient evidence to support.

969. UNCLOS, Article 88.
970. Bernard H Oxman, 'The Regime of Warships under the United Nations Convention on the Law of the Sea' (1984) 24 Va J Int'l L 809, 838; Umberto Leanza and Maria Cristina Caracciolo, 'The Exclusive Economic Zone' in David J Attard, Malgosia Fitzmaurice and Norman A Martínez Gutiérrez (eds), *The IMLI Manual on International Maritime Law: Volume 1 – The Law of the Sea* (OUP 2014) 192-193; Klein (n 920) 46-47; Pedrozo (n 961) 524. *See* Section 3.2.2 for a discussion on the sovereign rights and jurisdiction granted to the coastal State under the EEZ regime.
971. *See* Sections 1.3.1, 2.6.5 and 3.2.2.
972. UNCLOS, Article 58(3).
973. Charlotte Beaucillon, 'Limiting Third States' Military Activities in the EEZ: "Due Regard Obligations" and the Law of the Use of Force Applied to Nuclear Weapons' (2019) 34 IJMCL 128, 133; Klein (n 920) 49-50.
974. Klein (n 920) 47.

4.3.3.3 The Right to Self-Defence

ADIZs are predominantly explained as a tool for protecting national security, the idea being that a State will be able to perceive a threat from the air in advance. The right to self-defence is frequently explored as a possible legal basis for ADIZs on these grounds, and while it is still used as a justification,[975] it meets widespread criticism.[976]

The right to self-defence is recognised in Article 51 of the UN Charter, which states:

> Nothing in the present Charter shall impair the inherent right of individual or collective self-defence if an armed attack occurs against a Member of the United Nations.[977]

Both the threat that the right to self-defence is designed to address and the act of self-defence are not those that apply in the case of the establishment of ADIZs. It is the former of these that this section will examine in more detail. Specifically, it will demonstrate that even if the right to self-defence includes the right to act in the case of an imminent threat - as opposed to an armed attack - the 'threat' that ADIZs are designed to address is not the type of threat giving rise to the right to self-defence.

In terms of the latter, the right of self-defence exists as an exception to the prohibition against the use of force: it justifies the *use of force* by a State where that force would otherwise not be permitted under international law.[978] The principle of self-defence exists as an interim measure for States to protect themselves pending action by the UN Security Council, not as an ongoing tool to mitigate the risk of breaches of national security.[979] It does not envisage the establishment of a zone in international airspace for reporting and notification of aircraft, even if those aims are for the purpose of national security.

975. Peace and Security Research Unit at East Asia Institute, Interview with Min Gyo Koo, Associate Professor, Seoul National University (10 December 2013), available at www.eai.or.kr/main/english/search_view.asp?intSeq=8929&board=eng_multimedia accessed 17 January 2019.
976. *See*, for example, Head (n 915) 192; Kay Hailbronner, 'The Legal Regime of the Airspace above the Exclusive Economic Zone' (1983) 8(1) Air Law 30, 42-43; Papp (n 921) 45-47; Kaiser (n 952) 531-533; Cuadra (n 913) 501-504; Eugène Pépin, *The Law of the Air and the Draft Articles Concerning the Law of the Sea Adopted by the International Law Commission at Its Eighth Session* (A/CONF.13/4) – Extract from the *Official Records of the United Nations Conference on the Law of the Sea, Volume I* (Preparatory Documents), United Nations Conference on the Law of the Sea, Geneva, 24 February-27 April 1958, 70.
977. UN Charter, Article 51. The armed attack need not necessarily be carried out by regular armed forces for a State to have recourse to the right of self-defence (Christopher Greenwood, 'Self-Defence' (Max Planck Encylcopedia of Public International Law 2011) 11, referring to, *Military and Paramilitary Activities in and against Nicaragua (Nicaragua v. United States of America)*, Merits, I.C.J. Rep. 1986 (27 June) p. 14, p. 103 para. 195 ('*Military and Paramilitary Activities Case (Nicaragua v. United States of America)*')).
978. YILC (2001) Vol. II, Part 2, 74.
979. UN Charter, Article 51: '... until the Security Council has taken the measures necessary to maintain international peace and security'. *See also*, Christine Gray, *International Law and the Use of Force* (4th edn, OUP 2018) 48; Greenwood (n 977) 2.

4.3.3.3.1 *Not an Imminent Threat*

The right to self-defence arises in the case of an armed attack but, depending on interpretation, it may also apply in the case of an imminent threat. The former – an armed attack having occurred – is clearly not relevant when talking of the establishment of an ADIZ, and so if customary international law does allow for acts of self-defence in the case of an imminent attack, the question then is whether the establishment of ADIZs can be justified on the basis of an 'imminent threat'.

There is ongoing debate about whether the right to self-defence includes the right to act against an *imminent* threat as opposed to an armed attack.[980] The question of imminence is seen as an element of consideration of the necessity of the act of self-defence,[981] with necessity and proportionality being the well-established criteria for determining its legality.[982] States including the US, the UK and Australia claim that under customary international law the right to self-defence applies to an imminent threat.[983] The position is controversial not least because it goes against the literal interpretation of Article 51, which clearly requires that the right be exercised only 'if an armed attack occurs'. Opponents of an interpretation that includes the right to act against an imminent threat argue that 'the limits imposed on self-defence in Article 51 would be meaningless if a wider customary law right to self-defence survives unfettered by these restrictions'.[984] In pursuit of considering whether the establishment of ADIZs can be justified on the basis of the right to self-defence, this section will proceed on the basis of the more generous interpretation, encompassing an imminent threat.

980. *See*, for example, David Kretzmer, 'The Inherent Right to Self-Defence and Proportionality in Jus Ad Bellum' (2013) 24(1) EJIL 235, 247; Daniel Bethlehem, 'Principles Relevant to the Scope of a State's Right of Self-Defense Against an Imminent or Actual Armed Attack by Non-state Actors' (2012) 106 Am J Int'l L 1, 1; Marko Milanovic, 'The Solemani Strike and Self-Defence Against an Imminent Armed Attack' (EJIL:Talk!, 7 January 2020), available at www.ejiltalk.org/the-soleimani-strike-and-self-defence-against-an-imminent-armed-attack/ accessed 27 June 2019.
981. Jeremy Wright, 'The Modern Law of Self-Defence' (Speech delivered at the International Institute for Strategic Studies, London, 11 January 2017).
982. *Military and Paramilitary Activities Case (Nicaragua v. United States of America)*, p. 103 para. 194.
983. Brian J Egan, 'International Law, Legal Diplomacy, and the Counter-ISIL Campaign' (Speech delivered at the American Society of International Law, Washington DC, 1 April 2016): 'Under the *jus ad bellum*, a State may use force in the exercise of its inherent right of self-defense not only in response to armed attacks that have occurred, but also in response to imminent ones before they occur'; Wright (n 981): '... the long-standing UK view is that Article 51 of the UN Charter does not require a state passively to await an attack, but includes the "inherent right" – as it's described in Article 51 – to use force in self-defence against an "imminent" armed attack, referring back to customary international law'; George Brandis, 'The Right of Self-Defence Against Imminent Armed Attack in International Law' (Public Lecture delivered at the University of Queensland, Brisbane, 11 April 2017), available at www.ejiltalk.org/the-right-of-self-defence-against-imminent-armed-attack-in-international-law accessed 27 June 2019, 6: '... it is now recognised that customary international law permits self-defence not only against an armed attack that has occurred but also against one that is imminent. It has certainly been the long-held Australian position that acting in self-defence does not require a State passively to await attack'.
984. Gray (n 979) 124.

A State's right to self-defence under Article 51 of the UN Charter is a recognition of the right under customary international law.[985] Those in favour of the right of self-defence in the case of an imminent attack point to the Caroline case of 1837 as providing the foundation of the customary international law of self-defence.[986] This case involved the destruction of the US vessel, the *Caroline*, by British forces in US territory, and ultimately the vessel being sent over Niagara Falls. The legal test that has endured was part of a series of notes that formed the subsequent negotiations between the two States. In the correspondence, both States agreed that the exercise of the right of self-defence 'should be confined to cases in which the necessity of that self-defence is instant, overwhelming, and leaving no choice of means, and no moment for deliberation', a statement that established the concept of anticipatory self-defence, or self-defence in response to an imminent threat, in international law.[987]

Based on this, returning to the initial question of whether the establishment of ADIZs can be justified on the basis of an imminent threat, the short answer is no. If a State does indeed have a right to self-defence in the case of an imminent threat, it does not apply in the case of a mere possibility of a future attack by air, as ADIZs are established to address. The ambiguity around imminence instead arises in the case that a 'highly probable and severe threat exists', in which case a State might have the right to self-defence even if the threat is temporally remote.[988] Considering this, ADIZs fail to meet the test of necessity to be justified through the principle of self-defence, and more so, the future threat that ADIZs are employed to mitigate is so far removed from what can be considered as imminent that the principle of self-defence is not relevant.

4.3.3.3.2 Self-defence in the Case of Non-compliance with ADIZ Procedures

Another way of considering the legality of ADIZs under the principle of self-defence is in relation to the measures taken within ADIZs, where the armed attack or imminent threat is the failure of an aircraft to follow the procedures within the zone and the act of self-defence is the measure taken against the aircraft in response.

This proposition cannot be supported by international law, however. While the term 'armed attack' is not defined under international law, it is uncontroversial that it does not include non-military threats 'no matter how damaging they may be to that State's rights and interests'.[989] Failure to comply with ADIZ procedures cannot be framed as an armed attack or, consistent with the above analysis, as an imminent threat, at least not without accompanying factors that suggest such intent. As Kaiser

985. *Military and Paramilitary Activities Case (Nicaragua v. United States of America)*, p. 94 para. 176.
986. HL Deb 21 April 2004, Vol. 660, col 370: 'Article 51 recognises the inherent right of self-defence that states enjoy under international law. That can be traced back to the "Caroline" incident in 1837.'
987. Letter from Mr Webster to Lord Ashburton (Department of State, Washington, 6 August 1842).
988. Dapo Akande and Thomas Liefländer, 'Clarifying Necessity, Imminence, and Proportionality in the Law of Self-Defence' (2013) 107(3) Am J Int'l L 563, 565.
989. Greenwood (n 977) 9.

has noted, '[n]on-compliance with unilateral procedures within such an ADIZ does not in any instance indicate a hostile intent'.[990]

If an aircraft's failure to comply with orders is perceived as constituting a threat to national security, just as if it is seen as being a threat to the safety of other airspace users, there are protocols to follow under international civil aviation law to manage the threat, as will be explained in Section 4.3.5. ADIZs are irrelevant to implementing these protocols. Similarly, if an aircraft is used to conduct an armed attack or pose an imminent threat, as determined under international law, the right to self-defence applies regardless of an ADIZ being in place.

4.3.3.4 The Right to Establish ADIZs as Customary International Law

4.3.3.4.1 Academic Consideration

There is mixed opinion in academia as to whether a State has the right to establish an ADIZ under customary international law. Cuadra, writing in 1978, saw the practice as 'customary law in the making',[991] while Hailbronner, writing soon after, believed that this was doubtful.[992] Both authors indicated that the crystallisation, if it were to occur, would be in conflict with codified international law.[993] As discussed in Section 3.3.4.6, customary law can develop in conflict with codified international law, but the standard required to show its formation is more rigorous. In the context of ADIZs, Cuadra noted this, stating that:

> any legal basis for ADIZ's [sic] extending over the high seas must derive from some aspect of customary international law that is so fundamental a principle as to prevail over the will of the community of nations as expressed in these conventions.[994]

This is relevant in the case that, in establishing an ADIZ off its coast, the coastal State is acting in breach of a codified norm of international law. This will be considered below in Sections 4.3.6.1 and 4.3.6.2 in the context of, respectively, safety obligations under international civil aviation law and the principle of freedom of overflight under UNCLOS.

In contrast to Cuadra, O'Connell, arguing that the freedom of the seas is a fluid concept that shifts in accordance with the changing balance of the needs of the international community, states that 'the abstract freedom of the sea will not stand in the way' of States imposing ADIZs.[995] He furthermore describes ADIZs as an example

990. Kaiser (n 952) 531.
991. Cuadra (n 913) 485.
992. Hailbronner (n 976) 43.
993. Cuadra in reference to, among others, the Convention on the Territorial Sea and the Contiguous Zone 1958, and the fact that 'security' is not included among the purposes for which coastal States may exercise jurisdiction in their contiguous zones (Cuadra (n 913) 499); Hailbronner referring to the impending UNCLOS, in particular the decision to exclude security from the list of purposes for which States may act in their contiguous zone (Hailbronner (n 976) 43).
994. Cuadra (n 913) 500-501.
995. DP O'Connell, *The International Law of the Sea – Vol II* (OUP 1982) 796-797.

of 'where it is generally thought acceptable that States should insist upon certain conduct on or over the high seas'.[996] As discussed in Section 1.2.1, the freedom of the seas, and specifically freedom of overflight in this context, is not static; it must and it does adapt as our uses of the sea develop over time. Although it is abstract, in that there is no defined, exhaustive list of permitted or prohibited activities that fall within it, it is a foundational principle of the law of the sea and the unilateral exercise of jurisdiction over international airspace for the purpose of national security must be carefully considered in light of other rights and freedoms, which will be further examined in respect of ADIZs in Section 4.3.6.2. Seemingly contradictorily, O'Connell also recognises this, asserting:

> self-defence or national security is an insecure foundation for seeking to qualify the freedom of the seas, for it could lend plausibility to restraints that would not sustain the balance of the interests of the international community.[997]

In any case, O'Connell's comment suggests that he was of the opinion that the establishment of ADIZs had become customary international law, which is the purpose for which his observations above have been included at this point.

Today, views range from the right to establish an ADIZ having been crystallised as customary international law,[998] to it possibly having been crystallised,[999] to there being no evidence to support its crystallisation.[1000] The lack of comprehensive, publicly available ADIZ procedures from some States contributes to this absence of a consensus.[1001]

4.3.3.4.2 State Practice

As discussed in Section 3.3.4.2, the ICJ demonstrated a shift in its determination of State practice between the 1969 *North Sea Continental Shelf Cases* and the 1986 decision in the *Military and Paramilitary Activities Case*, to what seems to be a less rigorous threshold. Recalling this section, in the former, the practice was required to be 'extensive and virtually uniform', while in the latter, it was determined that it 'should, in general, be consistent with such rules'.[1002] Balancing these statements, the ILC has

996. O'Connell (n 995) 797.
997. *Ibid.*
998. Roach (n 921) 6; Su (n 906) 812-813.
999. Papp (n 921) 347.
1000. Haanappel (n 944) 28; Kaiser (n 952) 537.
1001. Su (n 906) 813-814 and 822-823. Cuba, Iceland, Indonesia, Panama, and the Philippines are mentioned, specifically in relation to whether their ADIZ procedures apply to transiting aircraft or only to aircraft that intend to enter national airspace (pp. 822-823). More generally, the author explains that 'some States have not published their rules for ADIZs in AIPs and some AIPs are difficult to access for the public' (p. 814).
1002. *North Sea Continental Shelf (Federal Republic of Germany/Netherlands; Federal Republic of Germany/Denmark)*, Judgment, I.C.J. Rep. 1969 (20 February), p. 3, p. 43 para. 74; *Military and Paramilitary Activities Case (Nicaragua v. United States of America)*, p. 98 para. 186.

indicated that the practice 'must be generally consistent' and 'sufficiently widespread and representative [but] ... need not be universal'.[1003]

Kaiser argues against the right to establish an ADIZ being customary international law on the basis that, although a number of States have established them, there is too great a variation in them for there to be sufficiently formed State practice and furthermore, the response of States to ADIZs does not reflect the existence of *opinio juris*, as to which *see* Section 4.3.3.4.3.[1004] Referring back to Section 4.3.1, Kaiser points out that in contrast to there being a customary international law, 'there is discrepancy in the understanding of States about the legal nature of an ADIZ [and] the positions of the US and Canada signify the archetypes of this discrepancies [sic]'.[1005]

The determination of whether State practice in the case of ADIZs is sufficient for the purpose of customary international law depends on how the divergence between States is viewed in terms of its significance. Arguing for the existence of sufficient State practice in the establishment of ADIZs, we know that there are a number of States[1006] that currently have, or have in the past established, ADIZs outside their territorial boundaries and that the purpose of these ADIZs is, at least formally, national security. In general, the zones require reporting conditions, radar and transponder requirements, and the obligation to follow the orders of certain national authorities. Beyond this though, there are significant variations in the practice, including in relation to: the breadth of the ADIZ; its confinement to the State's FIR or extension beyond into another State's; whether its procedures apply to transiting aircraft or only to aircraft flying into or out of the State's territory; whether they apply to military aircraft or civil aircraft, or both; purported enforcement measures in the case of non-compliance; whether an aircraft is required to report to the CAA or to a particular government ministry; which national authority issues orders to aircraft; how transparent the procedures are, including how and to what extent they are communicated to airspace users; whether the ADIZ is temporary or permanent; whether prior approval is required for aircraft to operate in the zone; and, of course, what information the procedures require the commander of the aircraft to impart and through which method.[1007]

When the ICJ, in the *Military and Paramilitary Activities Case*, determined that State practice 'should, in general, be consistent with such rules', it also added that it need not be in '*absolute rigorous* conformity' (emphasis added). Although this latter statement is in the negative, it indicates a high threshold in determining when State

1003. Michael Wood, 'Second Report on Identification of Customary International Law' (ILC 66th Session, 22 May 2014) 45.
1004. Kaiser (n 952) 537.
1005. *Ibid.* 537. In particular, the fact that Canada's ADIZ procedures apply to aircraft not intending to enter its national airspace, as to which *see* Section 4.3.1.
1006. *See* Section 4.3.2 (n 921). Noting that the number of States adopting the practice is only one element for consideration and a small number of States adopting the practice or a large number is not determinative either way (Wood (n 1003) 38).
1007. Many of these factors are considered and State practice compared in, Su (n 906) 834-835. As mentioned earlier, Su concludes that the right to establish ADIZ is customary international law despite these discrepancies in the establishment and operation of ADIZ between States. This is consistent with the divergence in academic opinion on the matter, where the opposite conclusion is reached based on the same factual circumstances.

practice is considered 'consistent': the practice does not have to demonstrate *absolutely* rigorous conformity, but it should meet a significant degree of conformity. As an example of what does not constitute sufficiently consistent practice, the ILC refers to the *Asylum Case*, in which the ICJ referred to practice which displays 'so much uncertainty and contradiction, so much fluctuation and discrepancy ... it is not possible to discern in all this any constant and uniform usage, accepted as law, with regard to the alleged rule'.[1008] This is not to say that this is the standard required for practice not to be sufficient; State practice in this category is *clearly* not State practice that gives rise to customary international law.

There are significant variations in the practice of ADIZ establishment. On the other hand, if the core elements of ADIZ – a zone extending into international airspace in which obligations additional to ATS requirements are imposed on aircraft for the, at least formal, purpose of national security – are evidence of State practice, with all of the surrounding discrepancies put aside, then on this basis alone, State practice may be sufficiently consistent for the purpose of customary international law.

4.3.3.4.3 Opinio Juris

One of the factors that Cuadra raises as support for the development of customary international law in respect of ADIZs is the lack of protest against the zones that existed back then.[1009] Certainly, this seems to have been the initial response to the US ADIZ, which has been described as 'one of quiet compliance'.[1010] In examining whether this has been the case in intervening decades, and what the current state of *opinio juris* is in relation to ADIZ, it is necessary to draw a distinction between compliance with the zones by military aircraft and other, predominantly civil, aircraft.

While highlighting the fact that military aircraft are the primary subjects of ADIZs, as the predominant security threat vis-à-vis civil aircraft and other State aircraft, Su states that military aircraft transiting ADIZs 'usually do not comply with voluntary identification measures in foreign ADIZs, except perhaps out of courtesy or cooperation between military allies'.[1011] This is consistent with reports of Russian and Chinese military aircraft operating in the ADIZs of South Korea and Japan,[1012] as well as Russia's flyovers in the US's ADIZ, mentioned in Section 4.3.3.1. US military aircraft are, again as discussed in Section 4.3.3.1, only compliant with a State's ADIZ procedures when they intend to enter the State's airspace. Given that most ADIZs also apply to transiting aircraft,[1013] US military aircraft also contravene ADIZs under these

1008. Wood (n 1003) 41, citing *Asylum Case (Colombia/Peru)*, Judgment, I.C.J. Rep. 1950 (20 November), p. 266, p. 277.
1009. Cuadra (n 913) 504.
1010. Head (n 915) 182.
1011. Su (n 906) 825.
1012. Josh Smith, 'Explainer: Competing Claims Make Northeast Asia Sea a Flashpoint' (Reuters, 25 July 2019), available at www.reuters.com/article/us-southkorea-russia-aircraft-explainer/explainer-competing-claims-make-northeast-asian-sea-a-flashpoint-idUSKCN1UK0NO accessed 28 November 2019; Jakhar (n 920).
1013. Su (n 906) 832.

circumstances, for instance, in China's ADIZ: the US has continued to 'assert US prerogatives' by operating its military aircraft in the ADIZs without complying with the prescribed procedures.[1014] On this basis, there is no evidence to suggest that there is *opinio juris* insofar as ADIZs apply to military aircraft. Considering both the national security purpose of ADIZs and that ATC procedures under international civil aviation law independently of ADIZs lead to the identification of civil aircraft in international airspace, this results in a peculiar situation insofar as the practical contribution of ADIZs in protecting national security. This is all the more so considering that coastal States have no greater enforcement jurisdiction in their ADIZs than they do in any other portion of international airspace.

The determination of *opinio juris* in respect of civil aircraft is more ambiguous. A State that believes its rights have been infringed by the unilateral exercise of jurisdiction will usually object upon the exercise of prescriptive jurisdiction, that is, in this case, upon the declaration of the establishment of an ADIZ:

> a State ordinarily protests as soon as another State makes undesirable assertions of prescriptive jurisdiction. The former State will not wait until the enforcement of these assertions, because it will believe that the latter will sooner or later go on to effectively enforce its laws.[1015]

The State's *initial* objection may not necessarily correspond with the State's subsequent actions, however, and indeed a State's *ongoing* verbal objections may not be consistent with their actions. Taking China's ADIZ again as an example, many States protested against the zone when it was established,[1016] but airlines of these same States comply with the procedures in the ADIZ. While the US specifically rejects China's ADIZ, it informed its commercial aircraft that it expected them to comply with the procedures in the zone.[1017] South Korea's aircraft also comply with the reporting requirements in China's ADIZ despite the State objecting to the zone. Korean Airlines and Asiana Airlines initially failed to comply but then did so once the South Korean government provided that its airlines may decide to comply for safety reasons.[1018] On the other hand, Japan Airlines and All Nippon Airways initially adhered to the

1014. 'China's Air Defense Identification Zone: Impact on Regional Security' (Centre for Strategic and International Studies, 26 November 2013), available at www.csis.org/analysis/chinas-air-defense-identification-zone-impact-regional-security accessed 3 November 2019: 'China Says US Should Respect China's Air Defense Zone' (Reuters, 23 March 2017), available at www.reuters.com/article/us-china-usa-defence-idUSKBN16U0SB accessed 26 October 2018: 'China said on Thursday the United States should respect its air defense identification zone (ADIZ), after Chinese officials warned a U.S. bomber it was illegally flying inside China's self-declared zone in the East China Sea. The Pentagon rejected the Chinese call and said it would continue its flight operations in the region.'

1015. Cedric Ryngaert, *Jurisdiction in International Law* (OUP 2015) 41.

1016. *See* Section 4.3.1.

1017. Rinehart and Elias (n 898) 16; Jennifer Thompson, Simon Mundy and Jung-a Song, 'Japan to Take up Spat over China Air Zone with US' (Financial Times, 2 December 2013), available at www.ft.com/content/d4be05c6-5a61-11e3-942a-00144feabdc0 accessed 16 March 2019.

1018. Demetri Sevastopulo, 'Q&A: What Is an Air Defence Identification Zone?' (Financial Times, 12 December 2013), available at www.ft.com/content/26cf55ce-58da-11e3-a7cb-00144feabdc0 accessed 10 May 2019.

procedures but then changed their position after pressure from the Japanese government to ignore them.[1019]

The discord between States' verbal protests and practical adherence to China's ADIZ procedures no doubt arises out of the States' primary obligation to ensure the safety of civil aviation.[1020] It may also be a recognition by States of the fact that failing to comply with China's ADIZ requirements could conflict with the procedures they impose in their own ADIZs, or that they comply with in another State's ADIZ. As outlined in Section 4.3.1, the vigorous protest of a State against a feature of one State's ADIZ may illicit little or no response from the first State in relation to the ADIZ of another State with the same feature. In an area that is heavy with political intentions, ascertaining *opinio juris* is particularly difficult and the above examples demonstrate that the assessment of *opinio juris* needs to take into account not just the protest or adherence by States but also the reasons behind them. This has been emphasised by the ILC in its statement that adherence to a rule, regardless of the frequency with which the adherence occurs, is not sufficient to indicate the existence of *opinio juris* but rather, 'the motivation behind a certain practice must be discernible in order to identify a rule of customary international law'.[1021]

It is proposed here, based on the above analysis, that there is currently insufficient evidence to argue that there is a customary international law right to establish an ADIZ. Both elements of customary international law – State practice and *opinio juris* – present hurdles in terms of the approach of States being inconsistent and conflicting, although demonstrating a sufficient standard of *opinio juris* at this stage is particularly problematic. Certainly, it is not present in relation to State aircraft, and for civil aircraft, the subjective intentions of States remain ambiguous.

4.3.4 The Persistence of the *Lotus* Principle

The 1927 *Lotus Case* of the Permanent Court of International Justice (PCIJ) is still the only case in which the PCIJ/ICJ has directly addressed the matter of jurisdiction.[1022] Despite the particular context of the case,[1023] the judgment became 'the main standard of reference for such conflicts [i.e. jurisdictional conflicts] in all legal areas' and continues to be 'the basic framework of reference for questions of jurisdiction under

1019. Sevastopulo (n 1018). Singapore Airlines, Cathay Pacific and Taiwanese airlines complied from the outset.
1020. *See* Section 2.2.2.3.
1021. Wood (n 1003) 58 and 56, respectively.
1022. Ryngaert (n 1015) 4.
1023. On this point, President Bedjaoui stated in his Declaration to the *Nuclear Weapons Advisory Opinion* that: 'The Court's decision in the "*Lotus*" case, which some people will inevitably resurrect, should be understood to be of very limited application in the particular context of the question which is the subject of this Advisory Opinion. It would be to exaggerate the importance of that decision of the Permanent Court and to distort its scope were it to be divorced from the particular context, both judicial and temporal, in which it was taken. No doubt this decision expressed *the spirit of the times*, the spirit of an international society which as yet had few institutions and was governed by an international law of strict coexistence, itself a reflection of the vigour of the principle of State sovereignty' (Declaration of President Bedjaoui on *Legality of the Threat or Use of Nuclear Weapons*, Advisory Opinion, I.C.J. Rep. 1996 (8 July), p. 226, p. 270 para. 12 ('*Nuclear Weapons Advisory Opinion*')).

international law'.[1024] The ICJ has recognised the *Lotus* principle in subsequent decisions[1025] and most recently, although not explicitly referring to the case, was seen to have reaffirmed the reasoning in *Lotus* in its *Kosovo Advisory Opinion*.[1026]

In the *Lotus Case*, France asserted the argument that 'the Turkish Courts, in order to have jurisdiction, should be able to point to some title to jurisdiction recognised by international law in favour of Turkey', whereas Turkey argued, in contrast, that a State is permitted to exercise jurisdiction 'whenever such jurisdiction does not come into conflict with a principle of international law'.[1027] In addressing the matter, the Court drew a distinction between prescriptive and enforcement jurisdiction or, respectively, the capacity to make law and the capacity to ensure compliance with the law, as outlined in Section 1.2.1.

Addressing enforcement jurisdiction, the Court made clear that it 'cannot be exercised by a State outside its territory except by virtue of a permissive rule derived from international custom or from a convention'.[1028] However, a State does have the right, the Court went on to declare, failing the existence of a rule under international law prohibiting it, to exercise jurisdiction in its territory for acts committed outside its national borders.[1029] In other words, a State may prescribe laws for acts outside its territory provided that there is no prohibition under international law.

The *Lotus* principle, as the Court's approach to extraterritorial jurisdiction is referred to, has met widespread criticism for its positivist approach to international law. Positivist theory, at its most simplistic, says that the law consists of that which has been posited; depending on the system, this may include, for example, legislation, common law and custom.[1030] A positivist understanding of international law says that the law is made by States for States; they 'enjoy unrestricted authority and freedom on the international plane, which flows from their statehood status and as an ontological consequence of (external) sovereignty'.[1031] The *Lotus* principle has continued to influence the reasoning of the ICJ, but more broadly, it is viewed as being outdated in

1024. Ryngaert (n 1015) 30 and 31.
1025. *See*, for example, *Nuclear Weapons Advisory Opinion*, p. 238 para. 21; *Military and Paramilitary Activities Case (Nicaragua v. United States of America)*, p. 24 para. 29.
1026. *Accordance with International Law of the Unilateral Declaration of Independence in Respect of Kosovo*, Advisory Opinion, I.C.J Rep. 2010 (22 July) p. 403, pp. 425-426 para. 56 ('*Kosovo Advisory Opinion*'). For discussion on the Court's reasoning in this Opinion as based on the *Lotus Case see*, Photini Pazartzis, 'Judicial Activism and Judicial Self Restraint' in Malgosia Fitzmaurice and Christian J Tams (eds), *Legacies of the Permanent Court of International Justice* (Martinus Nijhoff Publishers 2013) 332-333; Helmut Philipp Aust, *Complicity and the Law of State Responsibility* (CUP 2011) 68.
1027. *The Case of S.S. Lotus (France v. Turkey)* (1927) P.C.I.J. Series A, No. 10, p. 18.
1028. *Ibid.* pp. 18-19.
1029. *The Case of S.S. Lotus (France v. Turkey)* (1927) P.C.I.J. Series A, No. 10, pp. 19.
1030. Leslie Green and Thomas Adams, 'Legal Positivism' (Stanford Encyclopedia of Philosophy, 17 December 2019), available at plato.stanford.edu/entries/legal-positivism/# accessed 2 February 2020.
1031. Stéphane Beaulac, 'The *Lotus* Case in Context: Sovereignty, Westphalia, Vattel, and Positivism' in Stephan Allen, Daniel Costelloe, Malgosia Fitzmaurice, Paul Gragl and Edward Guntrip (eds), *The Oxford Handbook of Jurisdiction in International Law* (OUP 2019) 48.

an international legal order that has evolved into a more complex and collective-interest oriented system.[1032]

In its *Kosovo Advisory Opinion*, the ICJ asked the question not of whether Kosovo had a right under international law to unilaterally declare independence from Serbia but, consistent with the *Lotus* principle, whether it was prohibited from doing so by a rule of international law.[1033] Judge Simma, in his Declaration on the Opinion, criticised the Court's approach:

> The Court's reading of the General Assembly's question and its reasoning, leaping as it does straight from the lack of a prohibition to permissibility, is a straightforward application of the so-called *Lotus* principle. ... Under this approach, everything which is not expressly prohibited carries with it the same colour of legality.[1034]

Rather, he opines, the Court could have:

> explored whether international law can be deliberately neutral or silent on a certain issue, and whether it allows for the concept of *toleration*, something which breaks from the binary understanding of permission/prohibition and which allows for a range of non-prohibited options. That an act might be 'tolerated' would not necessarily mean that it is 'legal', but rather that it is 'not illegal'. ... The neutrality of international law on a certain point simply suggests that there are areas where international law has not yet come to regulate, or indeed, will never come to regulate.[1035]

In the *Nuclear Weapons Advisory Opinion*, the ICJ, expressly referring to the *Lotus* decision, considered that 'States are free to threaten or use nuclear weapons unless it can be shown that they are bound not to do so *by reference to a prohibition* in either treaty law or customary law' (emphasis added).[1036] President Bedjaoui, in his Declaration on the opinion, expressed his opposition to the Court's approach:

> The resolutely positivist, voluntarist approach of international law still current at the beginning of the century – and which the Permanent Court did not fail to endorse in the aforementioned Judgment [*Lotus*] – has been replaced by an objective conception of international law, a law more readily seeking to reflect a collective juridical conscience and respond to the social necessities of States organized as a community.[1037]

Finally, in their separate joint decision in the *Arrest Warrant Case*, Judges Higgins, Kooijmans and Buergenthal made clear their position that the *Lotus* principle is no longer the reference point for extraterritorial jurisdiction, stating that 'the dictum

1032. Beaulac (n 1031) 54; *see also*, as will be discussed below, Declaration of President Bedjaoui on *Nuclear* Weapons *Advisory Opinion*, pp. 270-271 para. 13.
1033. *Kosovo Advisory Opinion*, p. 438 para. 83: 'To answer that question, the Court need only determine whether the declaration of independence violated either general international law or the *lex specialis* created by Security Council resolution 1244 (1999).'
1034. Declaration of Judge Simma on *Kosovo Advisory Opinion*, p. 480 para. 8.
1035. Declaration of Judge Simma on *Kosovo Advisory Opinion*, p. 480 para. 8. p. 480 para. 9.
1036. *Nuclear Weapons Advisory Opinion*, p. 238 para. 21.
1037. Declaration of President Bedjaoui on *Nuclear Weapons Advisory Opinion*, pp. 270-271 para. 13.

represents the high water mark of laissez-faire in international relations, and an era that has been significantly overtaken by other tendencies'.[1038] These views are supported by those of academics who argue that State practice suggests that the *Lotus* principle may no longer be valid and that instead, it seems that 'the international community has embraced a more restrictive approach, by requiring that the asserting state rely on a permissive principle for the exercise of jurisdiction to be lawful'.[1039] These permissive principles refer to bases of jurisdiction including territoriality, personality, the protective principle, and universality.[1040]

If the *Lotus* principle stands, States have prescriptive jurisdiction to impose ADIZ unless prohibited by international law.[1041] Section 4.3.6 will examine whether there is a prohibition under international law on a State to establish an ADIZ. In doing so, it will consider the safety and procedural regulations under international civil aviation law and the principle of freedom of overflight. These have been chosen, once again, as the most commonly raised matters in international law in respect of ADIZs.

On the other hand, if we have moved beyond the *Lotus* principle, a permissive rule of international law is required for States to establish ADIZ in international airspace. This view is supported by Cuadra who claims that '[e]ven if there had been no protests whatever [to ADIZs], the unilateral adoption of any aspect of sovereignty on or above the high seas must have some foundation in international law if it is to be lawful'.[1042] Hailbronner also argues in favour of this view: 'States claiming to have acquired new rights have a burden of proof. They may rely on the Convention [UNCLOS] only to the extent that it explicitly grants regulatory competence and enforcement power.'[1043] As has been established in Section 4.3.3, there is no legal basis for coastal States to rely on to justify the establishment of ADIZs.

Before turning to consider the possible prohibitions on establishing an ADIZ, the following section will briefly address the coastal State's right to respond to foreign aircraft in their ADIZs in the case of non-compliance. As has been made clear here in this section, regardless of whether the *Lotus* approach to prescriptive jurisdiction is accepted or not, States may only exercise enforcement jurisdiction in their territories in respect of acts that take place in their ADIZs, unless there is a permissive rule under international law providing for extraterritorial jurisdiction.

1038. *Case Concerning the Arrest Warrant of 11 April 2000 (Democratic Republic of Congo v. Belgium)*, Judgment, I.C.J. Rep. 2002 (14 February) p. 3, p. 78 para. 51 (Joint Separate Opinion of Judges Higgins, Kooijmans and Buergenthal).

1039. Cedric Ryngaert, 'The Concept of Jurisdiction in International Law' in Alexander Orakhelashvili (ed), *Research Handbook on Jurisdiction and Immunities in International Law* (Edward Elgar Publishing 2015) 55; *see also*, Rain Liivoja, *Criminal Jurisdiction over Armed Forces Abroad* (CUP 2017) 60: 'Ultimately, the claims that *Lotus* is invalid seem well grounded in State practice'; Malcolm Shaw, *International Law* (6th edn, CUP 2008) 656.

1040. Ryngaert (n 1015) 29.

1041. For a brief discussion on the *Lotus* decision in relation to ADIZ *see*, Papp (n 921) 33-34.

1042. Cuadra (n 913) 505.

1043. Kay Hailbronner, 'Freedom of the Air and the Convention on the Law of the Sea' (1983) 77 Am J Int'l L 490, 520.

4.3.5 No Enforcement Jurisdiction in International Airspace

The Court in *Lotus* held that a State is not permitted to enforce their laws outside its territory unless there is a permissive rule in international law - a treaty law or customary law - providing them with the right to do so. This is true even in the case that the State has jurisdiction to prescribe their laws extraterritorially.[1044] The basis for this is the principles of non-intervention and the sovereign equality of States.[1045]

As a result, the prosecution of crew in the case of failure to comply with ADIZ procedures can only occur upon entry into the coastal State's national airspace. In the absence of being able to rely on any international law as a legal basis for ADIZs, including the enforcement of them, States are only able to justify actions taken against aircraft in their ADIZs that would otherwise be justified under international law. This section will examine the measures that States are permitted to take against aircraft in their ADIZs and the purposes for which they are permitted to do so.

International civil aviation law makes clear that States have a right to intercept aircraft in certain limited circumstances. Beyond these, including in the case of a failure to fulfil ADIZ requirements, there are no provisions for interception. Further to interception, the use of force against aircraft is expressly prohibited and the only justification for the use of force against them is the right of self-defence entailing, as it does, the stringent circumstances for it to be legitimate, as discussed in Section 4.3.3.3.

The prohibition on the use of force against civil aircraft is set out in Article 3 *bis* (a) of the Chicago Convention:

> every State must refrain from resorting to the use of weapons against civil aircraft in flight and that, in case of interception, the lives of persons on board and the safety of aircraft must not be endangered.

This article begins with the words '[t]he contracting States recognize ...', suggesting that it is a restatement of customary international law. This is so insofar as the article applies to an attack attributable to one State against an aircraft registered in another State, which amounts to a breach of the prohibition on the use of force, recognised as customary international law[1046] and as codified under Article 2(4) of the UN Charter.[1047] Cheng argues that Article 3 *bis* also applies more broadly than this though, as a prohibition against the use of force towards all civil aircraft, including a State's against its own, which is not within the scope of Article 2(4).[1048] Milde disagrees

1044. Ryngaert (n 1039) 58.
1045. The sovereign equality of States has been mentioned previously in Sections 3.3.4.4 and 4.2.4.1.
1046. *Military and Paramilitary Activities Case (Nicaragua v. United States of America)*, pp. 98-101 paras 187-190; *Legal Consequences of the Construction of a Wall in the Occupied Palestinian Territory*, Advisory Opinion, I.C.J. Rep. 2004 (9 July) p. 136, p. 171 para. 87.
1047. As discussed in Kimberly Trapp, 'Uses of Force Against Civil Aircraft' (EJIL:Talk!, 28 June 2011), available at www.ejiltalk.org/uses-of-force-against-civil-aircraft/ accessed 12 July 2017.
1048. Bin Cheng, 'The Destruction of KAL Flight KE007' in JWE Storm van 's Gravensande and A van der Veen Vonk (eds), *Air Worthy: Liber Amicorum Honouring Professor Dr IHPH Diederiks-Verschoor* (Kluwer 1985) 63.

with this position, however, arguing that the scope of Article 3 *bis* is restricted to foreign aircraft on that basis that if it were to be interpreted otherwise, 'such regulation would have exceeded the scope of the Convention which deals with international civil aviation'.[1049]

The rules for the interception of civil aircraft are set out in Annex 2 to the Chicago Convention.[1050] There are two elements to the interception rules that are key to ADIZs. The first is that interception is only to be performed as a last resort.[1051] The second is that the purpose for doing so should be limited to determining the identity of the aircraft or 'to return the aircraft to its planned track, direct it beyond the boundaries of national airspace, guide it away from prohibited, restricted or danger areas or instruct it to effect a landing at a designated aerodrome'.[1052] The first two of these – identification and returning an aircraft to its planned track – are possibly relevant in the case of ADIZs. Beyond these two purposes, a State cannot justify the interception of a civil aircraft in its ADIZ. Keeping in mind that interception is only to be used as a last resort, States would be required to first ascertain the aircraft's identification or direct the aircraft back to its stated flight plan, as the case may be, through communication with the aircraft via the applicable ATC unit. In the case that interception is necessary, given the specific purposes for which it may be conducted, it should be undertaken only to the extent required to achieve these purposes and the method of interception, including the proximity of the intercepting aircraft, should 'avoid any hazard for the intercepted aircraft'.[1053] A failure to adhere to these measures could also amount to the intercepting aircraft, as a State aircraft, breaching its obligation of due regard to the civil aircraft, which it owes under Article 3(d) of the Chicago Convention.[1054]

Furthermore, when it comes to the violation of the rules referred to in Article 12 of the Chicago Convention – recalling Section 2.7.2.2 – that is, those rules of international civil aviation law applicable in international airspace, the coastal State has no greater power to prosecute than any other State. Article 12 provides this expressly: '[e]ach contracting State undertakes to insure the prosecution of all persons violating the regulations applicable'. Thus, if a civil aircraft conducting a flight in international airspace fails to comply with, for example, its position reporting obligations pursuant to Standard 3.6.3 of Annex 2 to the Chicago Convention, the article clearly provides that it is formally the role of each State to take the relevant steps to prosecute the persons responsible.[1055]

1049. Michael Milde, 'Interception of Civil Aircraft vs. Misuse of Civil Aviation' (1986) 11 Ann Air & Space L 126.
1050. *See also*, ICAO Doc 9433, *Manual Concerning Interception of Civil Aircraft* (1990). This manual is a consolidation of ICAO provisions and special recommendations related to the interception of civil aircraft, which have been extracted from Annexes 2, 4, 6, 7, 10, 11 and 15, as well as PANS-OPS and PANS-ATM.
1051. Chicago Convention, Annex 2, Appendix 2, 1.1 (a).
1052. *Ibid.* Appendix 2, 1.1 (b).
1053. Chicago Convention, Annex 2, Appendix 2, 3.1.
1054. *See* Section 2.4.3 for discussion on the due regard obligation owed by State aircraft to civil aircraft.
1055. Niels van Antwerpen notes, in regard to the provision of air navigation services over international airspace, that the laws of the coastal State are relevant. In the case of an act or omission of an air navigation services provider, a victim may bring a claim for damages in the

State aircraft operating in another State's ADIZ are not protected by the above prohibitions and limitations relating to the use of force and interception, given that these aircraft fall outside the scope of the Chicago Convention and its annexes.[1056] In this environment, interception of military aircraft is not infrequently carried out in international airspace, whether in a State's ADIZ or beyond.[1057] There is no right to do so under international law but at the same time, there is no prohibition. Further to interception, the engagement of, i.e., the use of force against a State aircraft may be justified under the right to self-defence. Outside this exception though, State practice demonstrates that the use of force against a State aircraft amounts to a breach of Article 2(4) of the UN Charter.[1058]

The opposition by States to China's announcement that it would be willing to exercise enforcement jurisdiction within its ADIZ in the case of non-compliance with its ADIZ procedures is based on the fact that if it were to do so, it would be exceeding its jurisdictional powers. A State has no right to enforce its ADIZ in international airspace, and any action it takes in its ADIZ against another State's aircraft, be it a civil aircraft or a State aircraft, must be justified under international law as it applies in international airspace more broadly.

4.3.6 Prohibition under International Law

4.3.6.1 Safety Regulations under International Civil Aviation Law

The potential negative safety consequences of ADIZs most often stem from particular aspects of their management and of surrounding circumstances, including the political climate of the region, rather than from the presence of the zone itself. Furthermore, while nothing in international civil aviation law expressly provides States with the right to establish ADIZs, there is also nothing to prohibit them from doing so, either directly or indirectly. Based on these factors, ICAO's approach to ADIZs is to mitigate the safety risks they pose to the safety of international civil aviation. This approach is also

instance that the national law of the State providing those services (a coastal State) allows for such a claim. Reference here is made to *Blumenthal v. United States of America* (1960) 189 F. Supp. 439, in which damages were awarded by the US government in the case of wrongful death over the high seas (van Antwerpen (n 801) 98-99).

1056. Although, as recognised in the previous paragraphs and as addressed in Section 2.4.3, State aircraft are not completely excluded from the scope of international civil aviation law. For example, it is State aircraft that carry out the interception of civil aircraft and Article 3 *bis* of the Chicago Convention and the interception provisions under Annex 2 apply to them in carrying out these operations.

1057. In addition to the interception of Russian aircraft off the coast of Alaska in March 2020, as mentioned in Section 4.3.3.1, *see*, for example, 'Allied Fighter Jets Intercept Russian Aircraft' (NATO, 11 March 2020), available at www.nato.int/cps/en/natohq/news_174349.htm accessed 14 April 2020; Ben Blanchard and Yimou Lee, 'Taiwan Again Scrambles Jets to Intercept Chinese Planes, Tensions Spike' (Reuters, 9 February 2020), available at www.reuters.com/article/us-taiwan-china-defence/taiwan-again-scrambles-jets-to-intercept-chinese-planes-tensions-spike-idUSKBN2030AE accessed 14 April 2020.

1058. Oliver Dörr, 'Prohibition of Use of Force' (Max Planck Encyclopedia of Public International Law 2015) 24.

consistent with the fact that ICAO is a political forum,[1059] primarily tasked with the promotion of the safety of international civil aviation, and that ADIZs are attached to national security, a highly sensitive area sitting at the heart of State sovereignty.

This section will examine the safety implications of ADIZs in respect of the relevant SARPs in the Chicago Convention's annexes. It will consider whether ADIZs are consistent with the SARPs in Annex 11, setting out rules for the provision of ATS, particularly in the case of a State imposing an ADIZ that overlaps another State's ADIZ or FIR. The section will further discuss how the global approach towards greater civil-military integration aims to reduce the safety risks of ADIZs to international civil aviation by simplifying procedures. Finally, it will briefly explain why Article 12 of the Chicago Convention does not prohibit States from establishing ADIZs.

In a joint Working Paper to ICAO, the International Air Transport Association (IATA) and IFALPA raised the issue of an (unidentified)[1060] ADIZ that crossed the boundaries of two FIRs, leading to confusion of the ATC authorities in those FIRs.[1061] In addition, it reported, the ADIZ requirements were not clear, which created additional uncertainty regarding the procedures to be followed, both for the aircraft operating in the zone and the ATC. As a consequence, flights were ultimately arranged along alternative routes to avoid the area due to fear of interception in the zone.[1062] This is an extreme example of lack of coordination in the establishment of an ADIZ but, as mentioned in Section 4.3.1, the ADIZs of China, Japan, South Korea and Taiwan overlap and this necessarily also involves the overlap of ADIZs with FIRs. Overlapping ADIZs and ADIZs that extend across FIRs are less problematic when there is cooperation in their management, when there are good relations between the authorities administering the zones, such as between Japan and Taiwan,[1063] but they become a heightened safety risk when this is not the case.[1064] The increased cooperation required in the case overlapping ADIZs and FIRs adds to a matter that requires attention even where delimitation is clear: the Civil Air Navigation Services Organisation (CANSO) has reiterated through various best practice guides the need to improve 'the safe and efficient crossing of Flight Information Regions' and has highlighted this as a particular priority in the Asia-Pacific region.[1065]

Coordination complexities are also relevant within the boundaries of a coastal State's FIR where the ADIZ procedures require aircraft to follow the requests of, or

1059. Ruwantissa Abeyratne, *Regulation of Air Transport: The Slumbering Sentinels* (Springer 2014) 209.
1060. In consideration of the period around which it was established, and the general concerns expressed, it possibly refers to the ADIZ of Bangladesh, as discussed in Section 4.3.3.2.
1061. ICAO (n 905) 2.3.
1062. *Ibid.* 2.9.
1063. 'Japan Extends Air Defence Identification Zone into Taiwan Space' (BBC Monitoring Asia Pacific, 26 June 2010), text of report in English by Shih Hsiu-chuan on Taiwanese newspaper *Taipei Times* website on 26 June 2010 written, available at www.taipeitimes.com/News/front/archives/2010/06/26/2003476438 accessed 3 November 2019.
1064. Kaiser (n 952) 536: '... overlapping ADIZ lead to a non-coordinated practice of ICAO Member States which is detrimental to the safe, efficient and regular air navigation'.
1065. ICAO IP/13, *Automation Interface Between Flight Information Regions*, Presented by CANSO at the 28th Meeting of the Asia/Pacific Air Navigation Planning and Implementation Regional Group, Bangkok (11-14 September 2017) 1.1 and 2.1.

report to, an authority additional to the ATC unit, such as in the ADIZs off the coasts of China and the US.[1066] In accordance with ICAO's definition of 'ADIZ', provided in Section 4.3.2, an ADIZ necessarily imposes on aircraft '... special identification and/or reporting procedures *additional* to those related to the provision of air traffic services' (emphasis added),[1067] where these additional procedures are imposed by an authority other than the ATS provider. The additional authority that an ADIZ introduces into the affected portion of airspace requires consideration in respect of two main aspects of international civil aviation law. The first is the Standards contained in Annex 11, governing the responsibility of the control of flights and airspace, and the second is ICAO's aim to achieve global enhanced civil-military coordination.

There are two Standards in Annex 11 of the Chicago Convention that are relevant to the management of airspace by more than one authority.[1068] Standard 3.5.1 states that '[a] controlled flight shall be under the control of only one air traffic control unit at any given time' and Standard 3.5.2 provides that '*[r]esponsibility* for the control of all aircraft operating within a given block of airspace shall be vested in a single air traffic control unit' (emphasis added). Unlike Annex 2 in international airspace, a State may file differences for the Standards in Annex 11, meaning that these Standards are not necessarily fixed. Notwithstanding this, however, a literal interpretation of the terms does not necessarily prohibit the exercise of control by an additional authority. Specifically, they both refer to an *air traffic control unit* as opposed to using more general phrasing, in order to restrict the control to a single authority regardless of its purpose and thereby take into account the possibility of the operation of a military authority, for example, exercising control alongside the ATC unit. Second, as emphasised, Standard 3.5.2 sets out that responsibility must be vested in one unit, which does not necessarily restrict the provision of services or orders by additional units. Thus, despite the fact that the Annex seems to recognise the importance of aircraft communicating with only one authority in a given airspace, it falls short of considering this situation in respect of a non-ATC authority.

ICAO has, however, addressed this matter beyond the annexes, by encouraging coastal States to minimise the burden ADIZ requirements place on flight crew through enhanced coordination between the civil and military authorities administering the airspace.[1069] In this manner, aircraft would provide information to the ATC unit which would then communicate it directly to the military authority without further input being required from the aircraft. From an airline/pilot perspective, more streamlined communication channels are advantageous in terms of both efficiency and safety. IATA and IFALPA have, in the context of achieving greater civil/military cooperation, called for changes to ADIZ practices. They suggest that the flight plan and movement information are readily forwarded to the relevant military authorities, where required, and that States work towards the automation of authorisation procedures, an example

1066. *See* Section 4.3.2 for details of the specific authorities.
1067. Chicago Convention, Annex 4, 1-1 and Annex 15, 1-2.
1068. Kaiser briefly mentions what he refers to as 'the single control unit principle', in reference to the Standards that are discussed in this paragraph (Kaiser (n 952) 536).
1069. ICAO (n 965) 2.18.

of this being the generation of a clearance code in advance upon the initial submission of the flight plan.[1070] There is a strong preference expressed by IATA and IFALPA though, for military clearances and other authorisation procedures to be forgone, and they ultimately request States 'to obviate the need for pre-authorization for civil flights'.[1071]

Cuadra has suggested that ADIZs may, in one respect, lower the safety risk to aircraft by obviating the need for coastal States to conduct interceptions to identify aircraft as a result of the identification obligations that the zones impose.[1072] Given that identification and reporting procedures are common practice in aviation independently of ADIZs,[1073] it seems unlikely that this safety benefit would result, but even if it were to, it would be alongside the above coordination complexities and potential safety consequences that they entail.

One further matter under international civil aviation law is raised in relation to ADIZs regarding the management of airspace: the exclusive jurisdiction of ICAO pursuant to Article 12 of the Chicago Convention. Recalling Section 2.7.2.2, the relevant part of Article 12 reads, '[o]ver the high seas, the rules in force shall be those established under this Convention'.

As a result of this article, Head concludes that the only laws applicable to civil aviation in international airspace are those rules referred to in Article 12 and that therefore, coastal States are not permitted to exercise prescriptive jurisdiction to establish ADIZs: '[t]hus one state does not have the power within itself to enact regulations effective over the high seas'.[1074] Kaiser appears to agree with Head, stating that the purpose of this section of Article 12 is to 'prevent States from unilaterally mandating compliance with any other or additional rules which contravene this purpose'.[1075] Papp also raises the issue of Article 12 and considers its scope – noting that ADIZs relate to national security, which is outside the jurisdiction of ICAO – but he ultimately leaves the question open.[1076] Article 12 does provide ICAO with exclusive jurisdiction over the high seas but only in respect of those rules that fall within the scope of the article, including the Standards in Annex 2 together with the SARPs in Annexes 6, 10, 11 and 12, as to which *see* Section 2.7.2.2. ADIZs are not addressed by these annexes, either expressly or impliedly, and as a result, they are not within the exclusive jurisdiction of ICAO or otherwise governed by the scope of Article 12.[1077] As Cuadra notes on this matter:

1070. ICAO (n 905) 1.3, 2.10, 2.10 (a) and (b).
1071. *Ibid.* 2.10.
1072. Cuadra (n 913) 496.
1073. *See* Section 4.3.3.1.
1074. Head (n 915) 186.
1075. Kaiser (n 952) 535-536. Kaiser in fact refers to the 'third sentence of Article 11 of the Chicago Convention' here, but given the context – including the fact that he discusses Article 12 in the previous sentence – it is most likely that he is referring to Article 12.
1076. Papp (n 921) 40-41.
1077. *See also*, Section 3.3.3.1 for discussion on the distinction between the rules referred to in Article 12 and the rules applying to the provision of air navigation services in international airspace.

> When ICAO is silent on a given topic States are not precluded from formulating rules they have adopted on such topics, nor is it mandatory that States notify ICAO of rules they have adopted on such topics.[1078]

In the absence of a prohibition under international civil aviation law, ICAO policy materials instead aim to encourage States to impose their ADIZ procedures in the safest possible manner.

4.3.6.2 Freedom of Overflight

As discussed in Sections 2.6.5 and 3.3.3, legitimate restrictions to freedom of overflight are viewed narrowly by the international community. While airspace can be used in a way that leads to it being exclusive in practice, the exclusive use must be restricted geographically and in duration to what is strictly necessary for the activity. For portions of ADIZs that extend into the high seas, this can be understood on the basis of the 'due regard' obligation under Article 87(2) UNCLOS, which requires States to have, in exercising their freedoms of the high seas, a 'due regard' obligation for the interests of other States in their exercise of freedoms of the high seas.[1079] The right to establish ADIZs cannot be considered a freedom of the high seas. A high seas freedom applies – at least de facto – equally to all States, while the ability to establish ADIZs in international airspace necessarily only applies to coastal States. Thus, while determining the legality of ADIZs involves a balance of State interests, a consideration of the balancing of interests between the exercise of two high seas freedoms is not relevant to the discussion here. For an ADIZ that extends into the coastal State's EEZ, as discussed in Section 4.3.3.2, the zone cannot be justified by arguing that it achieves a balance between the rights established by UNCLOS of the coastal State in the zone and the freedom of overflight exercised by other States therein. The EEZ regime under UNCLOS provides no support for this argument without the formation of a customary international law to support such an interpretation.

Relying on the analysis of what exactly freedom of overflight entails, as presented in Sections 2.7.1 and 2.7.3.2, the question must first be asked of whether ADIZs do in fact interfere with freedom of overflight. This is particularly so given that – leaving aside the matter of enforcement jurisdiction which, as has been established, is the same in international airspace with or without an ADIZ – ADIZs do not per se physically prohibit or restrict aircraft from the airspace within the zone. The consideration of whether the establishment of an ADIZ is inconsistent with the right to freedom of overflight is not limited to physical restriction though and requires a broader perspective. Is it a violation of freedom overflight because it involves the unilateral imposition of requests or orders by one State in international airspace?[1080] Or does a violation

1078. Cuadra (n 913) 491. *See* Sections 2.6.5 and 3.2.2 for previous consideration of Article 87(2) UNCLOS.
1079. UNCLOS, Article 87(2).
1080. As Kaiser argues: Kaiser (n 952) 532.

require a certain degree of burden in its variation from standard procedure?[1081] Is it relevant that the unilateral measures are primarily for national security purposes, rather than being for the purpose of enhancing safety?

Freedom of overflight does not mean freedom from regulation,[1082] as is evident from Article 12 of the Chicago Convention. As indicated previously, identification and reporting procedures are standard at points throughout an international flight. Of course, then, the requirement of 'mere identification by foreign aircraft cannot be regarded as a restriction on the freedom of overflight'.[1083] It is also standard practice for pilots to file flight plans in advance,[1084] and to maintain radio contact en route. The issuing of clearances is also common practice for civil aircraft but under international civil aviation law, they are to be issued by ATC and are 'solely for expediting and separating air traffic'.[1085]

On top of standard ATC procedures, ADIZs impose additional parameters. As addressed in Section 4.3.6.1, ATC should be the only authority to which flights plans need to be submitted, as opposed to defence authorities, as seems to be required by China for certain flights. ADIZs also involve the obligation to comply with the orders of designated authorities, both when operating in the airspace and prior to entering the airspace, often defence bodies. For example, with reference to Section 4.3.2, a person operating an aircraft in the US ADIZ 'must ... comply with the special security instructions ... in the interest of national security', as issued by NORAD,[1086] while in China's ADIZ, they must comply with orders of the Ministry of National Defence.[1087] Furthermore, Bangladesh requires aircraft to receive military air defence clearance (ADC) numbers prior to entry into its ADIZ,[1088] as does India.[1089]

Drawing an analogy with vessels on the sea, the need to obtain prior clearance has been viewed as a violation of the right of innocent passage. UNCLOS provides a number of military activities that are prohibited from being carried out by a ship in

1081. As considered by Cuadra: Cuadra (n 913) 496: 'The procedural requirements themselves are not burdensome when viewed in the context of the system of air navigational aids, control, and aircraft-to-ground communication to which international (and even domestic) flights are normally subject.'
1082. 'Law, Conflict and Airspace: Understanding Air Defense Identification Zones' (Groningen University Blog, 17 January 2014), available at www.rug.nl/research/east-asian-studies/blogs/blog/blog-17-01-2014-law-conflict-and-airspace-understanding-air-defense-identification-zones accessed 13 May 2019.
1083. Hailbronner (n 976) 43.
1084. Chicago Convention, Annex 2, 3.3.1.4: 'Unless otherwise prescribed by the appropriate ATS authority, a flight plan for a flight to be provided with air traffic control service or air traffic advisory service shall be submitted at least sixty minutes before departure, or, if submitted during flight, at a time which will ensure its receipt by the appropriate air traffic services unit at least ten minutes before the aircraft is estimated to reach: a) the intended point of entry into a control area or advisory area; or, b) the point of crossing an airway or advisory route.'
1085. *ICAO* (n 784) 4.5.1.1.
1086. 14 C.F.R. §99.7.
1087. Announcement by the Ministry of National Defense, China (n 895).
1088. ICAO (n 965) 2.15.
1089. 'ENR-1.12 Interception of Civil Aircraft – Identification and Interception Procedures', available at aim-india.aai.aero/eaip/PUB/2012-04-01/html/eAIP/EC-ENR-1.12-en-GB.html accessed 2 July 2019.

another State's territorial sea,[1090] but the mere passage of a military ship is not deemed to be inconsistent with innocent passage.[1091] China, among many others, but as a high-profile State, requires prior authorisation for warships entering its territorial sea.[1092] The US has criticised this on the basis that it 'considers the establishment of an advanced authorisation or prior notification a "hindrance" to innocent passage'.[1093] Of course, this example involves the territorial sea as opposed to international airspace, and innocent passage rather than freedom of overflight. In this example though, it is the requirement itself that is relevant, and it is this that is transferable to the current context. The criticism from the US stems solely from the imposition of the requirement: the context and the effect that it has in practice are irrelevant.

It is proposed here that the additional requirements that are placed on aircraft in ADIZs differ from the regulations that apply to the operation of aircraft in international airspace in one principal manner. The regulations that apply, those SARPs in the applicable annexes pursuant to Article 12, apply *to facilitate the freedom of overflight.* By harmonising identification and reporting requirements, the provision of ATS, emergency procedures, among many other areas, these rules enable aircraft to exercise the right to freedom of overflight. As has been discussed, States may file differences to these SARPs with the exception of Annex 2,[1094] and in this respect a degree of unilateral prescription is permitted, but the varied practices are no less part of the legal framework to facilitate the operation of civil aviation in international airspace. In contrast, ADIZ procedures are unilaterally imposed for the purpose of national security and, in some cases, for other national interests such as territorial control. Furthermore, the procedures imposed can jeopardise the safety of international civil aviation, as addressed in Section 4.3.6.1.

The above considerations address *civil* aircraft. Freedom of overflight also applies to State aircraft, as do some States' ADIZ procedures. The above points focused on the additional impositions that ADIZs place on the operation of a civil aircraft in the zone. While 'many air navigation facilities and services are provided for and used by both civil and military aviation',[1095] State aircraft are not required to follow SARPs and are not subject to any reporting procedures in international airspace, as a result of their exclusion from the scope of the Chicago Convention and its annexes.[1096] On this basis, any requirement imposed in respect of the flight of a State aircraft in international airspace within an ADIZ is a violation of freedom of overflight.

The exclusion of State aircraft from obligations that apply to civil aircraft, such as identification and reporting, is necessary in order to be able to fulfil certain mission requirements. In these cases, it is the responsibility of the State aircraft to maintain

1090. As mentioned in Section 4.3.3.2 (n 967).
1091. Unlike the high seas freedom in Article 87, the instances in which the passage of a foreign ship 'shall be considered to be prejudicial to the peace, good order or security of the coastal State in the territorial sea', in accordance with Article 19 UNCLOS, are exclusive.
1092. Kaye (n 961) 8-12 (table) and 13.
1093. Sébastien Colin, 'China, the US, and the Law of the Sea' (2016) 2 China Perspect 57, 60.
1094. *See* Section 2.7.2.2.1.
1095. ICAO Cir 330, *Civil/Military Cooperation in Air Traffic Management* (2011) 1.3.2.
1096. *See* Section 2.4.1.

separation from civil aircraft as the State aircraft can be effectively invisible to ATC, having not filed a flight plan, established radio connection, or identified itself through cooperative surveillance systems.[1097] ADIZ procedures imposed on State aircraft restrict their operation in international airspace in a manner that the exclusion of this category of aircraft from the Chicago Convention safeguarded them from. In doing so, ADIZ procedures interfere with a State aircraft's freedom of overflight by restricting the international airspace in which it is able to undertake certain missions which are permitted under international law.

For these reasons, ADIZs are inconsistent with freedom of overflight, for both civil aircraft and State aircraft. They are an anomaly in international airspace as unilateral extensions of coastal State power, serving the interests only of that State, and to the detriment of other airspace users, at times in terms of safety, but necessarily in terms of limiting freedom of overflight.

4.3.7 In Summary: Legality of ADIZ

ADIZs have existed since the 1950s but there has been a renewed interest in them since the events of September 11, and States continue to establish and extend them today.

ADIZs have no foundation in international law, and States justify them using different legal bases, where the justifications reflect the requirements that the States impose in their own ADIZs. Although a State has the right to regulate the admission to or departure from its territory, and aircraft identification requirements are an accepted aspect of this, the establishment of a zone, as opposed to a point or a line as is standard for reporting requirements, is unnecessary to achieve this aim and thus, ADIZs cannot be justified on this ground. Neither can an ADIZ be justified on the basis of what a number of States claim to be their right to regulate military activities in their EEZ. The EEZ regime under UNCLOS is established for a specific purpose,[1098] and the coastal State's rights within the zone do not extend to restricting the mere exercise of freedom of overflight of military aircraft. The right to self-defence is a widely referred to but frequently rejected legal basis for ADIZs. The establishment of the zone is not self-defence under the definition of self-defence, which is an exception to the use of force, and the type of threat which gives rise to the right is not the type ADIZs are established in response to. Finally, the right to establish ADIZs does not have customary status. State practice remains varied but, more so, there is little evidence of *opinio juris* to indicate that the right is in the process of crystallising as a customary international law.

The international community is moving away from the *Lotus* principle, in which case a legal basis is required under international law for the exercise of prescriptive extraterritorial jurisdiction. The preceding sections have demonstrated that there is no legal basis that can be relied on to justify ADIZs. In the alternative, if the *Lotus* principle

1097. ICAO, *Guidelines to Airspace Users in Order to Raise Their Awareness on State Aircraft Operations Especially in the High Seas Airspace over the Baltic Sea* (Eur Ops Bulletin, 15 December 2015) 1.

1098. *See* Section 2.7.3.

still stands, a coastal State has the right to establish an ADIZ provided it is not prohibited by international law. In any case, in terms of enforcement jurisdiction, the actions a coastal State may take against an aircraft in international airspace within its ADIZ are the same as in any other international airspace.

Finally, ADIZs are prohibited by international law. Although they may pose a risk to the safety of civil aviation, they are not in violation of international civil aviation law, but rather of the principle of freedom of overflight. As a unilateral exercise of State power over international airspace for the purpose of, among other objectives, mitigating risks to national security, they impose control over the operation of civil aircraft and State aircraft that is not intended by, or consistent with, the understanding of freedom of overflight. As has been illustrated throughout this research, freedom of overflight does not mean freedom from regulation or even, in practice, free access to all international airspace at all times. The regulations and restrictions to access to international airspace though are specific and narrowly applied, relating to either safety and efficiency of international civil aviation or balancing the right of States to exercise their freedoms of the high seas. ADIZs are an anomaly in international airspace, with no legal basis in international law and in violation of the customary international law principle of freedom of overflight.

4.4 CONCLUSION TO CHAPTER

This chapter examined coastal State jurisdiction in respect of FIRs and ADIZs, considering its interaction with freedom of overflight in international airspace and whether the exercise of the jurisdiction is legitimate. It approached the question in relation to FIRs from a specific perspective: that of the application of the principle of non-discrimination to Annex 11, as the legal framework forming the basis for the responsibility of States in FIRs, including international airspace. The question regarding ADIZs was essentially whether they are legitimate under international law.

Contrary to the actions of Bahrain and the UAE, FIR responsibility does not give a coastal State the right to prohibit aircraft from international airspace within the FIR on the basis of the State of registration of the aircraft. This was clear as a result of there being freedom of overflight in international airspace, but this research set out to examine how international civil aviation law, considered in isolation, might prohibit such discrimination, specifically through there being an implied principle of non-discrimination in the rules applying to ATS provision. The rules forming the legal foundation for the allocation of responsibility for FIRs in Annex 11 do not include the principle of non-discrimination, and there is little support for an implied application of the principle on the basis of its importance to the rules governing air navigation in national airspace, but coastal State jurisdiction is very specific in the context of FIRs and must always be drawn back to technical and operational decisions for safety and efficiency purposes. Furthermore, the SARPs under Annex 11 are adopted by the ICAO Council whose objectives in developing principles for air navigation include avoiding discrimination between States. On this basis, if a State responsible for an FIR interprets its responsibility as permitting it to discriminate, without that decision being based solely on safety and efficiency considerations within the scope of Annex 11, it would be a breach of good faith.

In terms of ADIZs, it is clear that their presence does not affect the coastal State's enforcement jurisdiction in international airspace. The enforcement measures that a State may take in international airspace exist independently of ADIZs and are not specific to coastal States. The question of coastal State prescriptive jurisdiction in respect of ADIZs is more complicated and rests on the legitimacy of ADIZs. Even if no basis of jurisdiction is required for prescriptive jurisdiction in international airspace, ADIZs are a violation of the freedom of overflight, as has been demonstrated, and are therefore prohibited by international law. In the case that a legal basis is required for ADIZs under international law, the only possible grounds would be if the right of a coastal State to establish one has developed as a customary international law, in which case they would be legitimate regardless of any breach of freedom of overflight. This book has concluded that while evidence of sufficient uniformity of State practice could present a hurdle, establishing *opinio juris* currently stands as the greatest barrier to the demonstration of the right to establish ADIZs as being customary international law. This research concludes therefore that, based on the circumstances as they currently stand and the evidence available, ADIZs are not legitimate and that consequently, they do not provide coastal States with a basis for exercising jurisdiction in international airspace.

CHAPTER 5

Overflight of International Straits and Archipelagic Sea Lanes

5.1 INTRODUCTION

UNCLOS recognises, in addition to innocent passage through territorial sea, two other passage regimes: transit passage through international straits (hereinafter 'transit passage') and archipelagic sea lanes passage. While innocent passage does not apply to aircraft, both transit passage and archipelagic sea lanes passage have significant implications for overflight rights. In the lanes of transit passage and archipelagic sea lanes passage, the airspace retains its status as national airspace but the aircraft of other States have the right to fly through it without prior permission. As a result, these passage regimes are an exception to the special permission required under Articles 3(c), 6 and 8 of the Chicago Convention, applying respectively to State aircraft, scheduled services of civil aircraft and pilotless aircraft.[1099] While this research is focused on the rights of coastal States in *international* airspace, this chapter will briefly examine these two regimes applying to national airspace to the extent that they too – like the regimes in previous chapters – involve the consideration of anomalous and sometimes ambiguous rights of the coastal State vis-à-vis the overflight of aircraft of other States in the maritime areas off their coast.

Both passage regimes are applicable to State aircraft and civil aircraft alike; however, in practice they serve to provide access for State aircraft. This is because most States have negotiated overflight of each other's territory for civil aircraft through the Transit Agreement or through bilateral agreements for scheduled services, and through Article 5 of the Chicago Convention for non-scheduled flights.[1100] These sources of overflight rights are suspendable in the case of war though, as addressed in Section 2.6.1, and can be withdrawn in peacetime in the case a State denounces the relevant

1099. *See* Sections 2.3.3, 2.3.4 and 2.4.3.
1100. Only Dominica and Tuvalu are State parties to UNCLOS but not to the Chicago Convention.

treaty.[1101] In these situations, the transit and archipelagic sea lanes passage would allow for the continued right of overflight for civil aircraft through these portions of the suspending or withdrawing State's territory, as will be discussed in Section 5.5.

As a consequence of State – military – aircraft benefiting more so from the right of overflight under these passage regimes, the examples used throughout this chapter relate to events involving military aircraft. Furthermore, despite the application of the regimes to both civil aircraft and State aircraft, a closer examination of the provisions governing the designation of archipelagic sea lanes in Section 5.4.4.1 demonstrates that State aircraft were intended as the primary beneficiaries of the overflight provisions.

This chapter will begin, in Section 5.2, by outlining the common rights and duties in transit lanes and archipelagic sea lanes, for both aircraft and the State whose territorial sea the lanes fall within. The chapter will then examine the regime applying specifically to transit passage. Section 5.3.1 will first address the regime of non-suspendable innocent passage that applied prior to UNCLOS, with Section 5.3.2 demonstrating how concurrent developments under UNCLOS made the introduction of a more liberal passage regime particularly important for aircraft. The following section of the chapter (Section 5.3.3) will briefly consider the international straits that do not fall within the transit passage regime under UNCLOS before turning to examine its implications for overflight (Section 5.3.4). Lastly, in relation to transit passage, Section 5.3.5 will address the case of the Strait of Hormuz, which is an anomaly in that Iran, as one of the bordering States, applies the regime of innocent passage in the strait for States that are not party to UNCLOS.

The chapter will then turn to consider the regime under UNCLOS applying to archipelagic sea lanes passage. It will first briefly explain what an archipelagic State is under UNCLOS and why there are so few such States (Section 5.4.1), before outlining the implications for overflight of the recognition in UNCLOS of the concept of an archipelagic State (Section 5.4.2). The next section of the chapter will consider the main ambiguities in the text of UNCLOS insofar as archipelagic sea lanes passage concerns overflight. These include two matters that are tied to the military – State aircraft – basis of these provisions, as mentioned above. First, that the text indicates that air routes must be aligned with sea lanes through archipelagic waters (Section 5.4.4.1) and, second, that only approval from the IMO, as opposed to also ICAO, is required under UNCLOS for the designation of archipelagic sea lane air routes (Section 5.4.4.2). The final issue that will be considered specifically relating to archipelagic sea lanes passage is 'partial designation' and the implications of this for access to airspace by military aircraft. Finally, Section 5.5 will examine the right of overflight in transit and archipelagic sea lanes in the case of wartime, before concluding by highlighting the remaining areas of ambiguity in this area of law (Section 5.6).

The consequences of the lack of uniformity in the rules applying to transit passage in respect of some international straits, on the one hand, and in the ambiguity in the application of the UNCLOS rules for archipelagic sea lanes passage, on the other, results in a situation where there are conflicting views between the coastal States and

1101. For example, Article III of the Transit Agreement provides that '... any contracting State ... may denounce it on one year's notice'.

the States whose aircraft use the airspace over these maritime areas. This chapter complements the previous chapters of this research on this basis. The matters discussed in this chapter are not highly topical at this point in time, in that there are not frequent incidents arising out of the lack of uniformity or ambiguity in the application of the law, or particularly grave repercussions that stem from incidents that do occur. This will not necessarily always be the case though. For example, in the context of heightened political tensions between two or more States (e.g., South China Sea, Strait of Hormuz, Eastern Mediterranean Sea), such an incident could be the impetus for something much more serious. As stated in the previous chapter, an attack on an aircraft amounts to the use of force against the State of registry of the aircraft.[1102]

5.2 RIGHTS AND DUTIES OF AIRCRAFT IN PASSAGE AND OF COASTAL STATES

The key duties of the coastal States and of aircraft operating in each of these forms of passage are identical and are set out in Article 39 UNCLOS.[1103] Aircraft in transit passage and in archipelagic sea lanes passage must observe the rules of the air, as adopted by ICAO,[1104] and the coastal State may not file differences to them as they apply over the transit or archipelagic sea lanes.[1105] The article also provides that State aircraft 'will normally comply with such safety measures' and will operate with due regard for the safety of navigation.[1106] Soon after the adoption of UNCLOS, ICAO noted that 'normally' was not defined in the Convention but that a vote during the drafting process for its deletion from the article was defeated.[1107] Aircraft exercising their right of transit passage and archipelagic sea lanes passage are also required to 'monitor the radio frequency assigned by the competent *internationally designated* air traffic control authority' (emphasis added),[1108] as they are required to do over the high seas. This refers to the authority approved by the Council of ICAO under the applicable RANP,[1109] consistent with the arrangements in international airspace. Aircraft also have the duty to proceed without delay; to refrain from the threat or use of force against the coastal

1102. *See* Section 4.3.5.
1103. Under Article 54 UNCLOS the key duties of aircraft and ships in transit passage, and the duties of the States that border straits, apply *mutatis mutandis* to archipelagic sea lanes passage. The key duties are those in Articles 39, 40, 42 and 44. Article 40 applies only to vessels and is therefore not relevant to overflight.
1104. UNCLOS, Article 39(3)(a) for transit passage and Articles 39(3)(a) and 54 for archipelagic sea lanes passage.
1105. ICAO WP/5-1, *Secretariat Study on Agenda Item 5: Consideration of the Report of the Rapporteur on 'United Nations Convention on the Law of the Sea – Implications, if any, for the Application of the Chicago Convention, its Annexes and other International Air Law Instruments'*, Presented at the Legal Committee 26th Session, Montreal (4 February 1987), reproduced in (1987) 3 Int'l Org & L Sea: Documentary YB 243, 252.
1106. UNCLOS, Article 39(3)(a). The latter of which is a restatement of their obligation under Article 3(d) of the Chicago Convention.
1107. ICAO (n 1105) 254.
1108. UNCLOS, Article 39(3)(b) for transit passage and Articles 39(3)(b) and 54 for archipelagic sea lanes passage.
1109. ICAO (n 1105) 252.

State and from any other violation of the UN Charter; to refrain from any other activities external to expeditious transit unless necessary by force majeure; and, to comply with the relevant provisions of UNCLOS.[1110]

Coastal States bordering an international strait or archipelagic sea lane, whichever the case may be, are not permitted to impose their national civil aviation regulations in the areas of passage.[1111] They are restricted in their prescriptive jurisdiction concerning the passage to a limited scope of areas including, for the purposes of aviation, pollution control and, although far less relevant than to vessels, the prohibition of unloading commodities, currency or persons in contravention of certain national laws.[1112] The coastal States have the obligation not to hamper the passage, the requirement to adequately publicise danger to navigation or overflight that they are aware of within the strait or archipelagic waters; and, the inability to suspend the passage.[1113] Furthermore, UNCLOS provides the coastal State with very limited enforcement jurisdiction in transit lanes and archipelagic sea lanes, none of which relate to aircraft.[1114] As a result, Caminos explains, the coastal State is required to 'pursue the matter as a breach of international law through diplomatic channels and through other dispute settlement procedures'.[1115]

5.3 INTERNATIONAL STRAITS

5.3.1 Aircraft Excluded from Non-suspendable Innocent Passage

The beginning of the law applying to international straits under modern international law can be marked by reference to the 1949 case of *Corfu Channel (United Kingdom v.*

1110. UNCLOS, Article 39(1)(a)-(d) for transit passage and Articles 39(1)(a)-(d) and 54 for archipelagic sea lanes passage.
1111. P de Vries Lentsch, 'The Right of Overflight over Strait States and Archipelagic States: Developments and Prospects' (1983) 14 Neth Yearb Int Law 165, 200.
1112. UNCLOS, Article 42(1)(b) and (d) for transit passage and Articles 42(1)(b) and (d) and 54 for archipelagic sea lanes passage. These articles address, respectively, 'the prevention, reduction and control of pollution, by giving effect to applicable international regulations regarding the discharge of oil, oily wastes and other noxious substances in the strait'; and, 'the loading or unloading of any commodity, currency or person in contravention of the customs, fiscal, immigration or sanitary laws and regulations of States bordering straits'.
1113. UNCLOS, Article 44 for transit passage and Articles 44 and 54 for archipelagic sea lanes passage.
1114. UNCLOS, Articles 233 and 234 both apply only to vessels. Article 233 provides the States with enforcement jurisdiction in transit lanes over foreign ships – excluding those entitled to sovereign immunity (Article 236) – regarding protection of the marine environment (this also arguably also applies in archipelagic sea lanes, as to which *see*, Hugo Caminos and Vincent P Cogliati-Bantz, *The Legal Regime of Straits* (CUP 2014) 285). Article 234 provides prescriptive and enforcement jurisdiction of non-discriminatory laws applying to vessels for the protection of the marine environment in ice-covered areas.
1115. Hugo Caminos, 'The Legal Régime of Straits in the 1982 United Nations Convention on the Law of the Sea' (1987) 205 Recueil des Cours 19, 150. *See also*, for discussion on the absence of enforcement jurisdiction, Donald R Rothwell, 'International Straits', in Donald R Rothwell, Alex G Oude Elferink, Karen N Scott and Tim Stephens (eds), *The Oxford Handbook of the Law of the Sea* (OUP 2015) 123.

Albania) (*'Corfu Channel Case'*), in which the ICJ recognised as customary international law, the right of innocent passage through straits used for international navigation:

> It is, in the opinion of the Court, generally recognized and in accordance with international custom that States in time of peace have a right to send their warships through straits used for international navigation between two parts of the high seas without the previous authorization of a coastal State, provided that the passage is *innocent*. Unless otherwise prescribed in an international convention, there is no right for a coastal State to prohibit such passage through straits in time of peace.[1116]

This principle of customary international law was codified in the 1958 Convention on the Territorial Sea and the Contiguous Zone.[1117]

The 'non-suspendable' element of innocent passage in the straits under customary international law, as referred to in the *Corfu Channel Case*, is distinct from the power of the coastal State to act against non-innocent passage. As Guilfoyle explains, 'it is clearly arguable that under the non-suspendable innocent passage regime a coastal State retains its right to *prevent* non-innocent passage by individual foreign vessels' (emphasis in original).[1118] Non-suspendable innocent passage instead refers to a prohibition on the non-discriminatory cordoning off of any part of the strait. In contrast, under standard innocent passage, the coastal State has the right under UNCLOS to suspend the passage, in the form of a temporary restriction, 'if such suspension is essential for the protection of its security, including weapons exercises'.[1119]

Consistent with innocent passage, the non-suspendable innocent passage for international straits under customary international law does not apply to aircraft.[1120] Despite this, if both the State of registration of the aircraft and the State whose national airspace the aircraft is operating within – i.e., whose territorial sea the strait is a part of

1116. Merits, Judgment, I.C.J. Rep. 1949 (9 April), p. 4, p. 28. In this case, Greece considered itself to be at war with Albania and considering this, the Court concluded that Albania was permitted to regulate the passage of warships through the strait but not to prevent the passage or impose an obligation of special authorisation (p. 29). *See* Section 5.5.
1117. Convention on the Territorial Sea and the Contiguous Zone 1958, Article 16(4).
1118. Douglas Guilfoyle, 'Iran and the Strait of Hormuz: Some Initial Thoughts' (EJIL: Talk!, 2 February 2012), available at www.ejiltalk.org/iran-and-the-strait-of-hormuz-some-initial-thoughts/ accessed 17 January 2018.
1119. UNCLOS, Article 25(3).
1120. As indicated by the US in the context of transit passage in, United Nations Office for Ocean Affairs and the Law of the Sea, 'Law of the Sea – Straits Used for International Navigation: Legislative History of Part III of the United Nations Convention on the Law of the Sea' (1992) 33. This is also reflected – through absence of mention of aircraft – in the San Remo Manual on International Law Applicable to Armed Conflicts at Sea, adopted 12 June 1994 (International Review of the Red Cross, November-December 1995, No. 309, pp. 583-594) ('San Remo Manual'): 'In addition to the exercise of the rights of transit and archipelagic sea lanes passage, belligerent *warships* and auxiliary *vessels* may ... exercise the right of *innocent passage* through neutral international straits ...' (emphasis added) (para. 31) and, 'Neutral *vessels* may likewise exercise the right of *innocent passage* through belligerent international straits ...' (para. 32).

– are parties to the Chicago Convention and the Transit Agreement,[1121] then both civil non-scheduled and scheduled flights, respectively, have the right to overfly the airspace, notwithstanding any other restrictions that might be imposed by the State. Recalling Section 2.4, State aircraft are excluded from the Chicago regime and so, without further arrangements between the relevant States, such flights would not be permitted to operate through international straits under the regime of non-suspendable innocent passage.[1122]

5.3.2 Shifting Territorial Sea Boundaries: The Heightened Need for Transit Passage

The codification of a more generous right of passage through international straits under UNCLOS occurred simultaneously with the codification under this Convention of the right of a coastal State to claim a territorial sea of 12 nm, as opposed to the 3 nm which was previously recognised under customary international law.[1123] Most international straits are wider than 6 nm and so had high seas running through them prior to this change,[1124] but the extension led to over a hundred straits being encompassed by territorial sea,[1125] including ones that are strategically important for maritime States such as Gibraltar, Hormuz (Figure 5.1), Bab el Mandeb, Dover and Malacca.[1126]

1121. Recalling Section 2.3.3.1, this agreement, also known as the 'two freedoms agreement', provides for the exchange of the first two freedoms of the air, i.e., overflight and stops for technical purposes.
1122. United Nations Office for Ocean Affairs and the Law of the Sea (n 1120) 30-31 (Spain) and 62 (US).
1123. *See* Section 2.2.3.1 for discussion of the extension of the territorial sea from 3 nm to 12 nm.
1124. Bernard Oxman, 'Transit of Straits and Archipelagic Waters by Military Aircraft' (2000) 4 S J Int & Comp L 377, 384. The Singapore and Sunda Straits are, however, narrower than 6 nm.
1125. Karin M Burke and Deborah A DeLeo, 'Innocent Passage and Transit Passage in the United National Convention on the Law of the Sea' (1983) 9 Yale J World Pub Ord 389, 400, quoting Ronald P Cundick, 'International Straits: The Right of Access' (1975) 5 Ga J Int'l & Comp L 107.
1126. Kay Hailbronner, 'Freedom of the Air and the Convention on the Law of the Sea' (1983) 77 Am J Int'l L 490, 493.

Figure 5.1 Strait of Hormuz, Indicating the Loss of the High Seas Corridor with the Extension of the Territorial Sea

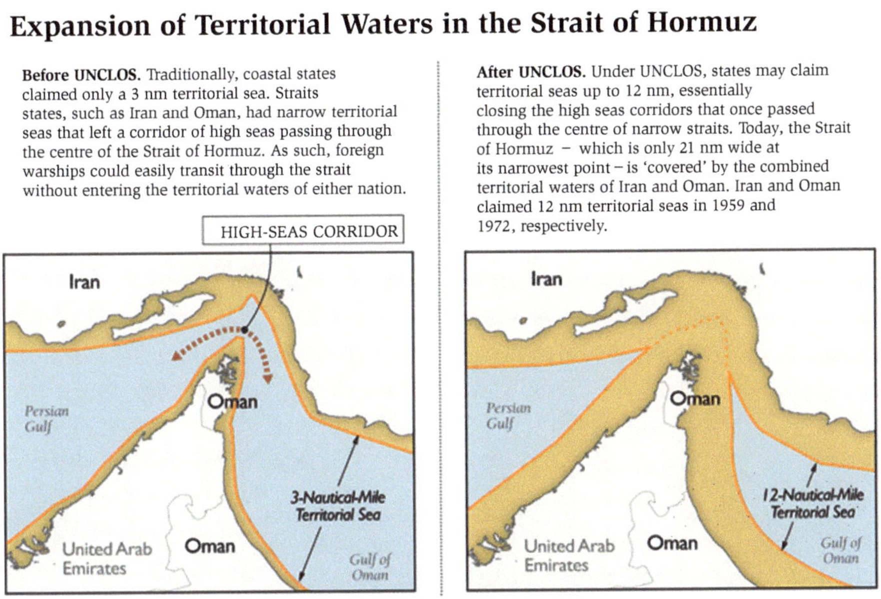

Note: Map locations and boundaries are approximate.
Source: US Department of State, Bureau of Oceans and International Environmental and Scientific Affairs, 'Iran's Maritime Claims,' *Limits in the Seas,* No. 114, 16 March 1994 (28 July 2011).

The coinciding adoption of these two elements – a comprehensive regime of transit passage and an increase in the breadth of the territorial sea – was aimed at ensuring that the extension of the territorial seas did not prohibit passage through certain straits that lost their high seas passage, particularly for military aircraft, which are regarded under Article 3 of the Chicago Convention as State aircraft. For those straits that are part of a State's EEZ or part of the high seas, the freedoms of the high seas – including freedom of overflight – apply as in any other part of the high seas and so are not relevant to the discussion on transit passage.[1127] Straits in this category are one of the four types of international straits excluded from the transit passage regime under UNCLOS, as will be addressed in the following section.

1127. Provided the high seas or EEZ route is of similar convenience to the routes through the territorial sea (*see* Section 5.3.3).

5.3.3 Exclusion of Certain International Straits from Transit Passage Regime

Before considering the application of the transit passage regime and its implications for overflight, this section will briefly set out the extent of transit passage in terms of the geographical requirements of an international strait in which transit passage applies. In addition to the type of strait mentioned above, that is, straits through which there are high sea routes or EEZ routes that are of similar convenience,[1128] UNCLOS excludes three other types of international straits from the transit passage regime: straits through which passage is subject to existing conventions;[1129] straits formed by an island off the coast of the mainland of a State, where there is a passage of similar convenience through the high seas or EEZ on the seaward side of the island;[1130] and, straits providing access between the high seas or an EEZ and territorial sea of a foreign State.[1131] The second of these four categories – straits subject to existing conventions – was adopted to maintain ingrained pre-existing treaties at the time of the drafting of UNCLOS and is not in wide application today.[1132] Passage through straits in this category is determined according to the relevant conventions. For straits in the final two categories, non-suspendable innocent passage applies, in the same manner as discussed above in relation to the *Corfu Channel Case*.[1133] In these two types of straits, as in other areas of the territorial sea where no passage is provided, overflight rights are obtained as for any other national airspace; that is, prior authorisation from the coastal State is required.[1134] Passage through the first category, however, is subject to the freedom of the high seas and applies as such to both ships and aircraft.[1135] As a result,

1128. UNCLOS, Article 36. This article applies in the case that an international strait is sufficiently wide so that at its narrowest point there is EEZ or high seas running through it. In this case, if those EEZ or high seas routes are 'of similar convenience' to the routes in the territorial sea portions of the international strait, the standard regimes of freedom of navigation and overflight in the EEZ/high seas and innocent passage in the territorial sea will apply (Caminos and Cogliati-Bantz (n 1114) 42).
1129. *Ibid.* Article 35(c). For example, the Turkish Straits, Bosphorus and Dardanelles, which are governed by the Montreux Convention of 1936, giving Turkey control over the straits in return for free passage. The original signatory States to this Convention are (in addition to Turkey) Bulgaria, France, Greece, Japan, Romania, the USSR, the UK and Yugoslavia (Jon M Van Dyke, 'Transit Passage Through International Straits' in Aldo Chircop, Theodore McDorman and Susan Rolston (eds), *The Future of Ocean Regime-Building: Essays in Tribute to Douglas M Johnston* (Martinus Nijhoff Publishers 2009) 204).
1130. *Ibid.* Article 38(1). Also known as the 'Messina exception', in recognition of its application to the strait between Sicily and mainland Italy.
1131. *Ibid.* Article 45(1)(b). For example, the Straits of Tiran, which connect the Red Sea and the Gulf of Aqaba, the latter of which is made up of the territorial seas of Egypt and Saudi Arabia.
1132. Stuart Kaye, 'Freedom of Navigation, Surveillance and Security: Legal Issues Surrounding the Collection of Intelligence from Beyond the Littoral' (2005) 24 Aust YBIL 93, 97. *See* above n 1129 for discussion of the Montreux Convention, as an example of a treaty of this kind currently in force.
1133. UNCLOS, Article 45(1) and (2).
1134. For Israel, in relation to the passage of its vessels, the application of non-suspendable innocent passage to the Straits of Tiran (*see* above n 1131) was particularly important considering that it would otherwise likely not have had the right of access to its territory through this body of water (Caminos and Cogliati-Bantz (n 1114) 54-55).
1135. UNCLOS, Article 36.

aside from any conventions governing individual straits, such as the Montreux Convention of 1936, there are only two instances where overflight without prior permission exists through international straits: first, where there is transit passage and, second, when there is a high seas or EEZ route through the strait.

5.3.4 The Result of Transit Passage on Overflight

UNCLOS expressly extends the regime of transit passage to aircraft: 'all ships and aircraft enjoy the right of transit passage'.[1136] Like non-suspendable innocent passage, and as mentioned in Section 5.2, the coastal State cannot suspend the right of transit passage. This is unequivocally provided under Article 44 UNCLOS – '[t]here shall be no suspension of transit passage' – and it means that States are not permitted to restrict or prohibit overflight in the airspace over straits in accordance with Article 9 of the Chicago Convention, as they are in other national airspace.[1137] Caminos and Cogliati-Bantz point out that the closure of the airspace in the Sunda Strait and the Lombok Strait by Indonesia in 1988 for 'the purpose of conducting air and sea tactical exercises' was consequently a violation of Article 44.[1138]

Transit passage through an international strait does not change the status of the seas that make up the strait; that is, they retain their status as the internal waters and territorial seas of the bordering States. UNCLOS makes this clear in stating that the transit passage regime 'shall not in other respects affect the legal status of the waters forming such straits'.[1139] It also stipulates that the sovereignty or jurisdiction of the States bordering the straits over such waters – the airspace, bed and subsoil – shall not in other respects be affected, but that it is to be exercised subject to the applicable part of UNCLOS (Part III) and to other rules of international law.[1140]

Transit passage under UNCLOS reflects the codification of the EEZ and so, further to the rule in the *Corfu Channel Case* which applies only to straits connecting specifically high seas, transit passage applies in straits that are 'used for international navigation between one part of the high seas or an exclusive economic zone and another part of the high seas or an exclusive economic zone'.[1141] Through these straits, in accordance with the regime of transit passage, aircraft and vessels enjoy 'freedom of navigation and overflight solely for the purpose of continuous and expeditious transit of the strait'.[1142] Despite the use of the term 'freedom' in this article, aircraft do not enjoy freedom of overflight in transit lanes. The obligations on aircraft to, for example, proceed without delay and refrain from engaging in activities that are not related to expeditious transit, as mentioned in Section 5.2, are indicative of this.

The regime finally adopted for transit passage in UNCLOS reflects a compromise between coastal States bordering international straits, in terms of their control over the

1136. UNCLOS, Article 38(1).
1137. Caminos and Cogliati-Bantz (n 1114) 232.
1138. *Ibid.*
1139. UNCLOS, Article 34(1).
1140. *Ibid.* Article 34(1) and (2).
1141. *Ibid.* Article 37.
1142. *Ibid.* Article 38(2).

straits in order to protect their marine resources and security interests, and maritime States, in respect of their ability to pass through the straits.[1143] The limitations on overflight that prevent transit passage from constituting freedom of overflight are one side of this compromise, in favour of States bordering international waterways such as Spain, Morocco, Malaysia and Indonesia, who contended during the drafting process that the regime of non-suspendable innocent passage should be maintained in international straits.[1144] These States were particularly concerned about the implications of providing access to foreign military aircraft. As Spain put forward:

> if a military aircraft overflew the waters of a narrow international strait at high altitude, it would be easy for it to carry out observations for military purposes of the territory and installations of the coastal States. The latter would be helpless to prevent such threats to their national security. In addition, of course, the territory of the coastal State would also be at serious risk in the case of an accident to such a military aircraft.[1145]

The adoption of the transit passage regime and its equal application to aircraft, in spite of these concerns, demonstrates the compromise from the other side. The fact that the rights of transit passage and archipelagic sea lanes passage continue to apply during armed conflict (*see* Section 5.5)[1146] makes these concerns particularly acute.

As will be seen in the following section, despite the ultimate adoption of an international codified transit passage regime, Iran has been reluctant to yield control in the Strait of Hormuz.

5.3.5 The Strait of Hormuz

Some States, including the US and the UK, support the view that transit passage under UNCLOS has attained customary status,[1147] but this is by no means widely accepted.[1148] This situation poses a problem considering that some States are not party to UNCLOS and do not recognise the customary status of the transit passage regime.

Oman has ratified UNCLOS, but Iran has not, and neither State is a party to the 1958 Convention on the Territorial Sea and the Contiguous Zone.[1149] As States bordering the Strait of Hormuz, they have also not concluded a specific treaty governing transit through the strait.

Both Iran and Oman dispute the applicability of the rule of non-suspendable innocent passage in the *Corfu Channel Case* to the Strait of Hormuz on the basis that it applies to straits connecting one part of the high seas to another part of the high seas,

1143. Burke and DeLeo (n 1125) 401.
1144. United Nations Office for Ocean Affairs and the Law of the Sea (n 1120) 31-32, 94, 36 and 134, respectively. Consider, for example, the Strait of Gibraltar and the Straits of Malacca.
1145. *Ibid.* 32. For further discussion on this matter in the drafting history *see*, Van Dyke (n 1129).
1146. San Remo Manual, para. 27.
1147. Guilfoyle (n 1118).
1148. Van Dyke (n 1129) 186-187.
1149. Iran is a signatory to the Convention though, as of 28 May 1958.

whereas the Persian Gulf does not contain high seas.[1150] Iran has also repeatedly voiced its opposition to the transit regime under UNCLOS having developed into customary international law.[1151]

Despite not being a State party, Iran is a signatory to UNCLOS and upon signing it, issued an interpretive declaration that it would grant the right of transit passage under Article 38 UNCLOS but only to those States that are parties to the said convention.[1152] Otherwise, Iran applies innocent passage to its area of territorial sea in the strait, as it applies in any other area of territorial sea.[1153] Notably, the US is not a party to UNCLOS. In June 2019, a US drone flying through the Strait of Hormuz was shot down by Iranian forces.[1154] The US declared that they were in international airspace at the time.[1155] As is so often the case with these highly politicised incidents, the facts are vague, and this event is just one of many arising out of ongoing tensions between the US and Iran, and one that goes beyond the interpretation of the law of the sea. It does, however, serve to illustrate that despite a widely accepted international legal framework for transit passage, which is generally uncontroversial, the application of the relevant law in certain straits and with regard to certain maritime States is complex, with potentially significant consequences for overflight.

Finally, although the above is presented as a problem in part arising from Iran not having ratified UNCLOS, doing so does not necessarily result in a harmonised approach considering that ratification of a treaty does not necessarily mean that a State adheres to all aspects of that treaty. Regarding transit passage under UNCLOS, Spain declared upon ratification that it did not adhere to the transit passage regime and that it would continue to apply its national laws in international straits.[1156] In addition, Greece, a State party to UNCLOS, issued a declaration that in practice provides that it has the responsibility to designate routes throughout its islands off its coast, in effect writing into the Convention additional or varied rules for transit passage by, as Turkey stated

1150. Andrea Gioia, 'Persian Gulf' (Max Planck Encyclopedia of Public International Law 2007) 31. This is presumably on the basis that Iran has declared an EEZ, which encompasses what existed of the high seas in the Gulf. This does of course mean that the Persian Gulf contains international airspace. Being encompassed by national airspace though, this makes little difference to overflight rights in the absence of transit passage for aircraft through the strait.

1151. *Ibid.*

1152. United Nations Treaty Collection, 'Chapter XXI: Law of the Sea, Declarations and Reservations', available at treaties.un.org/doc/Publication/MTDSG/Volume%20II/Chapter%20XXI/XXI-6.en.pdf accessed 26 July 2019. This is despite the fact that Article 38(1) UNCLOS provides that 'all ships and aircraft enjoy the right of transit passage', not just State parties to the treaty. *See also*, Nilufer Oral, 'Transit Passage Rights in the Strait of Hormuz and Iran's Threats to Block the Passage of Oil Tankers' (ASIL Insight, 3 May 2012), available at www.asil.org/insights/volume/16/issue/16/transit-passage-rights-strait-hormuz-and-iran%E2%80%99s-threats-block-passage accessed 1 February 2020.

1153. Geir Ulfstein, 'How International Law Restricts the Use of Military Force in Hormuz' (EJIL:Talk!, 27 August 2019), available at www.ejiltalk.org/how-international-law-restricts-the-use-of-military-force-in-hormuz/ accessed 3 November 2019.

1154. 'Strait of Hormuz: US Confirms Drone Shot Down by Iran' (BBC, 20 June 2019), available at www.bbc.com/news/world-middle-east-48700965 accessed 3 November 2019.

1155. *Ibid.*

1156. United Nations Treaty Collection (n 1152).

in its reply, allowing it to 'retain the power to exclude some of the straits which link the Aegean Sea to the Mediterranean from the regime of transit passage'.[1157]

The transit passage regime under UNCLOS has resulted in substantial uniformity for the passage of aircraft through international straits without the need for prior permission. Some coastal States, however, such as Iran, Spain and Greece, that border international straits falling within the scope of the UNCLOS transit passage regime do not apply this regime to the strait. This has implications for both navigation of vessels and overflight of aircraft through the strait. While uniformity in the rules is preferable for the safety and efficiency of both navigation and overflight, it is the conflict between the coastal State, in applying a different regime, and the State of nationality of the aircraft or vessel operating through the strait, in failing to accept, and therefore adhere to, the different regime, that potentially results in detrimental consequences. The incident above between the US and Iran provides an example of the implications for overflight.

5.4 ARCHIPELAGIC WATERS

5.4.1 What Is an Archipelagic State?

UNCLOS defines an archipelagic State simply as 'a State constituted wholly by one or more archipelagos', where an archipelago is 'a group of islands, interconnecting waters and other natural features which are so closely interrelated [that they] ... form an intrinsic entity'.[1158] Although this definition might suggest that there are a large number of archipelagic States, further conditions go some way in explaining why there are only nine States that have deposited charts or lists or geographical coordinates with the Secretary-General of the UN, as required under UNCLOS for an archipelagic State.[1159] These conditions apply to the drawing of the baselines of an archipelagic State and include, for example, that the water to land ratio inside the archipelagic baseline must be between 1 to 1 and 9 to 1, and that the length of baselines may not exceed 100 nm.[1160] Furthermore, as is clear from the definition of 'archipelagic State', it excludes States that comprise an archipelago in addition to land connected to a continent: the State must be *wholly* constituted by an archipelago or archipelagos.

1157. United Nations Treaty Collection (n 1152).
1158. UNCLOS, Article 46(a) and (b).
1159. *Ibid.* Article 47(9). These States are: Bahamas, Fiji, Indonesia, Jamaica, Papua New Guinea, the Philippines, Sao Tome and Principe, Seychelles, and Trinidad and Tobago. Despite this, other States have made archipelagic claims, including: Antigua and Barbuda, Cape Verde, Comoros, Kiribati, the Maldives, the Marshall Islands, St Vincent and the Grenadines, Solomon Islands, Tonga, Tuvalu and Vanuatu. On these points, *see*, Carlos Jiménez Piernas, 'Archipelagic Waters' (Max Planck Encyclopedia of Public International Law 2009) 20 and 21, respectively.
1160. UNCLOS, Article 47(1) and (2).

5.4.2 Coastal State Sovereignty over Archipelagic Waters and Sea Lanes

Returning to the definition of an archipelagic State, surrounding this 'intrinsic entity' is the territorial sea baseline, seaward of which the territorial sea begins.[1161] Prior to UNCLOS, an archipelagic State was required to delimit its territorial sea on the basis of each of its individual islands in accordance with the law applying to islands in general.[1162] As a result of the archipelagic sea regime under UNCLOS, States have, in addition to their territorial sea and their internal waters, sovereignty over their archipelagic waters,[1163] from the bed and subsoil up to and including the airspace.[1164] As with the territorial seas forming international straits under the transit passage regime, archipelagic waters are considered part of the territory of a State under Article 2 of the Chicago Convention, with the airspace above being national airspace.

ICAO has described the archipelagic State framework under UNCLOS as representing 'a profound innovation and progressive development of international law',[1165] not least in that it has led to the concept of 'territory' under Article 2 encompassing a far greater geographic expanse than was intended at the time of the drafting of the Chicago Convention. Despite this, upon the adoption of UNCLOS, ICAO did not consider an amendment to Article 2 to be necessary in light of the archipelagic waters regime. ICAO concluded that the archipelagic waters regime under UNCLOS instead resulted in an implicit shift in the interpretation of the term 'territory' under the Chicago Convention:

> Vast areas of the sea which were part of the high seas will become 'archipelagic waters' over which the archipelagic States will have sovereignty extending also to the airspace thereabove. Without any need for a textual amendment of the Chicago Convention, its Article 2 will have to be read as meaning that the territory of a State shall be the land areas, territorial sea adjacent thereto and its archipelagic waters.[1166]

Recalling Section 2.2.2.1, Article 2 stipulates that 'territory of a State shall be deemed to be *the land areas* and *territorial waters* ... under the sovereignty of such State' (emphasis added). It is proposed here that the term 'territorial waters', which is not used in UNCLOS and was also not used in the 1958 Convention on the Territorial Sea and the Contiguous Zone, necessarily refers more broadly to the maritime areas under the sovereignty of the State, rather than being synonymous with the more specific term of 'territorial sea', as used in UNCLOS and the 1958 Convention. This is the logical conclusion considering that internal waters, which are neither land areas nor territorial sea, have never been controversial in their inclusion within Article 2 of

1161. UNCLOS, Article 48.
1162. Convention on the Territorial Sea and the Contiguous Zone 1958, Article 10. Indonesia has not ratified this convention though, and in 1957 declared its archipelago part of its internal waters subject to innocent passage (P de Vries Lentsch, 'The Right of Overflight Over Strait States and Archipelagic States: Developments and Prospects' (1983) 14 Neth Yearb Int Law 165, 180).
1163. UNCLOS, Article 49(1).
1164. *Ibid.* Article 49(2).
1165. ICAO (n 1105) 253.
1166. *Ibid.* 254.

the Chicago Convention. Following this interpretation, 'territorial waters' under Article 2 of the Chicago Convention are those maritime areas referred to in Article 2(1) UNCLOS, setting out the extent of sovereignty of a coastal State beyond its land territory:

> The sovereignty of a coastal state extends, beyond its land territory and internal waters and, in the case of an archipelagic State, its archipelagic waters, to an adjacent belt of sea, described as the territorial sea.

This issue is still occasionally raised at the level of ICAO. In 2008, Indonesia brought the matter before the Legal Committee, arguing for a need to amend Article 2 of the Chicago Convention, but no further action on this has been recorded.[1167]

5.4.3 Archipelagic Sea Lanes

The right of innocent passage is enjoyed by ships through archipelagic waters outside sea lanes[1168] but, consistent with innocent passage in territorial seas,[1169] the right does not extend to aircraft. Archipelagic sea lanes provide aircraft (and vessels) with a right of passage through the archipelagic waters without affecting the archipelagic State's sovereignty over the lanes.[1170]

Archipelagic sea lanes passage is defined in Article 53(3) UNCLOS as:

> the exercise ... of the rights of navigation and overflight in the normal mode solely for the purpose of continuous, expeditious and unobstructed transit between one part of the high seas or an exclusive economic zone and another part of the high seas or an exclusive economic zone.

Importantly for overflight, the above definition necessarily means that aircraft also have the right to archipelagic sea lanes passage in the territorial sea surrounding a State's archipelagic waters, as further expressly provided in Article 53(1) and (4).[1171] If this were not the case, the right to exercise archipelagic sea lanes passage for aircraft

---

1167. ICAO WP/8-2, *Draft Report on the Work of the Legal Committee During its 33rd Session* (1 May 2008) 4.5-4.14.

1168. UNCLOS, Article 52(1). Although ships have the right to innocent passage through archipelagic waters, the designation of archipelagic seas lane passage is significant as there are a number of distinctions between the two, which make sea lanes more favourable. For example, the right of innocent passage can be suspended by the coastal State (Article 25(3)) but the right of archipelagic sea lanes passage cannot, although lanes can be substituted; and, when exercising their right to innocent passage, submarines and other underwater vehicles must surface and show their flag (Article 20), whereas in archipelagic sea lanes this is not required. In addition, prior notification and sometimes authorisation are required by some States for the innocent passage of warships, but this does not apply to the use of archipelagic sea lanes. For a discussion on these distinctions *see*, Hasjim Djalal, 'The Law of the Sea Convention and Navigational Freedoms' in Donald R Rothwell and Samuel Grono Bateman (eds), *Navigational Rights and Freedoms, and the New Law of the Sea* (Martinus Nijhoff Publishers 2000) 9.

1169. *See* Section 2.2.3.2.

1170. UNCLOS, Article 49(4).

1171. 'An archipelagic State may designate sea lanes and air routes thereabove, suitable for the continuous and expeditious passage of foreign ships and aircraft through or over its archipelagic waters *and the adjacent territorial sea*' (emphasis added) (Article 53(1)); and,

would be subject to the negotiation of access to the airspace in the territorial sea, as with access to national airspace in general. This is clear from Figure 5.2, which depicts the archipelagic State of the Philippines surrounded by its band of territorial sea. Having said this, the Philippines made a declaration upon signing UNCLOS that it considers archipelagic waters as similar to internal waters and thus that there is no passage through its territorial waters providing access to its archipelagic waters.[1172] The declaration was met with opposition by a number of States, including Russia and Australia.

Figure 5.2 The Archipelago of the Philippines Surrounded by the Philippines' Territorial Sea[1173]

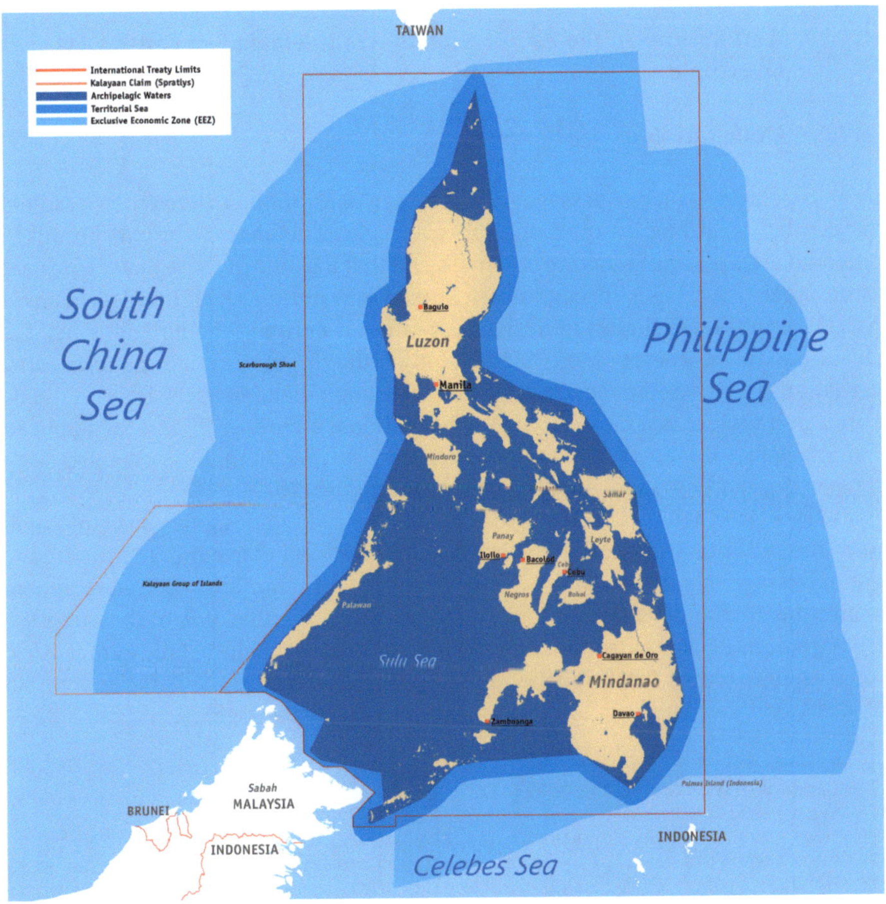

'Such sea lanes and air routes shall traverse the archipelagic waters *and the adjacent territorial sea* …' (emphasis added) (Article 53(4)). *See also*, ICAO (n 1105) 253.

1172. United Nations Treaty Collection (n 1152).

1173. *Source*: Roel Balingit (username: Namayan), available at commons.wikimedia.org/wiki/File:Ph_Territorial_Map.png accessed 12 February 2020.

As with transit passage, some States – such as the US – claim that archipelagic sea lanes passage is customary international law, but the variation in State practice in applying the regime suggests that this is unlikely to be the case.[1174] All States noted above in Section 5.4.1[1175] that have met the formal requirements of an archipelagic State, or that have registered but not met the formal requirements, are parties to UNCLOS, and therefore bound by its provisions. Like the Philippines though, Cape Verde and Sao Tome and Principe registered declarations to the archipelagic regime, in their case indicating a tacit rejection of archipelagic sea lanes passage.[1176] Indonesia's administration of its archipelagic sea lanes provides another example of what some States view as a variation from what is provided under UNCLOS, a matter that will be further discussed in Section 5.4.4.3.

5.4.4 Ambiguities in the Application of Archipelagic Sea Lanes Passage to Overflight

5.4.4.1 Designation of Air Routes

The archipelagic sea lanes passage regime under UNCLOS has, in practice, resulted in little conflict regarding its application to overflight. This may be in part because the number of archipelagic States is only small, and that just one of those States, Indonesia, has designated sea lanes through its archipelagic waters. As will be seen below, the UNCLOS provisions relating to designation are not entirely unambiguous insofar as they relate to overflight. More significantly though, like in international straits, international civil aviation generally operates through archipelagic waters on the basis of prior permission as it does through other national airspace,[1177] and the application of archipelagic sea lanes passage to overflight is predominantly intended for the purpose of providing State aircraft access through the seas.

Under UNLCOS, an archipelagic State has the right to designate sea lanes and air routes through the archipelago and once established, all ships and aircraft enjoy the right of passage in such sea lanes and air routes.[1178] Aircraft are required to adhere to the air routes, with deviations of up to 25 nm permitted either side of the route.[1179] In its designation of air routes, an archipelagic State must include 'all normal passage routes used as routes for international navigation or overflight'.[1180] If the State 'does not designate sea lanes or air routes', aircraft have the right to exercise passage

1174. Caminos and Cogliati-Bantz (n 1114) 472.
1175. *See* n 1159.
1176. United Nations Treaty Collection (n 1152).
1177. Pursuant to Articles 3, 5, 6 and 8 of the Chicago Convention, as addressed in Chapter 2.
1178. UNCLOS, Article 53(1) and (2). Article 41 UNCLOS governs the designation of sea lanes within international straits. Unlike its equivalent for archipelagic sea lanes, it does not provide States with the right to designate air routes over international straits. Greece and Morocco objected to this omission prior to the conclusion of UNCLOS, calling for coastal States to have the right to impose corridors for overflight in international straits, but their opposition on this point failed to impact the final outcome (Caminos (n 1115) *Note 386*).
1179. *Ibid.* Article 53(5).
1180. *Ibid.* 53(4).

'through the routes normally used for international navigation', in accordance with Article 53(12).

The wording in Article 53(12) requires attention in terms of its implications for overflight in that it provides only for the ongoing use of routes normally used for international *navigation*, which is specifically used in UNCLOS in respect of ships, whereas the term 'overflight' is used for aircraft. This is despite the fact that the first part of the article establishes that it applies in the case that either sea lanes or air routes have not been designated. Commentators have thus questioned whether this means that air routes are tied to sea lanes.[1181] The apparent coexistence is heightened by the wording of Article 53(1): 'an archipelagic State may designate sea lanes and air routes *thereabove* ...' (emphasis added).

ICAO has not commented on Article 53(1), but on Article 53(12) it stated, soon after the adoption of UNCLOS, merely that the provision 'preserves the factual status quo', meaning that 'the existing air routes will continue' in the case that the archipelagic State takes no action to expressly designate air routes. This suggests that ICAO either takes as a given that air routes follow the routes of navigation, or that the phrase 'routes for ... navigation' as it is used in Article 53(12) refers also to air routes. The latter is unlikely given that UNCLOS throughout is clear in its distinction between routes for navigation and air routes, and navigation and overflight.

De Vries Lentsch has considered the ambiguity, pointing out that in practice air routes and sea routes are established in accordance with the considerations of each mode of transport - air routes cover land, for example - and requiring them to be aligned has no practical benefit.[1182]

However, Kwiatkowska and Agoes provide logic to the literal interpretation of the text:

> The requirement that air routes must be above archipelagic sea lanes was dictated ... by the necessity to provide maneuvering possibilities for military aircraft while the naval forces of a particular fleet are passing through the sea lanes.[1183]

Thus, the symbiotic relationship between the sea lanes and air routes is intentional, but not relevant to international *civil* aviation. Quoting Kwiatkowska and Agoes once again:

> Civil aircraft could clearly not fulfill the condition of zigzagging above the archipelagic sea lanes and of overflying archipelagic waters without passing above archipelagic land (island) territory.[1184]

While international civil aircraft have a right to operate through air routes designated as archipelagic sea lanes pursuant to UNCLOS, in practice, these routes are

1181. Barbara Kwiatkowska and Etty R Agoes, 'Archipelagic Waters: An Assessment of National Legislation' in Rüdiger Wolfrum, Ursula E Heinz and Denise A Bizzarro (eds), *Law of the Sea at the Crossroads: The Continuing Search for a Universally Accepted Regime – Proceedings of an Interdisciplinary Symposium of the Kiel Institute of International Law, 10-14 July 1990* (Duncker & Humblot 1991) 144; de Vries Lentsch (n 1162) 211.
1182. *Ibid.*
1183. Kwiatkowska and Agoes (n 1181) 144.
1184. *Ibid.*

not designed with their navigation in mind and their flight paths will instead be dictated outside the scope of UNCLOS as for the operation of foreign aircraft in any other national airspace.

5.4.4.2 ICAO's Role in Approving Air Routes

Under Article 53(9), an archipelagic State is required to refer its proposals of designated sea lanes to 'the competent international organization', in this case the IMO,[1185] for adoption before the State designates them. The article refers only to sea lanes though, rather than also air routes, an omission ICAO addressed shortly after the adoption of UNCLOS. While it must be considered intentional, ICAO concluded, it noted that there is no record of the purpose of the omission and therefore:

> the prima facie interpretation must be that the archipelagic States would have no conventional duty to refer proposals on the designation of air routes over the archipelagic waters to ICAO for adoption.[1186]

For practical reasons though, ICAO indicated that archipelagic States should submit their air route proposals to their Regional Air Navigation Conference 'for eventual approval by the ICAO Council'.[1187] This also makes sense from a safety perspective given ICAO's role in approving RANPs and the fact that air routes are the foundation for the coordination of the provision of air navigation services as set out in those plans.[1188] The IMO has since formally recognised ICAO as a relevant party in considering archipelagic sea lanes proposals.[1189] Noting ICAO's consideration that there is no recorded intention for the omission, the reason may lie with the explanation above regarding the designation of air routes in archipelagic sea lanes being for the purpose of a military aircraft: given that State aircraft are outside the competence of ICAO, its involvement was not considered relevant.[1190]

5.4.4.3 Partial Designation

The rules for designation involving routes normally used for navigation and overflight are designed to help ensure archipelagic States maintain traditional routes through

1185. Caminos (n 1115) 166.
1186. ICAO (n 1105) 254.
1187. *Ibid.*
1188. 'Safety of Navigation: Designation of Certain Sea Lanes and Air Routes Thereabove Through Indonesian Archipelagic Waters – Note by Indonesia' (MSC 67/7/2 30 August 1996), in Barbara Kwiatkowska, Eric Molenaar, Alex Oude Elferink and Alfred Soons (eds), *International Organizations and the Law of the Sea – Documentary Yearbook 1996, Vol 12* (Martinus Nijhoff Publishers 1996) 727.
1189. IMO Resolution A.572(14), as amended, 'Amendments to the General Provisions on Ship's Routeing' (19 May 1998), Annex 2, 3.3: 'Upon receipt of a proposal for designating archipelagic sea lanes and before consideration for adoption, the IMO shall ensure that the proposal is disseminated to all Governments and ICAO so as to provide them with sufficient opportunity to comment on the proposal.'
1190. Kwiatkowska and Agoes (n 1181) 144. Having said this, ICAO plays a role in the coordination of civil and military traffic, and its involvement today in the designation process alongside the IMO is in this sense consistent with serving the interests of safety.

their archipelagos. It is in an archipelagic State's interest to minimise the designation of sea lanes through their archipelago though, as it retains greater control over non-sea lane designated waters.[1191] On the other hand, there are the interests of the States whose aircraft and ships benefit from a greater network of sea lanes to support both their commercial and military interests.[1192]

This tension has led to disagreements regarding Indonesia's designation of sea lanes. Indonesia designated north-south sea lanes through its archipelagic waters in 2002 but has not designated east-west lanes.[1193] The US and Australia object to the designation on the basis that they claim the east-west sea lanes to be routes normally used for navigation under Article 53(4) UNCLOS.[1194] Recalling Article 53(12), a State can use the routes normally used for navigation in the case that the archipelagic State has not designated routes, but this is the only permitted circumstance for the use of undesignated routes. In the case of Indonesia, however, the IMO has classified its designation of sea lanes as a 'partial designation' on the basis that it does not include the east-west lanes[1195] and, as a consequence, States are still permitted to use the east-west designation on the basis of Article 53(12).[1196] Indonesia has acknowledged that its designation is partial and accepts the right of vessels and aircraft to operate through 'routes normally used for navigation', but this public position is contrary to its domestic legislation.[1197] As acknowledged in Section 5.4.4.1, there is no evidence that this situation has resulted in concern for the operation of international civil aviation; however, it has impacted on foreign military operations, particularly those of the US who have operated in the east-west lanes, asserting what the US claims as its right to do so.[1198] In October 2016, the US reiterated its objection to the lack of designation by way of a diplomatic note to Indonesia.[1199] As at July 2021, this author is not aware of

1191. Chris Forward, 'Archipelagic Sea-Lanes in Indonesia – Their Legality in International Law' (2009) 23 Aust & NZ Mar LJ 143, 150-151.
1192. Carlos Jiménez Piernas, 'Archipelagic Waters' (Max Planck Encyclopedia of Public International Law 2009) 25.
1193. Caminos and Cogliati-Bantz (n 1114) 199-200.
1194. Tara Davenport, 'The Archipelagic Regime' in Donald R Rothwell, Alex G Oude Elferink, Karen N Scott and Tim Stephens (eds), *The Oxford Handbook of the Law of the Sea* (OUP 2015) 151.
1195. Arif Havas Oegroseno, 'Archipelagic States: From Concept to Law' in David J Attard, Malgosia Fitzmaurice and Norman A Martínez Gutiérrez (eds), *The IMLI Manual on International Maritime Law: Volume 1 – The Law of the Sea* (OUP 2014) 135.
1196. Caminos and Cogliati-Bantz (n 1114) 201. *See also*, Sam Bateman, 'Australia and Indonesia at odds at sea' (East Asia Forum, 26 June 2015), available at www.eastasiaforum.org/2015/06/26/australia-and-indonesia-at-odds-at-sea/ accessed 20 May 2018; Carlos Jiménez Piernas, 'Archipelagic Waters' (Max Planck Encyclopedia of Public International Law 2009) 27.
1197. 'Indonesian Archipelagic Sea Lanes' (Semaphore – Newsletter of the Sea Power Centre Australia, April 2005), available at www.navy.gov.au/sites/default/files/documents/Semaphore_2005_6.pdf accessed 25 June 2016.
1198. Davenport (n 1194) 151; Caminos and Cogliati-Bantz (n 1114) 200-201. A US military aircraft was met by Indonesia military aircraft while operating through the east-west sea lane.
1199. Robert Beckman, 'The Legal Regime Governing Passage on Routes used for International Navigation through Indonesian Waters' (Presentation delivered at the 42nd Annual Conference of the Centre for Oceans and Policy Cooperation and Engagement in the Asia Pacific Region, Beijing, 24-26 May 2018).

further steps having been taken towards a resolution of this matter between the two States.

5.5 OVERFLIGHT THROUGH TRANSIT AND ARCHIPELAGIC SEA LANES DURING ARMED CONFLICT

Sections 5.1 and 5.3.4 indicated that transit passage and archipelagic sea lanes passage continue to apply during a time of armed conflict. This is with the exception that a belligerent coastal State has no obligation to provide passage during an armed conflict for a vessel or aircraft of an enemy State.[1200]

Insofar as the passage of aircraft of neutral States[1201] is concerned, as a result of Article 44 UNCLOS, any provisions under air law that may lead to the suspension of the right of overflight during war, such as Article 89 of the Chicago Convention and Article I, Section 1 of the Transit Agreement, do not permit the coastal State to close an international strait[1202] and this applies equally to archipelagic sea lanes.[1203] In the case of suspension under these circumstances, transit and archipelagic sea lanes passage would continue to serve the operation of international civil aviation where overflight through other parts of the territory of the bordering States or archipelagic State would not be permitted.

The ICJ in the *Corfu Channel Case* made clear though that during a state of war, a belligerent State bordering a strait has the right to regulate - but not prohibit - the passage of warships through the strait,[1204] referring to neutral warships, and this is understood to extend also to merchant ships.[1205] Likewise, for neutral aircraft today, State practice suggests that a belligerent coastal State, while it may not prevent passage, has the right to impose regulations on overflight through transit lanes and archipelagic sea lanes during armed conflict, such as subjecting aircraft to visit and search.[1206]

Notwithstanding the above, Caminos and Cogliati-Bantz argue that in extreme circumstances, the State may be able to justify the closure of transit lanes or archipelagic sea lanes, with the legality of doing so determined on the basis of the rules on State responsibility, specifically circumstances precluding wrongfulness.[1207]

1200. Caminos and Cogliati-Bantz (n 1114) 21. As with many other aspects regulating the law of war, this is determined as a result of State practice. Note also, '[b]elligerents in transit or archipelagic sea lanes passage may not ... conduct offensive operations against enemy forces' (San Remo Manual, para. 30).
1201. That is, States that are not party to the conflict (San Remo Manual, para. 13(d)).
1202. Caminos (n 1115), 161.
1203. UNCLOS, Article 54. This article provides that Article 44, *inter alia*, applies *mutatis mutandis* to archipelagic sea lanes passage.
1204. *Corfu Channel (United Kingdom v. Albania)*, Merits, Judgment, I.C.J. Rep. 1949 (9 April), p. 4, p. 29.
1205. Caminos and Cogliati-Bantz (n 1114) 26.
1206. San Remo Manual, paras 115 and 125.
1207. Caminos and Cogliati-Bantz (n 1114) 30.

5.6 CONCLUSION TO CHAPTER

As a result of the regimes established under UNCLOS, the airspace over international straits and in archipelagic sea lanes is an anomaly in that it is part of sovereign airspace, but the rules applying to overflight are closer to those in international airspace. Like in the EEZ and the high seas, the Rules of the Air under Annex 2 of the Chicago Convention apply without exception and the coastal State cannot impose its national civil aviation regulations in the airspace. Furthermore, the coastal State may not hamper or suspend passage, even in the case of war, although State practice indicates that there is no obligation to permit the aircraft of an enemy State to pass through the lanes, and, possibly, in the case of exceptional circumstances, the coastal State also has the right to close the lanes to the aircraft of other States on the basis of the action being justifiable as a circumstance precluding wrongfulness.[1208]

Aircraft passing through an international strait or archipelagic sea lane do not require prior authorisation to pass through the airspace, but neither do they have the right to freedom of overflight: unlike in the EEZ or over the high seas, they must proceed without delay and, in doing so, they are forbidden from activities that are external to expeditious transit. While transit passage and archipelagic sea lanes passage apply to both civil aircraft and State aircraft, the regimes are, in practice, to the benefit of State – usually military – aircraft and as a result, the issues addressed in this chapter have consequences for these aircraft where they have little or no impact on international civil aviation. As discussed in Section 2.4.4, overflight of national airspace for State aircraft is largely negotiated on an ad hoc basis. Transit passage and archipelagic sea lanes passage enable such aircraft to operate freely between areas of international airspace without either the need for authorisation from the coastal States whose national airspace includes the international straits or archipelagic sea lanes they pass through or, the impractical detours that would be required if they were forced to avoid the airspace.

The regime under UNCLOS brings substantial uniformity to the legal framework applying to navigation in the airspace over international straits and archipelagic sea lanes. However, as demonstrated in this chapter, the application of the laws is not without conflict. In the case of transit passage, some coastal States have not accepted the application of the regime to their national airspace in the international strait. Where this is the case, the potential for conflict exists – as displayed in the Strait of Hormuz between the US and Iran – where the State of registry of the aircraft does not recognise the purported right of the coastal State to regulate the operation of the aircraft. In the case of archipelagic sea lanes passage, the designation of air routes has resulted in conflicting views between the coastal State, in this case Indonesia, and the States whose military aircraft operate in the airspace. As the case of Indonesia demonstrates, there is some ambiguity in the archipelagic sea lanes passage regime resulting from the failure to establish a contingency for the situation arising out of an archipelagic State designating some sea lanes but not including all normal passage routes. The concept of

1208. YILC (2001) Vol. II, Part 2.

'partial designation' has been accepted by the IMO to address this and to allow maritime States to operate in normal passage routes. In doing so, the IMO has arguably gone beyond the intention of UNCLOS[1209] and, although Indonesia has publicly accepted it, both its domestic legislation and actions in response to military aircraft operating in the east-west sea lanes indicate otherwise.

The tension between the conflicting rights asserted by the coastal State and the State of registry of aircraft navigating through international airspace, as has been addressed in the preceding chapters of this book, extends also to the context of archipelagic sea lanes and international straits which, despite constituting national airspace, involve rights that more closely resemble that of freedom of overflight. The consequences of this are negligible for international civil aviation but it remains to be seen whether and to what extent these legal issues result in greater conflict between States in future regarding the navigation of State, particularly military, aircraft.

1209. Davenport (n 1194) 151.

CHAPTER 6
Conclusions and Recommendations

6.1 CONCLUSIONS

The central research question of this book was: *what jurisdiction does a coastal State have over the operation of the aircraft registered in other States in international airspace adjacent to its coast?* In attempting to answer this question, this book addressed three principal matters, as those that were identified as involving ambiguity in terms of where the balance sits between the rights of the coastal State and the rights of the users of the airspace in the exercise of their freedom of overflight. This chapter will briefly address the main conclusions in the book on each of these matters before presenting, as the focus of the chapter, the overarching conclusions of the book. It will also provide some observations and recommendations based on these overarching conclusions.

6.1.1 Safety Zones

Article 60 UNCLOS provides the coastal State with the exclusive right to construct, regulate and use artificial islands, and installations and structures related to the exercise of its EEZ rights or that interfere with those rights, in its EEZ. This exclusive right exists *mutatis mutandis* on the continental shelf. This article also permits the coastal State to impose safety zones around their maritime constructions, to up to 500 metres from the perimeter of the construction, a distance which may be greater with the approval of the IMO, and which is required to reflect the nature and function of the construction. Within these safety zones, the jurisdiction of the State extends beyond that which the coastal State has in the EEZ or continental shelf more broadly, that is, outside the safety zones.

There were three broad matters that were discussed in Chapter 3 relevant to determining jurisdiction of the coastal State over the operation of aircraft in international airspace adjacent to its territorial sea. The *first* is the circumstances in which construction changes the legal status of a feature at sea in terms of shifting the delimitation of national and international airspace. The *second* is whether Article 60 can be interpreted as providing the right to extend safety zones to the airspace over maritime constructions or whether this has developed as a customary international law independently from the regime under UNCLOS. The *third* is, in the case that no such right exists to extend safety zones to the airspace, what rights does the coastal State have, if any, to prohibit, restrict or otherwise manage the overflight of the aircraft of other States in order to facilitate air traffic movement in and out of a maritime construction? This is particularly relevant in the case a State were to establish an artificial island in its EEZ for the purpose of a civil international airport, which would involve a consistent flow of traffic and therefore a need to impose measures to manage overflight on a sustained basis.

The potentially changing legal status of the sea was addressed in two ways: human modification to natural features beyond the territorial sea and human modification to the coastline of a land mass under the sovereignty of a State in the case that there are resulting changes to the delimitation of the airspace. The first of these discussed a series of cases culminating, most recently, in the *South China Sea Arbitration*, in which it was confirmed that a maritime feature retains its original legal status despite human modification. As a result of this, for example, a low-tide elevation in the EEZ or on high seas cannot become a natural island through construction, and it instead continues to exist in law as a low-tide elevation while also becoming an artificial island. This position is significant because it means that a State cannot use a low-tide elevation, or a permanently submerged reef, in order to claim national airspace over a maritime feature that, prior to the construction, did not generate claims to sovereignty. Furthermore, for the purposes of this book, it means that these features are relevant to the discussion on safety zones. The chapter also drew attention to the implication for the delimitation of national, and therefore international, airspace, as a result of human modification within a State's territorial sea. This discussion was raised in the context of its expected increasing relevance in light of rising sea levels as a result of climate change, where coastal construction and even island creation have been undertaken to protect affected communities.

The main body of Chapter 3 considered whether a coastal State may have jurisdiction in the airspace above its maritime construction through there being a right to extend safety zones around those constructions in its EEZ or on its continental shelf to the airspace above them. This chapter first considered the wording of Article 60, particularly Article 60(4), (5) and (6), which suggests that the safety zones are restricted to the sea itself. This conclusion was reached on the basis of the reference to 'navigation', as opposed to also 'overflight', the reference to 'ships' and not 'aircraft', and to the stipulation regarding the extent of the zones, that is, that it refers to a breadth around them but not to an altitude above them. Despite this, there are instances[1210] in which these laws have been interpreted as allowing for the extension of safety zones to the airspace above maritime constructions pursuant to these provisions. This is supported by a teleological interpretation of the laws: they are designed to protect the

1210. France, for example, as to which *see* Section 3.3.2.1, as well as in academic opinion, as to which *see* Rothwell, discussed in the same section.

safety of both the construction and users of the maritime space operating in the vicinity. On the other hand, the subsequent practice of States in implementing the law into their domestic jurisdiction overwhelmingly supports the literal interpretation of the text of the treaty, in applying only to vessels on the surface of the sea. This is furthermore supported by the drafting material to the 1958 provisions on safety zones, which form the basis for the UNCLOS provisions, and the fact that no amendments were made in respect of airspace in the provisions as they were included in UNCLOS. Based on the actions of the US in repeatedly overflying the 'prohibited airspace' above the artificial islands constructed by China in the South China Sea, this book also considered the possibility of the right to establish safety zones in the airspace above maritime constructions becoming customary international law and, in particular, it considered the role of the persistent objector and the development of regional custom, where only a small number of related States engage in the practice. In any case, this analysis was hypothetical as the present set of circumstances does not suggest that the right is forming as customary law.

A State has jurisdiction over the aviation operations themselves that are conducted to and from its maritime construction as a result of Article 60(1) and (2) UNCLOS. The management of air traffic is governed as it is with any other users of the airspace. In the case that a State constructs an artificial island in its EEZ or on its continental shelf for the purpose of establishing a civil international airport on it, a State would also undoubtedly have jurisdiction over that airport as a result of Article 60(1) and (2) UNCLOS. The State would not have jurisdiction over the airspace as a result of the construction of the artificial island though. It remains to be seen how States would respond to a proposal by a State to manage the airspace above an airport outside its territory, which would involve sustained use of the international airspace above it. At the least, it would involve amendments to the applicable RANP.

6.1.2 Flight Information Regions

This matter was examined in the scope of this book slightly differently from the other aspects. Instead of determining whether a costal State has jurisdiction in international airspace, it considered the scope of the coastal State's jurisdiction in the provision of its ATS, specifically in the context of whether the coastal State is prohibited under international civil aviation law from discriminating against aircraft operating in international airspace within the FIR for which it is responsible. In the absence of an explicit principle of non-discrimination applying to the provision of ATS under Annex 11 to the Chicago Convention, the chapter set out to examine whether there was an implied principle that applied, considering the context of Annex 11 within the broader international civil aviation law framework and the significance of non-discrimination to air navigation aspects in national airspace. The non-discrimination principle appears in the Chicago Convention several times. It is not an overarching principle though, as air transport matters are outside of its scope and, relying on a framework of, mostly, bilateral agreements, they are necessarily discriminatory. On this basis, access to national airspace from the outset is granted on a discriminatory basis.

Furthermore, the principle of non-discrimination, where it applies to air navigation, still leaves States with the discretion to discriminate against aircraft based on their State of registry in some instances. For example, the non-discrimination principle in respect of national aircraft and other States' aircraft in Article 9(a) applies only to aircraft engaged in scheduled services, while the access to air navigation facilities under Article 15 is subject to the exception in Article 68, that States have the right to designate the routes that any scheduled service may follow. The same right is included in the Transit Agreement in respect of the right of overflight. On this basis, it is difficult to argue that there is an overarching principle of non-discrimination in international civil aviation law which may implicitly apply to navigation in international airspace. In addition, while there are safety and economic arguments to be made for non-discrimination in international airspace, as are the purposes of non-discrimination in national airspace, the application of the principle is, in contrast to national airspace, not necessary to avoid discrimination in international airspace. Unlike in national airspace, jurisdiction in respect of air navigation in international airspace is narrowly defined: it is restricted to the provision of ATS, which involves decisions relating to technical and operational matters only for the purpose of safety and efficiency. This involves regulating the operation of air traffic and even, under certain circumstances, imposing temporary measures that restrict the operation of aircraft in certain parts of international airspace. These measures are consistent with the scope of jurisdiction of the coastal States provided that they are imposed for safety or efficiency purposes. Finally, Annex 11, as the legal foundation for the FIR responsibility in international airspace, is adopted by ICAO whose objectives in developing principles of international air navigation include the avoidance of discrimination between contracting States. For a State to carry out its responsibility in international airspace in a discriminatory manner would subsequently also be a breach of the principle of good faith.

6.1.3 Air Defence Identification Zones

Jurisdiction of the coastal State in respect of ADIZs was addressed in terms of prescriptive jurisdiction, or the right to establish ADIZs and thereby impose domestic regulations in the international airspace to which the zone applies, and enforcement jurisdiction, or the right to enforce the regulations in international airspace. As was made clear, even if a State has the right to establish an ADIZ, the zone does not provide the coastal State with enforcement jurisdiction in international airspace. On this basis, the coastal State has no right to act in international airspace in response to an aircraft that does not comply with its ADIZ requirements beyond the rights it has under international law in the absence of the ADIZ. These include, for example, limited circumstances under which a State is permitted to intercept a civil aircraft and, in the case of the use of force, the right to self-defence. This is so also for State aircraft, although there are no codified rules governing the interception of State aircraft and States frequently intercept the State aircraft of other States. As a consequence, the coastal State has no right in international airspace to act against an aircraft in the case it fails to comply with ADIZ procedures.

ADIZs are presented by coastal States as national security measures. They involve the exercise of prescriptive jurisdiction of the coastal State in international airspace in the case that the zone extends beyond national airspace. The specific procedures that apply to the zone differ between States but in any case, by definition, they involve 'special identification and/or reporting procedures additional to those related to the provision of air traffic services'.[1211] In determining whether a coastal State has the right to exercise prescriptive jurisdiction in international airspace by way of the establishment of an ADIZ, this book, on the one hand, considered whether there is a permissive rule under international law to serve as a legal basis for the right to establish ADIZs or, in the case that a permissive rule is not necessary, whether the establishment of such a zone is prohibited by international law. It found that there was no permissive rule and that ADIZs are not consistent with freedom of overflight.

In consideration of a permissive rule, four justifications for ADIZs were examined: the right of a State to establish conditions of admission to or departure from its territory based on the interpretation of Articles 11 and 3(c) of the Chicago Convention; the right of self-defence under customary international law, as recognised in Article 51 of the UN Charter; the right of a coastal State to restrict military activities in its EEZ based on the EEZ regime under UNCLOS, or in light of the right under customary international law; and, consideration of whether the right to establish an ADIZ is customary international law.

Regarding a State's right to establish the rules relating to entry and exit of its territory, it necessarily includes obligations that must be fulfilled outside the territory of the State but the identification purpose of ADIZs can be achieved through ATS and the creation of a zone is not a reasonable measure to achieve this purpose. Furthermore, most States apply their ADIZ procedures not just to aircraft entering or exiting their national airspace but also to aircraft with the intention of remaining in international airspace within the ADIZ. In terms of self-defence, the analysis clearly concluded that both the threat that the right to self-defence is designed to address and the act of self-defence are not those that apply in the case of the establishment of ADIZs.

The right of a State to regulate military activities in its EEZ was discussed in relation to ADIZs as far as the zones are limited to the EEZ boundary and only in terms of its application to military aircraft. In this respect, even if this basis was valid, it would not justify the establishment of ADIZs beyond the boundary of the EEZ or its application to civil aircraft or non-military State aircraft. Many coastal States regulate the military activities of other States in their EEZ in some way, including the overflight of military aircraft, although this is controversial and there is no express ground for doing so under UNCLOS. This chapter examined whether the obligation to have due regard for the coastal State's EEZ rights in the zone could be interpreted as encompassing the right to regulate military activities in the EEZ more generally. If the activities associated with the overflight impacted on the coastal State's rights and jurisdiction in the EEZ, this would be justified, as it would be for civil aircraft, but regulating overflight on the basis of national security interests would not fall within the

1211. Chicago Convention, Annex 4 (11th edn, July 2009) 1-1 and Annex 15 (16th edn, July 2018) 1-2. *See* Section 4.3.2.

scope of this right. Unlike vessels, aircraft are less likely to interfere with the coastal State's EEZ rights, even when undertaking military exercises. It is difficult to see how ADIZs, which apply to aircraft merely passing through the airspace, could be justified on this basis. On the other hand, the right of a coastal State to regulate the military activities of other States could develop as a customary international law to allow for regulation beyond instances interfering with the EEZ rights of the coastal State. At this stage, this is not the case however.

If a permissible law exists to support the right of the coastal State to establish ADIZs, the crystallisation of it as a customary international law is the most convincing argument, a matter that is reflected in the attention it has garnered in academic discussion. At the same time, there is great variation in State practice and finding that there is sufficiently uniform practice for the purpose of customary international law will depend on where the emphasis is placed on the elements of the establishment of the zones. The variation in practice is reflected in the very general definition of ADIZ provided by ICAO. Furthermore, there seems to be insufficient evidence of *opinio juris* for the purpose of customary international law. State aircraft rarely comply and, while civil aircraft tend to do so, discord between States' verbal objections to certain ADIZs and their expectation that their civil aircraft comply suggests that the intention behind the compliance may have more to do with ensuring the safety of international civil aviation than reflecting a belief that they are bound under international law to meet the requirements.

If the *Lotus* principle stands and coastal States are not required to rely on a permissive rule to exercise prescriptive jurisdiction in establishing ADIZs, they are still not legitimate as they are a violation of freedom of overflight. ADIZs cannot be validly construed as a balance of rights under UNCLOS, either in terms of freedoms of the high seas or in terms of coastal State rights in relation to other airspace users under the EEZ regime. Well-accepted instances of 'restrictions' that are consistent with freedom of overflight are all for one purpose: they facilitate freedom of overflight or the other accepted uses of the maritime space beyond territorial borders. This book also considered the consistency of the zones with international civil aviation law, considering the possible negative safety implications that ADIZs can bring about as a result of adding complexity to the procedures in the airspace. It ultimately found, despite this, that there was no inconsistency with the SARPs that govern the aspects of safety that ADIZs pose a risk to.

6.1.4 Transit and Archipelagic Sea Lanes Passage

UNCLOS provides a regime for overflight through international straits and archipelagic waters as a response to, respectively, the extension of the breadth of the territorial sea and the recognition of the concept of the archipelagic State that it codified. The correlating transit passage and archipelagic sea lanes passage ensured that States were still able to freely navigate from one body of the high seas, or the EEZ as was codified at the same time, to another. As explained in the chapter, while the right of passage applies to both State aircraft and civil aircraft, it is the former that generally exercises the right and who the passage is primarily designed to facilitate. Like in international airspace, aircraft do not require prior permission to fly through the airspace and the coastal States may not impose their national regulations to the operation of the aircraft; Article 12 of the Chicago Convention applies without exception, as in international airspace. Like in international airspace, the coastal States attempt to exercise greater control over the airspace that is subject to these passage regimes and, as with ADIZs, national security was a concern of States in the drafting process of the transit passage regime. This is demonstrated, for example, in the declarations and reservations that coastal States bordering international straits have with respect to the regime, as well as by the so-called partial designation by Indonesia of its archipelagic sea lanes.

6.1.5 General Conclusions and Recommendations

6.1.5.1 Fragmentation of the Law Governing the Use of International Airspace

The law of the sea and international air law are specialised areas of public international law. The contours of both areas are well recorded in treaty law, most notably UNCLOS and the Chicago Convention. They each contribute to the governance of overflight in international airspace. However, there are some areas that are not addressed by either, leaving States to interpret the silence or ambiguity through national legislation to complement the codified law. This was seen throughout this book in terms of the absence of an explicit statement on the application of safety zones to the airspace above maritime constructions and in relation to consideration regarding the legality of ADIZs, neither of which fit squarely within the competence of either authority. ICAO's lack of contribution to the drafting process of UNCLOS at the Third UN Conference on the Law of the Sea, from 1973 to 1982, was recognised in Chapter 1.[1212] On the other side, as was addressed in Chapter 3, the UK delegate during the drafting of the Second UN Conference on the Law of the Sea, in 1960, was against explicitly providing the coastal State with the right to extend safety zones to the airspace over maritime constructions on the basis of it not falling within the scope of the subject matter of the conference. It is difficult to know, as a result of this situation, whether subsequent silence by the IMO in its guidance material on safety zones in terms of their possible application to airspace is recognition that they are restricted to the sea or whether it is because it considers this aspect to be outside its competence.[1213] Furthermore, like with the regulation of passage through international straits and archipelagic sea lanes, ADIZs are focused on military aircraft, which generally pose a greater risk to national security than civil aircraft. As State aircraft fall outside the scope of the Chicago Convention, they are also outside the competence of ICAO.

1212. *See* Section 1.4.
1213. Considering, specifically, IMO Resolution A.671(16) 'Safety Zones and Safety of Navigation Around Offshore Installations and Structures' (19 October 1989) (*see* Section 3.2.1.2) and noting that the IMO is the global authority responsible for setting standards in respect of *shipping*.

These positions present a problem for the development of the law in that States are left to interpret the law without further guidance. Ambiguity in the law will always exist, and States are left to interpret the provisions of treaties in order to apply them in any case. The inclusion of subsequent practice in the application of a treaty as an element of the general rule of interpretation of that treaty in establishing agreement of the parties in its interpretation reflects this fact.[1214] At the same time, this is where an authority such as the IMO or the ICAO could play a constructive role in providing guidance on the text of the treaty. This is particularly so in the context of the topic of this book where the interests of coastal States collectively, in extending their jurisdiction into international airspace, are in direct opposition to users of the airspace, that is, State and civil aircraft exercising their freedom of overflight. The risk to freedom of overflight is even greater when justifications for the extension of jurisdiction are based on such broad concepts as 'national security'. A reduction in the fragmentation in the law between the law of the sea and international civil aviation law when it comes to governance of international airspace would help to alleviate this 'gap' in the law. On matters where this is possible, joint guidance material issued by the IMO and ICAO would help States to interpret the provisions of UNCLOS and the Chicago Convention.

6.1.5.2 ATS Providers as the Authority over International Airspace

Freedom of overflight is not defined in international law and what it entails is determined by the rights of other users of the maritime space. In the maritime areas adjacent to a State's territorial sea, the rights of the coastal State are relevant in determining what freedom of overflight involves. ICAO stated, upon the adoption of UNCLOS, that the EEZ regime has no impact on the rights of airspace users, but coastal States have, nevertheless, sought to extend their jurisdiction over the operation of aircraft in international airspace, at times justifying it based on their rights under UNCLOS, and at times relying on legal bases under international civil aviation law and public international law more broadly. There is no doubt that freedom of overflight, as a broad principle, is designed to evolve to fit the interests of States as their use of the maritime space develops. This book set out to determine where the balance sits at present in relation to areas that were identified as being ambiguous. It concluded, based on the areas it examined, that freedom of overflight is still narrowly defined; that is, the international community is reluctant to acknowledge the exercise of jurisdiction by States in international airspace. The exercise of jurisdiction by coastal States is presently restricted to the facilitation of the exercise of the freedom of overflight and achieving a balance between the freedom of overflight and other maritime freedoms.

Coastal States have prescriptive jurisdiction in international airspace within their FIRs in order to fulfil their responsibility for carrying out the provision of ATS in the area. Their responsibilities have their legal foundation in Annex 11 of the Chicago Convention and the RANP, which is established pursuant to the Annex. States that accept to provide ATS in international airspace may do so in a manner consistent with

1214. Vienna Convention on the Law of Treaties, Article 31(3)(b), as discussed in 3.3.2.2.

this Annex over its national airspace but again, this is restricted to circumstances in which the State deems it essential to enable it to fulfil its responsibility.[1215] In any case, the provision of ATS is for the purpose of the safety and efficiency of international civil aviation, thereby contributing to the facilitation of freedom of overflight.

A State may establish a danger area in international airspace for the purpose of notifying aircraft of potential safety risks resulting from the use of the maritime area. These danger areas are generally established in coordination with the ATS authority responsible for the FIR, but this is not an obligation when it is deemed by the State performing the activity that civil aircraft will not be at risk as a result of the absence of coordination.[1216] In addition to the requirements that the dimensions of a danger area are defined and that it is for a specified period of time, a State is not permitted to restrict or prohibit aircraft from international airspace by way of establishing a danger area. In practice though, a danger area will likely result in aircraft avoiding the affected airspace, on account of the risk to safety. Despite this, danger areas are accepted as being consistent with freedom of overflight and even more so, they are in some cases part of the corresponding obligation in exercising the freedom. Aerial military activities are part of freedom of overflight and in exercising this freedom, as with all freedoms, State have a due regard obligation under Article 87(2) to the interests of other States in carrying out their freedoms, whether freedom of overflight or otherwise. Danger areas may of course be established to protect international civil aviation from non-aviation-related maritime activities, but once again, the danger area is required as a result of the due regard obligation, and furthermore, its establishment facilitates international civil aviation by ensuring all aircraft are aware of safety risks.

Having said this, this book sees the possible development of customary international law in two areas as providing a significant shift in the concept of freedom of overflight if they were to crystallise. The first is the right of a coastal State to regulate military activities in its EEZ and the second is the right of a State to establish an ADIZ. Clear opposition to the former by the US provides a strong voice against the development of the law, positioning it as being in conflict with the freedom of overflight and navigation in the EEZ, but many States impose the practice, restricting the freedom of both navigation and overflight for national security purposes. These matters require assessment as they evolve.

Finally, a shift in the mentality of governments away from the idea of FIRs being linked to sovereignty, and towards prioritising them for the sole purpose of the provision of ATS – the purpose for which they exist – would assist in achieving the highest level of safety and efficiency for international civil aviation. This is particularly important over international airspace considering, as has been examined throughout this book, coastal States at times demonstrate a willingness to assert jurisdiction without a clear legal basis in international law.

1215. *See* Section 2.7.2.2.1.3.
1216. *See* Section 2.6.5.

6.1.5.3 *Environmental Implications Protecting Freedom of Overflight*

Environmental law may serve indirectly to protect freedom of overflight by restricting the establishment of larger and more permanent maritime constructions. While safety zones do not extend to the airspace above maritime constructions, the construction of airports or launch pads beyond the territorial sea, as expected in future, will require the establishment of danger areas in the airspace, at the very least. As has been identified, freedom of overflight at present is understood to be consistent with temporary danger areas that are restricted in their dimensions in relation to what is reasonable for the activity being undertaken. Furthermore, aircraft cannot be prohibited from the airspace: the danger area serves merely as a safety warning to other airspace users. At the same time, recognising that freedom of overflight is an evolving concept and that coastal States tend to attempt to expand their jurisdiction in the maritime areas adjacent to their national airspace, this position may undergo a shift. If, as identified in Chapter 3,[1217] a State wishes to construct a civil international airport beyond its territorial sea, a danger area would not be appropriate to ensure the safety of aircraft operating in the area and the State would need to negotiate with other States to establish jurisdiction for exclusive use of the airspace up to a certain altitude over the airport and in the airspace in its vicinity. This also applies to the launch of rockets if the platform was to be used on a regular basis. Closer examination on how this could be facilitated considering a balance of rights between the coastal State and users of international airspace in the case of such maritime constructions requires further attention.

States are required under Article 192 UNCLOS, among other environmental obligations, 'to protect and preserve the marine environment'. The Tribunal in the *South China Sea Arbitration* noted that China had, through its island-building activities, acted in violation of this provision, along with several other environmental protection provisions under UNCLOS. ITLOS similarly ordered Singapore not to engage in land reclamation that would result in significant harm to the marine environment.[1218] These regulations restrict the ability of a State to establish maritime constructions, certainly on a large and permanent scale, and may therefore serve, inadvertently, to minimise the subsequent jurisdiction over international airspace.

6.1.5.4 *Political Considerations and the Limitations of International Law*

The circumstances discussed in this book are highly political, as was established in Section 1.2.2, and reiterated throughout. National security unambiguously plays a key role for States in the imposition of ADIZs and in the desire to restrict traffic through international straits and archipelagic sea lanes. It is also a motive for a State to restrict overflight of maritime constructions where these constructions are part of a State's critical infrastructure, from oil rigs to airports. With reference to the notion of 'creeping

1217. *See* Section 3.4.2.
1218. *Land Reclamation in and around the Straits of Johor (Malaysia v. Singapore), Provisional Measures, Order of October 2003, ITLOS Reports 2003*, p. 10, p. 28 (*see* Section 3.2.2 (n 542)).

jurisdiction' as raised in Chapter 1, States are also driven by a desire to achieve greater control over the maritime domains adjacent to their coasts. State aircraft are often the targets of coastal State jurisdiction in international airspace both because they pose a greater risk to national security and because it is with State – military – aircraft that other States challenge the overflight restrictions and requirements imposed by coastal States. In the case of transit passage and archipelagic sea lanes passage, the regimes are designed to facilitate, primarily, the movement of State aircraft. Each of these considerations contributes to the politicised context in which the legal questions that have been addressed throughout this book are placed.

At a fundamental level, the involvement of State aircraft means that, insofar as international civil aviation is unimpeded, the matter falls outside of ICAO's normative powers. Even where international civil aviation is concerned, however, such as in the case of ADIZs, ICAO has not taken a position on their legality under international law. At the same time, ICAO appears to have contributed to the timely reversal of the prohibition of Qatari-registered aircraft from international airspace within the FIRs of its neighbouring States, with the change occurring soon after consultations took place. The law does not exist in a vacuum though and so violations of the law with strong political undercurrents tend not to be followed by unequivocal statements from ICAO clarifying the law.

On the other hand, freedom of overflight for both State aircraft and civil aircraft forms part of the law of the sea, being codified in UNCLOS. Section 6.1.5.1 addressed the issue of fragmentation and the fact that many of the legal questions addressed in this research sit on the boundaries of international civil aviation law and the law of the sea. In some respects though, the circumstances impact international civil aviation but the legal questions are more squarely positioned within the law of the sea. For answers to these questions under UNCLOS, adjudication of a dispute before ITLOS would be the ultimate procedure. The reach of this mechanism is restricted though, considering that key States such as the US and Turkey are not State parties to UNCLOS.[1219] Until, or if, clear statements are issued on these legal questions by the competent international organs, and even perhaps in spite of this, the interests of coastal States will continue to govern practical, and even legal, developments in this area.

Freedom of overflight is a fundamental principle in international airspace. At the same time, the interests of coastal States in extending their jurisdiction at sea, as considered in this book, are in direct opposition to the enjoyment of this freedom by other States. The practices of coastal States must, as a result, be closely scrutinised by the international community as to their legitimacy under relevant international law, including international civil aviation law and the law of the sea.

1219. Statute of the International Law of the Sea Tribunal (UNCLOS, Annex VI), Article 20.

Bibliography

Books

Abeyratne R, *Regulation of Air Transport: The Slumbering Sentinels* (Springer 2014).

van Antwerpen N, *Cross-Border Provision of Air Navigation Services with Specific Reference to Europe: Safeguarding Transparent Lines of Responsibility and Liability* (Kluwer Law International 2008).

Aquilina K, 'Territorial Sea and the Contiguous Zone' in David Attard, Malgosia Fitzmaurice and Norman A Martínez Gutiérrez (eds), *The Manual on International Maritime Law: Volume 1 – The Law of the Sea* (OUP 2014).

Aust HP, *Complicity and the Law of State Responsibility* (CUP 2011).

Bartsch RIC, *Aviation Law in Australia* (4th edn, Thomson Reuters 2013).

Beaulac S, 'The *Lotus* Case in Context: Sovereignty, Westphalia, Vattel, and Positivism' in Stephan Allen, Daniel Costelloe, Malgosia Fitzmaurice, Paul Gragl and Edward Guntrip (eds), *The Oxford Handbook of Jurisdiction in International Law* (OUP 2019).

Beaulac S, *The Power of Language in the Making of International Law: The Word Sovereignty in Bodin and Vattel and the Myth of Westphalia* (Martinus Nijhoff 2004).

Bederman DJ, 'Third Party Rights and Obligations in Treaties' in Duncan B Hollis (ed), *The Oxford Guide to Treaties* (OUP 2012).

Beyers M, *Custom, Power and the Power of Rules* (CUP 1999).

Brierly JL, *The Law of Nations* (6th edn, OUP 1963).

Buga I, *Modification of Treaties by Subsequent Practice* (OUP 2018).

Camilleri FA, *The Application of the High Seas Regime in the Exclusive Economic Zone* (Hamilton Books 2018).

Caminos H and Cogliati-Bantz VP, *The Legal Regime of Straits* (CUP 2014).

Carleton C, 'Problems Relating to Non-Natural and Man-Made Basepoints under UNCLOS' in Clive Ralph Symmons (ed), *Selected Contemporary Issues in the Law of the Sea* (Martinus Nijhoff Publishers 2011).

Chan C, Khan FN and Awan S, 'Bigger Issues in a Smaller World' in Blake Hudson, Jonathan Rosenbloom and Dan Cole (eds), *Routledge Handbook of the Study of the Commons* (Routledge 2019).

Cheng B, 'The Destruction of KAL Flight KE007, and Article 3 *bis* of the Chicago Convention' in JWE Storm van 's Gravensande and A van der Veen Vonk (eds), *Air Worthy – Liber Amicorum Honouring Professor Dr IHPh Diederiks-Verschoor* (Kluwer 1985).

Cheng B, *The Law of International Air Transport* (Stevens & Sons Ltd 1962).

Churchill R, 'The Piracy Provisions of the UN Convention on the Law of the Sea – Fit for Purpose?' in Panos Koutrakos and Achilles Skordas (eds), *The Law and Practice of Piracy at Sea: European and International Perspectives* (Hart Publishing 2014).

Constantinides A, 'Statehood and Recognition' in André Nollkaemper, August Reinisch, Ralph Janik, Florentina Simlinger (eds), *International Law in Domestic Courts: A Casebook* (OUP 2018).

Cooley A and Spruyt H, *Contracting States: Sovereign Transfers in International Relations* (Princeton University Press 2009).

Correia V, 'The Legacy of the 1919 Paris Convention Relating to the Regulation of Aerial Navigation' in Pablo Mendes de Leon and Niall Buissing (eds), *Behind and Beyond the Chicago Convention: The Evolution of Aerial Sovereignty* (Wolters Kluwer 2019).

Crawford J, *Brownlie's Principles of Public International Law* (9th edn, OUP 2019).

Crawford J, *The Creation of States in International Law* (2nd edn, OUP 2006).

Csabafi IA, *The Concept of State Jurisdiction in International Space Law: A Study in the Progressive Development of Space Law in the United Nations* (Martinus Nijhoff 1971).

Davenport T, 'The Archipelagic Regime' in Donald R Rothwell, Alex G Oude Elferink, Karen N Scott and Tim Stephens (eds), *The Oxford Handbook of the Law of the Sea* (OUP 2015).

Djalal H, 'The Law of the Sea Convention and Navigational Freedoms' in Donald R Rothwell and Samuel Grono Bateman (eds), *Navigational Rights and Freedoms, and the New Law of the Sea* (Martinus Nijhoff Publishers 2000).

Doganis R, *Flying Off Course: Airline Economics and Marketing* (4th edn, Routledge 2010).

Dörr O, 'Article 31 General Rule of Interpretation' in Oliver Dörr and Kirsten Schmalenbach (eds), *Vienna Convention on the Law of Treaties: A Commentary* (2nd edn, Springer 2018).

Espósito C, Kraska J, Scheiber HN and Kwon M (eds), *Ocean Law and Policy: Twenty Years of Development under the UNCLOS Regime* (Brill Nijhoff 2016).

Farrall J, 'Sanctions' in Jacob Katz Cogan, Ian Hurd and Ian Johnstone (eds), *The Oxford Handbook of International Organizations* (OUP 2016).

Franckx E, 'The Regime of Islands and Rocks' in David Attard, Malgosia Fitzmaurice and Norman A Martínez Gutiérrez (eds), *The Manual on International Maritime Law: Volume 1 – The Law of the Sea* (OUP 2014).

Gammeltoft-Hansen T and Aalberts T, 'Search and Rescue as a Geopolitics of International Law' in Thomas Gammeltoft-Hansen and Tanja Aalberts (eds), *The Changing Practices of International Law* (CUP 2018).
Gardiner R, *Treaty Interpretation* (OUP 2015).
Gavouneli M, *Functional Jurisdiction in the Law of the Sea* (Brill Nijhoff 2007).
Glanville L, *Sovereignty and Responsibility to Protest: A New History* (The University of Chicago Press 2014).
Goedhuis D, *Handboek voor het Luchtrecht* (Martinus Nijhoff 1943).
Gray C, *International Law and the Use of Force* (4th edn, OUP 2018).
Green JA, *The Persistent Objector Rule in International Law* (OUP 2016).
Grief N, *Public International Law in the Airspace of the High Seas* (Martinus Nijhoff 1994).
Grote Stoutenburg J, *Disappearing Island States in International Law* (Brill Nijhoff 2015).
Grotius H, *Mare Liberum* (Lodewijk Elzevir 1609).
Haanappel PCC, *The Law and Policy of Air Space and Outer Space: A Comparative Approach* (Kluwer Law International 2003).
Haanappel P, 'Aerial Sovereignty: From Paris 1919, Through Chicago 1944, to Today' in Pablo Mendes de Leon and Niall Buissing (eds), *Behind and Beyond the Chicago Convention* (Wolters Kluwer 2019).
Hakim C, *FIR di Kepulauan Riau Wilayah Udara Kedaulatan NKRI* (Penerbit Buku Kompas 2019).
Havas Oegroseno A, 'Archipelagic States: From Concept to Law' in David J Attard, Malgosia Fitzmaurice and Norman A Martínez Gutiérrez (eds), *The IMLI Manual on International Maritime Law: Volume 1 – The Law of the Sea* (OUP 2014).
Havel B and Sanchez G, *The Principles and Practice of International Aviation Law* (CUP 2014).
Heller PP, 'Air Space over Extended Jurisdictional Zones' in John King Gamble (ed) *Law of the Sea: Neglected Issues* (Law of the Sea Institute, University of Hawaii 1979).
Heraclides A, *Greek-Turkish Conflict in the Aegean* (Palgrave MacMillan Limited 2010).
Hobe S, Ruckteschell N and Heffernan D, *Cologne Compendium on Air Law in Europe* (Carl Heymanns Verlag 2013).
Hobe S, Schmidt-Tedd B, Schrogel K and Goh GM (eds), *Cologne Commentary on Space Law: Vol I* (Carl Heymanns Verlag 2009).
Honig JP, *The Legal Status of Aircraft* (Martinus Nijhoff 1956).
Huang J, *Aviation Safety and ICAO* (Kluwer Law International 2009).
Jennings R and Watts A, 'The Freedom of the High Seas' in Robert Jennings and Arthur Watts (eds), *Oppenheim's International Law: Volume 1 Peace* (9th edn, OUP 2008).
Kaye S, 'Maritime Security in the Post-9/11 World: A New Creeping Jurisdiction in the Law of the Sea?' in Clive H Schofield, Seokwoo Lee and Moon-Sang Kwon (eds), *The Limits of Maritime Jurisdiction* (Martinus Nijhoff Publishers 2013).
Klein N, *Maritime Security and the Law of the Sea* (OUP 2011).

Krisch N, 'Ch. VII Action with Respect to Threats to the Peace, Breaches of the Peace, and Acts of Aggression, Article 41' in Bruno Simma, Daniel-Erasmus Khan, Georg Nolte, Andreas Paulus and Nikolai Wessendorf (eds), *The Charter of the United Nations: A Commentary, Volume II* (3rd edn, OUP 2012).

Kwiatkowska B, Molenaar E, Oude Elferink A and Soons A (eds), *International Organizations and the Law of the Sea – Documentary Yearbook 1996, Vol 12* (Martinus Nijhoff Publishers 1996).

Kwiatkowska B and Agoes ER, 'Archipelagic Waters: An Assessment of National Legislation' in Rüdiger Wolfrum, Ursula E Heinz and Denise A Bizzarro (eds), *Law of the Sea at the Crossroads: The Continuing Search for a Universally Accepted Regime – Proceedings of an Interdisciplinary Symposium of the Kiel Institute of International Law, 10-14 July 1990* (Duncker & Humblot 1991).

Kwiatkowska B, *The 200 Mile Exclusive Economic Zone in the New Law of the Sea* (Martinus Nijhoff 1989).

Leanza U and Caracciolo MC, 'The Exclusive Economic Zone' in David Attard, Malgosia Fitzmaurice and Norman A Martínez Gutiérrez (eds), *The IMLI Manual on International Maritime Law: Vol 1 – Law of the Sea* (OUP 2014).

Liivoja R, *Criminal Jurisdiction over Armed Forces Abroad* (CUP 2017).

Mayer B, *The International Law on Climate Change* (CUP 2018).

McDougal MS and Burke WT, *The Public Order of the Oceans: A Contemporary International Law of the Sea* (New Haven Press 1987).

McNair, *The Law of Treaties* (OUP 1986).

Mendes de Leon P, *Introduction to Air Law* (10th edn, Wolters Kluwer 2017).

Merkouris P, 'Introduction: Interpretation Is a Science, Is an Art, Is a Science' in Malgosia Fitzmaurice, Olufemi Elias and Panos Merkouris (eds), *Treaty Interpretation and the Vienna Convention on the Law of Treaties: 30 Years On* (Martinus Nijhoff Publishers 2010).

Milde M, *International Air Law and ICAO* (3rd edn, Eleven International Publishing 2016).

Mouton MW, *The Continental Shelf* (Martinus Nijhoff 1952).

Nanda VP, 'Exercising Universal Jurisdiction over Piracy' in Michael P Scharf, Michael A Newton and Milena Sterio (eds), *Prosecuting Maritime Piracy: Domestic Solutions to International Crimes* (CUP 2015).

Nordquist MH (ed), *United Nations Convention on the Law of the Sea 1982: A Commentary – Volume II* (Brill Nijhoff 2011).

Nordquist MH (ed), *United Nations Convention on the Law of the Sea 1982: A Commentary – Volume III* (Brill Nijhoff 2011).

Nordquist MH, Grandy NR, Nandan SN and Rosenne S (eds), *United Nations Convention on the Law of the Sea 1982: A Commentary – Volume II* (Martinus Nijhoff 1993).

Noyes J, 'The Territorial Sea and Contiguous Zone' in Donald Rothwell, Alex G Oude Elferink, Karen N Scott and Tim Stephens (eds), *The Oxford Handbook of the Law of the Sea* (OUP 2015).

O'Connell DP, *The International Law of the Sea – Vol II* (OUP 1982).

Papadakis N, *The International Legal Regime of Artificial Islands* (Sijthoff 1977).

Pazartzis P, 'Judicial Activism and Judicial Self Restraint' in Malgosia Fitzmaurice and Christian J Tams (eds), *Legacies of the Permanent Court of International Justice* (Martinus Nijhoff Publishers 2013).

Piera A, *Greenhouse Gas Emissions from International Aviation: Legal and Policy Changes* (Eleven International Publishing 2015).

Poulantzas NM, *The Right of International Pursuit in International Law* (2nd edn, Martinus Nijhoff 2002).

Rothwell DR, 'International Straits', in Donald R Rothwell, Alex G Oude Elferink, Karen N Scott and Tim Stephens (eds), *The Oxford Handbook of the Law of the Sea* (OUP 2015).

Rothwell DR, 'Maritime Security in the Twenty-First Century: Contemporary and Anticipated Challenges for Australia and New Zealand' in Natalie Klein, Joanna Mossop and Donald R Rothwell (eds), *Maritime Security: International Law and Policy Perspectives from Australia and New Zealand* (Routledge 2010).

Ryngaert C, *Jurisdiction in International Law* (OUP 2015).

Ryngaert C, 'The Concept of Jurisdiction in International Law' in Alexander Orakhelashvili (ed), *Research Handbook on Jurisdiction and Immunities in International Law* (Edward Elgar Publishing 2015).

Schmalenbach K, 'Pacta Sunt Servanda' in Oliver Dörr and Kirsten Schmalenbach (eds), *Vienna Convention on the Law of Treaties: A Commentary* (2nd edn, Springer 2018).

Schofield C, 'The Trouble with Islands: The Definition and Role of Islands and Rocks in Maritime Boundary Delimitation' in Jon M van Dyke and Seoung-Yong Hong (eds), *Maritime Boundary Disputes, Settlement Processes and the Law of the Sea* (Brill Nijhoff 2009).

Schrijver N, *Sovereignty over Natural Resources: Balancing Rights and Duties* (CUP 2009).

Schubert F, 'Limits in the Sky: Sovereignty and Air Navigation Services' in Pablo Mendes de Leon and Niall Buissing (eds), *Behind and Beyond the Chicago Convention: The Evolution of Aerial Sovereignty* (Wolters Kluwer 2019).

Schubert F, 'Air Navigation' in Paul Stephen Dempsey and Ram S Jakhu (eds), *Routledge Handbook of Public Aviation Law* (Routledge 2017).

Shaw MN, *International Law* (6th edn, CUP 2008).

Sorel J and Boré Eveno V, 'Article 31 Convention of 1969' in Olivier Corten and Pierre Klein (eds), *The Vienna Conventions on the Law of Treaties: A Commentary (Vol I)* (OUP 2011).

Supancana IBR, 'Realignment of FIR from Singapore to Indonesia' in Pablo Mendes de Leon and Niall Buissing (eds), *Behind and Beyond the Chicago Convention: The Evolution of Aerial Sovereignty* (Wolters Kluwer 2019).

Symmons C, *The Maritime Zones of Islands in International Law* (Martinus Nijhoff 1979).

Treves T, 'UNCLOS and Non-party States Before the International Court of Justice' in Carlos Espósito, James Kraska, Harry N Scheiber and Moon-Sang Kwon (eds), *Ocean Law and Policy: Twenty Years of Development under the UNCLOS Regime* (Brill Nijhoff 2016).

Van den Bossche P and Zdouc W, *The Law and Policy of the World Trade Organization* (4th edn, CUP 2017) 342.

Van Dyke JM, 'Transit Passage Through International Straits' in Aldo Chircop, Theodore McDorman and Susan Rolston (eds), *The Future of Ocean Regime-Building: Essays in Tribute to Douglas M Johnston* (Martinus Nijhoff Publishers 2009).

Vella I, 'A New Advent for Renewable Offshore Resources' in Norman A Martínez Gutiérrez (ed), *Serving the Rules of International Maritime Law: Essays in Honour of Professor David Joseph Attard* (Routledge 2010).

Villiger ME, 'The Rules on Interpretation: Misgivings, Misunderstandings, Miscarriage? The "Crucible" Intended by the International Law Commission' in Enzo Cannizzaro (ed), *The Law of Treaties Beyond the Vienna Convention* (OUP 2011).

Villiger ME, *Commentary on the 1969 Vienna Convention on the Law of Treaties* (Brill Nijhoff 2009).

Wassenbergh HA, *Post-war International Civil Aviation Policy and the Law of the Air* (Springer 1957).

Weber L, *International Civil Aviation Organization* (Wolters Kluwer 2012).

Articles

Abeyratne R, 'Legal Issues of the Snowden Case: State Aircraft vs. Civil Aircraft' (2013) 62(4) ZLW 648.

Akande D and Liefländer T, 'Clarifying Necessity, Imminence, and Proportionality in the Law of Self-Defence' (2013) 107(3) Am J Int'l L 563.

Almond R, 'Clearing the Air above the East China Sea: The Primary Elements of Aircraft Defense Identification Zones' (2016) 7 NSJ 126.

Beaucillon C, 'Limiting Third States' Military Activities in the EEZ: "Due Regard Obligations" and the Law of the Use of Force Applied to Nuclear Weapons' (2019) 34 IJMCL 128.

Beckman R and Sun Z, 'The Relationship Between UNCLOS and IMO Instruments' (2017) 2 APOC 201.

Bethlehem D, 'Principles Relevant to the Scope of a State's Right of Self-Defense Against an Imminent or Actual Armed Attack by Non-state Actors' (2012) 106 Am J Int'l L 1.

Bourbonniere M and Haeck L, 'Military Aircraft and International Law: Chicago Opus 3' (2001) 66(3) J Air L&C 885.

Brock JR, 'Legality of Warning Areas as Used by the United States' (1966-1967) 21(3) The JAG Journal 69.

Burke KM and DeLeo DA, 'Innocent Passage and Transit Passage in the United National Convention on the Law of the Sea' (1983) 9 Yale J World Pub Ord 389.

Cáceres Rabionet I, Gracia García V and Rubio Galindo M, 'Indicators for Evaluating the Impact of Artificial Islands on Barcelona Coast' (2008) 36(3) Coastal Manage 254.

Caminos H, 'The Legal Régime of Straits in the 1982 United Nations Convention on the Law of the Sea' (1987) 205 Recueil des Cours 19.

Carpanelli E, 'The Siberian Overflights Issue' (2011) 11(23) Issues Aviation L & Pol'y 23.
Carroz J, 'International Legislation on Air Navigation over the High Seas' (1959) J Air L & Comm 158.
Cheng B, 'International Responsibility and Liability for Launch Activities' (1995) 20(6) A&SL 297.
Cheng B, 'The Extra-Territorial Application of International Law' (1965) 18 Curr Leg Probl 132.
Cheng B, 'The Right to Fly' (1959) 42 Trans Grotius Soc 99.
Cheng B, 'Crimes on Board Aircraft' (1959) 12 Curr Leg Probl 177.
Cobb Cooper J, 'The Chicago Convention – After Twenty Years' (1965) 19(3) U Miami L Rev 333.
Cobb Cooper J, 'Flight-Space and the Satellites' (1958) 7(1) ICLQ 82.
Colin S, 'China, the US, and the Law of the Sea' (2016) 2 China Perspect 57.
Cuadra E, 'Air Defense Identification Zones: Creeping Jurisdiction in the Airspace' (1978) 18 Va J Int'l L 485.
Davenport T, 'Island-Building in the South China Sea: Legality and Limits' (2018) 8 Asian J Int'l Law 76.
Dempsey PS, 'Flights of Fancy and Fights of Fury: Arbitration and Adjudication of Commercial and Political Disputes in International Aviation' (2004) 32(2) Ga J Int'l & Comp L 231.
Dunning WA, 'Jean Bodin on Sovereignty' (1896) Polit Sci Q 82.
Dutton PA, 'Caelum Liberum: Air Defense Identification Zones Outside Sovereign Airspace' (2009) 103 Am J Int'l L 691.
Fasullo JT and Neren RS, 'Altimeter-Era Emergence of the Patterns of Forced Sea-Level Rise in Climate Models and Implications for the Future' (2018) 115(51) Proc Natl Acad Sci USA 12944.
Fitzmaurice GG, 'The Law and Procedure of the International Court of Justice: Treaty Interpretation and Certain Other Treaty Points' (1951) 28 Brit YB Int'l L 1.
Forward C, 'Archipelagic Sea-Lanes in Indonesia – Their Legality in International Law' (2009) 23 Aust & NZ Mar LJ 143.
Franckx E, 'The 200-Mile Limit: Between Creeping Jurisdiction and Creeping Common Heritage – Some Law of the Sea Considerations from Professor Louis Sohn's Former LL.M. Student' (2007) 39 Geo Wash Int'l L Rev 467.
Franklin M and Porter S, 'Sovereignty over Airspace and the Chicago Convention: Northern Cyprus' (2010) 35(1) A&SL 63.
Freeland S, 'Fly Me to the Moon: How will International Law Cope with Commercial Space Tourism?' (2010) 11 Melb J Int'l L 1.
Gagain M, 'Climate Change, Sea Level Rise, and Artificial Islands: Saving the Maldives' Statehood and Maritime Claims Through the "Constitution of the Oceans"' (2012) 23(1) Colo J Int'l Envtl L & Pol'y 77.
Gallagher MG, 'Legal Aspects of the Strategic Defense Initiative' (1986) 111 US Mil Law Rev 11.
Guntrip E, 'The Common Heritage of Mankind: An Adequate Regime for Managing the Deep Seabed?' (2003) 4(2) Melb J Int'l L 376.

Haanappel P, 'Bilateral Air Transport Agreements – 1913-1980' (1980) 5(2) Md J Int'l L 241.

Hailbronner K, 'Freedom of the Air and the Convention on the Law of the Sea' (1983) 77 Am J Int'l L 490.

Hailbronner K, 'The Legal Regime of the Airspace above the Exclusive Economic Zone' (1983) 8(1) Air Law 30.

Harel A, 'Preventing Terrorist Attacks on Offshore Platforms: Do States Have Sufficient Legal Tools?' (2012) 4 Harv Natl Secur J 131.

Head IL, 'ADIZ, International Law, and Contiguous Airspace' (1964) 3 Alta L Rev 182.

Heijmans AMJ, 'Artificial Islands and the Law of Nations' (1974) 21(2) Neth Int Law Rev 139.

de Hoon M, 'Navigating the Legal Horizon: Lawyering the MH17 Disaster' (2017) 33(84) Utrecht J Int'l and Eur L 90.

Hulsroj P and Pecujlic AN, 'New in the Nest: The Danish Space Act' (2016) 41(3) A&SL 503.

Huttunen M, 'Unmanned, Remotely Piloted, or Something Else? Analysing the Terminological Dogfight' (2017) 42(3) A&SL 349.

Johnson DHN, 'Artificial Islands' (1951) 4(2) The Int'l L Q 203.

Kadelbach S, 'International Law Commission and Role of Subsequent Practice as a Means of Interpretation under Articles 31 and 32 VCLT' (2018) 46 QIL 5.

Kaiser SA, 'Legal Considerations about the Loss of Malaysia Airlines Flight MH17 in Eastern Ukraine' (2015) 40(2) A&SL 107.

Kaiser SA, 'The Legal Status of Air Defense Identification Zones: Tensions over the East China Sea' (2014) 63 ZWL 527.

Kaiser SA, 'No-Fly Zones Established by the United Nations Security Council' (2011) 60 ZLW 402.

Kashubsky M and Morrison A, 'Security of Offshore Oil and Gas Facilities: Exclusion Zones and Ships' Routeing' (2013) 5(1) Aust J Marit Ocean Aff 1.

Kasprzyk P, 'Legal Ramifications of the Investigations of the 2010 Polish President's Aircraft Accident' (2011) 36(3) A&SL 201.

Kaye S, 'International Measures to Protect Oil Platforms, Pipelines, and Submarine Cables from Attack' (2007) 31 Tul Mar LJ 377.

Kaye S, 'Freedom of Navigation, Surveillance and Security: Legal Issues Surrounding the Collection of Intelligence from Beyond the Littoral' (2005) 24 Aust YBIL 93.

Knauss JA, 'Creeping Jurisdiction and Customary International Law' (1985) 15(2) Ocean Dev Int'l L 209.

Kohl AW, 'China's Artificial Island Building Campaign in the South China Sea: Implications for the Reform of the United Nations Convention on the Law of the Sea' (2018) 122(3) Dickinson Law Rev 917.

Kretzmer D, 'The Inherent Right to Self-Defence and Proportionality in Jus Ad Bellum' (2013) 24(1) EJIL 235.

Kwiatkowska B, 'Creeping Jurisdiction Beyond 200 Miles in the Light of the 1982 Law of the Sea Convention and State Practice' (1991) 22 Ocean Dev & Int'l L 153.

Lamont CK, 'Conflict in the Skies: The Law of Air Defence Identification Zones' (2014) 39(3) A&SL 187.

Lathrop CG, Roach JA and Rothwell DR, 'Baselines under the International Law of the Sea: Reports of the International Law Association Committee on Baselines under the International Law of the Sea' (2018) 2(1-2) The Law of the Sea 1.

Lau H, 'Rethinking the Persistent Objector Doctrine in International Human Rights Law' (2005) 6(1) Chic J Int Law 495.

Lawrence WH, 'Superports, Airports and Other Fixed Installations on the High Seas' (1975) 6 J Mar L & Comm 575.

Macintosh A, 'Overcoming the Barriers to International Aviation Greenhouse Gases Emissions Abatement' (2008) 33(6) A&SL 403.

McLachlan C, 'The Principle of Systemic Integration and Article 31(3)(c) of the Vienna Convention' (2005) 54(2) ICLQ 279.

Mendes de Leon P and Molenaar EJ, 'Still a Mile too Far? International Law Implications of the Location of an Airport in the Sea' (2001) 14 Leiden J Int Law 233.

Milde M, 'Interception of Civil Aircraft vs. Misuse of Civil Aviation' (1986) 11 Ann Air & Space L.

Miron M, 'The Archipelagic Status Reconsidered in Light of the *South China Sea* and *Düzgit Integrity* Awards' (2018) 15(3) Indones J Int Law 306.

Osiander A, 'Sovereignty, International Relations, and the Westphalian Myth' (2001) 55(2) International Organization 251.

Oxman B, 'Transit of Straits and Archipelagic Waters by Military Aircraft' (2000) 4 S J Int & Comp L 377.

Oxman BH, 'The Regime of Warships under the United Nations Convention on the Law of the Sea' (1984) 24 Va J Int'l L 809.

Papp Z, 'Air Defense Identification Zone (ADIZ) in the light of Public International Law' (2015) 2 Pecs J Int Eur Law 28.

Pedrozo R, 'Military Activities in the Exclusive Economic Zone: East Asia Focus' (2014) 90 Int'l L Stud 514.

Rachovista A, 'The Principle of Systemic Integration in Human Rights Law' (2017) 66 ICLQ 557.

Robinson GS, 'Military Requirements for International Airspace: Evolving Claims to Exclusive Use of a Res Communes Natural Resource' (1971) 11 Nat Resources J 162.

Sands PH, Lyon JT and Pratt GN, 'An Historical Survey of International Air Law Since 1944' (1960-1961) 7(2) McGill L J 125.

Sands PH, de Sousa Freitas J and Pratt GN, 'An Historical Survey of International Air Law before the Second World War' (1960-1961) 7(1) McGill L J 24.

Schofield C and Schofield R, 'Testing the Waters: Charting the Evolution of Claims to and from Low-Tide Elevations and Artificial Islands under the Law of the Sea' (2016) 1 Asia-Pacific J of Ocean L & P 37.

Schubert F, 'State Responsibilities for Air Navigation Facilities and Standards – Understanding its Scope, Nature and Extent' (2010) J Aviat Manag 21.

Smith LJ and Leishman RJM, 'Up, up and Away: An Update on the UK's Latest Plans for Space Activities' (2019) 44(1) A&SL 1.

Sreejith SJ, 'Legality of the Gulf Ban on Qatari Flights: State Sovereignty at Crossroads' (2018) 43(2) A&SL 191.

Su J, 'The Practice of States on Air Defense Identification Zones: Geographical Scope, Object of Identification, and Identification Measures' (2019) 18 Chinese JIL 811.

Symmons C, 'Some Problems Relating to the Definition of "Insular Formations" in International Law: Islands and Low-Tide Elevations' (1995) 1(5) IBRU Marit Br 7.

Tanaka Y, 'The South China Sea Arbitration: Environmental Obligations under the Law of the Sea Convention' (2018) 27(1) RECIEL 90.

Tanaka T, 'Reflections on the Interpretation and Application of Article 121(3) in the *South China Sea Arbitration* (Merits)' (2017) 48(3-4) Ocean Dev & Int'l L 365.

Trevisanut S, 'Is There a Right to Be Rescued at Sea? A Constructive View' (2014) 4 QIL 3.

Van Dyke JM, 'Military Exclusion and Warning Zones on the High Seas' (1991) Marine Policy 147.

de Vries Lentsch P, 'The Right of Overflight over Strait States and Archipelagic States: Developments and Prospects' (1983) 14 Neth Yearb Int Law 165.

Zhang X, 'The Latest Developments of the US Freedom of Navigation Programs in the South China Sea: Deregulation or Re-balance?' (2016) 1 J of East Asia & Int'l L 167.

Zheng P, 'Justifications and Limits of ADIZs under Public International Law' (2015) 14(2) Issues Aviation L & Pol'y 183.

Thesis

Leclerc T, Les mesures correctives des émissions aériennes de gaz à effet de serre. Contribution à l'étude des interactions entre les ordres juridiques en droit international public (Ph.D. thesis, E.M. Meijers Instituut, Leiden University, 2017).

Studies and Reports

Burke EJ and Cevallos AS, 'In Line or Out of Order? China's Approach to ADIZ in Theory and Practice' (RAND Project AIR FORCE Strategy and Doctrine Program, 2017).

Dorst L, Oude Elferink AG and Ligteringen T, 'Recent Changes in the Dutch Baseline: The Inseparable Connection of Human Activities and Natural Processes' (2012), available at www.defensie.nl/downloads/brochures/2012/09/24/changes-dutch-baseline accessed 29 September 2018.

Grief N, 'The Legal Principles Governing the Control of National Airspace and Flight Information Regions and their Application to the Eastern Mediterranean' (European Rim Policy and Investment Council, 2009).

Hsu K, 'Air Defense Identification Zone Intended to Provide China Greater Flexibility to Enforce East China Sea Claims' (US-China Economic and Security Review Commission, 14 January 2014).

Kaye S, 'Freedom of Navigation in the Indo-Pacific Region' (Papers in Australian Maritime Affairs No. 22, Sea Power Centre Australia, 2008).

Lawrence SV et al., 'US-China Relations' (Congressional Research Service Report, 3 September 2019).

Mendes de Leon P, Correia V, Erling U and Leclerc T, 'Possible Legal Arrangements to Implement a Global Market Based Measure for International Aviation Emissions' (Study for the Directorate General Climate Action of the EU Commission, 2 December 2015).

Rinehart IE and Elias B, 'China's Air Defense Identification Zone (ADIZ)' (Congressional Research Service Report, 31 January 2015).

Vaugeois M, 'Settlement of Disputes at ICAO and Sustainable Development' (McGill Centre for Research in Air and Space Law Occasional Paper Series No. IV, June 2016).

'Offshore Energy Outlook' (International Energy Agency, 2018).

'Crash of Malaysia Airlines Flight MH17 Hrabove, Ukraine, 17 July 2014' (Dutch Safety Board, October 2015).

'Report on Occurrences over the High Seas Involving Military Aircraft in 2014' (EASA, 14 April 2015).

'Review of Selected Offshore Petroleum Regulatory Regimes: Offshore Helicopter Safety Inquiry' (Aerosafe Risk Management, Canada, 2010).

Blogs

Carpanelli E, 'To Overfly or Not to Overfly …? Autonomous Sanction in International Civil Aviation Amidst the Recent "Gulf Crisis" – Part II' (Blog of Groningen Journal of International Law, 25 September 2017), available at grojil.org/2017/09/25/to-overfly-or-not-to-overfly-autonomous-sanctions-in-international-civil-aviation-amidst-the-recent-gulf-crisis-pt2/ accessed 2 June 2018.

Green L and Adams T, 'Legal Positivism' (Stanford Encyclopedia of Philosophy, 17 December 2019), available at plato.stanford.edu/entries/legal-positivism/# accessed 2 February 2020.

Guilfoyle D, 'Iran and the Strait of Hormuz: Some Initial Thoughts' (EJIL: Talk!, 2 February 2012), available at www.ejiltalk.org/iran-and-the-strait-of-hormuz-some-initial-thoughts/ accessed 17 January 2018.

Kraska J, 'Military Activities on the Continental Shelf' (Lawfare, 22 August 2016), available at www.lawfareblog.com/military-activities-continental-shelf accessed 10 October 2019.

Milanovic M, 'The Soleimani Strike and Self-Defence Against an Imminent Armed Attack' (EJIL:Talk!, 7 January 2020), available at www.ejiltalk.org/the-soleimani-strike-and-self-defence-against-an-imminent-armed-attack/ accessed 27 June 2019.

Oral N, 'Transit Passage Rights in the Strait of Hormuz and Iran's Threats to Block the Passage of Oil Tankers' (ASIL Insight, 3 May 2012), available at www.asil.org/insights/volume/16/issue/16/transit-passage-rights-strait-hormuz-and-iran%E2%80%99s-threats-block-passage accessed 1 January 2016.

Oude Alink W, 'How "Safe" Airspace Was Not Safe: The Downing of Flight MH17' (Leiden Law Blog, 9 September 2014), available at leidenlawblog.nl/articles/how-safe-airspace-was-not-safe-the-downing-of-flight-mh17 accessed 18 July 2019.

Piera A, 'Reconciling CBDR with Non-discrimination: A Fundamental Requirement for ICAO's Global MBM Success' (Green Air, 23 September 2014), available at www.greenaironline.com/news.php?viewStory = 1983 accessed 3 November 2019.

Trapp K, 'Uses of Force Against Civil Aircraft' (EJIL:Talk!, 28 June 2011), available at www.ejiltalk.org/uses-of-force-against-civil-aircraft/ accessed 12 July 2017.

Ulfstein G, 'How International Law Restricts the Use of Military Force in Hormuz' (EJIL:Talk!, 27 August 2019), available at www.ejiltalk.org/how-international-law-restricts-the-use-of-military-force-in-hormuz/ accessed 3 November 2019.

'Law, Conflict and Airspace: Understanding Air Defense Identification Zones' (Groningen University Blog, 17 January 2014), available at www.rug.nl/research/east-asian-studies/blogs/blog/blog-17-01-2014-law-conflict-and-airspace-understanding-air-defense-identification-zones accessed 13 May 2019.

'Airline Ownership and Control Rules: At Once both Irrelevant and Enduring' (CAPA – Centre for Aviation), available at centreforaviation.com/analysis/reports/airline-ownership-and-control-rules-at-once-both-irrelevant-and-enduring-345816 accessed 3 July 2017.

News

Baglole J, 'Canada, Russia's Decision to Permit Polar Routes Promises to Cut Hours' (The Wall Street Journal, 8 June 2000), available at www.wsj.com/articles/SB960415817821812909 accessed 4 March 2018.

Barbosa RC, 'China Conducts First Sea Launch Mission with Long March 11 Launch of Seven Satellites' (NASASpaceflight.com, 5 June 2019), available at www.nasaspaceflight.com/2019/06/china-first-sea-launch-long-march-11-seven-satellites/ accessed 3 June 2020.

Bateman S, 'Australia and Indonesia at Odds at Sea' (East Asia Forum, 26 June 2015), available at www.eastasiaforum.org/2015/06/26/australia-and-indonesia-at-odds-at-sea/ accessed 20 May 2018.

Beech H, 'China's Sea Control Is a Done Deal, "Short of War with the US"' (The New York Times, 20 September 2018), available at www.nytimes.com/2018/09/20/world/asia/south-china-sea-navy.html accessed 10 October 2019.

Bergman J, 'This Is Why China's Airports Are a Nightmare' (BBC, 29 April 2016), available at www.bbc.com/capital/story/20160420-this-is-why-chinas-airports-are-a-nightmare accessed 8 May 2019.

Blanchard B and Lee Y, 'Taiwan again Scrambles Jets to Intercept Chinese Planes, Tensions Spike' (Reuters, 9 February 2020), available at www.reuters.com/article/us-taiwan-china-defence/taiwan-again-scrambles-jets-to-intercept-chinese-planes-tensions-spikeidUSKBN2030AE accessed 14 April 2020.

David L, 'NASA Proposes New Rules for Moon-Focused Space Rules' (Scientific American, 21 May 2020), available at www.scientificamerican.com/article/nasa-proposes-new-rules-for-moon-focused-space-race/ accessed 3 June 2020.

Foust J, 'Sea Launch "Frozen" after Ships Moved to Russia' (Space News, 24 April 2020), available at spacenews.com/sea-launch-frozen-after-ships-moved-to-russia/ accessed 3 June 2020.

de Gouyon Matignon L, 'Sea Launch and Launching States' (Space Legal Issues, 19 June 2019), available at www.spacelegalissues.com/sea-launch-and-launching-states/ accessed 23 June 2020.

Graham E, 'Australian Pilots Hit with Lasers During Indo-Pacific Exercise' (Australian Strategic Policy Institute, 28 May 2019), available at www.aspistrategist.org.au/australian-pilots-hit-with-lasers-during-indo-pacific-exercise/ accessed 10 October 2019.

Graham E, 'Southeast Asia's Neglected Navigational and Overflight Challenges' (The Interpreter, 27 February 2017), available at www.lowyinstitute.org/the-interpreter/southeast-asia-s-neglected-navigational-and-overflight-challenges accessed 13 August 2018.

Hakim C, 'A Strange Anomaly in Management of Airspace' (The Straits Times, 21 March 2016), available at www.straitstimes.com/opinion/a-strange-anomaly-in-management-of-airspace accessed 13 May 2019.

Jakhar P, 'Analysis: Why Is Airspace in East Asia Becoming Contentious?' (BBC Monitoring, 31 July 2019), available at monitoring.bbc.co.uk/product/c200zen7 accessed 14 November 2019.

Kaur K, 'Aviation's Shifting Centre of Gravity' (The Straits Times, 4 June 2016), available at www.straitstimes.com/singapore/aviations-shifting-centre-of-gravity accessed 16 March 2020.

Liddy M and Spraggon B, 'Before and After: China Builds Artificial Island in South China Sea' (Australian Broadcasting Corporation, 22 September 2015), available at www.abc.net.au/news/2015-09-22/south-china-sea-islands-before-and-after/6794076 accessed 12 June 2018.

Lubold G and Page J, 'American Military Aircraft Targeted by Lasers in Pacific Ocean, US Officials Say' (The Wall Street Journal, 21 June 2018), available at www.wsj.com/articles/american-military-aircraft-targeted-by-lasers-in-pacific-ocean-u-s-officials-say-1529613999 accessed 10 October 2019.

Macheras A, 'Here for the Long Haul: How Qatar Is Overcoming the Aviation Blockade' (The New Arab, 8 January 2018), available at english.alaraby.co.uk/english/comment/2018/1/8/how-qatar-is-overcoming-the-aviation-blockade accessed 12 April 2019.

Milne R, 'Scandinavians Warn Russia after Air Near-Miss' (Financial Times, 15 December 2014), available at www.ft.com/content/95751ff2-837e-11e4-8a84-00144feabdc0 accessed 12 June 2015.

Ming TE, 'Explained: What's Behind Indonesia's Move to Reclaim Control of Riau Islands Airspace from Singapore?' (South China Morning Post, 22 August 2019), available at www.scmp.com/week-asia/explained/article/3023918/whats-behind-indonesias-move-reclaim-control-riau-islands accessed 30 September 2019.

Mosher D, 'Elon Musk: "SpaceX is Building Floating, Superheavy-Class Spaceports" for Its Starship Rocket to Reach the Moon, Mars, and Fly Passengers Around Earth' (Business Insider, 17 June 2020), available at www.businessinsider.nl/elon-musk-spacex-starship-ocean-spaceports-offshore-engineer-job-posting-2020-6?international = true&r = US accessed 23 June 2020.

Page J, 'US Bomber Flies over Waters Claimed by China' (The Wall Street Journal, 18 December 2015), available at www.wsj.com/articles/u-s-jet-flies-over-waters-claimed-by-china-1450466358 accessed 10 October 2019.

Roulette J, 'Trump Administration Drafting "Artemis Accords" Pact for Moon Mining' (Reuters, 5 May 2020), available at www.reuters.com/article/us-space-exploration-moon-mining-exclusi/exclusive-trump-administration-drafting-artemis-accords-pact-for-moon-mining-sources-idUSKBN22H2SB accessed 3 June 2020.

Sevastopulo D, 'Q&A: What Is an Air Defence Identification Zone?' (Financial Times, 12 December 2013), available at www.ft.com/content/26cf55ce-58da-11e3-a7cb-00144feabdc0 accessed 10 May 2019.

Shin C, 'South Korea's Inevitable Expansion of Its ADIZ' (Asian Maritime Transparency Initiative, 8 December 2014), available at amti.csis.org/south-koreas-inevitable-expansion-of-its-adiz/ accessed 19 August 2019.

Smith J, 'Explainer: Competing Claims Make Northeast Asia Sea a Flashpoint' (Reuters, 25 July 2019), available at www.reuters.com/article/us-southkorea-russia-aircraft-explainer/explainer-competing-claims-make-northeast-asian-sea-a-flashpoint-idUSKCN1UK0NO accessed 28 November 2019.

Thompson J, Mundy S and Song J, 'Japan to Take up Spat over China Air Zone with US' (Financial Times, 2 December 2013), available at www.ft.com/content/d4be05c6-5a61-11e3-942a-00144feabdc0 accessed 16 March 2019.

'ICAO Welcomes Resolution of Gulf Airspace Restrictions' (ICAO, 7 January 2021), available at www.icao.int/Newsroom/Pages/ICAO-welcomes-resolution-of-Gulf-airspace-restrictions.aspx accessed 21 January 2021.

'Allied Fighter Jets Intercept Russian Aircraft' (NATO, 11 March 2020), available at www.nato.int/cps/en/natohq/news_174349.htm accessed 14 April 2020.

'US and Canadian Jets Intercepted Russian Reconnaissance Planes near Alaska' (Business Insider, 10 March 2020), available at www.businessinsider.com/us-canadian-jets-intercept-russian-reconnaissance-planes-near-alaska-2020-3?international = true&r = US&IR = T accessed 11 March 2020.

'Leaders' Retreat: Singapore and Indonesia Agree on Framework to Discuss Airspace Management, Military Training' (The Straits Times, 8 October 2019), available at www.straitstimes.com/politics/leaders-retreat-singapore-and-indonesia-agree-on-framework-to-discuss-airspace-management accessed 28 December 2019.

'Strait of Hormuz: US Confirms Drone Shot Down by Iran' (BBC, 20 June 2019), available at www.bbc.com/news/world-middle-east-48700965 accessed 3 November 2019.

'UAE and Bahrain Grant Qatar Airways New Routes' (Reuters, 9 August 2017), available at www.aljazeera.com/news/2017/08/uae-bahrain-grant-qatar-airwaysroutes170808161602538.html accessed 26 August 2019.

'Akbar al-Baker on the Gulf Crisis and Qatar Airways' (Al Jazeera, 14 June 2017), available at www.aljazeera.com/programmes/talktojazeera/2017/06/akbar-al-baker-qatar-airways170613020759574.html accessed 27 August 2018.

'Update 2 – Saudi Arabia Says Airspace Ban on Qatari Flights to Protect Citizens' (Reuters, 13 June 2017) available at www.reuters.com/article/gulf-qatar-flightsidUSL8N1JA1FK accessed 7 May 2019.

'China Says US Should Respect China's Air Defense Zone' (Reuters, 23 March 2017), available at www.reuters.com/article/us-china-usa-defence-idUSKBN16U0SB accessed 26 October 2018.

'South China Sea: China's Navy Told US Spy Plane Flying over Islands to Leave "Eight Times", CNN Reports' (Australian Broadcasting Corporation, 22 May 2015), available at www.abc.net.au/news/2015-05-22/us-spy-plane-in-south-china-sea-warned-to-leave-by-china/6488690?nw = 0 accessed 28 June 2015.

'US Fighter Planes Intercept Russian Combat Jets off Alaska, Sweden Protests "Violation"' (Deutsche Welle, 20 September 2014), available at www.dw.com/en/us-fighter-planes-intercept-russian-combat-jets-off-alaska-sweden-protests-violation/a-17936231 accessed 2 May 2015.

'China and Japan Trade Barbs after Close Encounter over South China Sea' (The Guardian, 25 May 2014), available at www.theguardian.com/world/2014/may/25/china-japan-jets-south-china-sea accessed 28 June 2015.

'China's Air Defense Identification Zone: Impact on Regional Security' (Centre for Strategic and International Studies, 26 November 2013), available at www.csis.org/analysis/chinas-air-defense-identification-zone-impact-regional-security accessed 3 November 2019.

'Military Experts Explain China's Air Defense Identification Zone' (People's Daily Online, 24 November 2013), available at en.people.cn/90786/8464466.html accessed 15 March 2019.

'China Establishes "Air Defence Zone" over East China Sea' (BBC, 23 November 2013), available at www.bbc.com/news/world-asia-25062525 accessed 5 May 2018.

'Japan Extends Air Defence Identification Zone into Taiwan Space' (BBC Monitoring Asia Pacific, 26 June 2010), text of report in English by Shih Hsiu-chuan on Taiwanese newspaper Taipei Times website on 26 June 2010 written, available at www.taipeitimes.com/News/front/archives/2010/06/26/2003476438 accessed 3 November 2019.

Interviews

Australian Broadcasting Corporation (Radio National, Late Night Live), 'Who Owns the South China Sea?' – Interview with Douglas Guilfoyle (14 July 2016), available at www.abc.net.au/radionational/programs/latenightlive/who-owns-the-south-china-sea/7629968 at 8:09 minutes, accessed 8 June 2018.

Peace and Security Research Unit at East Asia Institute, Interview with Min Gyo Koo, Associate Professor, Seoul National University (10 December 2013), available at www.eai.or.kr/main/english/search_view.asp?intSeq = 8929&board = eng_multimedia, accessed 17 January 2019.

Press releases

'E3 Joint Statement on the Situation in the South China Sea' (Press Release, 29 August 2019), available at www.gov.uk/government/news/e3-joint-statement-on-the-situation-in-the-south-china-sea accessed 10 October 2019.

'Canadian Air Defence Identification Zone Now Aligned with Canada's Sovereign Airspace' (Canada National Defence, News Release, 24 May 2018), available at www.canada.ca/en/department-national-defence/news/2018/05/canadian-air-defence-identification-zone-now-aligned-with-canadas-sovereign-airspace.html accessed 26 June 2018.

'Baird Concerned over China's Announcement of Air Defence Identification Zone' (Foreign Affairs, Trade and Development Canada, News Release, 2 December 2013), available at www.canada.ca/en/news/archive/2013/12/baird-concerned-china-announcement-air-defence-identification-zone.html accessed 3 November 2019.

'Declaration by the High Representative Catherine Ashton on Behalf of the European Union on the establishment by China of an "East China Sea Air Defence Identification Zone"' (European Union, Press Release, 28 November 2013), available at www.consilium.europa.eu/uedocs/cms_Data/docs/pressdata/EN/foraff/139752.pdf accessed 13 February 2016.

'China's Announcement of an Air-Defence Identification over the East China Sea' (Minister for Foreign Affairs, Julie Bishop, Press Release, 26 November 2013), available at www.foreignminister.gov.au/minister/julie-bishop/media-release/chinas-announcement-air-defence-identification-zone-over-east-china-sea accessed 3 November 2019.

'Announcement of the Aircraft Identification Rules for the East China Sea Air Defense Identification Zone of the People's Republic of China' (Ministry of National Defense, China, 23 November 2013).

'Statement on the East China Sea Air Defense Identification Zone' (John Kerry, Secretary of State, Press Statement, 23 November 2013), available at 2009-2017.state.gov/secretary/remarks/2013/11/218013.htm accessed 3 November 2019.

'Air Transport: Commission Welcomes Agreement on Siberian Overflights' (European Commission, Press Release, 1 December 2011), available at europa.eu/rapid/press-release_IP-11-1490_en.htm accessed 12 December 2018.

Speeches and Presentations

Beckman R, 'The Legal Regime Governing Passage on Routes Used for International Navigation Through Indonesian Waters' (Presentation delivered at the 42nd Annual Conference of the Centre for Oceans and Policy Cooperation and Engagement in the Asia Pacific Region, Beijing, 24-26 May 2018).

Brandis G, 'The Right of Self-Defence Against Imminent Armed Attack in International Law' (Public Lecture delivered at the University of Queensland, Brisbane, 11 April 2017).

Egan BJ, 'International Law, Legal Diplomacy, and the Counter-ISIL Campaign' (Speech delivered at the American Society of International Law, Washington DC, 1 April 2016).

Rothwell DR, 'Artificial Islands and International Law' (Presentation delivered at ANU College of Law, Canberra, 28 July 2015).

Wright J, 'The Modern Law of Self-Defence' (Speech delivered at the International Institute for Strategic Studies, London, 11 January 2017).

Dictionaries and Encyclopaedias

Cottier T and Müller JP, 'Estoppel' (Max Planck Encyclopedia of International Law 2007).

Dörr O, 'Prohibition of Use of Force' (Max Planck Encyclopedia of Public International Law 2015).

Gioia A, 'Persian Gulf' (Max Planck Encyclopedia of Public International Law 2007).

Greenwood C, 'Self-Defence' (Max Planck Encyclopedia of Public International Law 2011).

Jiménez Piernas C, 'Archipelagic Waters' (Max Planck Encyclopedia of Public International Law 2009).

Kemp D and Kemp P (eds), *The Oxford Companion to Ships and the Sea* (2nd edn, OUP 2006), available at www.oxfordreference.com accessed 20 November 2019.

Olufemi E, 'Persistent Objector' (Max Planck Encyclopedia of Public International Law 2006).

Oude Elferink AG, 'Artificial Islands, Installations and Structures' (Max Planck Encyclopedia of Public International Law 2013).

Roach JA, 'Air Defence Identification Zones' (Max Planck Encyclopedia of Public International Law 2017).

Stoll P, 'Continental Shelf' (Max Planck Encyclopedia of Public International Law 2008).

Vinuesa RE, 'National Treatment, Principle' (Max Planck Encyclopedia of International Law 2011).

Vöneky S, 'Armed Conflict, Effect on Treaties' (Max Planck Encyclopedia of Public International Law 2011).

International Hydrographic Organization, *Hydrographic Dictionary*, available at hd.iho.int/en accessed 2 February 2018.

Oxford English Dictionary, available at www.oed.com/view/Entry/191344?redirectedFrom=stratosphere#eid accessed 17 April 2019.

Websites

Airservices Australia, 'Commonwealth Games Airspace Procedure Guide', available at www.airservicesaustralia.com/wp-content/uploads/17-0067-BRO-Commonwealth-Games-airspace-new.pdf accessed 23 May 2019.

Australian Government, Department of Foreign Affairs and Trade, 'Diplomatic Clearances: Aircraft and Ships', available at dfat.gov.au/about-us/foreign-embassies/protocol/Pages/diplomatic-clearances-aircraft-and-ships accessed 5 January 2019.

Dutch Safety Board, 'More Attention Devoted to Overflying Conflict Zones', available at www.onderzoeksraad.nl/en/page/13613/more-attention-devoted-to-overflying-conflict-zones accessed 10 July 2019.

Eurocontrol, 'General Air Traffic', available at ext.eurocontrol.int/lexicon/index.php/General_Air_Traffic accessed 20 February 2019.

Eurocontrol, 'Operational Air Traffic', available at ext.eurocontrol.int/lexicon/index.php/Operational_Air_Traffic accessed 20 February 2019.

Eurocontrol, 'Governing Bodies', available at www.eurocontrol.int/info/governing-bodies accessed 1 August 2020.

European Defence Agency, 'Diplomatic Clearances', available at dic.eda.europa.eu/ accessed 3 January 2019.

Fédération Aéronautique Internationale (FAI), 'Statement about the Karman Line' (30 November 2018), available at www.fai.org/news/statement-about-karman-line accessed 4 August 2016.

Government of Canada, 'Global Affairs Canada: State, Military or Scientific Overflight Authorization', available at www.international.gc.ca/protocol-protocole/policies-politiques/overflight_clearance-autorisation_survol.aspx?lang=eng accessed 1 August 2020.

ICAO, '2017 Air Transport Statistical Results', available at www.icao.int/annual-report-2017/Documents/Annual.Report.2017_Air%20Transport%20Statistics.pdf accessed 12 March 2019.

ICAO, '2016 Air Transport Statistical Results', available at www.icao.int/annual-report-2016/documents/arc_2016_air%20transport%20statistics.pdf accessed 2 March 2019.

ICAO, 'About ICAO', available at www.icao.int/about-icao/Pages/default.aspx accessed 12 February 2020.

ICAO GIS, available at gis.icao.int/ accessed 14 July 2019.

ICAO, 'Current Lists of Parties to Multilateral Air Law Treaties – International Air Services Transit Agreement', available at www.icao.int/secretariat/legal/List%20of%20Parties/Transit$_EN.pdf accessed 13 November 2020.

ICAO, 'Current Lists of Parties to Multilateral Air Law Treaties – International Air Transport Agreement', available at www.icao.int/secretariat/legal/List%20of%20Parties/Transport_EN.pdf accessed 13 November 2020.

ICAO, 'Global Air Navigation Strategy', available at www4.icao.int/ganpportal/GanpDocument#/?_k=d978it accessed 4 August 2019.

ICAO, 'The Convention on International Civil Aviation: Annexes 1 to 18', available at www.icao.int/safety/airnavigation/NationalityMarks/annexes_booklet_en.pdf accessed 19 September 2018.

International Maritime Organization, 'Convention on the International Regulations for Preventing Collisions at Sea (COLREGs)', available at www.imo.org/en/About/Conventions/ListOfConventions/Pages/COLREG.aspx accessed 24 January 2018.

McGill University, 'MILAMOS Project', available at mcgill.ca/milamos/ accessed 3 November 2019.

NASA Science, 'Basics of Spaceflight: Planetary Orbits', available at solarsystem.nasa.gov/basics/chapter5-1/ accessed 3 June 2020.

Swedish Armed Forces, 'Diplomatic Clearances', available at www.forsvarsmakten.se/en/about/diplomatic-clearances/ accessed 18 March 2019.

Switzerland, Federal Office for Civil Aviation (FOCA), 'Diplomatic Clearances', available at www.bazl.admin.ch/diplomaticclearances accessed 1 August 2020.

United Nations, 'Non-self-governing Territories', available at www.un.org/dppa/decolonization/en/nsgt accessed 18 June 2019.

United Nations, 'Conference on Disarmament: An Introduction to the Conference', available at www.unog.ch/80256EE600585943/(httpPages)/BF18ABFEFE5D344DC1256F3100311CE9?OpenDocument accessed 13 March 2019.

United Nations, 'Table of Claims to Maritime Jurisdiction (as at 15 July 2011)', available at www.un.org/Depts/los/LEGISLATIONANDTREATIES/PDFFILES/table_summary_of_claims.pdf accessed 1 May 2018.

United Nations, 'UN Documentation: Researching UN Mandates', available at research.un.org/en/docs/mandates#s-lg-box-2829995 accessed 5 May 2020.

United Nations Division for Ocean Affairs and the Law of the Sea, 'UNCLOS Status Table', available at www.un.org/Depts/los/reference_files/UNCLOS%20Status%20table_ENG.pdf accessed 13 November 2020.

United Nations Office for Outer Space Affairs, 'Committee on the Peaceful Uses of Outer Space', available at www.unoosa.org/oosa/en/ourwork/copuos/index.html accessed 1 May 2018.

United Nations Treaty Collection, 'Multilateral Treaties Deposited with the Secretary General – Chapter XXI: Law of the Sea', available at treaties.un.org/pages/Treaties.aspx?id=21&subid=A&clang=_en accessed 13 November 2020.

United Nations Treaty Collection, 'Chapter XXI: Law of the Sea, Declarations and Reservations', available at treaties.un.org/doc/Publication/MTDSG/Volume%20II/Chapter%20XXI/XXI-6.en.pdf accessed 26 July 2019.

United Nations Treaty Collection, 'Chapter XXI: Law of the Sea, Declarations and Reservations – Chile', available at treaties.un.org/Pages/Declarations.aspx?index=Chile&lang=_en&chapter=21&treaty=463 accessed 3 February 2020.

US Coast Guard, 'IMO Maritime SAR Regions', available at www.dco.uscg.mil/Portals/9/CG-5R/nsarc/IMO%20Maritime%20SAR%20Regions.pdf accessed 25 October 2019.

US Department of State, 'Diplomatic Aircraft Clearance Procedures for Foreign State Aircraft to Operate in United States National Airspace', available at www.state.gov/diplomatic-aircraft-clearance-procedures-for-foreign-state-aircraft-to-operate-in-united-states-national-airspace/ accessed 1 August 2020.

US FAA, 'Entering, Exiting and Flying in United States Airspace', available at www.faa.gov/air_traffic/publications/us_restrictions/airspace/ accessed 14 February 2020.

Correspondence

Correspondence from Francis Schubert (Chief Corporate Officer and Deputy CEO, Skyguide, Adjunct Professor, Institute of Air & Space Law, McGill University) to the author, dated 19 February 2020.

Correspondence from Donald Rothwell (Professor of International Law, Australian National University) to the author, dated 20 December 2019.

Correspondence from Mike Boyd (Technical Officer, ICAO) to the author, dated 3 December 2019.

Email from Roland Dorsay to Pablo Mendes de Leon (6 November 2003).

Letter from Mr Webster to Lord Ashburton (Department of State, Washington, 6 August 1842).

Other

Katona S, '2014 High Seas Regional Assessment' (Ocean Health Index, 2014), available at www.oceanhealthindex.org/news/2014_highseas_assessment accessed 12 May 2018.

Declaration of the First Meeting of Equatorial Countries (Bogotá, 3 December 1976).

EU Diplomatic Clearance Technical Arrangement (DIC TA) Form, available at dic.eda.europa.eu/ accessed 13 March 2020.

'Indonesian Archipelagic Sea Lanes' (Semaphore – Sea Power Centre Australia, April 2005), available at www.navy.gov.au/sites/default/files/documents/Semaphore_2005_6.pdf accessed 25 June 2016.

International Law Association, 'Baselines under the International Law of the Sea', Final Report (2018).

'NATO Policy for Civil/Military Aircraft Operating in Support of NATO or NATO-led Missions and Operations' (NATO, 2016).

Resolution No. 1/2012 on Baselines under the International Law of the Sea, adopted at the 75th Conference of the International Law Association (Sofia, 26-30 August 2012).

San Remo Manual on International Law Applicable to Armed Conflicts at Sea, adopted 12 June 1994 (International Review of the Red Cross, November-December 1995, No. 309, pp. 583-594) ('San Remo Manual').

The Commander's Handbook on the Law of Naval Operations (Department of the Navy – Department of Homeland Security and US Coast Guard, August 2017).

US Department of Transportation, 'How to Become a Certified Air Carrier' (Information Packet, September 2012).

Table of Cases

International Court of Justice/Permanent Court of International Justice

Appeal Relating to the Jurisdiction of the ICAO Council under Article 84 of the Convention on Civil Aviation (Bahrain, Egypt, Saudi Arabia and United Arab Emirates v. Qatar), Judgment, I.C.J. 2020 (14 July), **168**

Appeal Relating to the Jurisdiction of the ICAO Council under Article II, Section 2, of the 1944 International Air Services Transit Agreement (Bahrain, Egypt and United Arab Emirates v. Qatar), Judgment, I.C.J. 2020 (14 July), **168**

Territorial and Maritime Dispute (Nicaragua v. Colombia), Judgment, I.C.J. Rep. 2012 (19 November), p. 624, **30, 96, 113, 114**

Accordance with International Law of the Unilateral Declaration of Independence in Respect of Kosovo, Advisory Opinion, I.C.J. Rep. 2010 (22 July), p. 403 ('Kosovo Advisory Opinion'), **49, 203**

Case Concerning Territorial and Maritime Dispute (Nicaragua v. Honduras), Reports of Judgments, Advisory Opinions and Orders, I.C.J. Rep. 2007 (8 October), p. 659, **96**

Legal Consequences of the Construction of a Wall in the Occupied Palestinian Territory, Advisory Opinion, I.C.J. Rep. 2004 (9 July), p. 136, **206**

Case Concerning the Arrest Warrant of 11 April 2000 (Democratic Republic of Congo v. Belgium), Judgment, I.C.J. Rep. 2002 (14 February), p. 3 ('Arrest Warrant Case'), **205**

Case Concerning Maritime Delimitation and Territorial Questions (Qatar v. Bahrain), Merits, Judgment, I.C.J. Rep. 2001 (16 March), p. 40, **96, 113**

Legality of the Threat or Use of Nuclear Weapons, Advisory Opinion, I.C.J. Rep. 1996 (8 July), p. 226 ('Nuclear Weapons Advisory Opinion'), **134, 202**

Arbitral Award of 31 July 1989 (Guinea-Bissau v. Senegal), Judgment, I.C.J. Rep. 1991 (12 November), p. 53, **12**

Military and Paramilitary Activities in and Against Nicaragua (Nicaragua v. United States of America), Merits, I.C.J. Rep. 1986 (27 June), p. 14 ('Military and Paramilitary Activities Case'), **49, 134, 194, 195, 196, 198, 199, 203, 206**

Case Concerning the Continental Shelf (Libyan Arab Jamahiriya/Malta), Judgment, I.C.J. Rep. 1985 (3 June), p. 13, **84, 133**

Case Concerning the Continental Shelf (Tunisia/Libyan Arab Jamahiriya), Judgment, I.C.J. Rep. 1982 (24 February), p. 18, **49, 84**

Western Sahara, Advisory Opinion, I.C.J. Rep. 1975 (16 October), p. 12, **22**

Nuclear Tests Case (Australia v. France), Judgment, I.C.J. Rep. 1974 (20 December), p. 253, **181**

Legal Consequences for States of the Continued Presence of South Africa in Namibia (South West Africa) Not Withstanding Security Council Resolution 276 (1970), Advisory Opinion, I.C.J. Rep. 1971 (21 June), p. 16 ('Namibia Advisory Opinion'), **137, 138**

North Sea Continental Shelf (Federal Republic of Germany/Netherlands; Federal Republic of Germany/Denmark), Judgment, I.C.J. Rep. 1969 (20 February), p. 3 ('North Sea Continental Shelf Cases'), **134, 135, 136, 198**

Case Concerning Right of Passage over Indian Territory (Portugal v. India), Merits, I.C.J. Rep. 1960 (12 April), p. 6, **135**

Fisheries (United Kingdom v. Norway), Judgment, I.C.J. Rep. 1951 (18 December), p. 116 ('Anglo-Norwegian Fisheries Case'), **30, 120, 135**

Asylum Case (Colombia/Peru), Judgment, I.C.J. Rep. 1950 (20 November), p. 266 ('Asylum Case'), **135, 136, 200**

Reparation for Injuries Suffered in the Service of the United Nations, Advisory Opinion, I.C.J. Rep. 1949 (11 April), p. 174, **39**

Corfu Channel (United Kingdom v. Albania), Merits, Judgment, I.C.J. Rep. 1949 (9 April), p. 4 ('Corfu Channel Case'), **223, 226, 227, 228, 238**

Legal Status of Eastern Greenland, Judgment (1933) P.C.I.J. Series A/B, No. 53, **22**

The Case of S.S. Lotus (France v. Turkey) (1927) P.C.I.J. Series A, No. 10 ('Lotus Case'), **11, 13, 153, 202, 203**

Arbitral Awards

In the *Matter of an Arbitration under the Arbitration Agreement Between the Government of the Republic of Croatia and the Government of the Republic of Slovenia, Signed on 4 November 2009 (Croatia v. Slovenia)*, P.C.A. Case No. 2010-04, 29 June 2017, **30**

In the Matter of the South China Sea Arbitration (Philippines v. China), P.C.A. Case No. 2013-19, 12 July 2016 ('South China Sea Arbitration'), **5, 10, 92, 96, 97, 103, 104, 109-113, 115, 117, 144, 149, 242, 250**

In the Matter of the Arctic Sunrise Arbitration (Netherlands v. Russia), P.C.A. Case No. 2014-02, 14 August 2015 ('Arctic Sunrise Case'), **92, 105, 108, 109, 149**

Air Service Agreement of 27 March 1946 Between the United States of America and France (USA v. France) (1978) XVIII R.I.A.A. 417, **48, 125**

Island of Palmas (US v. Netherlands) (1928) II R.I.A.A. 829, **20**

Award Between the United States and the United Kingdom Relating to the Rights of Jurisdiction of United States in the Bering's Sea and the Preservation of Fur Seals (1893) XXVIII R.I.A.A. 263, **118**

International Tribunal for the Law of the Sea

National Courts

Australia

Table of Legislation

France

Russia

United Kingdom

United States

Table of Treaties

Aeronautical Navigation Communications

Australia

Australia Aeronautical Information Service - AIP Supplement (SUP), XXI Commonwealth Games, Gold Coast, 2-18 April 2018, **186**

Bahrain

Kingdom of Bahrain NOTAM Summary (1 April 2020), available at www.bahrainaims.com/pdf/2020/Summary-01-04-2020.pdf, accessed 30 April 2020, **163**

Egypt

Arab Republic of Egypt Ministry of Civil Aviation NOTAM List (1 April 2020), available at www.nansceg.net/notam.pdf accessed 30 April 2020, **163**

India

'ENR-1.12 Interception of Civil Aircraft - Identification and Interception Procedures', available at aim-india.aai.aero/eaip/PUB/2012-04-01/html/eAIP/EC-ENR-1.12-en-GB.html accessed 2 July 2019, **213**

The Netherlands

Aeronautical Information Publication Netherlands, ENR 5 Navigation Warnings - ENR 5.1 Prohibited, Restricted and Danger Areas (28 March 2019), **132**

Singapore

Aeronautical Information Publication Singapore, GEN 1.2 Entry, Transit and Departure of Aircraft - 3.1.1.3 Civil Non-Scheduled Flights - Overflight (21 July 2016), **59**

United Arab Emirates

United Arab Emirates General Civil Aviation Authority Summary of NOTAM (26 April 2020), available at www.gcaa.gov.ae/en/ais/pages/notam.aspx, accessed 30 April 2020, **163**

United States

'ENR 1.12 National Security and Interception Procedures - National Security', available at www.faa.gov/air_traffic/publications/atpubs/aip_html/part2_enr_section_1.12.html#Para_1_8_4 accessed 2 July 2019, **188**

US Federal Register, Department of Transportation - FAA, 'Designation of Oceanic Airspace: Notice of Provision of Air Traffic Services in Oceanic Airspace' (Volume 80-No. 126, 1 July 2015), **162**

United Nations Documents

General Assembly Resolution

Security Council Resolutions

International Law Commission

International Civil Aviation Organization

Annexes

ICAO WP/295, *Establishment of Military Requirements and Restrictions on International Civil Aviation*, Presented by IATA and IFALPA at the 13th Air Navigation Conference, Montreal (28 September 2018), **184, 187**

ICAO WP/14325, *Report on the Outcome of the Meeting of the Special Group to Review the Application of ICAO Treaties Relating to Conflict Zones (SGRAIT-CZ)*, Presented by the Secretariat at the Council 206th Session (20 October 2015), **68**

ICAO WP/04 Secretariat, *Civil/Military Cooperation*, Presented by the Secretariat at the 1st Meeting of the ICAO Asia/Pacific Seamless ATM Planning Group, Bangkok (31 January-3 February 2012), **66**

ICAO WP/7, *Review of the Classification and Definitions Used for Civil Aviation Activities*, Presented by the Secretariat at the Statistics Division 10th Session, Montreal (16 October 2009), **41**

ICAO WP/8-2, *Draft Report on the Work of the Legal Committee During its 33rd Session* (1 May 2008), **232**

ICAO WP/64, *Fair and Equal Opportunities to Access the International Air Transport Market and the Problem of Airports' Congestion*, Presented by Bahrain, Egypt, Iraq, Jordan, Lebanon, Libyan Arab Jamahiriya, Morocco, Oman, Qatar, Saudi Arabia, Sudan, Syria, Tunisia, United Arab Emirates, Yemen and the Observer from Palestine at the 5th Air Transport Conference, Montreal (17 March 2003), **174**

ICAO WP/2-1, *Secretariat Study on 'Civil/State Aircraft'*, Presented by the Secretariat at the Legal Committee 29th Session, Montreal (3 March 1994), **51, 53**

ICAO WP/2, *Consideration of o\Other Items on the General Work Programme of the Legal Committee*, Presented by the Secretariat at the Legal Committee 37th Session, Montreal (12 July 2018), **57**

ICAO WP/2-6, *State/Civil Aircraft Definition and Its Impact on Aviation*, Presented by Poland, Bulgaria, The Czech Republic, Cyprus, Greece, Lithuania, Romania, Slovakia, Slovenia and Hungary at the Legal Committee 36th Session, Montreal (29 September 2015), **57**

ICAO WP/5-1, *Secretariat Study on Agenda Item 5: Consideration of the Report of the Rapporteur on 'United Nations Convention on the Law of the Sea – Implications, if any, for the Application of the Chicago Convention, Its Annexes and Other International Air Law Instruments'*, Presented at the Legal Committee 26th Session, Montreal (4 February 1987), reproduced in (1987) 3 Int'l Org & L Sea: Documentary YB 243, **2, 86, 91, 221**

ICAO WP/5-41, *Report by the Rapporteur on Agenda Item 5: Consideration of the Report of the Rapporteur on 'United Nations Convention on the Law of the Sea – Implications, If Any, for the Application of the Chicago Convention, Its Annexes and Other International Air Law Instruments'*, Presented at the Legal Committee 26th Session, Montreal (4 February 1987), reproduced in (1987) 3 Int'l Org & L Sea: Documentary YB 262, **75**

Other Materials

ICAO Summary of Discussions, *First Unassigned High Seas Airspace*, Special Coordination Meeting, Lima (24 July 2019), **82, 153**

ICAO, *ATM Contingency Plan: Africa and Indian Ocean Region* (July 2019), **69, 70**

Application (A) of the State of Qatar – Disagreement on the Interpretation and Application of the Convention on International Civil Aviation (Chicago 1944) and of Its Annexes, Submitted on Behalf of the State of Qatar by Its Agent, Essa Abdulla Almalki, Qatar Civil Aviation Authority Permanent Representative to ICAO (30 October 2017), **163**

ICAO IP/13, *Automation Interface Between Flight Information Regions*, Presented by CANSO at the 28th Meeting of the Asia/Pacific Air Navigation Planning and Implementation Regional Group, Bangkok (11-14 September 2017), **209**

ICAO European and North Atlantic Office EUR Doc 032, *Interim Guidance Material on Civil/Military Cooperation in Air Traffic Management* (2nd edn, 2016), **60**

ICAO, *Guidelines to Airspace Users in Order to Raise Their Awareness on State Aircraft Operations Especially in the High Seas Airspace over the Baltic Sea* (Eur Ops Bulletin, 15 December 2015), **215**

ICAO Council, *Procedure for the Amendment of Regional Air Navigation Plans* (18 June 2014), **166**

ICAO Cir 330, *Civil/Military Cooperation in Air Traffic Management* (2011), **214**

ICAO SN/12, *Harmonised Notification of Areas of Volcanic Ash,* Presented by Steven Hill at the 5th Meeting of the Aeronautical Information Services – Aeronautical Information Management Study Group, Montreal (10 October 2011), **69**

ICAO European and North Atlantic Office IP/03, *ICAO Provisions Related to Access to the High Seas*, Presented by the Secretariat at the 3rd Meeting of the European Air Navigation Planning Group Flexible Use of Airspace Task Force, Paris (16 January 2009), **69, 70**

International Maritime Organization

IMO Resolution A.572(14), as amended, 'Amendments to the General Provisions on Ship's Routeing' (19 May 1998), **236**

IMO Resolution A.671(16) 'Safety Zones and Safety of Navigation Around Offshore Installations and Structures' (19 October 1989), **99, 127, 247**

IMO, 'Sub-Committee on Safety of Navigation (NAV)' (55th Session, 27-31 July 2009), available at www.imo.org/en/MediaCentre/MeetingSummaries/NCSR/Pages/NAV-55th-session.aspx accessed 20 February 2020, **106**

Joint International Civil Aviation Organization and International Maritime Organization

International Aeronautical and Maritime Search and Rescue (IAMSAR) Manual, Volume I: Organization and Management (2016), **83, 156**

Division for Ocean Affairs and the Law of the Sea

United Nations Division for Ocean Affairs and the Law of the Sea, 'The United Nations Convention on the Law of the Sea: A Historical Perspective' (Paper Prepared for the International Year of the Ocean, 1998), available at www.un.org/depts/los/convention_agreements/convention_historical_perspective.htm accessed 21 August 2018, **26-27**

United Nations, Office for Ocean Affairs and the Law of the Sea, 'Law of the Sea – Straits Used for International Navigation: Legislative History of Part III of the United Nations Convention on the Law of the Sea' (1992), **223**

United Nations, Office for Ocean Affairs and the Law of the Sea, 'The Law of the Sea – Baselines: An Examination of the Relevant Provisions of the United Nations Convention on the Law of the Sea' (1989), **100**

Office for Outer Space Affairs

Working Paper of the Legal Subcommittee of the Committee on the Peaceful Uses of Outer Space, GOAR, 57th Session U.N. Doc. A/AC.105/C.2/L.302 (Vienna, 9-20 April 2018), **29, 33**

Committee on the Peaceful Uses of Outer Space, Promoting the Discussion of the Matters Relating to the Definition and Delimitation of Outer Space with a View to Elaborating a Common Position of States Members of the Committee on the Peaceful Uses of Outer Space: Working Paper Prepared by the Chair of the Working Group on the Definition and Delimitation of Outer Space of the Legal Subcommittee, 57th Session A/AC.105/C.2/L.302 (Vienna, 9-20 April 2018), **29, 33**

Dempsey PS and Manoli M, *Suborbital Flights and the Delimitation of Air Space vis -à-vis Outer Space: Functionalism, Spatialism and State Sovereignty*, A submission by the Space Safety Law and Regulation Committee of the International Association for the Advancement of Space Safety to the Legal Subcommittee of the Committee on the Peaceful Uses of Outer Space, Vienna, 9-20 April 2018, U.N. Doc. A/AC.105/C.2/2018/CRP.9 (29 March 2018), **33, 35**

National Legislation and Practice Relating to Definition and Delimitation of Outer Space – Note by the Secretariat A/AC.105/865/Add.1 (20 March 2006), **34**

Drafting Materials of Treaties

'38th Meeting of the Committee of the Whole – Extract from the Official Records of the United Nations Conference on the Law of Treaties, First Session (Summary Records of the Plenary Meetings and the Meetings of the Committee of the Whole)' A/CONF.39/C.1/SR.38 (Vienna, 26 March-24 May 1968), **140**

'Summary Records of the 26th to 30th Meetings of the Fourth Committee – Extract from the Official Records of the United Nations Conference on the Law of the Sea' Vol. VI (Fourth Committee (Continental Shelf)) A/CONF.13/C.4/SR.26-30 (Geneva, 24 February-27 April 1958), **107, 121**

Eugène Pépin, *The Law of the Air and the Draft Articles Concerning the Law of the Sea Adopted by the International Law Commission at Its Eighth Session* (A/CONF.13/4) – Extract from the *Official Records of the United Nations Conference on the Law of the Sea, Volume I* (Preparatory Documents), United Nations Conference on the Law of the Sea, Geneva, 24 February-27 April 1958, **23, 69, 75, 80, 81, 89, 121, 194**

Proceedings to the Chicago Convention, Illinois, 1 November-7 December 1944 (United States Government Printing Office 1948), **27, 28, 42, 46, 172, 176, 178**

Documents Relating to ICJ Proceedings

EU Documents

European Commission, 'Joint Communication to the European Parliament and the Council – Improving Military Mobility in the European Union' (Brussels, 10 November 2017, JOIN(2017) 41 final), **60**

Commission of the European Communities, 'Impact of the Third Package of Air Transport Liberalization Measures – Communication from the Commission to the Council and the European Parliament' (Brussels, 22 October 1996, COM(96) 514 final), **43**

Documents of Intergovernmental Organisations

Eurocontrol

AEROSPACE LAW AND POLICY SERIES

1. Erwin von den Steinen, *National Interest and International Aviation* (ISBN 90-411-2455-1).
2. Ludwig Weber, *International Civil Aviation Organisation: An Introduction* (ISBN 978-90-411-2622-1).
3. Niels van Antwerpen, *Cross-Border Provision of Air Navigation Services with Specific Reference to Europe: Safeguarding Transparent Lines of Responsibility and Liability* (ISBN 978-90-411-2688-7).
4. Brian F. Havel, *Beyond Open Skies: A New Regime for International Aviation* (ISBN 978-90-411-2389-3).
5. Jiefang Huang, *Aviation Safety through the Rule of Law: ICAO's Mechanisms and Practices* (ISBN 978-90-411-3115-7).
6. Marian Hoeks, *Multimodal Transport Law: The Law Applicable to the Multimodal Contract for the Carriage of Goods* (ISBN 978-90-411-3246-8).
7. George N. Tompkins, Jr., *Liability Rules Applicable to International Air Transportation as Developed by the Courts in the United States: From Warsaw 1929 to Montreal 1999* (ISBN 978-90-411-2646-7).
8. Daniel Calleja Crespo and Pablo Mendes de Leon (eds), *Achieving the Single European Sky: Goals and Challenges* (ISBN 978-90-411-3730-2).
9. Donal Patrick Hanley, *Aircraft Operating Leasing: A Legal and Practical Analysis in the Context of Public and Private International Air Law*, Second Edition, (ISBN 978-90-411-6050-8).
10. Mikołaj Ratajczyk, *Regional Aviation Safety Organisations: Enhancing Air Transport Safety through Regional Cooperation* (ISBN 978-90-411-5861-1).
11. Benjamyn I. Scott (ed.), *The Law of Unmanned Aircraft Systems: An Introduction to the Current and Future Regulation under National, Regional and International Law* (ISBN 978-90-411-6126-0).
12. Stamatis Varsamos, *Airport Competition Regulation in Europe* (ISBN 978-90-411-6831-3).
13. Katarzyna Malinowska, *Space Insurance: International Legal Aspects* (ISBN 978-90-411-6784-2).
14. John Milligan, *European Union Competition Law in the Airline Industry* (ISBN 978-90-411-6618-0).

15. Dejian Kong, *Civil Liability for Damage Caused by Global Navigation Satellite System* (ISBN 978-94-035-1171-9).
16. Pablo Mendes de Leon and Niall Buissing (eds), *Behind and Beyond the Chicago Convention: The Evolution of Aerial Sovereignty* (ISBN 978-94-035-1131-3).
17. Neta Palkovitz, *Regulating a Revolution: Small Satellites and the Law of Outer Space* (ISBN 978-94-035-1762-9).
18. Federico Bergamasco, Roberto Cassar, Rada Popova & Benjamyn I. Scott, *Cyber-security: Key Legal Considerations for the Aviation and Space Sectors* (ISBN 978-94-035-0110-9).
19. Luis Fernando Fiallos Pazmiño, *The International Civil Operations of Unmanned Aircraft Systems under Air Law* (ISBN 978-94-035-2854-0).
20. Merinda E. Stewart, *Freedom of Overflight: A Study of Coastal State Jurisdiction in International Airspace* (ISBN 978-94-035-3804-4).

9.951 51851CB00005B/12 [223319033]

www.ingramcontent.com/pod-product-compliance
Lightning Source LLC
Chambersburg PA
CBHW041308210926
51851CB00005B/12
9789403538044